J:C:A:V:VES MATTHESON.
Ableg: Brit: Secretarius, Eccles:
Cath: Hamb: Canonicus min: et
Chori Musici Director. Ət: xxxvii

Wahll. Pinx.                    C. Fritsch Sc: de Hambourg

# Johann Mattheson

## SPECTATOR IN MUSIC

BY

BEEKMAN C. CANNON

ARCHON BOOKS
1968

SBN: 208 00311 8
LIBRARY OF CONGRESS CATALOG CARD NUMBER: 68-8013
PRINTED IN THE UNITED STATES OF AMERICA

# PREFACE

THIS volume is the first in a new series of publications in the field of musical scholarship: the "Yale Studies in the History of Music." Our purpose is twofold: that musical scholars in Yale University may have a fuller opportunity to make known the results of their research; and that the study of the history of music in the academic institutions of this country may benefit by the achievements of youthful scholars. The editor of this series most earnestly believes that studies such as these must be maintained by colleges and universities. For at least two hundred years the history of music has received careful and honorable attention from more than one distinguished scholar, but it has never quite succeeded in gaining the place it should rightfully hold as companion to the other historical studies undertaken by our colleges.

In times long past music, as one of the liberal arts, had a secure place among academic studies. It then comprised a total knowledge of everything that related to music, and this knowledge was conveyed to the student in the form of a scholarly discipline without which no musical activity was of any avail. In the course of time, however, the science of music changed its meaning and and thereby forfeited the high place it held in institutions of learning. In recent years a return of this old discipline to the academic institutions has been sought—and, in various universities, both in this country and in Europe, with success. But a mere revival of the *Ars Musica* cannot bring back all the ideas which it once so fully embraced. Although the imitation of an old system of learning such as this would, certainly, be futile and mistaken, this fact should by no means exclude from our universities the maintainance of the study of music as an *Ars Liberalis*. Hence to regain for it its proper place amidst the commonwealth of scholars, we must stress that element in music which best quickens the nature of a liberal art—the history of music. Assiduous research into such history will, then, be the aim of the volumes published in this series, and we take pleasure and satisfaction in thus sharing in the attempt to establish the history of music as one of the liberal arts that a university represents.

There is good reason for further satisfaction that our new series can be opened with the work of a scholar only lately returned from service in the armed forces. Commander Cannon was in the United States Navy from May, 1941, through January, 1946. His study on Mattheson was the subject of his doctoral dissertation in 1939, and this publication is a partial fulfillment of the requirements for the Ph.D. degree at Yale University. The author collected all his material in 1938, chiefly in the libraries of Hamburg and Berlin. It is known that the archives of Hamburg were severely damaged by bombing; how much survives of the material used by the author in the Berlin *Staatsbibliothek* we have not been able to ascertain. This publication does, however, certainly contain a good deal of material that in all probability can never be recovered.

We are happy to express our gratitude to all those who so constructively shared in the publication of this book: to Dean Edgar S. Furniss, Provost of Yale University, whose continued interest made the inception of this series possible; to Professor Robert D. French, whose counsel has been an encouraging guide to the author for many years; to the late Professor Robert C. Bates, whose devoted friendship was the author's best advice and help; and to Mr. Beecher Hogan, whose masterly understanding of style has given to the following pages a good deal of their present form. We wish likewise to thank Miss Eva O'Meara, Librarian of the Yale School of Music for her generous help, and the members of the staff of the Sterling Memorial Library, particularly Miss Anne S. Pratt, to whose efforts we owe the view of eighteenth-century Hamburg reproduced in this book.

LEO SCHRADE.

*Yale University, December, 1946*

# INTRODUCTION

JOHANN MATTHESON—born in 1681—belongs to an age that, at the very moment of its decline, seemed to put forth all its strength into one last effort to procure some final form for human thought, some perfect skill for man's deed. His birth occurred within a decade that was to confer extraordinary distinction upon the history of music. Francesco Durante, Domenico Scarlatti, Francesco Feo, Niccolò Porpora, Leonardo Vinci, Jean Philippe Rameau, Georg Philipp Telemann, Christoph Graupner, Johann Sebastian Bach, Georg Friedrich Händel, and numerous others of lesser importance—all were born between 1680 and 1690. Italians led baroque opera to its last triumphant phase in Europe. Rameau gave to French opera its most convincing form by creating an entirely original transformation of its Italian prototype. Together with these Mattheson represents the last generation of baroque musicians.

While Mattheson was alive the music of his own country exhibited, both in style and in intention, a singular lack of unity. Bach was the unequaled and incomprehensible reorganizer of Protestant church music at a time when secular forms were almost wholly predominant. Händel swept aside the narrow, anachronistic traditions of German music and gained international rank in as many branches of composition as his generation could provide. Anxious to maintain the contact with generally recognized European forms, such as the opera, Christoph Graupner stood aloof from Bach's ideals. Telemann, artist of the rationalistic enlightment which finally numbered Bach himself among its victims, made the most of whatever the painfully strict limitations of German music during the baroque had to offer; he even lived long enough to witness its downfall. And another close witness, although he was never altogether aware of this breakdown, was Johann Mattheson.

German baroque music is indeed so diverse and contradictory that it can in no way be considered as the outgrowth of an unbroken, steadily developing ideal. The extreme individuality of its spokesmen was at continual variance with the general state of musicianship throughout Germany itself. Johann Mattheson knew this. He tried to eliminate the discrepancy, or at least to mitigate it. With this in mind, he wrote his many theoretical works.

The older he grew, the more he came to be concerned with the welfare of German music. He made every effort to absorb the total output of musical thought in all fields of musical knowledge. He studied English literature extensively, from the advantageous point of view of secretary to the English Resident in Hamburg. He studied French literature, philosophical and musical, and became one of the most eloquent advocates of Descartes' philosophy. He translated French treatises, reshaped them, combined them with Italian works and with German tradition, and thus presented to German musicians a complex and rounded knowledge which should have eliminated a good bit of their backwardness. He studied the Italians, reacted sensitively to their artistic achievements, examined the best of their literature, translated again, and tried to reconcile their ideas to German concepts. His profound knowledge of the actual situation of music in Germany gave him a superiority bordering on conceit that at times is not easy to put up with. This fact does not, however, diminish the importance of the man. Although in his generation there were numerous German writers who treated the material of composition theoretically, there were scarcely any who tried to search out the real reasons for the peculiar state of German music. But of writers who understood the problem, and who gave the full energy and power of their pens to emancipating German baroque music from its dreary isolation, there was, it would appear, but one—Johann Mattheson.

The contradictory phenomena in German culture during the baroque age were, however, not restricted to music alone. In more than one way this culture displayed pecularities that had no parallel. The Protestant Reformation in Germany was brought about by a resurgence of intense religious fervor. So unwieldly was the Holy Roman Empire of Charles the Fifth that the German princes were able to take advantage of the spirit of religious revolt and thus retard the natural political development of the "Nation" by turning it backwards toward a more medieval form of local autonomy. Their mutual ambitions and jealousies as much as their religious beliefs—at least during the period in which Protestantism had not as yet crystallized into definite dogmas—were responsible for their division into the two armies of the Catholic Empire and the Protestant States. Out of this finally grew the political and religious conflict that engulfed not only Germany but virtually the whole of Europe: manifestation of the struggle between religious freedom and authoritarianism, between centralized, absolute monarchy and the dying remnants of feudalism. The varying strength in the forces opposing one another, to mention only one of many factors, caused profound differences in the struggle as manifested in the Empire and in the other countries of Europe. In both England and France the ultimate effect was the triumph of the central authority of the State and the materialistic philosophy of which the Renaissance had been the original expression. In the German territories, on the other hand, a war of hideous destruction ended indecisively in the utter exhaustion of both forces, and marked the defeat of imperial power and the firm establishment of innumerable politico-ecclesiastical organisms.[1] The effect of this upon German spiritual life was to bring about a temporary cessation of the intense cultural activity which the impact of the Renaissance seems to have inspired at the end of the fifteenth and beginning of the sixteenth centuries. Alone of all the arts music remained alive— even though musical activities were severely curtailed, especially in middle Germany. The very strong religious mysticism which seems to have been the chief manifestation of German Protestantism, and which the material hardships of the Thirty Years' War seem only to have strengthened, found its chief means of expression in the music and poetry of Lutheran chorales.

From the conclusion of the Thirty Years' War to the beginning of the eighteenth century the reconstruction of German cultural

1. See the comprehensive work on the subject, C. V. Wedgwood, *The Thirty Years War* (New Haven, 1939).

life was connected almost exclusively with religious expression and thought. In neither Catholic nor Protestant Germany was the post-Reformation period characterized by that decline in the importance and strength of religious idealism which was evident throughout the rest of Europe. The intellectual life of France and England in the second half of the seventeenth century was conspicuous for the increasing number and predominance of secular systems of ideas, interpretations of existence, and forms of art. With the beginning of the eighteenth century these forces had become so supreme as to bear down all opposition to the institutions and habits of thought inherited from earlier times. As the result of this "Enlightenment" the spiritual idealism of the past was superseded by an attitude of rational scepticism.

The parallel intellectual movement which swept through Germany during the eighteenth century is known as the *Aufklärung*. Although it is the equivalent of the English word "enlightenment," this term has, because of its intrinsically German significance, a connotation that is not readily translated. With the revival of cultural life in the latter part of the seventeenth century, especially in the North of Germany, intellectual contact with other European countries came again into being. Gradually the new philosophy of these countries began to find its way into Germany through commercial and political relations that brought with them the knowledge of foreign art, literature, and manners. For the wider dissemination of these new ideas the publication of numerous translations of foreign works and the appearance of a large number of journals were chiefly responsible. But, while these ideas created skepticism and rationalism outside Germany, they were met and opposed, within it, by the innate strength of traditional beliefs, and became changed and absorbed by the existing doctrines of German Protestantism and Catholicism. The "classicism" of Haydn, Mozart, and the young Beethoven, and that of Goethe and Schiller at the end of the century were the last expression of these ideas.

It is, therefore, in the fusion of new ideas with old, which, opposed as they were to one another, still did not bring about the collapse or capitulation of traditional thought, that the German Aufklärung may be said to differ from the French or English Enlightenment.[2] It is natural that a movement of such scope should profoundly affect the esthetic, both practical and theoretical, of all the arts. The present study of the life of Johann Mattheson and of his philosophy as expressed in *Das Neu-Eröffnete Orchestre,* is an attempt to clarify the effect of the Enlightenment upon the musical life and thought of Germany in the first part of the eighteenth century.

2. In this book the term "Enlightenment" alone will be used regardless of its application to England, France, or Germany. The Enlightenment, as a European movement, has recently been expounded, briefly and excellently, by Benno von Wiese, "Kultur der Aufklärung" in *Handwörterbuch der Soziologie,* ed. by Alfred Vierkandt (Stuttgart, 1931), pp. 14–24.

# CONTENTS

# ILLUSTRATIONS

# JOHANN MATTHESON

## I

### Hamburg in the Seventeenth and Eighteenth Centuries

HAMBURG war eine edle von Gott überflüssig und reichlich gesegnete Stadt, ein schöner Lustgarten im irdischen Paradies." [1] Of all the states of the German Empire, Hamburg alone survived the horror and subsequent demoralization of the Thirty Years' War with scarcely an injury. In fact, secure behind her excellent fortifications,[2] Hamburg so grew and prospered that by the end of the seventeenth century she seemed to have no rival among the cities of Northern Germany. Although many large cities that were located on the chief routes, such as Leipzig, Munich, Frankfurt a/M, Breslau, Danzig, Bremen, Lübeck, experienced an amazingly quick recovery and enjoyed prosperity fairly soon after the war, Hamburg surpassed them all in impregnability and wealth.

Unquestionably the most salient single factor throughout the entire course of Hamburg's history is that of geography. Situated seventy miles from the mouth of the Elbe, she has always commanded the commerce of the greatest river of Northern Germany. The gradual increase in the volume and importance of river and maritime traffic in the seventeenth and eighteenth centuries caused a corresponding increase in the prosperity and size of the city itself. With the decline in influence of the Hanseatic League at the end of the sixteenth century,[3] Hamburg, violating the regulations of the League, had welcomed and tried to attract foreign industries and settlers from the neighboring countries of Europe.[4] Most prominent among these were the English Merchant Adventurers who were permitted to set up an "English

1. B. Schupp, *Der Unterrichtete Student* (Hamburg, 1669).
2. H. Reinke, Hamburg, ein Abriss der Stadtgeschichte von den Anfängen bis zur Gegenwart (Bremen, 1926), p. 82.
3. *Idem*, p. 81.
4. *Idem*, p. 66.

Court" in 1611.[5] In the troubled years of the Thirty Years' War
the city consequently continued, because of the industries within
her walls, to flourish.[6] After the peace of Westphalia, her in-
dustrial prosperity was increased by the good fortune that made
her the chief harbor for the import and export trade of all northern Germany.[7] Hamburg's wealth in commerce and possessions
naturally made her an object of envy to all the surrounding
states. Although Denmark and Sweden controlled respectively
the right and left banks of the lower Elbe and hence were able
to interfere with the passage of ships, neither was strong enough
seriously to menace the freedom of the city.[8] This was also se-
cured by the mutual jealousy and rivalry not only of these two
states but of the neighboring states of northern Germany as well.[9]
As the trade of Hamburg with each of those states and with
those across the sea became more important, the value of her
independence and peaceful relations with each one of them increased correspondingly. Thus, though each of her neighbors
desired Hamburg's enormous wealth for itself, the loss of her
freedom would have spelled ruin to all but the possessor, and
the city and the status quo were maintained through an excess of
rivalries—a paradoxical situation perhaps but a very fortunate
one for the development of Hamburg herself.

Since material existence was so dependent upon external circumstances, social life was obviously affected by those circumstances to no small degree. For many generations the mercantile
class, secure in its riches, had assumed the position of an aristoc-

5. *Idem*, pp. 65–66.
6. *Idem*, p. 89.
7. A contemporary English observer wrote of Hamburg: "It is at this Day the greatest *Emporium* in Germany. It has a great Trade, not only with the Empire, but likewise with most other countries in Europe; and Merchant-Ships come hither from the most consider-able Parts of the known World. Their Whale and Herring Fisheries are very flourishing. Of late Years they have erected Woollen Manufactures." *The Present State of Germany* (London, 1738), II, 131. See also Mattheson's report to the Lords of Trade on "the Herring-Trade" and "Wool-Manufactures" (pp. 40–41 of this book).
8. Reinke *op. cit.*, pp. 101–106.
9. The author of *The Present State of Germany* (II, 132) neatly describes this situa-tion: ". . . in the jealousy of the neighboring Princes, *viz. Denmark, Sweden, Holstein* and *Brunswick-Hanover* consist its chief security: but of all these *Denmark* is the Power this City has most to dread for that Crown lets no Opportunity escape to draw a little of their (superfluous) Cash from them."

racy. Wealthy foreign merchants added to its ranks, as did the
foreign residents maintained in the city by the chief states of the
Empire and by Hamburg's neighbors, England, France, Denmark and Sweden, to further the smooth course of trade and
diplomatic relations. In the country surrounding Hamburg, particularly in Schleswig-Holstein, there was a considerable number
of nobles, who, unlike those in other parts of the Empire, had
retained their independent rank and landed position. Since Hamburg was the largest and most desirable community in the entire region, many of these nobles not only spent their winters
there but also maintained residences inside her walls. These diverse groups formed an upper class which came to have more and
more the characteristics of the fashionable circles of London and
Paris.

If all these external circumstances combined to make Hamburg
the most prosperous free city of the Empire, its internal organization was admirably adapted to further this preëminence. The
actual form of this organization was in perfect agreement with
the precepts of Luther but, through pressure both political and
religious, it had assumed rather a character of aristocratic unity.
Luther's own realistic respect for the temporal power of the German princes made the affairs of his Church strictly subservient
to the will of the civil government. If the beliefs of both temporal
and spiritual rulers were not in agreement, the strength of this
governmental unity would be shattered. Both the teachings of
the Church and the city's organization of its material affairs had
contributed to the strong paternalistic governmental structure of
seventeenth-century Hamburg.[10]

The government of both civil and religious affairs rested in the
hands of the Senat, a hereditary body of twenty men chosen
from the leading families of the town [11] and presided over by four
Consuls and two Syndics. Working in conjunction with this body
but possessing considerably less power, was a Council of sixty
burghers, elected to represent the different parishes into which
the city was divided. The election of these representatives was,

10. Reinke, *op. cit.,* p. 48.
11. *Idem,* p. 75.

# 4 Johann Mattheson

however, rigidly limited to a mere handful of the citizenry—those who possessed the greatest amount of property. Church affairs were, on the other hand, in the control of the Geistliches Ministerium, which comprised the pastors of all the churches of Hamburg save the Dom, which was not controlled by the city. Their activities, except in theological affairs, were however dependent upon the will of the civil government or *Rath*. Nevertheless, unified by a balanced belief in and theory of government, the civil and religious administration of Hamburg was not only a natural and practical product of its own age but was even responsible for an unusually advanced "socialistic" policy, including the foundation of hospitals and charitable institutions of all sorts.[12]

The intellectual life of the town grew up almost entirely within the bounds of its closely interrelated institutions. Education was provided by the ancient Johannisschule, whose curriculum had been remodeled on humanistic principles. In 1616 a Gymnasium was founded, which corresponded in a general way to the universities of the time.[13] Both institutions were actually designed to prepare their students for a legal, governmental, or theological career. The Lutheran respect for learning and dialectic encouraged the development of scholars and teachers of eminence.[14] The strong taste for music, which Luther had declared "Die edle Gab GOttes," resulted in a marked growth and flowering of church music; and those who performed this music—organists, singers, instrumentalists—were likewise part of the municipal and clerical organizations, the instrumentalists being organized as *Stadtpfeifer* and *Rollbrüder* in the manner of a guild under civic jurisdiction.[15] Religious poetry also flourished in the work of writers such as Johann Rist and Paul Fleming.[16] Outside the influential sphere of the strict Lutheran organization the beginnings of an independent literary and musical expression might be dis-

12. *Idem*, p. 73.
13. *Idem*, p. 72.
14. Feodor Wehl, *Hamburgs Literaturleben im achzehnten Jahrhundert* (Leipzig 1856), p. 12.
15. Guido Adler, *Handbuch der Musikgeschichte* (Berlin-Wilmersdorf, 1930), pp. 447 f. Cf. Liselotte Krüger, *Die Hamburgische Musikorganisation im XVII Jahrhundert* (Zürich, 1933).
16. F. Wehl, *op. cit.*, pp. 14–15.

cerned, but they scarcely affected the orderly unity of Lutheran
Hamburg during the greater part of the seventeenth century.

Nevertheless the identical geographical factors which had contributed to the financial strength and made possible the essential
internal unity of Hamburg brought the city and its inhabitants
into contact with the life and thought of non-Lutheran Europe.
The vital forces at work in the France of Louis XIV and the
England of Charles II had little in common with the active concept of Lutheranism which prevailed in Hamburg. Nor did the
more immediate and equally important political or economic
circumstances of the city remain consistently favorable to its
stability. The effect of these forces and conditions upon the Elbe
port began to be noticeable by the beginning of the last quarter
of the seventeenth century. From 1675 to 1725, the period which
embraces the most important years of Johann Mattheson's career,
every aspect of Hamburg's life and institutional organization felt
the impact of disruptive forces. New elements which had had
no place in the unsophisticated seventeenth-century picture thrust
themselves forward. Interests appealing to the burgher aristocracy but which had been held down by traditional customs and
precepts profoundly colored and changed the intellectual life of
the town.

Externally the rise of Sweden to the rank of a major power
was a menace of no little magnitude. Denmark began demanding increasingly large subsidies as rewards for non-interference in
the city's commerce and, despite their payment, in 1686 attempted
to capture Hamburg. Since in the preceding few years the city
had allowed her defenses and military forces to deteriorate, her
freedom was preserved only by the intervention of Celle and
Brandenburg. Subsequent threats of force extracted even larger
sums from Hamburg's treasury, and Danish possession of the
right bank of the Elbe remained a menace to her trade.[17] Sweden
had recently come into possession of the left bank, and as a result
the passage of the city's merchant vessels was seriously imperiled.
The outbreak of the Northern War in 1712 brought to a climax
the dangers implicit in the situation. The conflict found England

17. Reinke, *op. cit.*, pp. 101–106.

and most of northern Germany allied against the combined forces of Russia and Sweden. Among the issues at stake, the possession or at least control of the valuable trade of Hamburg was one of the utmost importance to both sides.

It is therefore not surprising to find that activity on the part of the anti-Swedish allies, and of England in particular, whose share in the trade was perhaps the greatest, became at this time increasingly noticeable in the political affairs of Hamburg.[18] The importance England attached to the fate of the city was increased by the accession to the English throne of George I of Hanover. Hamburg directly commanded the lines of communications between England, Hanover, and northern Germany. Thus simultaneous interests of trade and politics combined to make Hamburg a center of international intrigue and a prey to diplomatic pressure from all sides during the period of conflict.[19] One of the first events of the Northern War was the occupation by the Hanoverian forces of the Duchies of Bremen and Verden whose territories commanded the left bank of the Elbe.[20] Although Russia and Sweden were suspected of planning to recapture these territories in 1715 and 1716, the menace potentially most dangerous to the security of Hamburg's overseas trade was removed.[21] Subsequently, in part through the mediation of the British Residents, all further attempts by Denmark and her ally, Holstein-Gottorp, to extort tribute from the city were held in check.[22] In the succeeding period of the eighteenth century the rise of Russian and the decline of Swedish power removed the menace

18. J. F. Chance, *George I and the Northern War* (London, 1909), p. 5.

19. The diplomatic and commercial papers of this period to and from the British Representatives in Hamburg are listed in Chance, "List of Diplomatic Representatives and Agents, England and North Germany 1689–1727," in *Notes on the Diplomatic Relations of England & Germany*, ed. by C. H. Firth (Oxford 1907), pp. 22–23, 28, 31. The manuscript in the possession of the Public Record Office in London for the period 1705–55 alone comprises Vols. 20–76, *State Papers, Foreign, Hamburg, and Hanseatic Towns*, and Vols. 62, 200, 204, 212, 217, 221, *State Papers, Foreign, Foreign Entry Books*.

20. Chance, *George I and the Northern War*, p. 29. Also Wolfgang Michael, *Englische Geschichte im achtzehnten Jahrhundert*, 4 Vols. (Leipzig 1896–1937), I, 730–731.

21. Chance, *George I and the Northern War*, notes on pp. 102, 149.

22. Reinke, *op. cit.*, p. 142. Because of Mattheson's connection with the British Residents, these events will receive somewhat more detailed examination below.

to the status quo of northwestern Germany. At the same time the principal reasons for Hamburg's prominence in international politics and diplomacy were also removed.

Meanwhile, the serious threats of these external events to Hamburg's unity found a parallel in the town's internal organization. During the last quarter of the seventeenth and the first quarter of the eighteenth centuries such bitter strife raged sporadically within the government of Hamburg as to produce conditions at times verging on anarchy. The origin of the quarrel was the property qualification, which, as has been seen, denied the franchise to all but the most wealthy inhabitants. The smaller burghers not illogically resented the autocratic tendencies of the government. The first indications of their dissatisfaction in 1665 had merely made the Rath become increasingly absolute.[23] Demands for more democratic government were, however, so persistent that in 1675 an imperial commissioner was delegated to arbitrate. He lowered the property qualification to 500 Reichsthaler. It was an empty gesture; his decree was ignored, and the resentment became intensified.[24] During the years 1686–90 the conflict was kept within bounds by a virtual dictatorship and by the external menace of the Danes.[25] After the death of Bürgermeister Meurer in 1690, however, violent discontent manifested itself. It culminated in 1698 with the issuing of a "Manifest Bürgerlicher Freiheit," and an actual revolutionary attack upon the government. In the ensuing conflict several members of the Rath were killed, and the remainder fled for their lives, thus depriving Hamburg of every shred of government. For eleven years anarchy pevailed; the city had no peace until the drawing up—with the aid of an imperial commission—of a new constitution in 1709.[26] Despite the liberal demands which had precipitated the struggle, the new constitution did no more than introduce a few minor governmental changes, and actually granted to the middle class scarcely any of the privileges they were struggling to get hold of.

23. *Idem*, pp. 118–122
24. *Idem*, pp. 124 f.
25. *Idem*, p. 135.
26. *Idem*, pp. 135–138.

Throughout the eighteenth century the government of Hamburg continued to become not only more autocratic but more plutocratic as well.

The civil conflict of these years was equaled and even furthered by religious dissension among the Lutherans. That there was considerable religious vitality in the second half of the seventeenth century is evidenced by the addition of great towers to three of Hamburg's principal churches, and by the uninterrupted production of church music.[27] But such "vitality" was often expressive of power and wealth rather than of religion. A curious commingling of a materialistic spirit with the forms of religion became characteristic of Hamburg society, as it did of most Protestant cities that flourished by commerce and trade.[28] The interests of Pastor Johann Balthasar Schupp (1610–1661) were pretty evenly divided between religious and mercantile concerns. The noble Hamburg Senators must have been inspired to profound contemplation of the state of their souls when, between prayers, they turned to the notations of the Stock exchange, printed conveniently on the last pages of Melchior Christoph Wöttgen's prayerbook, which showed on its title page a woodcut not of the church and its congregation but of Hamburg's exchange and the stockbrokers.[29] The materialism that had so firm a hold on religious forms may well have been at least one of the causes why two divergent parties and streams of thought became increasingly apparent in this period. The preoccupation of the one with theological and doctrinal matters seems to have stimulated the mystical and emotional reactions of the other. By 1693 the town was split into two religious camps, the orthodox majority under Dr. Mayer of the St. Jacobi Kirche, and the Pietist parishes of St. Nikolai and St. Michaelis under the inspiration of the teachings of Spener. The fanatical disagreements of these two groups were voiced through denunciatory sermons and pamphlets, by

27. *Idem*, p. 115.

28. See the discussion of this matter and its historical implications in the works of Max Weber and Troeltsch.

29. A copy of the *Geistreich Gebet Büchlein vor Reisende zu Land und Wasser sampt einen Ordentlichen Wegweiser durch ganz Teutschland,* by M. Ch. Wöttgen is in Hamburg, State Archives: HSt Arch H. 9. See also Heinrich Miesner, "Philipp Emmanuel Bach in Hamburg," Diss. (Berlin, 1929), p. 24.

riots in the streets and cabals within the very ranks of Hamburg's government.[30] Specifically the church was divided upon two issues. The first, which involved the making of a new *Gottesdienstordnung,* was settled in 1712.[31] The second, brought to the fore by the Hamburg Opera, which had been founded in 1678, revolved about dramatic tendencies in church music, and continued to be a subject for sharp controversy throughout the first half of the eighteenth century.

The rise both of opera and of dramatic church music is an indication of the social and intellectual changes noticeable in this period of Hamburg's disunity. Indeed, Hamburg's increasing international importance brought to it an ever larger number of foreign diplomats of considerable wealth, fresh from such fashionable centers as the capitals of England and France. It became customary also for the sons of Hamburg's native aristocracy to make the Grand Tour, and thus to come into closer contact with the elegant world of the European courts, where, as Pöllnitz says, they could easily pass for "Gentlemen of Holstein." [32] Resident foreign merchants increased the ranks of a society [33] which was becoming a small counterpart of that to be found in Paris and London. The men of Hamburg, dressed in the Parisian fashion, were spending more and more of their time in the newly established English coffee-houses; [34] foreign Residents, native burghers, and local nobility were attending balls and holding fêtes within fine mansions inside the city walls or in the immediately surrounding country.[35]

Influenced, perhaps, by the splendor of this non-mercantile aristocracy, the Hamburgers became more and more concerned with literature and art. Outside the sphere of Lutheran politics

30. Reinke, *op. cit.,* pp. 133 f.

31. Liselotte Krüger, *Die Hamburgische Musikorganisation,* p. 253.

32. C. L. Pöllnitz, *Memoirs, being the observations He made in his late Travels . . . ;* 2d ed. 4 Vols. (London, 1739–40), I, 52: "The Merchants [of Hamburg] are affable, civil; most of them in their youth travelled to the most remarkable Countries of *Europe,* where they then pass for Gentlemen of Holstein. There they learn that polite Air, and that Behaviour which one would wish to see in all gentlemen of good Families."

33. H. Stierling, "Leben und Bildnis Friedrich von Hagedorn," in *Mitteillungen aus dem Museum für Hamburgische Geschichte,* No. 2, Vol. 28, p. 30.

34. Reinke, *op. cit.,* p. 156.

35. Ernst Finder, *Hamburgisches Bürgertum* (Hamburg, 1930), p. 217.

and religion, the type of intellectual activity that was flourishing
in the rest of Europe made its appearance in their city. To the
divergent religious and political opinions that were altering and
splitting open the intellectual concepts of the past were added
the ideas of rational and classical French thinking. The *Cid* had
been translated for the Hamburg theater in 1650.[36] Thereafter a
school of poetry, inspired by Lohenstein, sprang to life and exhibited the same adulation of French classic drama that swept
through every civilized country of Europe. Pompous occasional
verses for weddings, birthdays, and fêtes, frequently set to music,
and the writing of books [37] became the fashion for every citizen
of taste and education.[38] The majority of these productions, both
as to subject and style, were vastly different from the traditional
religious poetry of the preceding generation.[39]

Simultaneous with the rise of English social and political influence in Hamburg was the growing popularity of English
philosophy and literature. Hamburg boasted the first weekly in
Germany: a translation and imitation of the *Tatler* and *Spectator
Papers* edited by Johann Mattheson in 1713–14.[40] Following in
its train in Hamburg and elsewhere numerous original imitations
of these publications appeared, of which the best and most famous was *Der Patriot,*[41] founded by the "Patriotische Gesellschaft,"
a literary society composed of the city's chief writers. Much of the
poetry of Heinrich Brockes and Friedrich von Hagedorn, the two
most eminent members of this group, both of whom had lived in
England, exhibited in style and in content the influence of the
poetry of Milton, Pope, and other English writers.[42] Translations

36. F. Wehl, *Hamburgs Literaturleben,* p. 28.
37. The most exaggerated of all dedicatory compliments is to be found in Johann
Mattheson's Dedication of *Der Vollkommene Capellmeister* to Ernst Ludwig, Landgraf of
Hesse: "Wenn GOtt nicht GOtt wäre, wer sollte billiger GOtt seyn, als unser Fürst?"
38. Ernst Finder, *Hamburgisches Bürgertum,* pp. 55–56. The Hamburg poet and writer,
Christopher Weichmann, published a collection of such verses in six volumes between
the years 1725 and 1738, entitled *Poesie der Nieder-Sachsen, oder allerhand, mehrentheils
noch nie gedruckte Gedichte von den berühmtesten Neider-Sachsen. . . .* Cf. also Alois
Brandl, *B. H. Brockes,* (Innsbruck, 1878), p. 26.
39. Reinke, *op. cit.,* pp. 113 f.
40. Cf. Bibliography No. 9.
41. It was published during the years 1724–28.
42. A. L. Brandl, *B. H. Brockes,* pp. 34–35.

of novels such as *Pamela* and of English works of all sorts appeared with more and more frequency in many learned journals, notably the *Niedersächsische Nachrichten von Gelehrte Sachen* (1729–34).[43] Philosophical and religious developments in England were followed with the keenest interest, and many of their often contradictory ideas were incorporated into the writings of more than one Hamburg *galant homme*. Throughout the first half of the eighteenth century these foreign intellectual influences subtly or openly were beating against and undermining the beliefs which Lutheranism had hitherto so strongly unified. Socially, politically, and intellectually, Hamburg during Johann Mattheson's life was a much more complex, less simply analyzed organism than it had been in the seventeenth century. That the traditional patterns of life and organization continued to dominate and hold together the entire community is indicative of their innate strength.

In no other particular aspect of Hamburg's life is the clash of new ideas and principles more revealing than in music. Because of the part music played in the life and thought of Johann Mattheson it is perhaps fitting here to discuss it as a distinct, albeit closely integrated, part of Hamburg's cultural existence.

In order to fulfil the musical requirements of seventeenth-century civil and religious life a highly developed organization had come into being. Music had played an important part in the doctrines of Luther.[44] Throughout the century its importance increased, and the requirements for the various forms of its expression became more complicated. To satisfy the demand for a sufficient number of instrumentalists and vocalists for all the chief

43. L. M. Price, *The Reception of English Literature in Germany* (Berkeley, Cal., 1932), p. 31.

44. The following is an excellent example of this attitude toward music: "Die Musika ist eine edle Kunst und ein grosses *Ornamentum* eines edlen *Ingenii*. Alle andre Künste und Wissenschafftten sterben mit uns. . . . Aber was ein Theologus und ein Musikus auf Erden gelernet hat, das practiciret er auch im Himmel, nehmlich, er lobet und preiset GOtt." Mattheson, *Grundlage einer Ehrenpforte,* Reprint, Kassel 1910, p. 304, quoted from B. Schupp, *Der Unterrichtete Student,* 1667. At the same time Mattheson gives evidence that he still holds to the system of *musica instrumentalis, humana, mundana* (*caelestis*), the musician continuing the real music on earth (*musica instrumentalis*) as celestial music (*musica mundana*). Also the statement that music is a noble genius has considerable significance.

churches in Hamburg the city organized and supported a corps
of singers who were attached to the churches and the schools,
and a guild of instrumentalists who were attached to the municipality itself.[45] They were kept busy not only with religious
ceremonies but also with civil festivities, which, as the dignity
and self-importance of the government increased, became more
numerous and elaborate. Secondly, the Lutheran emphasis upon
the spiritual importance of music made it an integral part of the
curriculum of the Johanneum.[46] Its students supplemented the
ranks of regular singers in the churches. The direction of musical
education and organization was placed in the hands of the cantor,
who was appointed by the rector and faculty of the school. The
office of cantor became an extremely influential one. By the middle of the century, in fact, the cantor had gained control over the
entire official musical organization of the town.[47] His appointment was therefore taken over by the municipal government,
with the secondary approval of the *Geistliches Ministerium.* Thus
the entire official musical life of the town became administered
by a single musician directly under the control of the government. The town cantor was entrusted with every aspect of this
not inconsiderable musical establishment, from the employment
of singers and instrumentalists to the provision of adequate and
appropriate music for the churches. During the years 1660–74,
under the cantorship of Christoph Bernhard, the system was
peculiarly successful.[48] Hamburg's musical reputation attracted
students from all Germany,[49] and the tradition of magnificent
church music for her organs and her singers was established.[50]

In 1678, only four years after the death of Bernhard, the Hamburg Opera was founded.[51] An institution of this sort could scarcely

45. L. Krüger's *Die Hamburgische Musikorganisation im XVII Jahrhundert* is an
authoritative account of this historical development.
46. Krüger *op. cit.*, p. 11.
47. *Idem*, p. 8.
48. *Idem*, p. 100.
49. *Idem*, pp. 8–9.
50. Adler, *Handbuch der Musikgeschichte*, pp. 691 ff.
51. The most comprehensive study on the subject of the Hamburg Opera is Walter
Schulze, "Die Quellen der Hamburger Oper (1678–1738). Eine bibliograph-statistische
Studie zur Geschichte der ersten stehenden deutschen Oper," in *Mitteilungen aus der
Bibliothek der Hansestadt Hamburg*, Neue Folge, ed. by Gustav Wahl, Vol. 4 (Hamburg-

have hoped to find any authority or position in a community ordered by Lutheran thinking. Nevertheless, prior to this period, the taste for the purely secular music which had spread over the rest of Europe had also begun to obtain a foothold in Hamburg, as is shown by the institution in 1660 of Weckmann's *Collegium Musicum.*[52] Outside Hamburg, opera had come to be, in the esteem of fashionable Paris, and later of London, the chief of the newer forms of artistic expression. It had many enemies, however, not only among the stricter clergy, but also, for reasons other than moral, among such freethinkers as St. Evremond.[53] Though it might deal with unchristian subjects, and at the same time be ridiculous to the rationalist,[54] its spectacular dramatic synthesis of all the arts satisfied the demands of a courtly, pompous, self-important society,[55] anxious to take advantage of the opera as the most effective medium of grandiose representation of, one might almost say, its very self. The Hamburg Opera appears to have been the inspiration of Hertzog Christian Albrecht von Gottorp, who had come to the city as an exile in 1676, and his Capellmeister, Johann Theile.[56] But Ratsherr Gerhard Schott, Licentiat Lütkens and Johann Reinken,[57] the famous organist of the St. Catharinen Kirche, were the actual organizers, and for the better part of its

Oldenburg, 1938). The repertory of Hamburg operas has never been correctly given, and errors have been carried on from one publication to another. Schulze consequently stresses the need for bibliographical clarification preliminary to any interpretation of the music itself. He skilfully investigates the *libretti*, the scores, and the collections of arias; he gives a complete list of the scores and anthologies of arias. His publication of thirteen documents, chiefly concerning the dispute between Schott and Kremberg, is of particular importance for the history of opera in Hamburg.

52. Krüger, *op. cit.*, pp. 97–98. For the best description of the Collegium Musicum in its early years see Max Seiffert, "Mathias Weckmann und das *Collegium Musicum* in Hamburg," in *Sammelbände der internationalen Musikgesellschaft* [abbreviated SIMG], II (Leipzig, 1900–1901), 110 ff. Mattheson, who apparently on the evidence offered by the *Chronicle of Hamburg*, by Conrad von Hövelen, dates the beginning of the Collegium Musicum erroneously 1688, mentions that "two noble amateurs of music started the Collegium Musicum together with Weckmann." This implies that the initiative seems to have come from the noble amateurs.

53. St. Evremond, "Lettre sur l'Opera."

54. He wrote of it: "Une sottise chargé de musique, de danses, de machines, de decorations, est une sottise magnifique, mais toujours une sottise." Quoted from Paul Hazard, *La Crise de la Conscience Européene* (Paris, 1935), II, 204.

55. *Idem*, pp. 203 ff.

56. Reinke, *op. cit.*, p. 117.

57. Krüger, *op. cit.*, pp. 254–256.

existence its artists were drawn from native sources. Its continued life was unquestionably made possible by the wealth and taste of the international Residents and of the scarcely less aristocratic burghers.[58]

The subject matter of the first operatic production was, happily, religious—a fact which prevented serious objection to the founding of the Opera.[59] For some years a primitive and simple form of dramatic music, the *Passionsmusiken,* had been presented in the churches.[60] and Theile's opera was much closer to the form of this passion music than to that of French and Italian opera proper.[61] Gerhard Schott, the real soul of the enterprise,[62] was a widely traveled and educated man, however,[63] and he was anything but satisfied with such a poor attempt as this. The three other works produced in 1678—although the text of one was written by Pastor Elmenhorst of the St. Catharinen Kirche—were frankly secular, as were those produced in subsequent years. Because of this, the inevitable opposition from the Pietistic elements in the city was not slow in making its appearance. But the orthodox elements in the Church were on the whole favorable to the institution, and the Opera became a matter of the utmost controversial importance.[64] During the years 1681–89 the controversy was fought out in Church and Government.[65] Schott's defense of the Opera,

58. Mattheson, in describing the proper social conditions for the existence of opera, is speaking of Hamburg when he writes: "Wenn aber Republicken, wegen der Menge und des Zuflusses von allerhand Leuten, viele *Requisita Scenica* bequemlich an die Hand geben, so ist eine geschlossene Zahl-reiche Gesellschafft das beste Mittel, der Sache auffzuhelffen. Die gute Ordnung und Einrichtung einer solchen Societät bringen dem gemeinen Wesen vielen Nutzen: weil durch berühmte Vorstellungen offt grosse Fürsten und Herren bewogen werden, . . . derselben häuffige Nahrung zuwenden. Wissenschaften, Künste und Handwercker fahren wol dabey, und der Ort macht sich so ausnehmend mit guten Opern, als mit guten Bancken: denn diese nützen, und jene ergetzen." *Der Musikalische Patriot,* p. 176.
59. *Der erschaffene, gefallene und aufgerichtete Mensch.*
60. H. Hörner, *G. P. Telemanns Passionsmusiken* (Borna-Leipzig, 1933), pp. 7–8.
61. It is described by E. O. Lindner, *Die erste stehende Deutsche Oper* (Berlin, 1855) I, 4–9. See also "Friedrich Zelle, J. Theile und N. A. Strungk. Zweiter Beitrag zur Geschichte der ältesten deutschen Oper," in *Wissenschaftliche Beilage zum Program des Humboldts-Gymnasium zu Berlin. Ostern 1891* (Berlin, 1891).
62. W. Kleefeld, "Das Orchester der Hamburger Oper," in *SIMG* 1899, p. 220.
63. Hans Schröder, *Lexikon der Hamburgischen Schriftsteller bis zur Gegenwart,* 8 vols. (Hamburg, 1851–83), VII, 13.
64. Krüger, *op. cit.,* pp. 254–257.
65. L. Meinardus, *Rückblick auf die Anfange der deutschen Oper in Hamburg* (Hamburg, 1878), p. 51.

after being debated by the theological faculties of Wittenberg and Rostock and by the Hamburger Senat, was overruled, and, for part of the year 1687,[66] the Opera was, in fact, closed. Despite continuous and vehement protests, it was opened in the following year, and with various vicissitudes for another fifty years.

The presence of an Opera in Hamburg profoundly affected the traditional musical organization of the town. The position of the Cantor was, of course, enormously weakened by the existence of a large body of musicians outside his jurisdiction. The use of operatic singers or instrumentalists in the churches was forbidden, even though many of them were far more accomplished than those under his control. Gerstenbüttel, the Cantor of this period, although a conservative, and individually opposed to the new institution and its music, was unable to take any definite stand in the controversy, since he was obliged to satisfy the musical demands of both parties in the church. Moreover, operatic style and forms were becoming more and more popular with performers, composers, and listeners alike. The Pietists found in the dramatic freedom of the operatic style a medium of expression for their subjective emotionalism.[67] As a result, even though they disapproved of any association with the theater, they were inspired to compose operas themselves. The very fact that this contradiction had failed to prevent the formation of an independent Opera, made it possible by the same token to institute individual public concerts of theatrical church music—that is to say, oratorios. In this way, if the official commands of the Senat barred an oratorio from the town churches, the production could be and still was performed privately, or in the Drillhaus or the Hamburger Domkirche which, as has been pointed out, lay outside the jurisdiction of the municipal government.[68] In this way the Church began to lose its position as chief purveyor of music. It could not withstand the competition of those other forms of musical production, which were the forerunners of the independent system of the present day. Like other older forms of Hamburg life, once completely controlled by Lutheranism, the musical

66. *Idem,* p. 56.
67. H. Hörner, *G. P. Telemanns Passionsmusiken,* pp. 32–33.
68. Eberhard Preussner, *Die Bürgerliche Musikkultur* (Hamburg, 1935), pp. 12–13.

organization of the Lutheran city-state had reached its period of decline and change. The musical scene, in fact, shows the same complex mingling of new and old forms and expressions as is to be found in all the other configurations of eighteenth-century life in Hamburg.

It is against this background that the life of Johann Mattheson must be viewed. The extreme diversity of his interests and activities brought him into contact with virtually all the different aspects of Hamburg society and culture. His musical ability was apparent from his childhood; he gained his chief musical education from the Opera, the vehicle of the baroque style and its new musical ideas. Unwilling to adjust himself to the traditional system of making a musical livelihood in the musical organization of Lutheran Hamburg, he entered into the realm of international affairs and diplomacy as secretary to the British Resident. In addition to the comfortable income he received from this post, he earned a profitable and independent living as composer, performer, and teacher of music. In the upper circles of Hamburg he was a familiar figure. Notwithstanding his predilection for secular music, his innate religious sentiments, in which love for church music was implicit, impelled him to accept the position of Director of Music in the Domkirche. Although he was grossly underpaid for the numerous duties of this position, he enjoyed a freedom, while he had it, which enabled him to apply his advanced musical theories to the composition of numerous oratorios. Since popular demand called for repeated performances of the oratorio outside the Dom, they were also presented in the Drillhaus, and thus played their part in establishing the modern form of the public concert. The borderline between sacred and secular music was in many ways scarcely discernible, and Mattheson had a considerable share in the foundation of modern concert life. He was a man of considerable, if somewhat conventional literary taste and ability, and translated a number of English political pamphlets and literary works that were of importance to the intellectual life of northern Germany. He devoted much of his energy to the writing of the books on musical theory and composition, philosophy, and criticism, which have been his chief claim to the attentions of posterity. A Lutheran, whose faith was unshaken by his familiarity with rationalistic and anti-religious doctrines, his last act was symptomatic of all he had lived for: the bequeathal of his entire fortune for the building of a magnificent church organ to the glory of music, of himself, and of his Maker. His biography can in no wise be anything but a significant part of the history of eighteenth century musical culture.

# II

## The Life of Johann Mattheson

### I

#### EARLY YEARS

JOHANN MATTHESON was born September 28, 1681.[1] The following day he was taken by his parents to their parish church, the St. Nikolai-Kirche, and baptized.[2] Of his parents and ancestry nothing is known except what Mattheson himself wrote in his autobiography.[3] From this published account and the notes he added to it after his sixtieth year it is clear that neither of his parents was prominent in Hamburg society. His father was a tax-collector, which suggests that he may have enjoyed some official status. But he seems to have been wealthy enough to give his son a fairly expensive education. His mother came from the neighboring town of Rendsburg, in Schleswig-Holstein; she was "of good sturdy stock." Because of his own substantial position at the time he wrote his life, it is apparent that Mattheson was disposed to improve upon his pedigree.[4] In his autobiography he

1. His baptism is recorded in the *Nicolai Tauffen Register*, 1676–95, Hamburger Staats Archiv III 4 E. under the date of September 29: "Johannis Mattheson K.[ind], Johannis."

2. *Grundlage einer Ehrenpforte* (Hamburg, 1740; Reprint, Kassel, 1910), p. 187: "Seine lieben Eltern, haben ihn demnach in der S. Nicolai-Kirche bey öffentlicher Procession den 29. Sept. tauffen lassen." (The full titles of Mattheson's works will be found in the bibliography; the titles will be abbreviated in the text.)

3. The sources of our knowledge of the life of Johann Mattheson are, regrettably, limited to the account he writes of himself in the third person in the *Ehrenpforte*, in notes written by him after the publication of this volume, in manuscript material scattered through his collected documents in the Hamburger Stadt-Bibliothek, etc.—in other words, most of the material for his biography comes from him. In the following pages, the *Ehrenpforte* account has been extensively used, as is inevitable. Since it is obviously based on his own *Denckbücher*, it may be considered accurate within human limitations. What his vanity prompted him to exaggerate can be readily discerned and evaluated by any careful reader.

4. *Ehrenpforte*, p. 187: "Sein Vater, Johann, war Accise-Einnehmer; sein Gros-Vater ein wohlversuchter Kriegesmann; sein Aelter-Vater Stadtschreiber in Wismar &c.; das Geschlecht aber kömmt aus Norwegen her. Seine Mutter, Margarethe, war eine gebohrene Höling, aus Rendsburg, von gutem, alten, handfesten, ditmarser-Stamme."

therefore included a detailed description of the Mattheson coat of arms which, it is to be feared, he invented; in his unpublished notes, he wrote of men of importance who bore different forms of his own name. After his mother's pedigree, however, he added partly in regret, partly in pride, "Il faut avoir bien peu de vertu, quand on ne peut faire estimer que par celle de ses ancêtres! *Arlequiniana* p. 191." [5] The Matthesons, in short, were not members of the aristocracy of Hamburg.

Despite this, Mattheson's early education was a very good one. He was instructed in the precepts of his religion by many special Protestant teachers.[6] After the death of his two other brothers he attended the Johanneum with the sons of Hamburg's leading families.[7] Paul Georg Krüsike, the Sub-Rector of the school, was a scholar of high rank, famous for his Latin and Greek poems and for his philological works.[8] From him, Mattheson learned Latin and Greek; other subjects he learned from the Rector, Johann Schultze.[9] Since his father wished him to enter the profession of Law, his formal scholastic education did not continue beyond the Johanneum. In fact, when he was nine years old two "famous jurists, Dr. Schneegass and Dr. Kellner, held two *Collegia* [10] with him. Outside of school young Mattheson had lessons in the fashionable accomplishments of dancing, drawing, and arithmetic, as well as in riding and fencing.[11] Of far greater importance than

5. *Idem,* Anhang, p. 10.

6. *Idem,* p. 187: ". . . auch hernach ungemein wohl und christlich erzogen, mittelst verschiedener, besonderer, evangelischer Lehrer, die zu erst im Hause, hernach auf der Nähe gehalten." In view of the position of his father, it is doubtful that house-instructors were engaged, as Mattheson's remark might suggest.

7. *Ibid.:* "Nachdem seine zween Brüder gantz jung verstorben, haben sie diesen ihren einigen Sohn in die berühmte hiesige Johannisschule gesandt. . . ."

8. Edmund Kelter, *Hamburg und sein Johanneum im Wandel der Jahrhunderte* (Hamburg, 1929), p. 88.

9. *Ehrenpforte,* pp. 187–188: ". . . er, nebst der lateinischen und griechischen Sprache, anfangs durch den damahligen Sub- und hernach Conrector, Paul Georg Krüsike, aus Schleswig, in der Dichtkunst, absonderlich in der lateinischen, so dann durch den Rector, Johann Schultze, aus Garleben, in andern Disciplinen, mit Fleiss unterrichtet worden."

10. *Idem,* pp. 188–189: "Ob ihn nun zwar diese reitzende Arbeit von förmlicher Besuchung andrer hohen Schulen abhielt . . . zumahl, da ihn sein Vater hauptsächlich der Rechtsgelehrsamkeit gewidmet hatte, und er denn auch, zu solchem Ende, eben um diese Zeit, 1690, zwey Collegia bey berühmten Juristen, D. Schneegass, und D. Kellner, nacheinander mithielt."

11. *Idem,* p. 188: ". . . dabey er denn auch im Tantzen, Reissen, Rechnen, . . . so ferner, bey heranwachsenden Kräfften, im Fechten bey dreien Meistern, im Reiten &c. seine

these, however, was his musical education, which began when he was seven. Johann Nicolaus Hanff, *Kapellmeister* of the Bishop of Lübeck, taught him the clavier and composition for four years; from an unknown musician named Woldag he learned how to sing, and he states that he was also instructed in the playing of the gamba, violin, flute, and oboe.[12]

From this recital it appears that the remarkable activity of his mature life was inaugurated in his earliest youth. At the age of nine, he had already become somewhat of a musical prodigy: he was "possessed of a pure and lovely soprano voice, which was heard in different churches"; he played his own "compositions," if such a title can be given to the production of so youthful a student, and "he was often heard playing the organ (although his feet could not yet reach the pedal); he also accompanied his singing in specially arranged compositions with a thorough-bass." [13])

His ability seems to have been sufficient to attract the attention of Gerhard Schott, who at that time was managing the Hamburg Opera. Schott who, until he died in 1702, continued to take an interest in him, introduced him to the theater.[14] Although Mattheson's private music lessons continued with three other masters successively—they taught him how to write church-music, fugues, and counterpoint—he felt that this new connection with the art

Übungen hatte." To the disadvantage of the *curriculum*, subjects such as dancing, etc. were introduced even in the best schools at the beginning of the eighteenth century. Instruction in music suffered severely from these novelties. Instructors were also appointed to teach "anständige Tragung des Leibes und geschichte Komplimente." See Arne Werner, "Musik und Musiker in der Landesschule Pforta," in *SIMG* VIII (Leipzig, 1906–07), pp. 536, 545.

12. *Ehrenpforte*, p. 188: "Im siebenten Jahr seines Alters machte man mit ihm den Anfang zur Musik, mittelst getreuer Anweisung eines hauptehrlichen Mannes, der Johann Nicolaus Hanff hiess, und vorhin Hochfürstl. Capelldirector des Bishoffs von Lübeck zu Eutin gewesen war; Dieser unterrichtete ihn vier Jahr auf dem Clavier und in der Setzkunst; ein andrer, Nahmens Woldag, zu gleicher Zeit, in der Singekunst; dabey er denn auch im Tantzen, Reissen, Rechnen, auf der Gambe, Violine, Flöte und Hoboe . . . seine Übungen hatte."

13. *Ibid.*: "Nachdem er sich, bey so zartem Alter, 1690, mit einer umfänglichen, hellen und lieblichen Discantstimme, auch selbsteigener Composition, wie sie denn gewesen seyn mag, und von seiner Jugend gefordert werden mögte, in verschiedenen Kirchen, anbey gar offt mit Orgelspielen (ungeachtet die Füsse das Pedal noch nicht erreichen konnten) als ein neun-jähriger Knabe hören liess; auch sodann, in besonders-Angestellten Concerten, sich selber, bey seinem Singen, alles vorgelegt mit dem Generalbass accompagnirte."

14. *Ibid.*: ". . . gefiel er dem Hrn. Gerhard Schott, . . . dermaassen, dass er den Knaben auf Theater brachte, und biss an sein Ende, welches den 25. October 1702. erfolgte, mit grossem Nutzen gebrauchte."

of the opera was of much greater benefit to him than his regular musical studies, or, indeed, any of his other lessons. In the opera be found an entire "musical University," whose greatest attraction—discounting the study of French, English, and Italian, which he by no means neglected—was the opportunity it offered to learn composition.[15] In fact, his passion for music was, by this time, absorbing his entire attention, and the "operatic High-School" was making a profound and lasting impression upon his life and musical ideas.

Mattheson's musical education did not, it would appear, run entirely parallel to traditional lines. This tradition rested on the organization of school and church. Where Mattheson lays his emphasis is on private lessons. No matter whether or not this information is based on actual fact, he obviously wants to give the impression that his musical education was not intimately related to any established institution. He mentions the Johanneum only in passing. But nowhere save at the Johanneum could he have received any regular musical instruction.

The study of music at the Johanneum was regulated by a decree of 1635 which was still in force when Mattheson attended the school. The principal emphasis lay in the study of choral music, in singing *"figuraliter,"* that is, in the manner of the contrapuntal style established by the compositions of the sixteenth century. It was in this school that the *Kantorei* arose. This institution was devoted to the cultivation of choral music, in close conjunction with the Lutheran church, of which, in fact, the Kantorei was a direct outgrowth. The Johanneum provided the music for the five chief churches in Hamburg. The nature of the choral music was not altogether contemporaneous. Old-fashioned works from the reper-

15. *Idem,* p. 189.: "Er hatte zwar, durch Anführung seines zweiten, dritten und vierten Lehrmeisters in der Musik, Nahmens Brunmüller, Prätorius und Kerner, schon vorlängst Kirchenstücke gesetzet, Fugen und Contrapuncte, in grosser Anzahl, ausgeführet. . . . so gestund er doch gar gerne, dass ihm die Singspiele in der That eine musikalische Universität wären, . . . und dass er diesenfalls (da indessen seine übrige Bestrebungen nicht an die Seite, sondern, nebst gründlicher Erlernung der frantzösischem, engländischen und italiänischen Sprachen, frisch fortgesetzet wurden) die lange Zeit seiner Opern-Verrichtungen desto weniger bedauerte, da ihm solche die allerbeste Gelegenheit gegeben, sich in der Composition mehr, als auf den gewöhnlichen Academien geschiehet, umzusehen."

tory of the Kantorei were sung whenever motets were needed in the service.[16] Now Mattheson must have come into contact with the musical training at the Johanneum. But he mentions only Brunmüller, Prätorius, Kerner as his teachers in the composition of "Kirchenstücke, Fugen and Contrapuncte," and in this connection makes no reference to the Johanneum at all. That he must have meant, not the counterpoint of his own age, but obsolete vocal polyphony, is to be concluded from his own remark that he was not wanting in teachers; if he did not learn anything they had to tell him, it was not their fault.

Indeed, there is a marked element of contradiction in Mattheson's musical education. He evaded the tradition or, to say the least, he seems to have been in no way interested in what it had to offer. The Kantorei did not suffice. The style of music and the repertory of compositions which they accepted in no way agreed with the esthetic of truly contemporaneous, secular music. The difficulty lay in the great field opened up by the baroque opera. The music of the Kantorei and that of the opera were altogether irreconcilable, and Mattheson, the child of his age, speaks almost exclusively of the operatic parts of his musical education.[17] This conflict between traditional training and the actual style of music was severely felt in Germany wherever and whenever Italian opera intruded into the established forms of musical life.

Unquestionably the glamour and magnificence of the Hamburg Opera, which was at this time entering upon its most glorious days, appealed with peculiar power to Mattheson. Moreover, the narrowness of Cantor Gerstenberg's musicianship had gone far toward discrediting the regular institutions of musical education.[18]

16. A decline in good choral singing is clearly indicated by Karl Röhlk, *Geschichte des Hauptgottesdienstes in der evangelisch-lutherischen Kirche Hamburg's* (Göttingen, 1899), p. 33, who refers to a complaint expressed in the *Kantoreiordnung* of 1675 that "in Hamburg good choristers are wanting."

17. Of special interest is Mattheson's version of the musical education of Reinhard Keiser. *Ehrenpforte,* article "Keiser," p. 126: Keiser is said not to have had any particular instruction; what he possessed he owed almost exclusively to "the grace of nature" and to "fruitful studies of some of the best Italian compositions." The statement is important. The creative talent appears to be a boon of heaven. The doctrine of genius manifests itself, and for the training of genius no convention seems to be fitting; hence the pride in being a self-taught person.

18. For Gerstenberg see below.

The Kantorei had gone to pieces; the musicians were disunited. Whatever talent there was turned to operatic or other secular forms of music. It took the vigor and versatility of a Telemann to re-organize Hamburg's musical life and adjust the abuses that had grown up during Gerstenberg's tenure of office. But never again did the Cantor of Hamburg conduct the musical training of the school, once the backbone of all musical activities. Telemann as well as Karl Philipp Emmanuel Bach appointed substitute teachers at the Johanneum, a duty which the Cantor himself, according to con-tract, was obliged to fulfill. The center of gravity had long since shifted away from the old choral institutions; they were now in a plight which in any event would have scarcely attracted a youth such as Mattheson, particularly when the opera had all the attrac-tion and all the support of society. From the foundation of this institution in 1678, the elaborateness of its productions was unheard of, rivaling those of Paris itself.[19] The operatic performances im-pressed even the fastidious taste of Jean François Regnard when, in 1681, he visited Hamburg: "Les opéra n'y sont pas mal repré-sentés; j'y ai trouvé celui d'Alceste très beau." [20] Strungk, the lead-ing operatic composer at this time, was also Kapellmeister at the Hanoverian Court, where Italian and French operas were played.[21] Although not musically "modern," his operas had been the reason for the outbreak of opposition on the part of the clergy.[22] This must also have added to young Mattheson's excitement. It was in 1693, three years later, however, that the extraordinary Johann Sigismund Kusser became chief composer. The arrival of this man marked a new epoch at the opera and also in Mattheson's youthful musical experience, for as Mattheson writes, he "imported a kind of singing unknown up to that time, and took great pains to improve everything in the performance of music, and to adjust

19. Ludwig Meinardus, *Rückblicke auf die Anfänge der deutschen Oper in Hamburg* (Hamburg, 1878), pp. 34–35.

20. Jean François Renard, *Oeuvres* (nouvelle édition) (Paris, 1789), I, 27.

21. Hermann Kretzschmar, *Geschichte der Oper* (Leipzig, 1919), pp. 146–147. For plans of stage and theater at Hanover, see Theodor Wilhelm Werner, "Agostino Steffanis Opern-theater in Hannover," in *Archiv für Musikforschung* (Leipzig, 1938), III, 65–79. For Strungk's activities at Hamburg, see Fritz Berend, "Nicolaus Adam Strungk" Diss. (Mu-nich, 1913), pp. 46 ff.

22. Cf. p. 14.

it to the genuine Italian taste; for this reason and because he also showed a leaning toward the French style, he has won great praise."[23]

Kusser was indeed a most cosmopolitan, well-traveled musician; he had studied under Lully in Paris; he had gone "twice to Italy in order fully to acquire the style in use there";[24] he was, also, associated at Hanover with the Italian, Agostino Steffani.[25] He was, in fact, forced to become cosmopolitan, so hopelessly restricted were musical conditions in Germany, which, since 1600, had grown more and more remote from the leading musical style, namely, the Italian. In search for it many a German musician went away "because Germany appeared to him too narrow."[26] He therefore brought with him an idiom for writing opera that was enriched by forms of expression unknown at Hamburg—the *da capo* aria, the use of dance forms in the composition of arias, *Basso Ostinato* accompaniments, and instrumental *Ritornelli*,[27] all characteristics of structure that had marked the new baroque style ever since it originated in Italy together with the opera. These innovations caused the oldest singers to become students again.[28] Under Rein-

23. *Ehrenpforte*, p. 189: ". . . bevorab, da der unvergleichliche Director, Johann Sigismund Cousser, eine bisher unbekannte Art zum Singen einführte, und sich äusserst angelegen seyn liess, in der practischen Musik alles zu verbessern, und nach dem ächten welschen Geschmack einzurichten; deshalber ihm auch, und dass er der frantzösischen Manier zugleich sehr zugethan gewesen, billig ein grosses Lob gebühret."

24. Johann Gottfried Walther, *Musicalisches Lexicon* (Leipzig, 1732), *sub verbo* "Cousser."

25. G. Adler, *Handbuch der Musik Geschichte* (Frankfurt-am-Main, 1924) article by Robert Haas, p. 675.

26. "Endlich, weil ihm Teutschland zu enge geschienen, ist er nach England gegangen"; see Johann Gottfried Walther, *Musicalisches Lexicon* (Leipzig, 1732), *sub verbo* "Cousser."

27. G. Adler, *Handbuch der Musik Geschichte*, p. 675. Ludwig Schiedermair, *Die Deutsche Oper* (Leipzig, 1930), p. 65. See Irmtraud Schreiber, "Dichtung und Musik der deutschen Opernarien," Diss. (Berlin, 1934), pp. 34 ff.

28. Mattheson, *Der Musikalische Patriot*, p. 181: "Die neue Sing-Art wurde zu dieser Zeit eingeführet, und musten die ältesten Sänger Schüler werden." The singers were unprepared for the Italian style. On the other hand, the Italian singers at times refused to have a share in performances of works in the German style. As a result of a quarrel Strungk met with open resistance when he wanted Italians to sing his sacred works at Dresden; he had to be satisfied with German singers. See Friedrich Zelle, "J. Theile und N. A. Strungk. Zweiter Beitrag zur Geschichte der ältesten deutschen Oper," in *Wissenschaftliche Beilage zum Programm des Humboldts-Gymnasiums zu Berlin, Ostern 1891* (Berlin, 1891), p. 13; Moritz Fürstenau, *Zur Geschichte der Musik und des Theaters am Hofe der Kurfürsten von Sachsen* (Dresden, 1862), I, 301; also Fritz Berend, *N. A. Strungk,* pp. 76 f.

hard Keiser, who became chief operatic composer in Hamburg a year later, the new stylistic elements were synthesized with the native tradition of song. Keiser, whom Mattheson considered the greatest operatic composer in the world,[29] became the mainstay of the opera. He increased the size and expressiveness of its orchestra,[30] and he far excelled his associates in the composition of music.[31] Mattheson himself wrote that no one wished to hear anything unless this "galant" composer had written it,[32] and it is easy to surmise the enormous effect Keiser's personality and music must have had on the youth.

Mattheson records his first appearance upon the stage as taking place in 1690 in Johann Wolfgang Franck's *Aeneas,*[33] the ninth opera to be produced in Hamburg that year. Franck, another one of the German musicians who left their homeland to go to England, had a share in the early development of opera in Hamburg. One year after its opening he produced his extraordinary work *Die drey Töchter Cecrops,* composed for Ansbach in 1679 (?), with numerous cuts in Hamburg (1680).[34] Presumably Mattheson's

29. Mattheson's poem on the death of Keiser, *Ehrenpforte,* pp. 133 f., is headed: "Als der grösseste Opern-Componist von der Welt, den 12. Sept. 1739. von der Welt Abschied nahm, hegte man darüber folgende Gedancken." In *Ehrenpforte,* p. 129, M. calls Keiser "le premier homme du monde."
30. Klefeld, "Das Orchester der Hamburger Oper," in *SIMG* I (Leipzig, 1899–1900), p. 286.
31. Schiedermair, *Die Deutsche Oper,* p. 69.
32. *Ehrenpforte,* p. 189: ". . . wolte niemand was anders hören oder machen, als was dieser galante Componist gesetzt hatte."
33. Mattheson, *Der Musicalische Patriot,* p. 180, MS. note in his own copy: "In diesem Jahre, im 9ten seines alters, sang der Verfasser des Musik. Patr. zum erstenmahl auf den Theater, und zwar bey Vorstellung der A. 1680 verfertigte 9te Oper *Aeneas.*
34. The work is now available in *Das Erbe deutscher Musik. Zweite Reihe: Landschafts-denkmale: Bayern;* Vol. 2 (1938), ed. by Gustav Friedrich Schmidt. Mattheson later compiled a list of Hamburg's operas in *Der Musikalische Patriot* (1728) which is, however, neither complete nor correct. See also Moller, *Cimbria literata* (1744), II *passim.* On Franck's Hamburg activities see Richard Klages, "Johann Wolfgang Franck," Diss. (Hamburg, 1937), pp. 20 ff. On Franck in England see William W. Barclay Squire, "J. W. Franck in England," *The Musical Antiquary* (1912), pp. 181–190. Walter Schulze, *Die Quellen der Hamburger Oper* (Hamburg-Oldenburg, 1938), expresses doubts that the Hamburg *Cecrops* is the same as the Ansbach *Cecrops.* Johann Moller, *Cimbria literata* (1745), art. "Franck," attributes the Hamburg work to Franck; Mattheson, *Musikalischer Patriot,* to Nikolaus Adam Strungk; so also Michael Richey. The editor of *Cecrops* now assumes the two versions to be by Franck, although the Hamburg libretto is cut to half the length of the Ansbach opera. Irmtraudt Schreiber, "Dichtung und Musik der deutschen Opernarien," Diss. (Berlin, 1934), p. 40, note 43, speaks incorrectly of merely "a few changes."

active connection with the organization continued for the next few years, although we have but one reference to it—made thirty years later. The elaborate staging of these baroque operas provided many opportunities for the use of ambitious young performers. At any rate Mattheson recalled how, when he played—as he often did— the part of a flying angel, the "machinemaster" always made use of the formula: "Let the boy down in the name of Heaven."[35] At the age of fifteen, he was sufficiently accomplished to play solo female parts. His debut took place in 1696 at Kiel, to which town Schott sent the entire Opera company for the three weeks of the annual Fair, both that year and the following one.[36] According to Pöllnitz, Hamburg was "a perfect Desert at that moment of the year. For every body hurries to this Fair, because 'tis there that they are commonly paid their Rents, that Leases are renew'd with the Farmers and that Money is let out to Advantage."[37] It was therefore a profitable occasion for the Opera, which on its tour in 1696 gave thirteen performances at Kiel.[38] The next year Mattheson's voice had changed, for he played the part of a man, "and no one had any more doubts thereof."[39]

He remained a member of the Opera company until 1705, playing in the last seven or eight years chiefly principal parts, "not without the universal and great enthusiasm of the audience."[40] His first opera, the *Plejades,*[41] was written and produced in 1699, when he was eighteen; he took the lead, directed the entire production, and "occasioned pleasurable wonder among people."[42] Three years

35. Mattheson, *Der Musikalischer Patriot*, pp. 155–156: "wie ich in meiner Jugend offt einem fliegenden Engel vorstellete, der damahlige Machinen-Meister allezeit diese Formul zu gebrauchen pflegte: 'Lasst den Knaben herab, in GOttes Nahmen.'"

36. *Ehrenpforte*, p. 190: "Als er 1696. und 1697. die Opern im Kiel mit zieren halff, sang er das erstemahl Frauens-Partien, und es wurde, wegen des Geschlechts, manche Wette gewonnen, oder verlohren."

37. Pöllnitz, *Memoirs*, IV, 283.

38. L. Meinardus, *Rückblick*, p. 26.

39. *Ehrenpforte*, p. 190: "Das andremahl that er schon, als ein Mann, und niemand zweifelte mehr daran: denn die Stimme hatte sich verändert."

40. *Idem*, p. 188: ". . . [er] stellte, die letzten 7. oder 8. Jahre über, fast immer die Hauptperson vor; nicht ohne allgemeinen und grossen Beifall der Zuschauer."

41. Cf. Bibliography No. 1.

42. *Ehrenpforte*, p. 190: "Anno 1699. verfertigte er seine erste Oper, Plejades; machte in derselben die Haupt-Partie: dirigirte das gantze Wesen, und setzte viele Leute in eine vergnügte Verwunderung."

later, in the most lavish season of the Opera's existence,[43] his *Porsenna* [44] was presented as well as the *Victor,* an opera in three acts, of which he wrote the second.[45] In 1704 his third full-length opera *Cleopatra* [46] was staged. Although the only opinion of Mattheson's ability as a singer and actor that has survived is his own, his reputation was probably greater in these capacities than in that of composer. He himself was sufficiently convinced of his own merits and popularity as a singer to take issue, at the age of eighty, with a slightly derogatory description of his talent which he found in Mainwaring's life of Händel.[47] In his translation of this work he appends the following note to the offensive passage:

> To say that he [Mattheson] sang only occasionally is symply ridiculous, when the statement is made of a man who remained on the stage for fifteen years, who nearly always played the chief rôle and whose natural manner of singing, whose gestures and whose action—all of which are most essential in every opera—aroused in the audience feelings of fear and terror, pity and lament, joy and pleasure.[48]

He states elsewhere that his performances were the cause of so much envy and jealousy in 1702 that he found it necessary often to guard himself against his enemies with the sword.[49] His playing of Antonius in his opera *Cleopatra* was, he is pleased to say, so natural that his suicide called forth cries of horror from the spectators.[50] Mattheson's account of these years of his life as an opera-

43. *Idem,* Article on Raupach, p. 283n. "Es wurden im Jahre 1701. vier, und 1702. gar zehn neue Opern . . . auf den Schauplatz gebracht, welches vielleicht in der Welt niemahls geschehen seyn mag."
44. Cf. Bibliography No. 2.
45. Cf. Bibliography, No. 4.
46. Cf. Bibliography No. 5.
47. [Mainwaring], *Memoirs of the Life of the late Georg Frederic Händel,* (London, 1760), p. 31: "the principal singers [in Hamburg] were CONRATINI and MATHYSON. . . . MATHYSON was no great singer, for which reason he sang only occasionally; but he was a good actor, a good composer of lessons, and a good player on the harpsichord . . ."
48. *Georg Friderich Händels Lebensbeschreibung.* Bibliography No. 183, p. 22: "Dass er [Mattheson] nur gelegentlich gesungen haben sollte, ist lächerlich von einem zu sagen, der in 15 Jahren nicht vom Theater gekommen, auch sowol durch ein ungekünsteltes Singen, als durch seine Geberdekunst oder Action, welche in allen Singespielen das Wesentliche ist, bey den Zuschauern bald Thränen, bald Freude und Vergnügen erwecket hat."
49. *Ehrenpforte,* p. 191: "Aus solchen Ursachen sahe er offt die Nothwendigkeit, sich seiner Neider mit dem Degen zu erwehren."
50. *Idem,* p. 192: ". . . er ahmte darin die Person des Antonius so natürlich nach, dass die Zuschauer, bey der verstellten Selbstenleibung, ein lautes Geschrey erhuben. . . ."

singer is full of tales of duels and disagreements with his fellow musicians.[51] Whether they were caused by jealousy of his abilities, as Mattheson implies, or annoyance at his only too evident conceit it is impossible to state, but the latter of these two hypotheses would seem to be the more plausible in the light of subsequent events.

Although Mattheson's time must have been very fully occupied during his period of operatic prominence, he nevertheless was absorbed in many other activities, both musical and social. In the winter of 1700–1701 Graf von Eckgh, the imperial ambassador to Hamburg, held each Sunday in his palace a series of concerts. Mattheson is careful to state that he was not a mere "member of these concerts but, with Eberhard Reinwald, the great violinist, a director, and likewise musicmaster to the Count's youngest daughter." [52] His own musical reputation was unquestionably growing, for he was invited to Lübeck in 1703 by the President of the Rath as a possible successor to the great organist of the *Marienkirche,* Dietrich Buxtehude. He made this expedition with young Händel, "making many double fugues in the carriage," and both displayed their talents on the organ and harpsichord.[53] Despite the eminence of this post, it does not, however, seem to have attracted young Mattheson, who like Händel was envisaging at this time a career, not connected with the traditional position of cantor or organist. In the following year, the Opera being temporarily closed, he set out upon what was to be a grand concert tour, culminating in London, which at that time was becoming a Mecca for young musi-

51. *Idem,* p. 191: "Den ersten Kampf hielt er mit einem eifersüchtigen, und sonst wohl-geübten Räuffer, am 13. Jun. dieses 1702ten Jahrs, . . . Es fielen hernach noch mehr dergleichen Händel vor. . . ." And p. 192: "Bey seiner Heimkunfft . . . erweckte ihm der Neid einen neuen Fehder. . . . Mit demselben muste er am 9ten Julii einen formlichen Zweikampff in offenem Felde halten. . . ." See also below.

52. *Idem,* Article on Keiser, p. 132. "Erwehnte Concerte wurden alle Sonntage, den Winter über, 1700. 1701. mit solcher Pracht und Herrlichkeit gehalten, dass ich, an Königl. Höfen dergleichen Überfluss bey Assembleen gesehen zu haben, mich nicht erinnere. . . . Ich war nicht nur ein Mitglied desselben Concerts, sondern mit Eberhard Reinwald, dem starcken Violinisten, ein Director, und zugleich Musikmeister des gräflichen jüngsten Fräuleins."

53. *Idem,* p. 94: "Wir reiseten auch den 17. Aug. desselben 1703. Jahrs zusammen nach Lübeck, und machten viele Doppelfugen auf dem Wagen, *da mente, non da penna:* Es hatte mich dahin der Geheime Raths-präsident, Magnus von Wedderkopp, eingeladen: um dem vortrefflichen Organisten, Dieterich Buxtehude, einem künfftigen Nachfolger auszumachen. [Buxtehude died in 1707.] Wir bespielten daselbst fast alle Orgeln und Clavicimbel. . . ."

cians. But he got only as far as Amsterdam. While there, he held "many excellent concerts in the *Dule* before the magnificent Portuguese Jews, who conducted themselves like Kings and Queens," [54] He also performed for two hours on both organs of the great *Pfarrkirche* in Harlem for the Bürgermeister and heads of the government, and he sang and played on the clavichord and harpsichord. They too offered him the post of organist at that great church, with "an income of 1500 Gülden," but again he refused this offer, the reason being probably the same that made him decline the position at Lübeck.[55] His trip was discontinued because of trivial illness and the entreaties of his parents and friends, especially young Händel, that he return to the reopened Opera.[56] The opportunity to compete for still another important post was offered him in 1705 in the St. Catharinen Kirche in Hamburg. Under the celebrated organist Johann Adam Reinken this church had the reputation of having the best music in northern Germany.[57] But Mattheson spurned this also "because truth to tell he was disposed to be something else than an organist." [58]

54. *Idem*, pp. 191–192: "Wie die Opern 1704. aus gewissen Ursachen still lagen, that Mattheson eine Reise nach Holland: Vorhabens, von dannen weiter nach England, Frankreich und Italien zu gehen. In Holland versuchte er die besten Orgelwercke; hörte die künstlichsten Spieler; hielt zu Amsterdam verschiedene starcke Concerte auf der Dule, in Gegenwart der prächtigen, portugisischen Juden, die sich als Könige und Königinnen aufführten."

55. *Idem*, p. 192: ". . . wäre bald gar Organist an der grossen Pfarrkirchen zu Harlem geworden: wie der denn daselbst, in Gegenwart der Bürgermeister und Schöpfen, am 17. Märtz, Nachmittags, über zwo Stunden, auf beiden in selbiger Kirche befindlichen Wercken zur Probe spielte; hernach aber sich, in einem eigentlich dazu angestellten Concert, auf dem Flügel und Clavichordio, mit der Stimme hören liess. Worauf ihm folgendes Tages, durch die Ratsherren von Saanen und Geerlingen, der Dienst, mit 1500 Gülden Einkommens, angetragen wurde."

56. *Idem*: "Die vornehmste Ursache, warum die Reise nicht weiter, als Leiden, fortgesetzt werden konnte, war nicht nur eine kleine Krankheit. . . ." Article on "Händel," p. 94: ". . . erhielt ich den 21. Märtz in Amsterdam einen solchen verbindlichen und nachdrücklichen Brief von Händel aus Hamburg, der mich vorzuglich bewog, den Rückweg wieder nach Hause zu nehmen." (He quotes part of said letter on page 94.)

57. J. S. Bach came to Hamburg in 1704 to meet and hear Reinken play. Philip Spitta, *J. S. Bach* (London, 1899), I, 196–200.

58. *Ehrenpforte*, p. 194: "Indessen wurde er, den 17. April ohne sein Gesuch, von dem zeitigen Oberalten und Vorstehern der Kirche S. Catharinen, Nahmens Hökenkamp, zur Anwartschafft auf den einträglichen Organistendienst, welchen der abgängige Johann Adam Reinken besass, und zum Probespielen erfordert; allein, . . . verbat, und weil auch, die Wahrheit zu sagen, Mattheson sich zu etwas anders, als einem Organisten, aufgelegt zu seyn befand. . . ." The *St. Catharinen Kirchen Archiv* contain no reference to any such

His reputation as a musician, thanks both to the Opera and to his private efforts, must have won him recognition and position in the higher circles of Hamburg society, a fact deeply satisfying to his intense vanity. Already at the age of twelve, while he was page-boy to the Graf von Güldenlöw, the "Vice-König" of Norway, and brother of the king of Denmark, he had become acquainted with the brilliance and splendor of the life in Hamburg's most aristocratic circles, and had been allowed to associate with von Güldenlöw's children.[59] His musical ability must have accounted for this honor, for he remembered later the generosity of the noble guests, who never threw less than a ducat to him after he had played on the harpsichord.[60] In his autobiography he described his chief impression of this experience with such vividness that its effect upon him may be clearly seen:

> To wear a white plume in his hat, an ornamented velvet, a silver cutlass, etc. filled the lad's heart with delight. Since his father, however, objected to life at court, especially to that in Copenhagen, he annulled the contract which already had been drawn up; and Johann shed bitter tears because he had to give away the lovely finery. Of such things is misery made.[61]

After this, young Johann must have seized upon every possibility offered to him to mingle with such patrician society. Musical functions such as the Graf von Eckgh's concerts were exciting opportunities for an ambitious young man. In 1703, at one of the Graf's concerts, he was introduced to the celebrated Gräfin Aurora von Königsmarck, the mistress of Augustus the Strong of Saxony.[62]

---

invitation. No compositions for the organ composed by Mattheson have survived, but it is inconceivable that he wrote none.

59. *Idem*, p. 189: "Anno 1693. erlebte Mattheson, als ein Knabe von 12. Jahren, das Glück, dem Vice-Könige in Norwegen, und Brudern Christians V., Königes in Dännemarck, dem Grafen von Güldenlöw dermaassen gefallen, dass ihn dieser Herr als einen Edel-Knaben aufnehmen, mit seinen Kindern ferner erziehen. . . ."

60. *Idem*, p. 190: "Keiner von den Fürstl. und Gräfl. Gästen warff ihm weniger, als einen Ducaten, in das Clavier-Lädgen, so, dass er offt nicht wuste, was er mit dem Golde anfangen sollte; aber die andern Pagen wusten es desto besser, und zwackten es ihm bald, mit Karten und Würffeln ab."

61. *Ibid.*: "Die weisse Feder auf dem Hute, die sammittene verbrämte Kleidung, der silberne Hirschfänger u. d. g. machten dem Burschen das Hertze gross. Weil aber dem Vater das Hofeleben, zumahl in Kopenhagen, wiederrathen wurde, hub er den bereits schriftlich-verfasseten Contract wieder auf, und Johann weinte bitterlich, wie er seinen geliebten Staat ablegen muste. Das sind Fatalitäten!"

62. *Idem*, p. 191: "Nicht nur die vornehme und liebreiche Gesellschafft einer gewissen

This notorious lady was not only a famous beauty, but an intelligent patron of the Arts, to whom Mattheson dedicated his first treatise on music ten years later.[63] She also was the author of the libretto to Franck's "Die drei Töchter Cecrops." In his autobiography he comments as follows on his association with the *Gräfin:* "This is not the time nor place to discuss what profit, both outward and inward, a young man can draw from association with [persons of the fair sex] ladies irrespective of the suspicions malevolent people will have."[64] He was perhaps even spurred to emulation by his great admiration for Reinhard Keiser, who was not only the musical leader of the town, but who was also acting the "grand seigneur"— in a manner that was ultimately to lead to his ruin.[65]

In the meantime, while continuing to sing at the Opera until early in the year 1705, Mattheson appears to have become dissatisfied with this method of gaining a livelihood, and discouraged by the prospects it afforded for the future. The personality of Reinhard Keiser dominated the entire organization so completely that there was scarcely any possibility of immediate advancement for a young musician. Mattheson's relations with his fellow members of the Opera seem to have been anything but amicable, due—as has already been observed—to his pride and his overbearing manners. In December, 1704, he fought a duel with his friend Händel. No harm was incurred by either, since, happily, Mattheson's sword was shivered upon the coat-button of his opponent; indeed their friendship was soon afterward wholly restored.[66] Nevertheless his

adelichen Dame, sondern die Ehre, mit der Gräfinn Aurora von Königsmarck, zum erstenmahl bekannt zu werden, genoss Mattheson den 5ten October, und ersten December 1703."
63. *Das Neu-Eröffnete Orchestre;* Bibliography No. 27.
64. *Ehrenpforte,* p. 191: "Was der Umgang mit solchen Personen des schönen Geschlechts (es mögen auch übeldenckende argwöhnen, was sie wollen und lieben) einen jungen menschen für äuserlichen und innerlichen Nutzen bringet, ist nicht zu beschreiben, auch hier der Ort nicht dazu." See Möller, *Cimbria literata,* II, 430.
65. Hermann Kretzschmar, *op. cit.,* p. 148.
66. This quarrel with Händel Mattheson describes in both his article on Händel and his autobiographical article in the *Ehrenpforte.* In the former, and much fuller, account, Mattheson's temperament and conceit seem to be responsible for the disagreement; in the latter, however, he insinuates that Händel was infuriated by being supplanted by Mattheson as tutor to Cyrill Wich. It is probable that the two accounts together present a correct picture of the actions of two hasty young men. I quote them in full:
*Ehrenpforte,* Article on Händel, pp. 94–95: "Am 5. Dec. obbesagten Jahres, da meine dritte Oper Cleopatra aufgeführet wurde, und Händel beym Clavicimbel sass,

unpopularity at the Opera seems to have outlasted his active connection with it, and was most surely based on personal and not on musical grounds. This may be seen in the fate of his two later contributions to the operatic repertoire. The first of these, *Boris Godenow,*[67] of which he composed both text and music in 1710, was not performed at all;[68] the second, *Die geheimen Begebenheiten Henrico IV,*[69] was produced a year later, but the difficulties which were placed in its way and which prevented it from having a fair hearing compelled him to publish a number of arias from it "to do Justice, not only to all men, but likewise to myself."[70] In view of these circumstances it is not surprising that he should have terminated his career as singer at the Opera when a position of a more promising nature presented itself. In November, 1704, he was appointed tutor to Cyrill Wich, the son of the English Resident in Hamburg, and three months later gladly bade farewell to the stage[71]—after

---

entstund ein Misverständniss; . . . Ich dirigirte, als Componist, und stellte zugleich den Antonius vor, der sich, wohl eine halbe Stunde vor dem Beschluss des Schauspiels, entleibet. Nun war ich bisher gewohnt, nach dieser Action, ins Orchester zu gehen, und das übrige selbst zu accompagniren: welches doch unstreitig ein jeder Verfasser besser, als ein andrer, thun kann; es wurde mir aber diesesmahl verweigert. Darüber geriethen wir, durche einige Anhetzer, im Ausgange aus der Oper, auf öffentlichem Marckte, bey einer Menge Zuschauer, in einen Zweikampf, welcher für uns beide sehr unglücklich hätte ablauffen können; wenn es GOttes Führung nicht so gnädig gefüget, dass mir die Klinge, im Stoffen auf einem breiten, metallen Rockknopf des Gegners, zersprungen wäre. Es geschah also kein sonderlicher Schade, und wir wurden, durch Vermittelung eines der ansehnlichsten Rathsherren in Hamburg, wie auch der damahligen Opern-Pächtern, bald wider vertragen. . . ."

*Idem,* p. 193: "Denn, es hatte vorhin ein gewisser, und schon genannter Mann [Händel] diesen Posten zur Helffte bekleidet, nehmlich, so viel die Musik oder den Unterricht auf dem Clavier betraff; . . . daher er denn auf Mattheson einen heimlichen Groll warff, und mit demselben Groll, bey der ersten Adventswoche, in der letzten Vorstellung der Opera, Cleopatra, vor Weihnacht lossbrach. . . ."

67. Cf. Bibliography No. 19.

68. *Ehrenpforte,* p. 197. ". . . selbige [*Boris*] aber, aus gewisser Ursachen, dem Theatro zu überlassen Bedencken trug. Sie ist also nicht aufgeführet worden. . . ."

69. Cf. Bibliography No. 20.

70. Dedication (to Cyrill Wich) of *Arie Scelte,* Bibliography No. 21: ". . . but I dare say, Sir, you were not aware of the Trick the Box-keepers intended to play me, which would have pretty well drained my Purse if your generous family had not furnished me with the means to thwart their pitifull desseins. . . . You are not ignorant with what a negligence the envy, or the malice, or the Ignorance of some people has endeavoured to make this Musick performed. . . ."

71. *Ehrenpforte,* p. 193: "Anno 1705. den 17. Febr., nachdem er den Nero, in einer Oper gleichen Nahmens [by Händel], mit Nachdruck vorgestellet, und Ende gut alles gut gemacht hatte, von der Schaubühne seinen ordentlichen Abschied, und richtete forthin sein Augenmerck auf etwas wichtigeres, dauerhaffteres und gültigers."

having taken part in nearly two thousand performances.[72] His new position gave Mattheson a considerable salary, the entire charge of the education of young Cyrill, whom his father, Sir John Wich, wished to see as his successor, and the title of *Hofmeister* to the Embassy. It is small wonder that Mattheson felt that he was entering upon a period of lasting good fortune.[73]

The connection with the Wich family offered a number of new possibilities for advancement. In addition to the social and material benefits accruing from the position, Mattheson was left almost wholly free to further his own private musical reputation and career. In 1705 he was sufficiently famous to have twenty students, of whom the majority paid five or six *Thalers* "in solid gold." He was also commissioned to compose the music for a French operetta to be given at a special fete on the occasion of the return of the Königsmarck family to their estate in Plön outside of Hamburg. Young Mattheson's income from all these activities presently became a sizable one, and he wasted no time in establishing himself in a way of life which he made conform as best he could to that of a Hamburg gentleman:

There were a couple of riding horses in the stable; to alleviate a melancholy hour there were fine clothes worthy of one of the positions at court upon which others had more than once pinned their vain hopes; and there were the *"Kramer company"* as well as the ratskeller with their social obligations . . . This much is certain: that at various times of two persons one would have liked to acquire the title of Reichsfreiherr, the other of count in Italy for him; if only the property and income of such noblemen could also have been put, along with the titles, on paper or parchment.[74]

72. *Idem*, Article on Dreyer, p. 54: ". . . da ich bey nahe 2000. Opernvorstellungen und Proben in Hamburg, Kiel und Braunschweig, mehrentheils als Haupt-Person, mit beigewehnet habe. . . ." Mattheson's inevitable citation of dates, statistics etc. may be explained again by the fact that he kept a *"Denkbuch,"* which has unfortunately disappeared, but which he used in the preparation of his "memoirs." Cf. *idem*, p. 200: "In seinen Denkbüchern. . . ."

73. *Idem*, p. 193: "Den siebenten November dieses Jahres 1704. liess der damahlige Königl. Gros-Britannische Gesandte im niedersächsischen Kreise, Hr. Johann von Wich, unsern Mattheson, zur Unterrichtung seines Sohnes, welcher dem Vater hernach in der Würde gefolget ist, berufen, und, gegen ein ansehnliches Jahrgeld, zur allgemeinen Aufsicht und Erziehung, also Hofemeister, bestellen: welcher Beruf denn auch der wahre Anfang seines dauerhafften Glückes. . . ."

74. *Idem*, p. 194 note: "Ein paar Reit-Pferde nach einander auf dem Stall; schöne Kleider für einen betrübten Sinn, die sich zum gräfl. Stande, dazu andre sich zwei-

While Mattheson was officially tutoring young Cyrill Wich he took the opportunity to study with great care the language, history, law, and politics of England.[75] Although both Händel and he were successively chosen as Cyrill's instructors because of their musical ability—their young pupil was both interested and talented in this art [76]—Mattheson's industry and intelligence won his promotion in 1706 to the position of secretary to the English Resident.[77] With an annual salary of two hundred thalers, he was now able to have the "costliest table in the town," and the prestige of such a connection procured him "much honor from many eminent persons."[78] The consequences of accepting this post, however, were much more far reaching to the later life of Johann Mattheson than he seems at first to have realized. He had been presented not only with a virtually permanent source of income, but also with a social position which brought him into contact with English manners and thought in the most cosmopolitan city in Germany. Had Wich been supplanted in his diplomatic station in Hamburg, it would not have been difficult for Mattheson to make himself invaluable in routine matters to his successor. In addition to these advantages he had found a continuous, exacting, and at times arduous occupation with which he was to be actively concerned until he was sixty years old and over.

Sir John Wich, Mattheson's employer, was the son of a diplo-

mahl vergebliche Hoffnung machten, nicht übelschickten; die Kramer-Compagnie und der Rathskeller, forderten ihre Pflicht einhelliglich. . . . So viel ist gewiss, dass, von zwo verschiedenen Personen, zu verschiedenen Zeiten, die eine ihm gerne den Reichsfeiherrl., die andere aber den gräfl. Titel, auf italiänischen Fusse, erkaufft hätte; wenn nur die Güter und Einkünffte mit dabey auf dem Papier oder Pergament gestanden wären."

75. *Idem*, p. 195: "Wie er sich hiernächst insonderheit, mit allem Ernst, auf die engländische Sprache, Geschichte, Rechte und Staatskunde legte. . . ."

76. Two compositions from Mattheson's hand for two *cembali* were written for his pupil; see Bibliography Nos. 7 and 8. That Cyrill also composed music is suggested by Mattheson's remarks in his dedication of the *Arie Scelte*, No. 21: ". . . since that in dedicating to you the Airs of my Opera I do but entertain you in a great measure with compositions of your own, being indebted to you for two of the most exquisite Pieces, and for a very fine Chorus. . . ."

77. *Ehrenpforte*, p. 195: ". . . beehrte ihn der Herr von Wich, am 6. Jan. 1706. mit dem Character, mit der wircklichen Verrichtung, und mit den Einkünfften seines Secretars."

78. *Idem:* "Er hatte hiebey den köstlichsten Tisch in der Stadt, und bald darauf auch seine Zimmer in des Herrn Gesandten Hause, samt aller andern Bequemlichkeiten, und vieler Ehre von geehrten Leuten."

mat,[79] and had been the English Resident in Hamburg since 1702. He was rewarded for the conscientiousness with which he fulfilled his office by being made Envoy Extraordinary to Hamburg, Mecklenburg-Schwerin and Holstein-Gottorp in 1709 [80] and, if one may judge by the efficiency of his letters and reports to the Secretary of State for the Northern Province in Whitehall, as well as by Mattheson's account of his activities, his advancement was well deserved. Although the honor and prestige of the English Resident in Hamburg may have outweighed their actual diplomatic value,[81] Sir John was not one to shift the entire business and responsibility of his position to the shoulders of his young secretary, of whom, on the other hand, much was expected. Immediately upon his appointment Mattheson set himself to study international law, especially as it concerned maritime and trade regulations, to examine international trade and related subjects, and to seek out the best information concerning the affairs of the European states. None of these matters could be learned, he remarked, in universities; one had to be one's own instructor.[82]

At first Mattheson's task was mainly secretarial, that is, he transcribed and prepared the various types of letters and reports sent in not inconsiderable number from Hamburg to England. This correspondence on the whole may be divided into three categories. The "Official Despatch" letters, written by the Resident to the

79. Accounts of the Wich family (spelt Wyche or Wiche in secondary sources, but always Wich by Mattheson and by both John and his son) are to be found in G. E. Cockayne, *Complete Baronetage 1707–1800*, p. 68, *The Dictionary of National Biography*, LXIII, 193–194, and Burke's *Extinct & Dormant Baronetcies of England*, p. 587.

80. J. F. Chance, "List of Diplomatic Representatives," pp. 22, 28, 31.

81. Hubert Stierling, "Leben und Bildnis Friedrich von Hagedorn" (Hamburg, 1911), p. 89. A letter from Hagedorn to his brother dated 17 Nov., 1741, speaks of the enviable position of the Resident, Cyrill Wich, in Hamburg: "Urteile daraus, wie wenig es an Leuten fehlen muss, die darum werben, und wie sehr mancher wohlverdienter englischer Minister die täglichen drey Pfund Sterling und die 300-Equipage-money, die ein englischer Resident hat, hier zu verehren wünschet, wenn er kein sonderliches Vermögen hat, das ihn, ohne Dienst und Character in Engelland hinlänglich etablieren kann. . . ."

82. *Ehrenpforte*, p. 195: ". . . [hatte er Gelegenheit] die allgemeinen Rechte, nebst den besonderen See- und Handlungs-Gesetzen, die Welthändel, samt andern dahin gehörigen Wissenschafften, vernehmlich aber die besten Nachrichten von den Angelegenheiten der europäischen Staaten hervorzusuchen. . . . Das waren abermahl solche Dinge, die man ihm auf Universitäten nicht würde haben beibringen können, und worin er also sein Selbstlehrer seyn muste: denn Grotii Buch weiss Papier ist hier noch immer der beste Auctor."

principal Secretary of State for the Northern Province, contained
data, drawn from correspondents in every part of the Continent or
from other Residents in Hamburg, regarding political events in
the various countries, the relative size and power of the various
armies and their movements; gave information concerning British
commerce and trade agreements with Hamburg and the other
Hanseatic towns, the affairs of British commercial nationals trad-
ing with or residing in Hamburg; and, finally, detailed the arrival
and departure of notables, both British and Foreign, and a number
of particular matters of importance which were discussed from
time to time. The "Official News Letters," sometimes called "Circulars," were much the same as these, but were merely sent regularly
in the packet for Whitehall, and used probably as sources for the
foreign news items in the *Whitehall Gazette*.[83] After his first few
years in office Mattheson was entirely responsible for the composition of these circulars.[84] The third category were letters of
much the same sort but written formally, even personally, to under-
secretaries of state, requesting their interest in matters of promotion
or the like.[85]

In the same year in which he became secretary, Mattheson was
also entrusted with activities of a more responsible nature. These
included journeys on Wich's business to Hanover, where he took
advantage of the occasion to make the acquaintance of various
well-known musicians, to Quedlinburg and Obersachsen, to Leipzig, to Bremen twice, and to Hanover again in August.[86] In the
following year he journeyed to Altranstadt on a mission to Charles

83. *State Papers* 104/212, 8 July 1712, St. John directs Wich to send either Tilsen or
Hare "Letters of News and Common Occurances proper for the gazette apart from your
letters to me."

84. This is a logical supposition since these letters were unsigned, and were almost invariably in Mattheson's handwriting.

85. Since I have been unable myself to make an examination of this correspondence
in the London Public Record Office, the above information and all of that which has to
do with these letters is taken from a report prepared for me by Mr. Ashley Olmsted.

86. *Ehrenpforte*, p. 195: "Den 5ten Junii dieses Jahres muste er, in gewissen, wichtigen
Geschäfften, nach Hanover reisen, woselbst er beiläufig die dasigen Virtuosen, absonderlich
aber die auserlesenste Bande Hoboisten hörte, auch mit dem berühmten Farinelli, Venturini
&c. Bekanntschafft machte. Er ging von da nach Quedlinburg, und, in Amts-Verrichtungen,
weiter nach Obersachsen, da denn Leipzig nicht vergessen wurde; und kehrte, über gedachten Quedlinburg, wieder zurück nach Hamburg. Den 18. August. ging er mit Com-
missionen nach Bremen; den 22. von da nach Hanover; den 24. wieder nach Bremen, und
so den 28. nach Hamburg: um von seinem Gewerbe Bericht abzustatten."

XII, who was at that time becoming more and more of a potential danger to the nations of Northern Europe. From there he went on to Leipzig, where in an official capacity he attended a musical celebration in honor of Queen Anne's Name Day, in which to his disgust, he took part only as Mattheson the diplomat and not as Mattheson the musician.[87] All this shows that the position of Sir John's secretary involved many more occupations than that of merely drafting letters—occupations which did bring him into some sort of contact with the "elect" of northern Germany. The presence of the Imperial Commission in Hamburg in the year 1708 meant that the English Resident, who acted as "middleman," [88] and his secretary, were unusually busy, and Mattheson himself had the honor of addressing a speech of welcome to the Graf von Schönborn, the leader of the delegation.[89]

Although it is scarcely necessary to recount all the events of his secretarial career, certain of them lend interest to the somewhat even tenor of Mattheson's life. His own good fortune was inevitably linked with that of Sir John, which, during this period of excitement caused by fear of Charles XII and the Northern War, underwent several crises. On being raised to the rank of Envoy Extraordinary in 1709,[90] Wich's daily income was increased from three pounds to five, and he was good enough to add an annual one hundred thalers to the stipend of his secretary.[91] On the strength of

87. *Idem*, pp. 195–196: "Anno 1707. wurde er abermahl, in geheimen Königl. Angelegenheiten nach Obersachsen versandt, zu der Zeit, wie sich der König von Schweden, Carl XII., zu Altranstadt aufhielt. . . . Dass er, von dort aus, Leipzig aufs neue besuchen nicht unterlassen habe, ist leicht zu erachten: zumahl bei einer feierlichen Begehung des Nahmens-Tages seiner Königinn Anna, da er im Pauline mitten unter Gesandten sass, und eine schöne lateinische Ode von Kuhnau anhörte; sich aber nicht mercken lassen durffte, dass er lieber mit gesungen, oder mitgespielt, als die Gravität mit ausgerecktem Nacken da gehalten hätte."

88. *Idem*, p. 196: "Im Jahr 1708. nahm die, wegen der hamburgischen Zwistigkeiten so der Rath mit den Bürgern hatte, angeordnete grosse Kaiserl. Commission ihren Anfang, dabey denn die fremden Gesandten, absenderlich aber die engländischen, als Mittelsmänner, und ihre Secretären, alle Hände vell zu thun bekamen."

89. The two-page manuscript of this address, entitled "Matthesons Glückwünschungs Rede an Graf v. Schönborn 4 Junii, 1708," is among his manuscripts in the Hamburger Stadt Bibliothek. Mattheson noted in his later hand on the outside: "dergleichen Anrede hat Mattheson noch vielmehr gehalten an Keiserl. u. Königl. Minister bey deren Ankunft und andere Gelegenheit."

90. G. F. Chance, "List of Diplomatic Representatives," pp. 22, 28, 31.

91. *Ehrenpforte*, p. 197: "Im Junio dieses Jahrs [1709] erklärte die Königinn den Herrn von Wich zum ausserordentlichen Abgesandten. . . . Und weil daduch dessen

this improvement in his outward circumstances, Mattheson promptly married Catharine Jennings, the daughter of the rector of the parishes of Calsten, Blackland, and Cherill in Wiltshire.[92] Mattheson makes only three references to his wife: he mentions the marriage, "which took place in the presence of a very distinguished company in the so-called English Court";[93] he notes, without comment, her death; and his only other allusion to Catherine's existence might well have been penned by Pepys:

"Children she bore none; but of pleasure not always resulting from children, she gave much."[94]

Mattheson's life for the next few years ran on in the fulfilment of his regular duties as secretary to the Resident. In 1713[95] came the

---

ordentliche Einkünffte, von 3. auf 5. Pfund Sterling. täglich anwuchsen, legte er auch der Besoldung seines Secretars noch hundert Reichsthaler jährlich zu." (A Thaler was equal to 3 *Kurantmark;* Cf. Walter Horace Bruford, *Germany in the Eighteenth Century* (Cambridge [England], 1935), p. 330.

92. *Ehrenpforte*, p. 197: "Darauf sich dieser den 25. August, in GOttes Nahmen, ehelich verlobte mit der wohlgebehrenen Catharina, einer Tochter des weiland hochwürdigen Johann Jennings, Rectoris oder Hauptpastoris der Kirchspiele Calston, Blackland und Cherill, in der Graffschafft Wiltshire. . . ."

No further record of Catharina Jennings has survived. How she came to Hamburg and in what capacity remains a mystery. No information of importance regarding her father, the Rector, has come to light. In response to my inquiries, the Registrar of the Diocese of Salisbury has made some researches into the Register of the Bishop, the Subscription Books, etc. From the first he discovered that the parish of Calstone had been in the Jennings family's possession for at least two generations prior to this John. He found the record of the Institution of John Jennings to Calstone in the Subscription Books, under the date of February 26, 1668/9, as well as to that of Blackland, for the same date, in the Dean's Register of Institution—Blackland was a "peculiar" of the Dean of Salisbury. John apparently died in 1702, for there is a record of the Institution of his successor to Calstone in the Register of the Bishop. There happens to be no bundle of Presentations for the year 1669, and the transcripts of the Registers of Calstone, though searched, yielded no information of significance. The Registrar also could offer no information regarding the Parish of Cherill.

93. *Ibid.:* "Die Hochzeit wurde den 9. October, in sehr vernehmer Gesellschafft, auf dem so genannten engländischen Hofe gehalten." None of the records of the "English Court" in Hamburg have survived. Cf. Heinrich Hitzigrath, *Die Kompagnie der Merchants Adventurers und die englische Kirchengemeinde in Hamburg 1611–1835* (Hamburg, 1904). Also William E Lingelbach, "The Merchant Adventurers at Hamburg," in *American Historical Review*, Vol. IX, no. 2, January, 1904).

94. *Ibid.* "Kinder hat sie nicht gebraucht; aber tausend Vergnügen: welches offt bey Kindern fehlet."

95. *Idem,* p. 198. In 1711 "ein Handlungs-Tractat zwischen England und Hamburg." In 1712 the occupation of Stade by the Hanoverian forces (see G. F. Chance, *Great Britain and the Northern War*, p. 29) caused Mattheson to write: "Was hiebey für Schreibens Berichten, Hin- und Hersendens. (auch Kundschafftens) vorgefallen, ist leicht zu erachten."

moment of his greatest glory. Despite the Northern War and the burning by the Swedes,[96] of Altona, the next-door neighbor of Hamburg, Sir John Wich departed for London, probably to recover the funds the British Government owed him, and also to ensure the succession of his son to his position in Hamburg.[97] He had left his secretary in charge, and when he unexpectedly died in London, Mattheson was obliged to assume the position of *"Subdelegati"* in the name of the younger Wich, who was not yet eighteen years old.[98] At the same moment Hamburg was visited by the plague—the last ever to visit northwestern Europe—in which it is estimated that at least one eighth of the city's population perished.[99] The Wich family took refuge outside the town, as did many others of Hamburg's most distinguished inhabitants,[100] but Mattheson remained at his post, apparently unmoved by any sense of danger. During the ensuing month of uncertainty as to whether young Wich would indeed inherit his father's position, Mattheson continued to send the necessary letters in Sir Cyrill's name.[101] He also did everything in his power to prepare the young man for the hoped-for eventuality, which, after the writing of a great number of letters to influential people, at last took place on March 15, 1714. Four days later, Mattheson had the satisfaction of conveying the new credentials to the presiding Bürgermeister.[102]

No further doubts or uncertainties of position eluded the career of either Wich or his secretary for the next twenty-seven years.

96. *Ibid.* "Unsere Unruhen um Hamburg her nahmen indes mehr zu, als ab; die Schweden steckten Anno 1713. Altona in Brand. . . ."

97. The letters of Sir John and Cyrill Wich to Lord Strafford (British Museum, the *Strafford Papers*, Ms. 22, 216) from 1711 to 1714 are full of pleas for the payment of the funds owed them.

98. *Idem*, p. 199: "Da den 21. Junii der Herr Abgesandte nach England reisete, allwo er leider! den 27. Octob., im 42. seines Alters, starb, . . . vertrat Mattheson die Stelle eines Subdelegati zum erstenmahl, Nahmens des jungen Hrn. von Wich, welcher, . . . noch nicht 18. Jahre erreichet hatte."

99. Ernst Finder, *Hamburgisches Bürgertum,* pp. 179–182.

100. *Ehrenpforte*, p. 199: ". . . die Pest in Hamburg so starck wütete, dass ich die wichiche Familie auf einem ausserhalb der Ringmauer belegenen Garten eines vornehmen Rathsherrn enhalten muste. . . ."

101. *State Papers* 82/30, 31.

102. *Ehrenpforte*, p. 200: "Anno 1714. den 15. Märtz die Königlichen Credentzbriefe, welche den 14. Febr. datirt waren, mit dem Residenten-Character glücklich einliefen, und den 19. darauf, durch Matthesons Hand, dem präsidirenden Burgermeister, Hrn. Johann Lütjens L. mit gewöhnlichen Formalitäten überreicht wurden."

From the evidence of letters and of Mattheson's autobiography, several outstanding events color his otherwise routine existence. In 1715, because of the uprising in Scotland, the English Resident was instructed to apply to the Senat of Hamburg for permission to have all Scotch vessels suspected of carrying arms seized in the harbor of Hamburg.[103] One was found bound for Waterford, and in Wich's letter of October 1715 (written, of course, by Mattheson) he reported:

My Secretary has this moment come from aboard the said Ship, and has actually seen in the bottom of the Vessel great heaps of Cannon Balls; but time would not permit him to make any further search this night, the rest of the Ship's loading being cover'd over Pipe Staves. . . .[104]

Mattheson reported himself as the hero of this event, the forbidden cargo having been discovered by his "dutiful watchfulness," and added that many people had no idea of what the Minister of Great Britain might do, and "may form from this explanation at least a small picture of the important business imposed upon him and his own deputy." [105]

In the following years Mattheson frequently took over the entire responsibility of the Residency when business or illness occasioned Wich's absence. In 1719, Sir Cyrill having journeyed to Göhre to wait upon His Majesty, the King of England, Mattheson took it upon himself to answer several important communications concerning the herring trade and wool manufactures of Hamburg. His letter, written on October 27, presents an excellent picture of his efficiency and the type of work he was called on to perform. He writes in part:

Sir

Whilst Mr. Wich has been absent from hence, I have receiv'd two letters for him, written by the Lords Commissioners of Trade, which I have open'd

103. *State Papers* 82/32.
104. *Ibid.*
105. *Ehrenpforte*, p. 201. "Da denn, unter andern, durch Matthesons schuldige Wachsamkeit, ein mit dergleichen verbotenen Waaren beladenes scotländisches Schiff in dem Hamburger Hafen entdecket, in Verhafft genommen, und die Landung, so meist in Stück-Kugeln bestund, confiscirt wurde. Viele Leute begreiffen nicht, was ein Grossbritannischer Minister in Hamburg sagen will; die können sich aus diesen Erzehlungen wenigstens ein kleines Bild von den wichtigen Verrichtungen machen, die ihm und seinem Stellvertreter obliegen."

and found, that the first concern'd the Herring-Trade, and the second the Wool Manufactures. . . .

By the first, the Lords of Trade desire to know: what quantity of British Hering is yearly imported at Hamburgh, and how that of this year did prove? &c. Upon this point, having imploy'd some People experienc'd in such matters, I now have the honour to tell you that the yearly quantity of British Herıng, brought hither, amounts to about 150 till 200 Lasts, and that the Fish we had this year, prov'd very good, and much better than heretofore. By the second Letter their Lordships are desirious to have exact accounts and specifications of what Woollen-Manufactures, as well British as dutch, have for the three Last yeares past, pay'd the Customs at Stade. Upon this point, Sir, I am not yet in a condition to give the least Satisfaction; but have committed a Gentleman at Stade to go next week down to that place and do his best, to get the desir'd accounts and specifications, as exact and particular as will be possible for him. . . .

This, Sir, I have thought in some measure necessary to write to you, that if you think it fit, it might be communicated *ad interim* to the Lords of Trade, till at Mr. Wich's return, he shall himself answer every article of the said Letters more fully and satisfactory.

I am with Respect

Sir,

Your most humble servant

JMattheson

Hamburgh
Oct. 27. 1719.[106]

In 1720 Mattheson again visited Leipzig in order to convey to Count Flemming, the General in charge of the Saxon forces, a large English subsidy. Wich explained this mission in a letter probably written to Lord Stanhope, at that time Secretary of State for the North:

. . . J'ai envoyé mon Secretaire à Leipzick avec les seixante mill ecus pour le Comte de Flemming, parti en Lettres du Change et quinze mill Ducats en Or; Comme le Comte de Flemming m'a prié de me Servir des Voyés les plus Seures pur lui faire tenir cette Somme; ainsi[?] j'ai cru qu'ai etoit necessaire d'envoyer un Homme auquel je pourois me fier avec une Somme de cette importance. . . .[107]

Mattheson's own account of this expedition dwells upon the splendid reception he was accorded, the magnificent entertainment at

106. *State Papers* 82/36.
107. *Ibid.*, 82/37. Wich to [Stanhope?], 23 Avril, 1720.

which the fantastic Count Flemming treated him with so much honor that the other officers all sought his friendship, and the basket of the best Tokay wine given him at his departure.[108] Although the satisfaction of playing such a momentarily honorific role as this, and the pleasure of fraternizing with the eminent English noblemen who were repeatedly passing through Hamburg,[109] must have flattered Mattheson's vanity, the petty tasks of correspondence began to elicit from him more than one expression of annoyance. One of these is particularly eloquent in its description of the secretarial round and the secretary's reaction to it. The occasion for this outburst was the labor involved in the proper apprehension of Lord Duffus in 1716, who was guilty of taking part in the Stuart uprising of the previous year.[110] The presence in Hamburg, shortly before, of the Czar and the King of Denmark had already given him much to do, and had perhaps exhausted his patience.[111] On the tenth of July, just after their departure, the nobleman was arrested as he left the theater. Ten days later he was dispatched to London, but Mattheson had to investigate all his treasonable writings.[112] He writes:

108. *Ehrenpforte,* p. 206: "In Leipzig zog ihn der Herr General-Feldmarschall, Graf von Flemming, nicht nur an seine Tafel, bey grosser und vornehmer Gesellschafft, sondern erwies ihm auch sonst so viele Ehre, dass gar Oberstern und Generals sich um seine, als eines vermeinten Günstlings, Freundschafft bewurben. Beym Abschiede beschenkte ihn der Herr Graf, (weil er sonst keine Belohnung annehmen wollte) mit einem Korbe voll des besten Tockaier-Weins, und sandte ihm ein gantzes Antahl, mit einem eigenhändigen Schreiben begleitet, zu Wasser nach Hamburg nach."

109. *Ibid.:* "Mylord Carteret . . . fand an unsers Mathesons Musik selche Lust, dass er einst zwo gantzer Stunden, ohne von der Stelle zu weichen, bey ihm sasz und zuhörte. . . ."

Also p. 194: "Der Hertzog, Anton Ulrich [von Braunschweig] unterhielt sich etliche mahl bey der Tafel mit Mattheson, den er zu sich winckte, von der Musik und von den theatralischen Sachen mit ihm redete: ist das der Hamburger? war seine erste Frage &c."

110. G. E. Cockayne, *Complete Peerage,* III, 192–193, describes the career of this nobleman, Kenneth Sutherland, Lord Duffus, who, though lodged in the Tower of London after his arrest, was set free without trial in 1717.

111. *Ehrenpforte,* p. 202: "Da den 28. May der König von Dänemarck durch Hamburg auf das Vorwerck Ham fuhr, und mit dem Czaaren daselbst Unterredung hielt, machte selches viel Nachdenckens, Forschens und Berichtens."

112. *Ibid.:* "Den 10. Jul. wurde der rebellische Lord Duffus, durch die Grossbritannische Gesandschafft, in Hamburg gefangen genommen, als er aus der Comödie kam; den 15. nach Haarburg gebracht; den 24. aber auf ein engländisches Schiff nach London ausgeliefert. Die Untersuchung aller verrätherischen Schrifften dieses Lords fiel Mattheson zu, welcher auch absonderlich dafür belohnet wurde."

It is easy to imagine the time and labor such matters take, together with the reports that must constantly be made. Because of the great number of subjects to be treated, many an important event can only be mentioned in passing; but as a brief sample I may mention that today it may be stone and lime, tomorrow singing and playing, the day after tomorrow throne and crown. These matters have been daily bread of a hard-working man. They did not arise at regular, stated intervals; on the contrary, they usually seemed to crop up all at once. When, for instance, several long awaited orders came in all at the same time, or, when a special messenger arrived: "Away with the music! Drop the ruler; Fetch the code from there—the one for deciphering secret messages! Get the other one! There! Spread the one for writing the reply over that long table!" And all has to be neatly copied, dated, subscribed, signed, provided with headings, numbered, protocolled, filed, neatly folded, firmly packed, well sealed, properly addressed, safely despatched with instruction for the messenger etc. Alas! If it so chanced that such respectable labor could be speedily finished (also under special circumstances it often took as many weeks or months as it did hours or days at other occasions) and the courier of the State had departed, pell mell, with his weighty briefcase—ah, with what happy leisure were the lines again drawn . . . How sweet was the very sight of a half-finished composition for *viole da gamba* and *flutes traversers*, an *aria* that was perhaps to be sung by Mademoiselle Püchon or *Signore* Campioli! Merely seeing the pleasant melody and humming harmony on paper, drew from the languishing heart that wonderful word of Clinias: *Mansuefio*. But a moment! The historian has almost become a rhetorician. This must not be. Mattheson, the author of this, pinched me, pulled me by the sleeve, in disapproval of such flowery language.[113]

113. *Idem*, pp. 202–203: "Man kann leicht dencken, was für Arbeit und Zeit zu solchen Sachen, und den davon abzustattenden Berichten, gehöret. Wir müssen hier, wegen der vielen Materien, über manche wichtige Begebenheit hinwischen, und nur in einer kleinen Probe zeigen, wie heute Stein und Kalck, morgen Sang und Klang, übermorgen Thron und Kron eines arbeitsamen Mannes Vorwürffe gewesen sind. Und das geschah nicht zu gewissen, bestimmten Zeiten; sondern mehrentheils unvermuthlich, wenn z. E. etliche ausgebliebene Posten auf einmahl ankamen, oder etwa ein Expresser anlangte. Fort! mit den Noten. Weg! mit der Bleischnur. Die eine Cypher dort her! um geheime Schrifften aufzulösen! die andre auf jenem langen Tische ausgebreitet, um mit dergleichen Schrifften wieder zu antworten; alles hernach fein ins reine gabracht; datirt; subscribirt; paraphirt; rubricirt; numerirt; prottocollirt; registrirt; sauber gefalten; fest gepackt; wohl versiegelt; gehörig adressirt; sicher spedirt; den Boten instruirt &c, O, ha! —Fügte es sich dann, dass solche hochgebotene Arbeit bald ihre Endschafft erreichte, (wiewohl sie auch bey andern Umständen, nicht selten, statt Stunden oder Tage, so viele Wochen oder Monathe erforderte) und der Staats-Courier, mit seinem wichtigen Briefbündel, über Hals und Kopf, abgefertigt war; ach! wie ruhig liessen sich denn die Fächer abmessen; ja, wie süss lächelte nicht ein halbfertiger Satz von Gamben und Traversen, den irgend eine Püchen oder ein Campioli singen sollte? die Sichtbarkeit der angenehmen Melodie und säuselnden Harmonie, auf dem blessen Papier, lockte schon aus dem schmeltzenden Hertzen das beträchtliche Wort des Clinias: *Man-sue-fi-o*. Doch halt! der Geschichtsschreiber wäre hier bald zum Redner geworden. Das soll nicht seyn. Mattheson zupft

On reading the last sentences of this passage, no one can fail to see that Mattheson's prime concern was by no means the labor which, for nearly forty years, he devoted to the English Resident in Hamburg; that, no matter how satisfactory the perquisites of an Ambassadorial secretary, Mattheson would not allow them to interfere for long in the pursuit of his favorite art. For the first two years of his secretaryship he seems to have been entirely engrossed in his work, but then the record of musical activities reappears in his autobiography. In 1708 he composed "Sonates, à 2 & 3 Flutes sans Basse."[114] In the same year, the gambist, Abel, who was the father of the more famous Karl Friedrich Abel and an associate of J. S. Bach at the Court of Cöthen,[115] came to Hamburg and gave some concerts with Mattheson in the Drillhaus.[116] A year later Mattheson received the first municipal recognition of his musical talents. He was commissioned by the Hamburger Rath to write the music to a text by the Syndic, Lucas von Bostel, for the annual *Petri-Mahl,* the great holiday of the Hamburg government. For this work he received twelve ducats, and was presented with a golden medal.[117] His two unsuccessful operatic projects, already mentioned, followed in the next years. He was also commissioned to write a number of serenatas for various private festivities.[118] His reputation increased by his first musical treatise of a definitely

---

mich, der ich dieses aufsetze, starck beym Ermel, und will von solchen Blümlein nichts wissen."

114. Bibliography No. 11.

115. E. L. Gerber, *Historisch-Biographisches Lexicon* (Leipzig, 1790–92), p. 3, Bach probably wrote his *Viola da Gamba* Suites for Abel.

116. *Ehrenpforte,* p. 196: "Es kam sonst in diesem Jahre der berühmte engländische Altist, Abel, mit welchem Mattheson, im October, verschiedene starcke, doch keine geistlichen Concerte, in so genannten Drillhause, und auf dem Niedernbaum, anstellete." (The "Drillhaus" was Hamburg's great public hall at this time, in which public concerts were beginning to be given. Cf. Preussner, *Die Bürgerliche Musikkultur,* where there is an illustration of it on page 157.)

117. *Ehrenpforte,* p. 197: "Im Jahre 1709, wurde unserm Mattheson die umfängliche Musik zu dem jährlichen Petri-Mahl E. E. Raths der Stadt Hamburg aufgetragen, welche er auch am Tage Matthiä vollzog, und vom Magistrat mit einer goldenen Medaille von 12. Dukaten am Gewichte beschencket wurde. Weil es nun eine öffentliche, Stadtkündige Verrichtung war, und die Worte im Druck erschienen, zehlen wir sie billig mit. Der Herr Syndicus, Lucas von Bostel, nachmahls Bürgermeister, hatte die Verse gemacht." Cf Bibliography No. 18.

118. Bibliography Nos. 31, 32, 34, 35, etc.

# The Dom

popular nature, published in 1713,[119] for later in that year he began
to teach thorough bass to three of the town's most eminent citizens,
and to give general musical instruction to a fourth.[120] The coronation of George I of England in 1714 was naturally celebrated
with due magnificence, and Mattheson collaborated with König,
who later became Court Poet at Dresden,[121] in a Serenata and
Illumination.[122] Clearly his secretarial career was not in the least
interfering with his musical activities.

2

## THE DOM

Up to the year 1715, Mattheson had pursued two of the three
possible courses which eighteenth-century Hamburg offered to
the creative musician. For a time he had been a member of the
Opera, and subsequently, as composer and teacher, he had earned
an independent livelihood. But despite the growth in popularity,
or better, respectability of these two careers, Mattheson had per-
sistently refused to follow the third, namely, the profession of municipal and ecclesiastical musician. In towns such as Hamburg,
the continued vitality of religious belief still left the civil and
ecclesiastical musical organization the dominant one. Lutheran
church services provided the greatest and steadiest demand for
musical writing, and, in most cases, the instrumentalists and vocalists at the disposal of the churches were, or at least they had been in
the past, admirable performers. Nevertheless Mattheson had defi-

119. *Das Neu-Eröffnete Orchestre,* Bibliography No. 27.
120. *Ehrenpforte,* p. 200: "Am 9. November nahm er den jungen Herrn von Som,
hernach Licentiaten und hamburgischen Syndicum, in welcher Würde er auch gestorben
ist, samt zween Herren Winckler, zu Scholaren im Generalbass an: einer dieser ist Doctor
der Rechten, und wegen seiner Advocatur sehr berühmt; der andre Licentiat und Secretar
am Dom-Capitel. Zu ihnen fügte sich hernach ein Herr de Dobbeler, itzund Stadt-Secretar
und Licentiat die zu ihm ins Haus kamen, und guten, auch wohlvergoltenen Unterricht
empfingen."
121. Schröder, *Lexicon der Hamburgischen Schriftsteller,* IV, 121–126.
122. *Ehrenpforte,* p. 200: "Da auch hernach auf Ihrer Maj. Krönungfest, den 15. Nov.
ein grosses Mahl angestellet wurde . . . verfertigte [Mattheson] dazu eine grosse Serenate,
davon der nicht weniger grosse Dichter Joh. Ulrich König &c. die Verse machte." Cf. Bibliography No. 31.

nitely spurned the only opportunity offered him to become a member of the regular musical organization of Hamburg. Not only did he feel himself superior to the position of mere organist, but also it is probable that he was bitterly opposed to the conservatism of Cantor Gerstenbüttel, under whom he would have had to serve. Above all, his musical instinct had made him aware that an incongruity existed between the traditional German organization of music and the predominant forms of Italian origin. His enthusiasm for the theatrical style of operatic music left him with very little patience for old-fashioned ecclesiastical music. It seemed to him not only dull, but, indeed, unworthy for the worship of God, in that it did not employ modern improvements in musical learning.[123]

The problem was insoluble: while Gerstenbüttel lived, these "improvements" could not possibly be introduced into church music. At the same time, Mattheson's ardor in clinging to his opinions may have militated against his being offered the kind of position he felt suitable to his talents. Within the walls of the city, however, there luckily existed an organization which was completely independent of the Hamburg municipality. This was the Domkirche. In the year 1715 Mattheson suddenly applied for—and received—the reversion of the directorship of music in the Dom. The peculiar position this church held in all the affairs of Hamburg must be understood before this unexpected action on the part of the British Resident's busy young secretary can be explained.

The Dom, or Cathedral, was an imperial and ecclesiastical foundation that was considerably older than Hamburg itself. The Middle Ages had witnessed endless disputes between the rising authority and power of the municipality of Hamburg and that of the Bishop of its Cathedral.[124] The reformation had offered an opportunity for the solution of this old and vigorous rivalry, but Imperial procedure was so cumbersome that nothing truly practical had ever been arrived at. When the foundation was secularized,

---

123. Cf. p. 116 where will be found an analysis of these sentiments which were expressed in the introduction of *Das Neu-Eröffnete Orchestre*, Bibliography No. 27.
124. L. Reinke, *Hamburg, ein Abriss der Stadtgeschichte*, pp. 20 and 38.

it reverted to the direct possession of the Empire instead of to Hamburg proper, and was attached politically to the newly created neighboring duchies of Bremen and Verden.[125] In the process of secularization the ecclesiastical method of administration of the Dom's property had, however, been retained. The so-called *Domkapitel* [126] administered the finances and provided for the continuance of religious services in the church itself. Titles to a hundred or more benefices remained in the gift of the Domkapitel, and most frequently were given as sinecures and marks of honor to members of Hamburg's leading families—the honor of the canonicates making up for the greatly depleted income attached to them.[127] And the Dom continued to maintain this independent, albeit impotent, position in the very middle of the city of Hamburg—until it was finally destroyed by fire at the beginning of the nineteenth century.

During the first half of the eighteenth century, however, this institution was a factor of considerable importance in the political, ecclesiastical, and, particularly, musical affairs of the city. Up to the outbreak of the Northern War its political connection with Bremen and Verden made it a stronghold of Swedish influence.[128] After the loss of these territories to the Hanoverian forces, it naturally came under the aegis of England and Hanover, who did not hesitate to make use of its sinecures to further their political ends.[129] Although the church was physically one of the largest

125. *Idem*, pp. 48–49.
126. The old form of this word is "Dom Capitel"; I have, however, used the modern form throughout my text.
127. Ludwig von Griesheim, *Die Stadt Hamburg in ihrem politischen, ökonomischen und sittlichen Zustand* (Hamburg, 1760), pp. 33–34: "Hamburg hat in seinen Ringmauern einen Dohm, der sehr alt ist . . . auch gehören unter die Dohm-Herren-Curien viele Häuser, mit abgesonderter Gerichtsbarkeit und Nutzungen, doch mit wohl eingerichteten Verträgen. Der Dohm hat aber nach der Reformation manche Schmälerung seiner Einkünffte erlitten. . . . Er hat zwölf Dom-Herren; doch wird bey diesem Stift weder auf den Adel, noch dessen Ahnen-Zahl gesehen . . . und viele Canonici. . . . Zu so bequeme Tituls, mit so weniger Beschwerlichkeit, finden immer Liebhaber. Ich will nicht sagen, durch eine Art von Negoce; die Simonie ist im Jure Canonico zu hesslich abgeschildert; aber man kann doch zu einem Canonicat gelangen, ohne sich über die Wissenschaften examiniren zu lassen."
128. Krüger, *Die Hamburgische Musikorganisation*, p. 242, note 831.
129. Griesheim, *Die Stadt Hamburg*, p. 35: "Chur-Hanover exercirt als Schutzherr verschiedene Gerechtsame bey Ernennung eines Canonici, in personeller Gerichtsbarkeit, auch in Dohm- Rechtshändeln."

in Hamburg, it possessed no official parish or parishioners. Its pastor was a personage of no importance, and took no part in the orthodox-pietist controversies raging in the Geistliches Ministerium at the time. Nevertheless the members of the Domkapitel and the possessors of its secularized benefits were members of Hamburg's most illustrious families. If any of the other inhabitants of the city attended its services, they were probably persons who had some social connection with the institution or were foreigners who had no affiliation with any of the regular parishes. Because of this somewhat anomalous position, it would appear that the Dom had little to attract a congregation save its music.

The Rath had never succeeded in gaining control over the civil or ecclesiastical actions of the Dom; neither had its musical subordinate, the town cantor, ever gained control over the Dom's music. An agreement had been made in the preceding century between the Domkapitel and the Hamburg Government whereby, in return for a small sum, the Dom was to receive the necessary singers and instrumentalists from the municipal organization for a full musical service in each quarter of the year.[130] All matters of directing this music, however, remained in the hands of a special _Domcantor,_ who was remunerated by the possession of one or more canonicates. Naturally this person had to be chosen from among its composers. This situation, which was a fairly constant menace to the authority of the cantor, was a perpetual source of irritation throughout the entire career of the conservative Gerstenbüttel. He attempted to force his way into power by applying for the possession of a canonicate, but all his applications elicited the same response—he must wait for a vacancy. His request was never granted, although three different directors of music were appointed before Mattheson was.[131] Two of these had been composers for the Opera,[132] which is a reasonably clear indication of the musical taste of the Domkapitel at that time.

Thus matters stood in 1715 at the time of Mattheson's application. The Dom's Director of Music was Friederich Nicolaus Braun, who

130. Krüger, _Die Hamburgische Musikorganisation,_ p. 35.
131. _Idem,_ pp. 241–243.
132. Nicolaus Strungk, 1674–78; Johann Wolfgang Franck, 1682–86.

had held the position for the past twenty-nine years, and who was now an old man.[133] He had preserved the freedom of the Dom's music, but he had done nothing to make it distinguished, nor had he contributed much to the musical prestige of his position to make up for the material perquisites it lacked. Outside of the freedom of musical action which differentiated this position from all other music-ecclesiastical ones in Hamburg, and which was perhaps fostered by the presence of a musically enlightened congregation, it appears to have offered but small attraction for a man of Mattheson's self-importance. Whether he was invited by members of the Domkapitel (one of them was studying thorough bass with him at that time) [134] cannot be ascertained, but may well be surmised. According to the records of the Domkapitel,[135] he submitted his application for the survivance to the cantorship on July 18, 1715. A month later, in compliance with the recommendation of the Swedish Envoy to Hamburg [136] the application for the reversion of Braun's post was finally granted.[137] Since Braun retained the position and the income until his death, which occurred three years later, Mattheson received no immediate benefit of any sort whatsoever by this act, and was forced to await the first vacant liv-

133. Mattheson published a short biographical notice of him in his *Ehrenpforte*, pp. 25–26.

134. *Ehrenpforte*, p. 200: "Am 9. November [1713] nahm er . . . zween Herren Winckler, zu Scholaren im Generalbass an; . . . der andre [ist] Licentiat und Secretär am Dom-Capitel."

135. *Protokol des Dom Capitels*, 1715, p. 480. 8 July, 1715: Convenere in low Capitulari: "Joh. Mattheson übergab Unterdienste: Littr. um die Survivance auf des alten Brauns Cantoris S[t]elle, bey hiesiger Cathedral-Kirche: Conclusum: So verlesen, und nimt der Deca: über sich, mit dem Cantori Brauns daraus zu reden."

136. *Idem*, p. 481, 1 August, 1715. "Relation von Mattheson Survivance: Joh. Mattheson's Survivance halber, hätte geredet, welcher der geneigten Communication gedancket u. gebethen, dass zu seinem prä-juditz, hier unter nichts mögte verhängt werden; Worauf der Deca regieret, dass er Canonicatum cum pertinentiis ad dies vita behalten, und ihn nichts priejudicirliches wiederfahren solte." Although no longer a possession of Sweden's, her wishes might still be of importance to the Domkapitel. See above.

137. *Idem*, p. 485, 29 Aug. 1715. "Mattheson erhält die Survivance auf das Cantorat: Ihre Excell. der Königl. Schwedische Envoye Hr. von Rohtleib gesteiger Erges (?) Selber behändiget und zu obtenierung sothaner Survivance demelir recommendiret.—Unanimi Consensu Supplicanti die gesuchte Survivance ad Cantoratum Cathedralem, sive praejudicio des jetzigen Cantoris Brauns hiemit ertheilet." Mattheson recorded the receipt of this decision in the *Ehrenpforte* (p. 201). "Den 29. August darauf erhielt er von Dom-Capitel die Anwartschafft, auf das *Directorium musicum,* und auf das demselben anhängige Canonicat, bey der Cathedral-Kirche [zu kommen]."

ing. In November, the "Vicarius in Petro" having conveniently died, his Canonicate was presented to him, thus providing him with an official status.[138] Mattheson inaugurated his career as director of music by composing an oratorio for the Christmas Festival,[139] which was celebrated in the Dom, according to the notation on his score, on December 27, 1715.[140] Both the music and the text of this oratorio contain none of the more startling or dramatic elements of the majority of his later church compositions. The story of the Nativity according to St. Luke is here narrated by the tenor Evangelist, and there is no dramatic personification by the other soloists or chorus. Although the composition itself was conservative, its production violated a fundamental principle of the church: three of the soloists were not only singers at the Opera, but were also women. When he had the benefit of the services of Mme. Keiser, the leading operatic soprano in Hamburg,[141] for the production of an oratorio in the following year, he mentioned this extraordinary innovation with obvious pride.[142] Never before had women been permitted to take part in the formal music of the Lutheran churches in Hamburg. Mattheson had already in 1713 advocated the use of professional singers because they would make possible an improvement in church music, as was illustrated, according to him, by the enlightened customs of Venice.[143] Some years later he recorded

138. *Protokol des Dom Capitels* 1715, pp. 503–504, 21 Nov. 1715. "Joh. Mattheson wird Vicarius in Petro: . . . St. Catharina in Petro, so obitu gratiis Georgii, vacant werde, ruf Joh. Mattheson, um supplica dich Mattheson pro conferenda Vicaria perdicta, et solutione statutorum. Soll die Vicarie dem Presentate conferiret werden." Mattheson writes, *Ehrenpforte*, p. 201: "Am 21 Nov. nahm er Besitz von der *Vicaria tertia ad Altare Stae Catharinae in Petro*, und Schwur dem Capitel."

139. *Ehrenpforte*, pp. 201–202: "Den 12. Dec. wurde ihm aufgetragen, eine vollstimmige Kirchenmusik, auf das bervorstehende Weihnacht-Fest, im Dom anzustellen, welche auch mit gutem Fortgang vollzogen ward. . . . Es sangen dabey Madame Rischmüller, Mademoiselle Schwartz u. Mademoiselle Schober." The first and last of these were known as "tüchtige Sängerinnen," according to Enst Lindner, *Die erste stehende Deutsche Oper*, p. 49.

140. Bibliography, No. 37.

141. Lindner, *Die erste stehende Deutsche Oper*, p. 138.

142. *Ehrenpforte*, p. 203: "Den 17. Sept. hielt er Musik im Dom, und führte Madame Kayser [Keiser] aufs Chor, welches, ausser obigem Exempel, zuvor in keiner hamburgischen Kirche geschehen war, dass ein Frauenzimmer mit musiciret hätte; hinführo aber im Dom allemahl, bey seiner Zeit, geschah."

143. *Das Neu-Eröffnete Orchestre*, p. 206: "Zu verwundern ist das *Republiquen* nicht

that he had not been able to introduce this custom without considerable opposition, even from the intelligent members of the
Domkapitel,[144] but added that in the end "they could not hear
and see enough." From the notations in his scores written in the
next eight years, it is, however, clear that he was able thereafter
to make use of opera singers of both sexes. There remain no records
of the engagement of these singers or of any of the monetary ar-
rangements involving either them or the instrumentalists necessary for many of Mattheson's elaborate scores.[145] And yet he must
have been able somehow to acquire the requisite funds from non-
official sources, which suggests that the Dom's congregation was
indeed drawn from admirers of the opera and of operatic church
music.[146]

Although Mattheson's first oratorio bears no trace of the technique of dramatic style, those he wrote in 1716 show an astonishing
advance in this direction. In the first of these, *Die Gnädige Sendung
Gottes*,[147] both text and music abandon the older narrative style,

an den Königen aller *Republiquen,* ich meine an dem klugen und *delicieusen Venedig*
ein löbliches und rühmliches Exempel in Anbauung dergleichen *Seminarien* zu GOttes
Ehre und der Menschen Wohlgefallen, nehmen; sondern im Gegenteil die *Dona Dei*
fast mit Füssen treten unter nichtigen, *scrupuleusen* und heuchlerischen Verwand bei
Frauen-Zimmer zur Kirchen-Music *admittiren,* und den Gottesdienst also des besten
Ornats berauben wellen." Concerning the musical activities of women in Venice, see
Kathi Meyer, "Der chorische Gesang der Frauen mit besonderer Zezugnahme seiner
Betätigung auf geistlichen Gebiet. 1. Teil bis zur Zeit um 1800," Diss., Leipzig (Mittenwald, 1917). Mattheson fully realised that the soloistic art of modern music required
new schools of musical training. He certainly had the Italian conservatories in mind when
he referred to Venice.

144. Der Vollkommene Capellmeister, p. 482: "Ich weiss, was mirs für Mühe und
Verdruss gekostet hat, die Sängerinnen in der hiesigen Dom Kirche einzuführen. Anfangs wurde verlangt, ich sollte sie bey Leibe so stellen, dass sie kein Mensch zu
sehen kriegte; zuletzt aber konte man nie genug hören und sehen."

145. Only one reference to the remuneration of a singer occurs in the records of the
Domkapitel during the period of Mattheson's directorship. *Protokol des Dom Capitels*
cl. VIII, no. VI, 1717–1728, p. 430: "Dr. Senior referiret dass er . . . dem Sänger
Möring auf Rev. Capituli gleichfalls 4 mk. an Kronen gegeben."

146. In discussing the low state of the Dom music after his departure Mattheson
makes some significant comparisons which imply that he had singers for six Sundays in
the year, for which each was paid 7 thaler. *Ehrenpforte,* p. 212 n. ". . . sind erbötig,
sechsmal im Jahr, wie gewöhnlich, d. i. sowohl Pfingsten, Johannis und Michaelis, als
zu obbenannten dreien Zeiten [auf Weihnacht, zur Passionszeit, und auf Ostern], ihre
Dienste des endes zu leisten, damit jede Person doch wenigstens 6. Thaler, und zum Weih-
nachten den siebenden bekomme."

147. Bibliography No. 41.

and each of the seven soloists as well as the various choruses are dramatic personifications.[148] In the second, *Chera, Oder die Wittwe zu Nain*,[149] the dramatic intentions of opera are strikingly evident. It was written for the sixteenth Sunday after Trinity; the text is based upon the story of Christ's raising of the dead son of the widow of Nain.[150] Around the deathbed of the young man are gathered his mother and the bearers of his coffin. After they have lamented, he sings an aria of joyful resignation to death, and is welcomed in Heaven by a chorus of angels. In the meantime the allegorical figures of "Belief" and "Devotion" attempt unsuccessfully to comfort the weeping widow. At last Jesus, surrounded by his followers, appears and bids her cease her lamentations and have faith in Him. In response to her promises He raises her son—an act which is the occasion for an aria of trumph sung by "Belief." The oratorio is concluded by a fervent duet between Chera and her son, and a chorus of joy sung by "the Church." Both the text and music conform with Neumeister's definition of a cantata as part of an opera, with arias and recitatives "put together." [151] It would seem that this "theatrical" oratorio was a popular one, since Mattheson records two further performances of it, in 1719 and 1722.[152] Within a year of his assuming control of the Dom's music he had thus been able to produce results in the Dom, and to set a standard which his predecessor, Braun, had certainly never approached.

The year 1717 was musically the most active of his career as the Dom's director. In addition to providing music for the four specified occasions required by the old agreement between the Domkapitel and the Hamburg Rath, he wrote an oratorio for the ordination service of two priests in Altona,[153] and a secular cantata in honor

148. *Ibid.*
149. Bibliography, No. 42.
150. Luke 7. 11–18.
151. G. P. Hörner, *Telemanns Passionsmusiken*, p. 26.
152. The following table is inscribed on the last page of the score *Chera:*

|  |  |  | Chera | Neaniscus | der Glaube |
|---|---|---|---|---|---|
| zum erstenmahl | aufgeführt |  | Ao. 1716. | Keiserin | Hasz | Petzholt |
| " ander " | " |  | Ao. 1719. | Endradi | Grünwald | Arnoldi |
| " drittenmahl | " |  | Ao. 1722 | Mlle. | Möhring | Riem- |
|  |  |  |  | Monjou |  | schneider |

153. Bibliography No. 52.

of the Domkapitel.[154] Two other events of this year were the cause of extraordinary celebrations in Hamburg, in which, of course, the Dom took part. The first of these was the defeat of the Turks before Belgrade by Prince Eugene. In the composition of the oratorio for this occasion, *Der Siegende Gideon*,[155] which contains nine full choruses and twelve extensive arias, Mattheson records having consumed four days.[156] Though it was a most elaborate score, he had but six days in which to rehearse it, and as though this were not excitement enough, he very nearly lost his life by being drowned as he was crossing the Elbe to fetch some extra singers.[157] The second event, which took place scarcely a month later, was the great "Evangelische Jubel-Fest" on October 31. Ten days earlier the indefatigable composer submitted to the Domkapitel for approval the text and music of his oratorio for this service.[158] It was entitled *Der reformirende Johannes*,[159] and most appropriately described the actions of Luther under the guise of John the Baptist. It is by far the longest of Mattheson's oratorios, and he declares that it was hailed as a masterpiece.[160]

When his predecessor, Braun, died the following year Mattheson at once received his correct title and its accompanying emolument.[161] Although his autobiography contains countless refer-

154. Bibliography No. 53.
155. Bibliography No. 56.
156. On the title-page of his score he wrote:
    "Cominciato    15 Settembre
    e finito    19    detto    1717"
157. *Ehrenpforte*, p. 204. "Er gerieth aber den 23. September in sehr grosse Wassergefahr, durch Sturm und Ungewitter: woraus ihn GOtt sichtbarlich errettete. Er wollte nehmlich einige Sänger zur Verstärckung holen, und fuhr deswegen mit einem kleinen Nachen über die Elbe, bey schönem Wetter hin; bey sehr bösem her."
158. *Protokol des Dom Capitels 1717*, p. 680: 21. Octob. 1717. "Der Deca . . . produciret die Texte einer project d. Music vom Rev. Capit. vice Cantore, Mattheson. . . ."
159. Bibliography No. 57.
160. *Ehrenpforte*, p. 205: "Man hielt diese *piece* [Bibl. No. 63] und die Jubel-Musik für ein Paar Meisterstücke."
161. *Protokollum des Dom Capitels 1718*, p. 720, 24 Martii 1718: "Mattheson pro canonicatus minoris a cantoratus admissione Deliberatio cum Conclusc: Der Memorial vorlesen, folgendes Protocollum vom 7 Julÿ 1687. Wie es mit der Cantore Brauns gefalten nachgesehen, u. welchem nach der Statuten-Gelder, im gleich die halbe Gebühr des Kirchen-Dienstes remittiret, und produciret Dn. Decanus Capitulationem so mit der vorigen Cantoris seiner collationiret und mir durch gedachter Mattheson vollenziehen zu lassen, commitiret quod factum."

ences to his monetary affairs throughout his life, it never mentions
this aspect of his relations with the Domkapitel. Expediency perhaps accounts for this unusual omission, for from what he wrote
elsewhere it is clear that he and the Domkapitel did not always see
eye to eye. In describing the life of Reinhard Keiser who followed
Mattheson as Domcantor, he did not hesitate to state exactly what
income his successor received, and exactly what his opinion on the
subject was. He writes: "Since the title of *Canonici minoris & Cantoris cathedralis* sounds well, many people fancy that it carries
with it a large income. Let them here be informed, however, that
said income ordinarily did not amount to 24 Thaler annually." [162]
In order to corroborate this statement, he thereupon gives a tabulation of his own annual receipts.[163] The actual expenses involved
by the receipt and possession of his canonical had cost him twice
the amount of its income, which outrage he describes in a burst
of vituperative rhetoric: "God of money, father belly, blessed
paunch, and loathing of music! The annual fees for copying cost
me twice as much as I earn. And for this, go down upon your
knees and you have to take a costly Latin oath." [164] Whether or not
Mattheson assumed the directorship in full knowledge of the
truly paltry payment he was to receive for his pains cannot be said.
It is surprising, however, that he neglected to state his idealistic
motives—did any occur to him—in taking on the position. Al-

Mattheson alluded to this event in the *Ehrenpforte* (p. 204): "Als nun am 11. Märtz
der bissherige Director in Dom gestorben, nahm Mattheson am 24. den feierlichen Besitz
von seinem Canonicat, mit einem abermahligen Eide."

162. *Ehrenpforte*, p. 130: "Und weil die *Praedicata* eines *Canonici minoris* & *Cantoris
cathedralis* hoch klingen, dencken viele Leute es werden auch grosse Einkünffte dabey
vermacht seyn. Aber sie lassen sich hier berichten, dass sich solche Einkünffte, ordentlicher
Weise, jährlich nicht auf 24. Thaler erstrecken."

163. *Idem*, pp. 130–131: Mattheson concludes it: "Machen also 71 fl. 6 sh. eines gantzen
Jahres Memorien. Davon gibt man dem Bringer jedesmahl 2 sh. oder mehr. bleiben 70 fl.
14 sh. übrig."

164. *Idem*, pp. 131–132: "Das sogenannte Canonicat, oder die *Praebenda minor*, hat mir
An. 1718. den 24. Märtz, an Statutengeldern 46 fl. 2 sh. . . . den 11 May darauf, *pro redi-
mentis Memoriis, pro Calendis &c.* 65 Fl. 5sh., den Bringern, der Distributionen etc. in
zehn Jahren wenigstens 5 fl. zusammen 122. fl. 5 sh. gekostet. Mit was für Kräutlein man
dabey zu thun hat, das lässt sich besser mündlich, als schrifftlich berichten. Kennzeichen
der Verwerfung sind jederzeit diese gewesen: Goldklumpen der GOtt! Vater Bauch!
lieber Wanst! und Hass der Musik! Mir hats jährlich an Schreibgebühr zweimahl so viel
gekostet, als eingebracht. Und dafür muss man einen theuren, lateinischen Eid auf den
Knien leisten . . ."

though in his capacity as secretary as well as private music-teacher he was earning a more than adequate income, the records of the Domkapitel show that he by no means remained mute on the subject of his salary. From 1715 to 1719 he received his small remuneration without protest, but in each of the two succeeding years he demanded an annual increase of 12 thalers. By both of these petitions the Domkapitel remained unmoved.[165] Undaunted by his lack of success, Mattheson renewed his efforts two years later, enlisting in his aid Graf van Schlaff, the Hanoverian Resident.[166] Despite the influence of this important personage the Domkapitel replied that they could not accede to his request since they lacked funds.[167] Some seven months later, however, they did present Mattheson with an additional 4 thalers.[168]

In the meantime, no matter how much he resented this treatment, Mattheson devoted much of his time and energy to the composition of a number of oratorios for the Dom, which followed the same pattern as those of the preceding years. In 1718 he set to music the passion text, entitled *Der für die Sünde der Welt gemart-*

165. *Protokol des Doms cl. VIII no. VI*, pp. 126–127. 16. Mai, 1720: "Mattheson pro augmentando Salario

Dr. Decan, prod. Joh. Matthesons Cantoris dieselbe Vorstellung dass zu den beliebten 30 Rthl. noch jährlich 12 zugeleget werden mögten. . . ." *Idem*, p. 213. 27. Märtz, 1721: "Mattheson pro augmentando Salario

Joh. Mattheson Ecclesia Cathed. Canter übergab ein Unterdienst Gesuch, dass ihm zu denen jährl. beliebten 30 Rthl. annoch 18 Rthls. zugeleget werden mögten." *Ibid.*, "Concl.—Bleibet es bey dem einmahl beliebten Quanto."

166. *Idem*, p. 395. 1. Martii, 1725: "Dr. Decan. reassumirte des Hrn. Cant. Matthesons Memoriale in pto. der Memorien-Gelder des ihm der Königl. und Chur-Fürstl. Resident Gf. Schlaff per Secretar. behändigen Sachen und zu Capitul verlesen, ereilen um die Memorien-Rechnungen gäben, dass mit selbigen durch-gehends es schlecht Stünde, ist die Sache in Deliberation genommen, und doch in ausgefallen, da andere Bediente, ratione Salarii, mit denen Erbgiften wie der Zustand es mit sich brächte, friedlich und vergnügt seyn musten, supplicant auch solches ihm würde gefallen lassen biss etiam die Distribution reichlicher ergeben könte: welches dem Secretario gedachten Hrn. Residenten Schlaff in Interart zu hinterbringen committiret."

167. *Protokol des Doms*, p. 398. 22 Martii, 1725: "Secretarius referirte—dass vigore Protoc. vom 1sten hujus praemia Salute dem Königl. Gross Britannischen und Chur-Hannoverischen Residenten Gf. Schlaff Neu Capituli Conclus. wegen des Cantoris Matthesons hinterbracht, welchen resalutanden in Antwort gegeben, weilen der Rechnungen schlechten Zustand es von dieses mahl nicht leiden wolte, Supplicanten zu gratificiren Neu Capitulum sich dessen Persohn ins Künftige recommendiret seyn lassen möchte."

168. *Idem*, p. 430: 1. Novembr., 1725: "Dr. Senior referiret, dass er den Cantori Mattheson 4 Rthl. an Kronen . . . auf Rev. Capituli gegeben. . . ."

*erte und sterbende Jesus.*[169] by the poet Heinrich Brockes, and produced it in the Dom on Palm Sunday before "several thousand listeners." [170] This particular poem was a most popular one, having been already set by Keiser, Händel, and Telemann; according to the Foreword to the printed text for the performance of Händel's version it was repeatedly performed that year in Hamburg.[171] Shortly after this Mattheson composed and produced another oratorio for Easter, carefully adding in his autobiographical account that none of these compositions were "usual church-pieces, but composed entirely dramatically, and with all the attributes of a full *Actus,*" and also that at the performances of such music the collections were "at least three times as large as formerly." [172] The death of Charles XII of Sweden in 1719 provided the occasion for what he said was the most successful of his oratorios. Doubtless because of the Dom's former political connection with Sweden a memorial service, solemn with "funeral pomp, the pulpit, choir, and stalls of the chapter being draped with black," [173] was held on February 26, five days after the King's death. The text for Mattheson's oratorio, entitled *Das Betrübte Schweden,*[174] contained personifications of "Fame," "Fate," "Sorrowing Sweden," "the weeping Elbe River," which together with the sentiments expressed are far more suggestive of a contemporary court fête than a Lutheran memorial service—orthodox or pietist! Undeniably its ex-

169. Bibliography No. 58.

170. *Ehrenpforte,* p. 204: "Unter den Anmerckungen von Anno 1718. findet sich, dass er im Februario die berühmte brockesische Passion in die Musik gebracht. . . . Am Palmsonntage führte er oberwehntes Passions-Oratorium, mit dem Beifall vieler tausend Zuhörer, sehr starck besetzet, im Dom auf."

171. *Idem,* Article on Händel, p. 96. "Von diesem *Oratorio* wurde, in einem gedruckten Vorberichte, 1719. folgendes gemeldet: '. . . Des Herr Keisers Musik ist ehedessen schon unterschiedene mahl, mit der grössesten Approbation, aufgeführet worden. Des Herrn Mathesons dies Jahr zu zweien mahlen (!) gehörte Musik hat den Zuhörern derselben ein unsterbliches Andencken seiner *Virtù* überlassen. Nun aber ist man Willens, Künfftigen Montag (in der Stillen Woche) des Herrn Händels, und Dienstags des Herrn Telemanns Musik aufzuführen &c.' "

172. *Idem,* p. 204: "Man muss nicht meynen, dass dieses Wesen aus gewöhnlichen Kirchenstücken bestehet; sondern alles ist dramatisch abgefasst, und von ziemlichen Umfange, wie ein völliger Actus. Partituren zu 20. 30. und mehr Bogen. Es ist auch um diese Zeit bemercket worden, dass, bey Haltung einer solchen Musik, wenigstens dreimahl so viel, als sonst, in den Gottesdienst gekommen ist."

173. These are Mattheson's words. *Ibid.:* ". . . mit sehr anständigem Trauer-Gepränge, bey schwartz-bezogener Kantzel, Chor, Herren-Sitzen &c."

174. Bibliography No. 63.

aggerated pomposities were rich in the emotional expressions for
which Mattheson's musical style was most suited. His score achieved
an objective dignity which may well have "affected the several
thousand listeners so deeply to attention and pity, that hardly one
stirred, not even those who knew and cared for music but little."[175]
That at the same time there may have been those within Hamburg who were still unconvinced of the efficacy and appropriate-
ness of the theatrical style of *Das Betrübte Schweden* is suggested
by Mattheson's apologetic remarks appended to his enthusiastic
account of its reception.[176] Although the many oratorios he continued to compose for the Dom in the next nine years were all
written in this same style to a greater or less degree,[177] Mattheson
remained on the defensive: the Forewords to two oratorios written
in 1720 and 1721 [178] are both powerful pleas entered on behalf
of theatrical church music. Up to the latter year he wrote an extraordinary number of oratorios in rapid succession, the cataloguing
of which caused him to exclaim with characteristically naïve conceit: "Only new and important compositions are listed here, and
not incidental smaller compositions. How could so great an amount
of music possibly be mentioned?" [179]

In 1722 the town Cantor Gerstenbüttel died, leaving a vacancy
of which Mattheson may well have been covetous.[180] Telemann

175. *Ehrenpforte*, pp. 204–205: "Das Epicedium, so er um diese Zeit, auf den Tod
Carl XII. Königs von Schweden, verfertiget . . . bewegte etliche tausend Zuhörer so
ungemein, zur Aufmerksamkeit und Mitleiden, dass sich fast keiner rührte; und auch die
nicht, welche sonst keine Musik kennen noch lieben." Dramatic music in connection with
solemn occasions had already been made use of, especially in Italy. One of the first compositions of this kind in the new dramatic baroque style is the mass Monteverdi composed
on the obsequies of Cosimo II Grand Duke of Tuscany (1621).
176. *Idem*, p. 204 n. He is quoting from Bonnet's *Histoire de la Musique*, IV, 121:
"Du moment qu'elle [music] emeut & penetre un honet homme, elle est admirable; il
n'est plus besoin de raisonnement." Mattheson adds: "Hergegen, wo man von einem
Oratorio oder Dramate sagen kann, dass auch die besten Gönner im Gemüthe keine
Aenderung davon spüren, sondern eben so klug weggehen, als sie gekommen sind; da taugt
die Musik nichts."
177. Cf. Bibliography Nos. 60, 61, 64, 65, 71, 72, 74, 75, etc.
178. *Die durch Christi Auferstehung bestätigte Auferstehung aller Todten*, Bibliography
No. 71, and *Der Blut-rünstige Kelter-Treter*, No. 74.
179. *Ehrenpforte*, p. 207 n.: "Man bemercket hier nur die neuen und grossen Compo-
sitionen, nicht aber alle kleinen Neben-Musiken. Wie wäre es auch möglich?"
180. *Idem*, pp. 207–208: "Unser Telemann, welcher, statt des am grünen Donnerstage
dieses Jahrs verstorbenen Joachim Gerstenbüttels, Cantor in Hamburg worden war, hielt
den 17. September seine erste Musik Vormittags in der Catharinen-Kirche, und Mattheson

was given the position, and his appointment signalized the triumph of dramatic church music in Hamburg; for his music was as modern as Mattheson's in every respect. The controversy on the nature of church music, however, was still being fought out in Lutheran Germany at large. In 1727, Joachim Meyer, a member of the theological faculty at Göttingen,[181] published a pamphlet attacking the new music. Triumphant in the local success of his musical principles, Mattheson did not hesitate to publish a reply, ruthlessly excoriating Meyer's conclusions.[182] By no means the first of his musical writings to be published, it was nevertheless the first which discussed a problem having a close bearing upon his own musical position. So strong were his feelings on this point that in 1728 he issued a journal, *Der Musicalische Patriot,*[183] which was entirely devoted to the justification of secular and ecclesiastical theatrical music. The violence of his personal sentiments in these two publications stirred up equally violent reactions. One pamphlet in particular, *Ein paar derbe Musicalische-Patriotische Orfeigen,*[184] made such sarcastic and vitriolic allegations concerning Mattheson's music and his capacities as Dom-Director that he demanded from the Domkapitel a public statement in attestation of his good services.[185] The resultant *Testament* he immediately published in his

des Nachmittags im Dom. Bey dieser Veränderung hegten viele Leute die Gedancken, der letztgenannte würde einen Mitwerber abgeben: wie denn die Patronen unter der Hand selbst Vorschub dazu thaten; allein er verlohr deswegen nicht ein eintzigen Schritt, u. machte nicht die geringste Bewegung: hätte es auch niemahls angenommen; maassen er sich, bei seinen höhern Würden und reichlichern Einkünfften, weit besser und freier befand, als bey dergleichen sehr mühsamen Schuldiensten."

181. *Unvergreiffliche Gedancken über die Neulich eingerissene Theatralische Kirchen-MUSIC* . . . Cf. Bibliography No. 100.

182. *Der neue Göttingishe Aber Viel schlechter als Die alten Lacedämonischen, urtheilende EPHORUS.* . . . Cf. Bibliography No. 100.

183. Bibliography No. 107.

184. "Ein paar derbe Musicalische Patriotische Ohrfeigen Dem Nichts weniger als Musicalischen Patrioten und nichts weniger als Patriotische Musico, Salv. venia Hn. MATTHESON, Welcher zum Neuen Jahr eine neue Probe seiner gewohnten Calummianten-Streiche unverschämter Weise an den Tag geleget hat, In Wiederherstellung seines verlohrenen Gehörs und Verstandes Und zu Bezeugung schuldiger Danckbarkeit Auff beyde Backen In einem zufälligen *Discours* wohlmeynend ertheilet Von Zween Brauchbahren *Virtuosen, Musandern* und *Harmonie.* Erstes Gespräche. Anno MDCCXXVIII." [8] pages. Among the numerous assertions this pamphlet made is the following: "*Har.* Er hat ja auch einmahl in der Kirche ein Duett selbst mit gesungen und sich dabey um einen Thon verstiegen, dass die Leute wegen des Übelklanges theils die Ohren zustoppfen, theils zum Temple hinaus lauffen müssen."

185. *Protokol des Doms cl. VIII no. VI, 1719–28.,* pp. 621–622. 11 Martii 1728. "Der

*Musicalische Patriot,*[186] along with other expressions of admiration and approval from various people, including Sir Cyrill Wich.[187] Shortly after this episode, Mattheson surprised the Domkapitel by a petition to be relieved of his duties as director of music.[188] His reasons for resigning what was normally a lifetime's occupation were many. Chief among these was a physical disability, deafness. This misfortune had not by any means made its appearance suddenly, but had been becoming more acute for a number of years. In 1705, at the age of twenty-four, he first became aware, "in the midst of his happiness and good fortune," of an impediment to his hearing.[189] Although Mattheson makes no references to it in the next few years, the author of the abovementioned pamphlet knew of it and did not hesitate to hold it up to obloquy and scorn.[190] In addition to the weakness of his hearing

Decanus referiret, dass Mr. Mattheson ihm die Visite gegeben un gesuchet, dass da er durch ein gewissen Impressum gegen seine Musicalischen Patrioten sich touchirt befindet Rev. Capitulum ihm dahinder ein Attestatum seiner guten Aufführung und gründlichen musicalischen Wissenschaft verschreiben möge. . . ."

186. *Der Musicalische Patriot*, p. 104: "Ferner ist,' sub dato den 11. Mertz dieses Jahrs, vom Hoch-Ehrwürd. Dom-Capitul alhier . . . unter dero *Secretarii* Hand, & *quidem ex speciali Mandato*, ein Instrument eingesandt: 'Darin *Rev. Capit.* die gute Aufführung ihres *Directoris Chori Musici*, als an welcher nichts auszusetzen, und die gründliche, musicalische Wissenschafft desselben, mit völliger Zufriedenheit zu attestiren beliebet hat.' "

187. *Idem,* pp. 103–104. Wich wrote in part: ". . . Dass gedachter Johann Mattheson . . . die gantze 24. Jahr lang, da er täglich unsre wichtigsten Geschäffte verrichtet, mit Uns an einer Tafel gespeiset. &c. sich also verhalten und aufgeführet, wie es einem getreuen, redlichen, gewissenhaften, fleissigen, bescheidenen, und, nebst der Music zum höchsten Grad, in verschiedenen andern Studien, Sprachen und Künsten wolgelehrten, *expediten*, verschwiegenen und geschickten *Secretario* zusteht . . ."

188. *Protokol des Doms cl. VIII no. VI, 1719–28,* 9. Sept., 1728. See below (Note 195).

189. *Ehrenpforte,* p. 195: "Aber, aber, in solchem besten Lauff seines Glückes und Gewinnes hatte er das Unglück, dass ihn in diesem Jahr erst eine kleine Verstopffung des Gehörs überfiel, davon er lange Zeit ein Geheimniss machte, und eben dadurch verursachte, dass das Übel, wiewohl damahls mehrentheils nur auf einer Seite, Wurtzel fasste, auch nach und nach mehr zu, also abnahm. . . ."

190. *Ein paar derbe Ohrfeigen* attributes his deafness to the following mishap: "Er wollte nehmlich einer solchen Gottheit des Sonntags unter der Predigt einmahl, auff dem Hemde knyend, seine Verehrung abstatten, zum Unglücke aber war der Platz durch einen andern schon besetzt, dass er mit einer langen Nase abziehen muste. Aus Eifersucht und Neugierigkeit nun getrieben, kehrte er wieder zurücke und applicirte sein unglückseliges Ohrsloch so genau an das Schlüssel-Loch der Kammer-Thüre, dass die bey offenstehenden Fenstern durchgehende *penetrante* Hohlung der Luft, wozu die *Alteration* über die Untreue seines angebeteten Götzen-Bildes auch etwas beygetragen haben mag, senien [*sic*] Gehör-Organis einer höchst-*fatalen* Streich versetzte, und er bey seiner nach Hausekunft, nachdem ihn vorher bedüncket, als ob eine Canoni für seinen Ohren lossginge, sich dieses einem Musice so desiderablen Sinnes verlustig sahe."

and possibly because of it, he had had a serious misunderstanding with his singers.[191] A year earlier, he had again attempted without success to have his salary increased.[192] At the same time his secretarial occupations were as demanding as ever, and he was devoting more and more time and energy to various literary occupations. Thirty-two oratorios had come from his pen in thirteen years, and although the quality of his music did not decline or the apparent ease of his inspiration forsake him, it is not remarkable that his position as Dom-Director had become a heavier burden than he could carry.

Mattheson's relations with the Domkapitel concerning this matter seems to have occupied much time throughout the year 1728. In April he asked to have a temporary substitute appointed to direct the performances of the necessary music in the Dom.[193] Within two weeks the Kapitel acceded, naming a musician named Muchsel, for six months.[194] Only three months later, however, at the first meeting of the Kapitel in September,[195] Mattheson submitted his formal resignation. He had brought it to their unwilling attention through the good offices of a third person, Geheimrath von Grooth.

191. *Protokol des Doms cl. VIII no. VI, 1719–28*, p. 618, 26 Febr. 1728. "Der Decanus produciret Mr. Johann Matthesons abgenöthigte Verstellung gegen einige Sänger aufm Thumb-Chor, so verlesen. Communicetur."

192. *Idem*, p. 547, 8 Maji 1727. "Dr. Decanus produciret Cantoris Matthesons dienstliches Memoriale darinnen derselbe weilen Rev. Capitulum sein Salarium zu verbessern nicht resolvieren wollen desfalls seinen andern Verschlag gethan um dadurch einiges massen soulagiret zu vor den, so verbessern und vor der Hand bey dem Alten es zu lassen beliebet."

193. *Idem*, p. 632, 29 April 1728. "Der Senior produciret der Cantoris Mattheson eingehandter Schreiben, dahin gesend, dass da er zugestossener Unpässlichkeit halber sich künftigen Sommer der Trum und bade der unentbehrl. bedienen müste Rev. Capitulum ihm die Güte zu erzeigen geruhen möchte, ihm ad interim eine Persohn zu adjungiere, welche seine Vices auf hiesigen Chor vertreten könne, vor er denn dazu Mr. Muchsel Rev. Capitulo voltu anrecommendiret haben, so verlesen."

194. *Idem*, p. 634, 13 Maji 1728. "Der Senior Dr. Meurer referiret dass jüngsten Protokolls zufolge er Mr. Muchsel auf ein halb Jahr die Verwaltung der Dom Music aufgetragen viel ihre sich desfalls bedancket und sich Rev. Capitulo de meliori recommendiret."

195. *Idem*, p. 667, 9 Sept. 1728. "Der Decanus produciret Mr. Mattheson Canonici Minoris et Directoris Chori Musici Cathedralis gehorsamstes Ansuchen pro Conservatio, so ihm von mir Secretario allhier überliefert nun aber von dem H. Regierungs Rath von Bardenfleth ante Conventum aingehändiget werden, wie der H. von mir mit unserm Umständen vernehmen würden. Secretarii Relation einigen Matthesons Memorial.
"Ego referiren hierauf, dass der H. von Bardenfleth mich ante Conventum zu sich fordern lassen, und mir Mr. Matthesons Memorial überliefert mit bitte solches nicht zu erwehnen, dass Ihre Excell. der H. Geheim Rath von Groot welches dem H. Regierungs Rath Gedachtes Memorial um er mit Recommendation Rev. Capituli zu stellen zu lassen, zugesandt, gern sahe, dass wenn er thunlich der H. Matthesons Petito deferiret würde."

The government of the Dom was not given to making rapid decisions or acting quickly. In this instance, having discussed the matter at one meeting, they concluded that there was no reason why the difficulties could not be solved, and refused to act upon the matter.[196] From the records of the next meeting, on September 23, it is clear that the Kapitel was not at all disposed to be deprived of their director's services.[197] Annoyed by this turn of events and unmoved by the efforts of Wich and others, to whom the Kapitel turned in their dilemma, Mattheson resorted to direct action. This took the form of an "impertinent letter" to the Domkapitel, which upon the consent of the mediators, obligated them to grant his release.[198] He thus severed all official connections with the church, although he retained for life his *Vicariat*.[199]

196. *Idem*, p. 668. "Ich nahm das Memorial an, versicherte dabey, dass Rev. Capitulum Mr. Mattheson gar nicht zumöge (?), zu resignieren, und verlangte er unteromisliche Musiquen von ihm ein er vorhero aufgeführet, erzehlte die Uhrsache und die Umstände des Misverständnisses zwischen ihm und die Musicanten, und nahm er ad referendum an.

"Dass hierauf das Memorial verlesen und folgendes Decret. Auf übergebenes Memorial Mr. Mattheson Canonici minoris und Directoris Chori Musici Cathedralis decretiret ein Hochw. Thumb-Capitul, dass wenn er seiner Capitulation zufolge unser emislische [blot] Musiquen nach ein [blot], in der Thumb-Kirchen aufzuführen vermögend mögen [blot], er in dem geruhigen Besitz seines Directori verbleiben konte."

197. *Idem*, p. 670, 23 Sept. 1728. "Der Decanus produciret hierauf Mr. Mattheson geziemende Vorstellung in pto. der Thumb-Music so verlesen und folgendes drauf decretiret. Auf Mr. Mathesons Directoris Chori Musici Cathedralis abermahlig übergebenes Memorial decretiret ein Hochehrw. Thumb-Capitul, dass Supplicans Seiner Capitulation Zufolge die ordentliche Music in der hiesigen Thumb-Kirchen am instehenden Sontag aufzuführen schuldig im wiedrigen weiter ergehen würde."

198. *Idem*, p. 676, 14 Oct. 1728. "Secretarii Relation von Mr. Mattheson Chori Musici Cathdr. Directore. Ego referire dass Mr. Mattheson Director Chori Musici Cathedralis am verwichenen Sonntag vor 14 Tagen als d. 24. Sept. mir einen impertinenten Brief zugesandt in welchen er sich zugleich auf Ihre Excell. H. Geheimen Rath von Groot und H. Envoye von Wich sich verziehet, und mich bittet diesen Brief meinen H. Obere vorzuzeigen. Wie ich nun hiervon bereits in vergangener Session extra Protocollum referiret mir auch extra Protocollum commitiret obbenannten Hl. aufzuwarten und Matthesons unbescheidenen Brief vorzuweisen, als referire seiner, dass ich diesen Commisserio gemäss geliebet un von beyden Herren gebeten, dass ein nicht ungütig verwerden möchten, von Rev. Capitulum itzo genöthiget wurde Mr. Mattheson seinen Abschied zu geben. Der H. Geheim Rath und der H. Envoye danckten beyde die Bezeugung des Egards, und wie ersterer mich versicherte, dass, da dem [blot] er sich vor Mr. Mattheson nicht herum interessiren würde, so bezeugt, dass er sich nicht meliren wurde in dass was Rev. Capitulum mit Mr. Mattheson vornehmen möchte.

"Ist darauf diese Sache reassumiret, und weil er der Capitulation nicht genügen geleistet seiner Dienste erlassen worden, zu welchem Ende denn ihn folgendes Decretum durch der Gabe Träger Lillie insinuiret werden soll. Weilen Mr. Mattheson Directo Chori Musici Cathedralis seiner Capitulation kein Genügen geleistet: als decretiret Ein Hochehr. Thumb-Capitul, dass er hiemit seiner Dienste erlassen seyn solle."

199. Mattheson reported this entire episode briefly, *Ehrenpforte*, pp. 211–212: ". . . er-

It is true that Mattheson had taken advantage of his position to compose a large amount of church music, which, according to his lights, represented the best medium for the worship of God. But his cantorship can in no way be compared to any of the similar positions occupied by his contemporaries in other parts of Germany. Nor did it have the same significance in his own life. If no record of the contemporary reaction to his music has survived except his own, there is still no reason to suppose that his music was anything but popular, or his directorship anything but a source of material, if not artistic, satisfaction to the Domkapitel. They appointed a successor immediately: Reinhard Keiser, who was admirably equipped to provide for the Church the same kind of music as had Mattheson himself. To a man as sensitive as Mattheson was about his music and his theories this opportunity to write and perform his compositions exactly as he wished was a highly desirable one, and since he had become during these years the chief defender and exponent of the "new music," his experience at the Dom may be taken as the initiation he needed, fully to convince himself of the validity of his theories. Thus considered, those years of service became a turning-point of very great importance in his artistic career.

## 3

### MATTHESON—CRITIC AND AUTHOR

The period of Mattheson's life from his thirtieth to his sixtieth year was one of great intellectual industry and material prosperity. His secretarial tasks continued to yield him a comfortable income. His own musical reputation and interests kept pace with his career as Dom-Cantor. Even before his church music had demonstrated his real ability as a writer of oratorios he had been commissioned to write five secular cantatas or serenatas for important

hielt er, wegen mercklicher Schwäche des Gehörs, so wohl, als in Betracht einiger Mishelligkeiten unter den Sängern, am 15. October dieses Jahrs 1728. seine Erlassung vom Dom-Chor, . . . mit Beibehaltung seines Vicariats, welches er nun schon 25. Jahr besitzet, und einer von den Senioren ist."

social festivities. One of these in 1714 had been produced at the Opera by Sir Cyrill Wich in honor of the coronation of George I.[200] Wich's letter of November 16, 1714, to the Secretary of State for the North suggests the scale of this entertainment: "Hier, Mylord je regalai tous les Ministres etrangers, au nombre de 50. sur l'heureux sujet du Couronnement de Sa Majesté. Premierement je les menai à un Opera que j'avois fait faire exprès; apres je leur donnai a souper, et enfin la Fête se termina par un Bal, qui dura jusq'à ce matin. . . ."[201] Between 1715 and 1720 Mattheson wrote eight more serenatas of various size and complexity, the most elaborate being *La Gagarina,* which was produced in honor of the Russian Envoy to Hamburg, Prince Gagarin.[202] In most instances these were performed by the same singers from the Opera whose services Mattheson made use of for his music at the Dom.[203]

Probably because of his popularity as composer for the most brilliant entertainments given by and for Hamburg society, he was, in 1719, asked by the Duke of Schleswig-Holstein to become his Capellmeister—a distinction which Mattheson was not slow in accepting. Although a few months later two of his serenatas were performed before His Highness,[204] there is no indication that this title, which Mattheson used proudly for much of his life, required from him any services whatsoever. That Duke Carl Friedrich was one of the most impecunious princes in northern Germany accounts perhaps for the lack of enthusiasm in the account Mattheson wrote of receiving the honor.[205] In subsequent comments written upon this matter he reveals the real reasons for his receipt of the appointment: the high favor in which Sir Cyrill Wich stood with

200. *Die Frohlockende Themse, Auf das Höchsterfreulichste Krönungs-Fest Des Aller-Durchlauchtigsten, Grossmächtigsten Königs.* . . . Bibliography, No. 31.

201. *State Papers* 82/31.

202. *Den verewigten Ruhm und Rahmen Des Durchl. Fürstl. Hauses Gagarin.* Bibliography No. 34.

203. Mattheson made a habit of noting the names of the singers in the scores of many of his serenatas.

204. *Der Verlohrne und wiedergefundene AMOR,* Bibliography No. 66 and *Die Vergnügte Nacht,* No. 67.

205. *Ehrenpforte,* p. 205. "Den 15. Junii traffen Ihro Königl. Hoheit, der hochseel. Hertzog von Holstein, Carl Friedrich, in Hamburg ein, und den 30. erhielt Mattheson von dere erstem Minister Nachricht, dass Ihro Hoheit ihn zu dero Capellmeister ernennen würden. Den 3. Julii wurde er, solcher wegen, zur Audientz und zum Hand-Kuss gelassen, empfing auch den 4. darauf seinen Bestallungs-Brief."

His Highness of Schleswig-Holstein, and the Duke's accommodating Resident in Hamburg, who indiscreetly said to Mattheson: "J'en pourrois faire autant pour vous, mais vous n'étez pas *accomodant*. (C'est à dire, vous ne sauriez appeller blanc ce qui est noir);" to which Mattheson retorted that he would rather be a Capellmeister without commission than a Resident without pay![206] Mattheson's reply has, also, musical implications. Johann Sebastian Bach took precisely the same attitude when he attributed the greatest importance to his title of *Hofkapellmeister* at Dresden. The courts, devoted to modern operatic and instrumental music, bestowed on musicians far greater renown than ever could come from the position of cantor. Hence, many composers placed as much emphasis on titles that involved no duties as did Mattheson.

In this period Sir Cyrill's quick-tongued secretary also wrote and published a small amount of instrumental music. After the flute sonatas of 1708, came a sonata in G major for the harpsichord, first published in 1713, with the subtitle: "dedié à QUI LA JEUERA LE MIEUX," and republished in 1729.[207] It was an extremely popular work, and is remarkable chiefly for its unusual form and for the brilliant virtuosity it demands.[208] In the year following the appearance of this sonata, his *Harmonisches Denckmahl, aus Zwölf erwählten Clavier-Suiten* [209] was published in London, with an alternative title-page, in German and French for the editions issued respectively in Germany and in England. In the brevity of the forms and the simplicity of the writing the style of these suites is utterly unlike that of the sonata. The English publisher sang their praises in glowing terms:

. . . As the Harpsichord [he said] is an Instrument yet capable of Greater Improvement, so the following Pieces claim a Precedence to all others of this Nature; not only that they are composed by one of the Greatest Masters of

206. *Idem,* Anhang, p. 15: "Um diese Zeit stund bey dem Gottseel. Hertzog, Carl Friedrich, der Herr von Wich dermaassen in Gnaden, dass er nur sprechen durffte, so geschah was er verlangte. Unter andern erfuhr es auch der *Hr. de Hartoghe,* welcher zum Holsteinischen *Ministre* in Hamburg ernannt, und bey solcher Gelegenheit zu *Mattheson* gesagt ward: J'en pourrois etc. . . . Niemals ist ihm der grösseste Lobspruch so angenehm gewesen, als dieser ehrenreiche Verweiss. Indessen wurde er doch, ohne Vermittelung Capellmeister, welches ihm damals lieber war, als ein unbezahlter Resident zu seyn."

207. Bibliography No. 28.

208. Cf. Max Seiffert, *Geschichte der Klaviermusik* (Leipzig, 1899), I, 343.

209. Bibliography No. 30.

the Age, in a Taste altogether Pleasing, and Sublime; but as they are peculiarly adapted to that Instrument and Engraved with an Exactness, which cannot be Equal'd by Any of this Nature yet extant. . . .

In 1720 Mattheson published a set of twelve suites or sonatas for flute or violin with thorough bass, entitled *der Brauchbare VIRTU-OSO, . . . mit zwölf neuen Kammer-Sonaten, auf der Flute Traversiere, Der Violine und dem Claviere.*[210] The first words of this curious title were applicable only to the long preface to this edition, which is a bitter attack upon the ignorance of conservative, "incompetent" musicians. This music, too, has an ease and a simplicity which indicate that it was designed for the amateur musical circles of Hamburg. His next venture in instrumental music did not take place until fifteen years later, when he published the first part of *Die wol-klingende Finger-Sprache, in Zwölff Fugen,* the second part appearing two years later.[211] Although written with two or three subjects, these fugues have none of the innate contrapuntal complexity of Bach's, and require but little technique on the part of the performer. It is unlikely that any of this music achieved much renown outside of the immediate community of Hamburg, for whose particular musical needs these compositions seem to have been designed.

Appearance in public continued to absorb his attention, the most notable being a concert given with Keiser in 1716.[212] References to his students repeatedly occur in his autobiography. In 1719 he was teaching a pair of "growing scholars in thorough-bass, who made no profession of it";[213] in 1720 and 1721 Jantzen, the organist in Bremen, came to him for a number of lessons in composition;[214] in 1721 he held a second "Collegium melopoëticum"

210. Bibliography No. 69.
211. Bibliography No. 129 and 135.
212. *Ehrenpforte,* p. 202: "Den 1. April hielt er, in Gesellschaft des Capellmeisters Keiser, ein grosses Concert auf dem niedern Baumhause." In A. C. Benthner's *Jetzt lebendes Hamburg* (1725, p. 110) Mattheson and Keiser have both the distinction of being classified as "Virtuosi."
213. *Idem,* p. 206: "Er hatte dabey noch ein Paar erwachsene Scholaren im Generalbass, die keine Profession davon machten, und zu ihm kamen."
214. *Ibid.:* "Im August kam ein Organist von Bremen, und liess sich von Mattheson in der Setzkunst unterrichten, gegen reichliche Bezahlung." Mattheson added the name *Jantzen* after the word *Organist* in his notes (*Idem,* Anhang, p. 15).
*Idem,* p. 207: "Den 16. August kam der obgedachte bremische Organist wieder, und hohlte mehr Unterricht. Acht zwo-stündige Lectiones bezahlte er mit 10. Reichsthalern."

for two practical musicians; [215] between 1724 and 1727 he apparently held similar classes for young students, some of whom were amateur and some professional musicians, giving in the last year seventy-five two-hour sessions, for which he received 100 thalers. [216] The popularity enjoyed by Mattheson as a musician seems evident from the verses which were written on the occasion of his publishing *Das Beschützte Orchestre* in 1717. [217] Hamburg's leading poet, Barthold Heinrich Brockes, wrote as follows:

> Non, MATTHESON, c'est trop! tu n'es donc plus content
> De charmer les esprits, d'enchanter nos oreilles,
> De rendre sous tes mains un Clavecin parlant,
> L'on te voit ₊entasser merveilles sur merveilles:
> Ce que jusqu'à présent on a crû impossible
> Ne l'est plus; ton esprit nous rend un ton visible,
> Nous voyons un concert, nous oyons par nos yeux,
> En lisant tes ecrits, un chant melodieux: . . .

Michael Richey, a professor in the Hamburg *Gymnasium* and a writer of local prominence, made a number of flattering comparisons.

> Will Keiser Geist sich ausser Keisern zeigen,
> Will Hendels Kunst in mehr als Hendeln steigen,
> Wann *Mattheson* nur Wunder componirt;
> Muss Ohr und Hertz in Lust entzücket stehen,
> Muss *Orpheus* selbst noch in die Schule gehen,
> Wann *Mattheson* die Saiten zaubernd rührt. . . .

Mattheson's references to the monetary rewards from these musical pursuits are numerous. They appear, indeed, to outweigh

215. The first he held in 1719. *Idem,* p. 206: "Mattheson hielt in diesem Jahr mit einem sehr geschickten jungen Menschen ein ordentliches *Collegium melopoëticum,* täglich zwo Stunden." The second (*Idem,* p. 207): "Den 17. gedachten Monaths [Febr.] fing er ein zweites *Collegium melopoëticum* mit zween wircklichen Practicis an."
216. *Idem,* p. 209: ". . . da hub sich ein neues *Collegium de Melodica* für zween junge Herren an, deren einer hernach *Doctor juris* geworden ist."
*Idem,* p. 210: "Ein abermahliges lehrreiches *Collegium melodicum* wurde, mit dem Eingange des Jahres 1727., dreien Zuhörern gehalten, deren einer unsers berühmten Professoris, des Hrn. Richey, einiger Sohn war. . . . Die beiden andern machten bereits von der Musik Profession, und hatten das *plus ultra* zum löblichen Zweck. Einer davon ist Organist in Grönungen, der andre an einem Orte in Holstein, geworden. Der Versammlungen, jede von zwo Stunden, waren 75, und währten biss in November. Das Honorarium bestund in 100. Thalern."
217. Bibliography No. 47.

all other considerations at times, for it is perfectly obvious that he was enjoying the process of becoming a rich man. With the exception of his music for the Dom, his other compositions and musical services were extremely profitable.[218] He often received extra "honoria" for unusual secretarial labors, such as the treaty between Denmark and Holstein in 1711, for which he was given 300 thalers.[219] Several of his literary ventures he mentions as being also highly profitable, particularly the two journals, the *Critica Musica,* begun in 1722, which after three years netted a "pure gain of 200 Thalers," [220] and the *Musicalische Patriot,* which brought him over 450 marks in 1728.[221] The acquisition of this wealth naturally affected Mattheson's mode of life. His chief aim, though never expressed openly, was apparently the successful and lucrative investment of these sums. In 1714 he was seized with "the desire to undertake a different kind of composition or construction, and to build a house for his own use; he therefore bought . . . a plot on the so-called Kamp, in a still, pleasant, airy, high neighborhood, and layed . . . the first stone for it in God's name." [222] Having finished and occupied this house, he soon bought another site and on it erected a house which he offered for rent.[223] House-building having proved a profitable form of investment in a city whose population was rapidly increasing, he bought another piece of land in 1721 and erected seven apartments on it.[224] Mattheson's

218. In his serenata, *Der Verlohrne und wiedergefundene AMOR,* Bibliography No. 66, Mattheson noted: "Le Compositeur eut 50 Ecus."

219. *Ehrenpforte,* pp. 197–198: "Das erste, so 1711. vorfiel, war, dass der sogenannte Collateral-Vergleich zwischen Dänemarck und Holstein . . . förmlich unterschrieben wurde. Wegen dabey gehabter, vielfältiger Mühe, bekam der Secretar Mattheson . . . den 7. Juli. dreihundert Reichsthaler, *jussu Serenissimi,* zum Geschenck."

220. *Idem,* p. 209: ". . . endigte hernach den zweeten Band seiner Critick [*Critica Musica*] am 28. Sept. mit einem reinen Gewinn, von 200. Reichsthl., eignen Verlags."

221. *Idem,* p. 211 n. "Er hat bisher, die Verlags-Kosten abgerechnet, 454. Marck 3. sh. eingebracht, und es ist nur noch ein eintziges Exemplar übrig."

222. *Idem,* p. 200: "Im May, ob er gleich an einem Fieber danieder lag, kam ihm doch die Lust an, eine andere Setzkunst oder Compositions-Art vorzunehmen, und ein eigenes Haus zu bauen; Kauffte sich daher den 12. besagten Monaths einen Platz auf dem sogenannten Kamp, in einer stillen, lustigen, lufftigen, hohen Gegend, und legte den 31. darauf in GOttes Nahmen, den ersten Stein dazu."

223. *Idem,* p. 202: "An 1716. den 19. Märtz erkauffte Mattheson einen umfänglichen Gartenplatz, ausserhalb der Stadt, zur Helffte, und componirte ein neues Gebäude darauf, um es zu vermiethen."

224. *Idem,* p. 207: "Hausgeschäffte wurden dabey so wenig bey Seite gesetzet, dass

preoccupation with monetary affairs, which all these operations seem to connote, became, in 1728, the butt for attack in the pamphlet *Ein Paar derbe Ohrfeigen,* which declared that he "reckoned day and night to see if the surplus [from his publications] after the expenses would yield enough for another house." [225] Mattheson himself was possibly unconscious of this trait. After a friend died owing him 1,000 thalers, he turned, as was his pious wont, to the Bible, and read the prophetic and comforting words from *II Chronicles* 25, 9: " 'The Lord is able to give thee much more than this.' Therefore [he continues] he consoled himself immediately for the loss of his money, and deplored only the loss of his friend." [226]

Such an attitude of candid materialism was not, in fact, at all unusual within the confines of Hamburg. The distinguished poet Brockes was also a Senator and the recipient of a very handsome income from trade. The literary circle which surrounded him, and with which his schoolmate Mattheson was well acquainted,[227] consisted entirely of men of substance. It was characteristic of this

---

er den 14. Julii einen Platz erhandelte, der an sein Haus stiess, und den 6. October anfing, sieben Wohnungen, samt einen Stall, darauf zu bauen."

225. *Ein Paar derbe Ohrfeigen:* ". . . In der That nichts anders denn darum hat er eine menge Subscribenten zusammen gebettelt, damit er ihren Thaler auff den Fall, dass sein fürtreffliches Werck . . . ins Stecken gerathen sollte . . . und darum rechnet er Tag und Nacht, ob nicht der Überschuss nach Abzug derer Unkosten ihm noch ein Haus mehr abwerfen könne."

226. *Ehrenpforte,* p. 212: "Ein Freund starb ihm in seinen Armen, in seinem eigenen Hause, den 5. Febr., und nahm 1000 Rthlr. *Banco* als ein Anlehn, mit sich ins Grab. Wie nun Matthesons Gewohnheit war, und noch ist, alle Abend ein Capitel aus der Bibel u. einen Psalm zu lesen, fand er II. Chron. XXX [he corrected it to Chapter XXV, v. 9. in his notes] die Worte: Der HErr hat noch mehr, denn das ist, das er dir geben kann. Darüber verschmertzte er alsobald den Verlust seines Geldes; und beklagte nur den Verlust seines Freundes."

227. Mattheson proudly mentions his acquaintance with Brockes on three occasions. (1). *Ehrenpforte,* p. 198: "Unter seinen grössesten Ergetzlichkeiten zehlet er den angenehmen und erbaulichen Umgang mit dem grossen Brockes, und es findet sich, in seinen Denckbüchern, der 14. Jul. u. 27. Octobr. vor allen bemercket, weil er an selbigen Tagen die Vergnügung gehabt, diesen vortrefflichen Mann, und ehemaligen Schulgenossen, in seinem Hause zu sehen und zu bewirthen."

*Idem,* (2)., p. 200: "In seinen Denckbüchern hat er sonst noch einen am 13. Märtz [1714] von den Herrn Brockes empfangenen Besuch angeschrieben, und dabey, als was merckwürdiges, verzeichnet, dass ihm dieser Herr, Tages vorher, 24 Bouteillen Rheinwein verehren lassen."

*Idem,* (3), p. 204. "Den ersten Tag dieses Monaths [Febr. 1719] hat er abermahl bemercket, weil er an selbigem die Ehre gehabt, den Herrn Brockes bey sich zu sehen: für welchen schönen Mann er jederzeit mehr Liebe und Hochachtung hat, als für andre."

society to form smaller separate groups for the reading and discussion of various efforts by its members. Mattheson was an active participator in these clubs; in 1730 he states that he founded his third, which, "because of the number of its membership, bore the name of the seven free Arts." The death of one of the members caused its discontinuance two years later,[228] but in that same year, 1732, Mattheson founded yet another, which was called the "Orden des guten Geschmacks," and which likewise had seven members.[229] The motto of this society, taken from Horace's *Ars Poetica,* was "Concordia Discors." Its "Kantzler"—a man considerably younger than Mattheson—was the distinguished poet Friedrich von Hagedorn, known to his fellow-members as "Maro." [230] According to a list Mattheson made in 1759, the proceedings of this society were preserved in several volumes among his works; they have since disappeared.[231] From an isolated fragment found among his manuscripts in Hamburg, it appears that the members

228. *Idem,* p. 213: ". . . er stifftete dabey zur Lust, im Märtz [1730], eine Gesellschaft, die wegen ihrer Zahl, den Nahmen der 7. Freien Künste bekam. Der schwere Beinbruch aber eines Mitgliedes, und hernach der Tod gar, machten nach 2. Jahren ein Loch darin. Er hatte sonst in seinen jüngeren Zeiten schon zwo dergleichen Gesellschafften errichtet, mit welchen es immer desto ehender zum Ende gereichte, je angenehmer sie waren."

229. *Idem,* p. 215: "Im Nov. [1732] errichtete Mattheson eine neue, gelehrte Gesellschafft, von 7. Mannspersonen, und nannte sie den Orden des guten Geschmacks. Er wollte aber nicht länger, als ein Jahr schmecken. *Tout ce qui plait ne dure pas long temps.* Kurtz und süss wars. Das ist gewis[s]."

230. Mattheson dedicated his translation of Elizabeth Rowe's *Friendship in Death* (Bibliography No. 121), to this society, and noted in his copy the following details:

"Motto: Concordia Discors
Horatius discordum concerdum nominet Symphoniam discordam.—de Art. Poet.
Hr. Secr. Friedrich von Hagedorn, Kantzler, unter dem Namen *Maro.*
Hr. Kammerath Johann Legtho, unter dem Namen *Pylades.*
Hr. Secr. u. Licentiandus Christian Phil. Krieger, genannt *Tribonarium.*
Hr. Joh. Phil. Praetorius, als *Platus.*
Hr. Joachim Lorgeist, Z. V. L., namens *Calaïs.*
Hr. Johann Wolff, genannt *Symmachus.*
Hr. Secr. Heinr. Frie. Pilgram, genannt *Aeros."*

Although Mattheson himself is not mentioned, it is clear from a manuscript (see below) that he made an eighth member, under the name of *Aristoxenus,* which he assumed about this time in some of his published works. Cf. Bibliography No. 137.

231. *Nachrichten aus dem Reiche der Gelehrsamkeit* (Hamburg, 1759), p. 704, no. 52, in the list of Mattheson's literary works: "Tagebuch des Ordens vom guten Geschmack, gestiftet durch M., von Hagedorn ein Mitglied gewesen, Drey Bände in einem. Hamb. 1733 & 34. 4 to Maj. Ms. vielen Merckwündigen Beylagen."

of the society amused themselves by such literary diversions as im-
provising upon a basic verse form with a refrain.[232]

This atmosphere of casual literary composition and intellectual
badinage profoundly affected the form and scope of Mattheson's
literary production. In addition to his various works on musical
subjects, a number of other books and pamphlets came, in disor-
derly profusion, from his never idle pen. His actual literary career
may be said to have started with the writing of the News Letters
sent by the British Resident to London. Of little intellectual interest and importance to him, they were, however, the first routine
expression of an interest in English affairs that lasted all his life.
In the first half of the eighteenth century English thought and literature fought with that of France for the dominant place in the
interests of intelligent Germans. In Hamburg, needless to say, the
former was supreme. It is therefore not surprising that Mattheson's first regular productions were in no way connected with music, but were actually translations from the English.

The first of these was published in 1708, and is entitled: *Die Vermittelst eines künstlich eingerichteten und gantz accuraten
AUTOMATONS, oder von selbst-gehenden Uhrwercke zu findende LONGITUDO* . . . etc.[233] This curious volume, of which
Mattheson finished only the first half, was apparently written by
a watch-maker from London named John Carte, who was at this
time living in Hamburg. The title, of spectacular length, promised

---

232. "Sammlung der Gesellschaft Gedichte, in Leben un[d] Geben, von ihrem Archi-
vario und Vorhänger Triboniano; welcher sie deroselbe, mit Versicherung seiner be-
reitwilligen Dienste in der 29. Zusammenkunft überreichet. Gedruckt bey dem Sammler
selbst, mit etwas abgemissten Littern."
Thirty-four nine-line stanzas follow, written by the different members. The first of these,
by Mattheson, being headed:

> "*Vom Aristoxeno, autore dieser Sätze und Gegensätze.*
> "Wer mit eitel Lust betracht
> Und die Wercke nimt in Acht,
> Die des Chöpfers Hand gemacht,
> Der ist wohl zu leben!
> Aber unter allen Wercken,
> Die wir mit Vernunfft bemercken,
> Ist doch ein süszes Weibgen nur
> Die allerschönste Creatur
> Die er uns gegeben."

233. Bibliography No. 12.

chapters which would demonstrate the latest facts of reckoning by longitude, the history of clocks and their mechanism, and other fascinating information. Mattheson was inspired by this work to compose, as a preface to his translation, a poem of heroic couplets. It shows that his knowledge of English left not a little to be desired and that his poetic ability was hardly the equal of his inspiration.[234]

UPON *LONGITUDE, FOUND OUT* BY MR. JOHN CARTE

Thy Title Page all Artists must surprise
With joy, to see at last before their Eyes
Their Goddess brought to light, long sought with pain
By all the learned, but still sought in vain.
All knew she was in being, but not where:
Invisibly she liv'd as in the Air:
But thy *Automaton* has chalk'd the Way
And her abode most lively do's display.
Thrô Labyrinthian mazes so the Clew
Of *Adriadne* did to *Theseus* shew
The Path exact, which to the *Centaur* led,
Whereby in his attempt the Hero sped.
As a new Starr seamen will thee revere,
And henceforth on the main securly steer
Their flying Bark's from Port to Port, nor may
Distracting storms henceforth confound their Way.
The Travellour by Land his Path now knows'
In different Regions as he onward goes,
Taking his Observation from the Sun
Or Moon's Eclipses, as his Way does run.
Insurers gains will now by Sea abate
And Merchants more securly run their fate;
The Distances of Regions now no more
Will be obscure as has been heretofore.
This thy design thou teachest in a stile
Not tedious, but deverting all the while.
Those other Theams on which thy Book dos treat
Serve but to make they Title Page compleat,
Or to illustrate it, or lead the Way,
To prove its Truth, as light dos prove the day.
Thy Readers cannot tire, their exercise
Being as various as thy Theam likewise.

234. A complete German version of this poem is printed on the opposite pages from the English.

Sometimes thou leadst 'em round the World by Sea,
Then round by land, while yet at home they be;
Then lifts them up above the Earthly Sphaere
Among the Planets, shew'st them what's done there,
What influences each upon us sheds
By day, or when upon our feather beds.
Sometimes thou charmst them on upon the Wing
Of Poetry, and then thy Theam dost sing,
Turning their Travell from all sence of pain
And prompting still, to travell on again.
For when thou singst thy numbers so do flow
As Brooks along the Banks do prattling go,
Transporting so thy Readers with the song,
That, thô at home, they think they move along.
Let this suffice to frontispice the dore
Thy Book will show them all these things and more.

For three years after making this translation Mattheson published nothing. Then in 1711 appeared his translation of the sermon preached by John Robinson, Lord Bishop of Bristol, on March
8, 1710, the anniversary of Queen Anne's accession to the throne.[235]
Mattheson had had considerable contact with Robinson in 1707
and 1708 when, as British Ambassador to Sweden, he had been sent
to Hamburg to assist the Imperial Commission.[236] From the pompous foreword by Mattheson, it is clear that he intended his work to
be a compliment to that successful diplomat.[237] A year later he
translated another pamphlet of contemporary importance. The
plague which broke out seriously in Hamburg in 1713 was then
beginning to alarm the city by its proximity, and this pamphlet
outlined the beneficial qualities of tobacco as a plague-remedy.[238]
He dedicated it to Garlieb Sillem, who was directing the fight
against the epidemic, and explained that at the suggestion of Bishop
Robinson, he had forthwith undertaken the task from a "patriotic
Intention." Although he found his effort well repaid,[239] he turned

235. Bibliography No. 22.
236. J. F. Chance, "List of Diplomatic Representatives and Agents, England and North
Germany 1689–1727," p. 22.
237. D.N.B. XLIX, 24.
238. *Die Ausbündig-schönen Eigenschafften Der . . . Americanischen Tobacks-
Pflantzen; . . .* Bibliography No. 23.
239. *Ehrenpforte*, p. 198: "Die Sache verlohnte sich der Mühe sehr wohl."

from such bizarre subjects in his subsequent translations, which, for the next three decades, were of tracts dealing with political and commercial matters, or of works of purely literary interests. Although this was the period of Mattheson's greatest activity as diplomatic secretary, no sign of abatement in his energetic career as a writer is evident. In the two years, 1716 and 1717, he translated five tracts which dealt with the Jacobite uprising and with the Swedish plot. The latter had been revealed by the opening of the correspondence of the Swedish Ambassador to England, Count Gyllenborg,[240]—a highly unethical procedure which the British Government justified by a full publication of the communications between the Ambassador and the arch-conspirator, Baron Görtz, on the Continent.[241] Swedish influence had scarcely been destroyed in Hamburg at this time, and the translation of the Gyllenborg correspondence occasioned great excitement: it netted its translator a profit of 25 thalers.[242] Wich was naturally interested in bolstering up the reputation of the new government in England as much as possible, and probably encouraged or even suggested the dissemination of these particular pamphlets. And not only did the Swedish affair have to be justified, but the government's success against the Jacobites had also to be publicized. One of Mattheson's tracts consequently contained news despatches of the defeat of the rebels in Scotland,[243] another recorded the trial and sentence of the Jacobite Lord Derwentwater and his fellow conspirators,[244] and a third in 1723 provided German readers with the entire proceedings against Christopher Layer, which brought to light his extraordinary conspiracy.[245]

240. Bibliography Nos. 39, 40, 48, 49, 50.
241. *Letters which passed between Count G., the barons Gortz, Sparre and others, relating to the design of raising a rebellion in his Majesty's dominions, to be supported by a force from Sweden*. London, 1717. Cf. Michael, *Englische Geschichte im Achtzehnten Jahrhundert*, I, 741.
242. *Ehrenpforte*, p. 203: "An 1717. übersetzte er in 2. Tagen 8. gedruckte Bogen, und bekam vom Verleger 25. Thaler dafür. Es waren die Görtzische und Gyllenborgische Briefe 4to.
243. *Extract Der Zeitungen aus Gross-Britannien, So der hiesige Königliche Ministre, Herr von Wich, mit gestriger Post erhalten* . . . 1716, Bibliography No. 39.
244. *Anrede des Lord Gross-Meisters, Bey Verurtheilung James Grafen von Derwentwater, Bibliography No. 40*.
245. *Die Neu-Entdeckte Gross-Britannische Haupt-Verrätherey*, Bibliography No. 84.

The tracts which Mattheson translated after 1719 were preëminently concerned with economic and political problems, and the effect of political events upon them. In 1720, immediately after the collapse of the system of John Law in France, Mattheson translated a pamphlet,[246] which outlined its fallacies and the reasons for its downfall. In a sharply pointed dedication to the Government of Hamburg, he declared that: "although not all of it, most of it is applicable to this place."[247] Mattheson took advantage of the local interest of this piece, and made it a vehicle for the expression of his own undisguised opinions, but his other translations were more temperate. For the most part they seem to suggest official sanction if not encouragement. In 1727 continental affairs appeared to throw doubt upon the wisdom of maintaining any link between the foreign interests of England and Hanover. In particular the secret alliance between the Emperor and the King of Spain was the occasion of much criticism. The Whig policy as to this issue was defended in detail by Bishop Hoadly in a tract entitled *An Enquiry into the Reasons of the Conduct of Great Britain* which Mattheson immediately translated.[248] Because of the definite stand taken by its author upon central European affairs it was inevitably a matter of intense interest to Hamburg, and Mattheson declared that it "made a great stir with the Imperial Ministers."[249] He also translated in the same year a philippic entitled *The Evident Approach of a War,* which was especially designed to gain the support of the mercantile interests because of the improvement of trade which would follow a war.[250] This, he admits, was made at the request of the British Court,[251] and he further noted—evidently in proof of its

246. *Betrachtung des Neuen Finanz-Wercks,* Bibliography No. 70. The title of the original pamphlet has evaded discovery.

247. "Und ob gleich nicht alles, so wird doch das meiste auch hiesigen Ortes *applicable* seyn."

248. *Untersuchung der Ursachen, welche Gross-Britannien . . . bewogen haben. . . .* Bibliography No. 101.

249. *Ehrenpforte,* p. 210: "Die Übersetzung von engländischen Staats-Sachen, welche von ihm den 6. Febr. heraus kam . . . machte bey den kaiserlichen Ministern viel Aufsehens."

250. *Die Augenscheinliche Herannäherung eines Krieges. . . .* Bibliography No. 102.

251. *Ehrenpforte,* p. 210: "Diese Übersetzung geschahen zum Vortheil des Grossbritannischen Hofes, auf dessen Befehl, und mit des Königes gnädigster Aufnahm."

popularity—that he had great difficulty in acquiring a copy in 1743, when another conflict appeared to be at hand.[252] In the following years he translated several similar documents,[253] the last of which appeared in 1731. In this year, Wich being absent in England, Mattheson was in entire charge of British affairs in Hamburg. His duties were very trying: he had to investigate a violent and bloody riot which took place among some British sailors in the city,[254] and to combat the influence of a series of pamphlets attacking the British government, which unexpectedly and in great numbers appeared in the Hamburg book-stalls. Disturbed by these simultaneous happenings, he made his final defense of the State to whose interests he was so much devoted by translating *Considerations on the Present State of Affairs in Europe.*[255] That there should be no possible doubts in the minds of his readers as to his intentions, the following explanation of his motives was published in the *Niedersächsische Nachrichten von Gelehrten Sachen,* this may well have been written by Mattheson himself since he became at about this time an important contributor to that periodical:

Recently so many calumnies against the Government of Great Britain in London have appeared, that it is deemed necessary to print several pages in its defense, so that the thoughtless and easily persuaded may be no longer led by the nose by these shameful exudations. In order to place these considerations before the eyes of the German Staats-Welt . . . Mr. Secretary Mattheson has published an applicable English pamphlet, here translated. . . .[256]

252. *Idem,* Anhang, p. 17: "Ao. 1743. war dieses Buch für Geld nicht mehr zu bekommen u. der Verfasser selbst erhandelte ein Exemplar im Ausruf theuer genug. *Patri* in Guben hat es von ihm für einen Ducaten bekommen."

253. Bibliography Nos. 111, 112, and 113.

254. *SP* 82/48 (Bremen), 13 Oct. 1731, Letter from Wich to [Harrington]: ". . . They write me from Hamburg, that four English Mariners, quarreling with some Sailors belonging to the Ship Apollo, have been barbarously stabbed with Knives by the Indians. . . . My Secretary having made Application to the Judge, he immediately gave Orders to proper Officers to search after the Murderers. . . ."

255. *Betrachtungen über den Gegenwärtigen Zustand der Europäischen Staats-Geschäffte. . . .* Bibliography No. 118.

*Ehrenpforte,* p. 213: "Da auch der Grossbritannische Hof um diese Zeit mit anzüglichen Schrifften angegriffen wurde, und zu derselben Abfertigung eine Schutz-Schrifft drucken liess, wurde [dies] unserm Mattheson aufgetragen. . . ."

256. No. 14, 1731, 19 Feb.: "Es sind neulich so viele Schmäh-Schrifften wider die itzige Gross-Britannische Regierung in London herausgekommen dass man für nöthig

Since Mattheson acted in this instance on his own authority, this statement perhaps indicates the extent of his own feeling of responsibility as a British agent in Hamburg. The furtherance of British prestige did not present to him any problem of divided allegiance, for the well-being of Hamburg and that of England were clearly linked together. Since the commercial prosperity of his city depended materially upon the foreign policy of Great Britain, the immense contemporary interest in these translations can be easily surmised.

Thanks to his concern and connection with English political affairs it was not unnatural that Mattheson should develop a considerable—and discriminating—taste for English literature. He first evinced this interest as early as 1713, when he began to publish a weekly magazine, *Die Vernünfftler.*[257] Of the hundred odd numbers which appeared between June 21, 1713, and May 26, 1714, all but seven are translations of articles in the *Tatler* and *Spectator Papers.* He adapted all of them to the local Hamburg scene, which, despite his explanation in the first issue that he was merely a translator of the papers, inevitably created the impression that he was their original author. Seven papers from his own pen heightened this impression, since they even quoted letters from his readers. The reception of the magazine, as well as his story of the inception of the idea, he recounts with interesting details in what appears to be the rough draft of a letter to Sir Richard Steele, dated December 26, 1713.[258]

Sir,                                            Mr. Steele. Dec. 26, 1713.
   If I did not think you were too well us'd to receive Letters from unknown hands, I should not importune you with this; but, may be, the distance from which I write to you, if nothing else, will make this my application more uncommon than others, and consequently more acceptable. To be short, Sir,

---

erachtet hat, zu deren Vertheidigung einige Bogen drucken zu lassen, damit der unbedachtsame und leicht überredete gemeine Mann nicht länger durch die schändlichen Ausschläge bey der Nase geführet werden möge. Um nun diese Grund-Sätze, samt dem frevelhafften Betrieb der Uebel gesinnten auch der Teutschen Staats-Welt vor Augen zu stellen, hat der Herr Secretair Mattheson eine dahin gehörige Engeländischen Schrifft dieser Tagen hier verdolmetschet drucken lassen. . . ."

257. Bibliography No. 29.

258. It is unfortunately not known whether this letter ever reached its destination.

I have made bold, to translate some of your incomparable Speculations into ye German language, and if you will give me leave I'll tell you how.

My Country is this Town, and thô, besides some parts of Germany & Holland, I have never travell'd much, except in a few Mapps & Books, I allways had, and still have a great desire to see England. It is 12. years agoe, when I was on the way, but fell sick at Leyden and lost my oportunity, which since that time I never could regain: as I was bred in Musik from my Infancy, with somewhat more than common success, I hid the little scrapes of Greek & Latin, which young people are oblig'd to swallow down before they understand 'em, and having a natural aversion for the three great Professions, that are followed by so many insignifecant Creatures, you call by the name *Umbrae,* apply'd my self very earnestly to the noble art before mention'd and to some reigning languages. This procur'd me a wellcome in the Family of the *Honbl.* Mr. Wich, Her *Mtyes* late Envoy Extr. in the Circle of Lower Saxony, who finding me capable for more things than touching the Spinet or contriving a Contrapunct, was pleas'd to make me his Secretairy, which place both honourable and profitable I have continu'd in these last 7. [sic] years, till Death has bereav'd me of a Gentleman, that was more my Friend and Compagnon than Master. During this my imployment I had frequent Occasion to peruse your English polite autors, and among the rest, Sir, your delicious and usefull Lucubrations, which so pleas'd me, bey[ond] all what I ever read, that it came in my head, to gratifye my contrymen with a Translation of some of the choicest Pieces, and give 'em a Taste of the true English humour & Witt. Vices & Follyes are every where at home, and some of my stubborn Hamburghers grew out of humour, as soon as any thing aproaching their own Character appear'd. You will easily guess, Sir, that I told 'em, in a Preface, the work was nothing else but a Translation, and onely adapted to the present Circumstances as well as to the Place, wherein we live, whose manners are quite different from the Docility of the English world. But nothing would do, they fancy'd to know so well, who was Clarissa, who Chloe, who Cynthio, who Nocturnus(?), &c. that they found their own Pictures where they were not. Some, who pleas'd themselves with the Sport, gave me several Hints, a few of which I made use of, in 2. or 3. Papers of my own; but my angry readers, discovering the difference between a Translation and a Composition would give the former no more credit, and cry'd I attacked the Princes of Learning such as Scaliger, Salmasius &c. out of my own accord, and falsely hid myself behind an English autor; upon this several Lampoons came out against the Translator, none of which I answer'd, nor ever will by the Pen; but shall find my time to aquit myself of that debt very reputably. All this Story, Sir, tends to nothing else, but to beg your pardon, for the Liberty I have taken to interpreting some of your uncommon thoughts to my ungrateful contrymen without yr, consent. The number of Papers, which I publishe'd and term'd by a german name signifying as much as the French word *Raisonneur* amounting near an hundred I shall put a stop to it at the Conclusion of the Century, since I find my paines so very ill bestow'd, and this Soil too barren for sowing any such precious Seed, as yours, upon it.

The Gentleman, that will have the honneur to deliver you this Letter, Sir, will attest the truth of all what is said here by adding more circumstances to it and all the favour I beg of you, is, to let me know, by a few lines from your Hand, (which I shall have leave to publish at the end of the last Piece) that you are not at all displeas'd with what I have undertaken, but rather that you like my good dessign, and (which I leave to yr. choice) desire me to go on. If I thought there would be the least unreasonableness in this my demand, I should never make it, but Mr. Phrygenius, who knows my integrity, will convince you that my intentions are sincere. Therefore be pleas'd, Sir, to do me the honour, onely in general Termes to approve of what I have translated out of your Tatlers and Spectators, which will be very satisfactory to me, and stop the mouthes of some ignorant People, [who] undeservedly call me the author whereas I am but a meer Translator, and with all veneration [259]

> Sr
> Mr. Philipps & Mr. Forbes
> will also give you my Character
> if requir'd.

If Steele ever received this letter, he might have taken the Hamburger's criticism of the translator as a real tribute, for Mattheson's version indeed reproduced the spirit of the originals to a remarkable extent.[260] The concluding number was published, however, without any statement from Steele.

Perhaps because of the "barrenness of Hamburg's soil," Mattheson made no further translations of purely literary works for ten years. Then in 1723, he published a translation of Defoe's *Moll Flanders,* dedicating it, possibly because of his scorn for his "stubborn Hamburghers," to a member of the local aristocracy, the Freyherrin von Schmettau.[261] In the dedication he declared that the story had so deeply moved him that he had determined to make public the translation which he had begun for reasons of "private pleasure." [262] He also confessed that he had omitted or shortened

259. Cf. The *Tatler, Bibliography* No. 29.

260. Karl Jacoby's *Die ersten moralischen Wochenschriften Hamburgs am Anfange des achtzehnten Jahrhunderts* contains a partial analysis of the contents of *Die Vernünfftler.*

261. Bibliography No. 85.

262. [Dedication, p. 3.]: ". . . hat mich die Historie der Moll Flanders so bewegt dass

certain passages to avoid offending "innocent ears," but recommended the moral precepts to be found in the book.[263] It seems doubtful whether this tale found much of any popularity in Hamburg or Germany at large, for none of Mattheson's contemporaries mentioned it, and no other translation appears to have been made until nearly two centuries later.[264]

Mattheson's next effort took a considerably different turn. In 1724, the year of its publication jn England, he translated the first volume of Bishop Burnet's *History of His Own Time*.[265] The labor involved in this prodigious work (his version runs to 936 pages) occupied him for sixty-nine days, including Sundays and "maildays" when, as might be expected, his time was pretty well occupied in other activities.[266] He was, moreover, sufficiently interested to begin work on the second volume as soon as it appeared ten years later,[267] as well as, immediately after publication, the pamphlet by Bevil Higgens denouncing Burnet's book.[268] In the meantime he published three other translations of not inconsiderable size and interest: in 1726 a *Life of Mary Stuart*, in 1728 *The Travels of Cyrus* by Chevalier Ramsay, one of the most popular of all the contemporary "philosophical" travel-books (to judge by its numerous editions in English and French) and, in 1734, the moralistic *Friendship in Death* by Elizabeth Rowe.[269]

The last of the literary translations undertaken by Mattheson was Richardson's *Pamela*. He published half of it in two volumes in

ich nicht umhin gekönnt, solche in meiner Übersetzung, die nur Anfangs eine privat-Lust zum Zweck gehabt, öffentlich ans Licht zu geben."
263. Vorbericht, No. 4: "Man hat so gar einige Umstände, keusche Ohren nicht zu beleidigen, theils ausgelassen, theils um ein merkliches verkürtztt: und weil aus der ärgsten Historie gemeiniglich der beste Nutz zu ziehen, ist solcher hin und wieder, mit kurzen Moralien angedeutet worden."
264. T. M. Hatfield, "Moll Flanders in Germany," *Journal of English and German Philology*, XXXII (1933), pp. 61–63.
265. *Bischof Burnets Geschichte, die er selbst erlebet hat.* . . . Bibliography No. 89.
266. *Ehrenpforte*, pp. 208–209: ". . . übersetzte solches in 69. Tagen, Sonntage und Posttage blieben ohne dergleichen Arbeit, und sind also nicht mit dazu angewandt, aber doch mit gezählet."
267. Bibliography No. 130.
268. Bibliography No. 136.
269. *Die Geschichte von dem Leben und von der Regierung MARIAE, Königinn der Schotten.* . . . Bibliography No. 98. *Des Ritters Ramsay Reisender CYRUS.* . . . Bibliography No. 108; *Freundschafft im Tode.* . . . Bibliography No. 121.

1742,[270] and completed it the following year. In the dedication he explained that the "inordinate desire" of his readers had forced him to issue the first part before he had completed the whole.[271] Indeed the news of the rapturous reception of Richardson's novel in England and France must have reached Hamburg[272] and incited Mattheson to edify his countrymen with all possible speed. Their enthusiasm was fully as unalloyed as that of *Pamela's* readers elsewhere; it was furthermore spurred on by Mattheson's friend Brockes, who wrote a number of poems in praise of it.[273] Mattheson jotted his own reaction to the work on the front page of his copy of the first volume:

> Cet ouvrage enrichit les Librairies;
> Il passe la Mer, et procure à son auteur célèbre une éspèce d'immortalité.
> Il y a pourtant de certains defauts; mais ils sont excusables.

Possibly it was the recognition of these "certain defects" which prevented him from making his translation complete, for he omitted a number of the letters contained in the third and fourth volumes of the original, and merely summarized their contents. At the beginning of his last volume he frankly confessed as to the liberties he had taken with the English text, and added that the last two volumes of the original were so inferior to the first that, "in my opinion they do not merit a word for word translation."[274] To excuse this condensation, he elaborately describes the labor demanded of the translator of such a work:

270. *Pamela oder die belohnte Tugend.* . . . Bibliography Nos. 142 and 143.
271. "Maassen die Begierde der Leser so gross gewesen, dass man sie unmöglich, bis zum völligen Abdruck, hat aufhalten können; sondern gezwungen worden ist, ihnen, bey der neurigen Ostermesse, nur einige Bogen davon, zum Vorschmack und zur Probe, in die Hände zu spielen."
272. The review of the first volume of *Pamela* in the *Hamburgische Berichte von den neuesten gelehrten Sachen,* 1742, pp. 246–247, wrote in part: "Diese Schrift hat sich in Engeland und Frankreich einen allgemeinen Ruhm erworben; so gar die Geistlichen in Engeland haben dieselben ihren Gemeinen von der Kanzel angepriesen. . . ."
273. *Irdisches Vergnügen in Gott,* IX, 553–558. The first of these reads as follows:
"Das was man, von der wahrend Tugend, in hundert tausend Büchern lehret,
Wird, durch der Pamela Betragen, auf eine solche Weis' erkläret,
Dass der nicht nur kein tugendhaftes, kein menschliches Herz im Busen hegt,
Denn diese tugendhafte Schöne zur Tugendliebe nicht bewegt."
274. "Sind sie, meines Erachtens, einer völligen Uebersetzung von Wort zu Wort nicht Werth."

Who will think, or believe without further explanation, that a work such as this merely to be translated must be read in its entirety seven or eight times? Nonetheless, it is only too true. First curiosity impels one to read the book through as quickly as possible and purely for pleasure; this everyone does. While translating, however, you read the book a second, third, and fourth time, paragraph by paragraph, sentence by sentence, with considerably greater care and with very much less pleasure. This, and what is to follow few people do. The fifth time, and perhaps repeatedly, you have a final reading of the manuscript before turning it over to the printer. You read the book the sixth time when you correct the first galleys of each fascicle; the seventh time with particular attention when you get the second galleys; the eighth time when the sheets come clean from the press, and you find that there are still errors that have to be expunged.[275]

The accumulation of feeling of this passage explains why Mattheson terminated his career as translator of English literature with *Pamela*.[276]

But translating was not the only way in which Mattheson continued to show his interest in English thought and literature. In the years 1731–35—years which seem to have been among the most uneventful of his life—he was one of the chief contributors to the *Niedersächsische Nachrichten von Gelehrte Sachen*.[277] This learned journal was similar in form and content to many others of the day: *The Present State of the Republic of Letters in England,* and the *Memoires de Trevoux* in France. It contained articles on matters of intellectual interest, and "news-reports" of books published in the various important cities of Europe. None of the contents was signed, but Leisner, the editor, counted Mattheson as a

275. Wer bedencket wohl, ja, wer glaubt es wohl, ohne Auslegung, dass ein solches Werck, wie dieses (andrer wichtigerer Erfordernisse zu geschweigen) wenn es nur schlechterdings uebersetzet werden soll, eine sieben-bis achtmalige gantze Durchlesung haben will? Und dennoch ist es mehr, als alzuwahr. Denn, Erstlich bringt uns die Neubegierde dazu, dass wir es auf das schleunigste, und mit Lust, durchgehen: das thut ein jeder. Zum andern, dritten und vierten geschiehet es ja bey der Uebersetzung selbst, und zwar, mit weit grösserm Bedacht; doch viel weniger Lust, zwey bis dreimahl Stück oder Satz-weise. Das, und was folget, thut ein jeder nicht. Fünftens, bey der Nachschung des geschriebenen Exemplars, ehe es in die Presse gegeben wird, wo nicht mehr, doch gewiss einmahl. Sechtens, bey der Ausbesserung des ersten Abdrucks eines jeden Bogens. Siebendens, mit besonderer Aufmercksamkeit bey dessen Revision. Achtens, wenn der Bogen rein aus der Presse kommt, und noch die Druck fehler auszuziehen sind. . . ."
276. After this Mattheson published but one other translation: that of Mainwaring's *Life of George Frederick Händel*, which he undertook in 1761, at the age of eighty. Bibliography No. 183.
277. Bibliography No. 117.

82     *Johann Mattheson*

most important contributor, since he was responsible for all the literary news from England.[278] In his reports, which occupied the majority of the space in each of the bi-weekly issues, he revealed himself as thoroughly well informed of contemporary intellectual controversies. The various works which animated the discussions of Deism, such as Bott's *Morality Founded in the Reason of Things* or Tindal's *Christianity as Old as the Creation,* received much attention.[279] In the issues for 1733 he also described the contents of such journals as *The Craftsman, Mist's Journal, The London Journal and Free Britain,* etc. Unfortunately, however, despite the years of "enlightenment" which had intervened between Mattheson's first efforts to "gratify his countrymen with a . . . Taste of the true English Humor & Witt," the "stubbornness" of his fellow Hamburgers again forced him to terminate the efforts he was making in their behalf. Coming on an article entitled "A Dissertation on gloves, showing their Antiquity and use in the several Ages of the World," in the *Present State of the Republic of Letters,*[280] he translated it, his version appearing in several numbers of the magazine.[281] This was his swan-song; not long afterwards he resigned as contributor, apparently,—judging, at least, from the regretful announcement of the editor—because of the outspoken disapproval of the journal's readers, who felt themselves insulted and their time wasted by any such triviality as the how and the why of gloves.[282]

278. *Niedersächsische Nachrichten von Gelehrte Sachen,* Vorrede, 1732: "Unter denselben [contributors] verdient der berühmte Herr Capell-Meister und Secretar Mattheson vor allen andern ein öffentliches Lob. Von dem Kommen die Auszüge des Englischen Present State, wie auch die übrigen Nachrichten aus London, und dasjenige so von der Music und Theatralischen Sachen handelt, her. Ihm haben die Leser den ordentlichen, vollständigen, und gründlichen Bericht der in England vorgefallenen neuen zur Gelehrsamkeit gehörenden Sachen zu dancken. . . . Man gesteht es gerne, dass sein Beytrag einen grossen und wichtigen Theil der Nieders. Nachr. ausmacht."

279. *Idem,* Nos. 10, 11, 14, etc.

280. October, 1732, Vol. X, Article XXII, pp. 289–302.

281. His translation was entitled: "Abhandlungen von Handschuhen," and was printed in Nos. 46–48, and 50 in the edition of 1733.

282. *Niedersächsische Nachrichten,* Vorrede, 1734. "Nun darin sind wir von unserm ehemaligen Vorhaben gegen das Ende des vorigen Jahres abgewichen, dass wir kein englisches oder frantzösisches Journal nach der Ordnung mehr durchgenommen haben. . . . Nunmehro wenden wir uns zur Beantwortung verschiedener Einwürffe, die von günstigen und ungünstigen Lesern gegen einige Artickel der *Niedersäschen Nachrichten* beygepflogener Unterredung sind gemacht worden, und welche vornehmlich un-

The various translations which came from Mattheson's pen had a significant bearing on the dissemination of English literature and ideas in Hamburg and in Northern Germany. But they are notable mainly as another indication of his inexhaustible energy and the catholicity of his taste. The thirty years (1710–40) in which the most important of these works had seen the light witnessed also the publications of the majority of his treatises on music. It was to these musical writings that Mattheson dedicated his best energies and deepest thought, with the result that, taken together, they form an encyclopedic exposition of musical life, art, and thought in the Germany of the eighteenth century.

Mattheson first manifested an interest in what he called *"Musicam didacticam & theoreticam"* [283] in 1713, two years before he became director of music in the Dom, by publishing *Das Neu-Eröffnete Orchestre.*[284] He designed this book to be not only an "introduction" to, but a thorough exposition of the theory and practice of music. Unlike previous treatises which dealt with the same material, it was written in a popular style—one that deliberately avoided the obscurities of traditional musical parlance. In it Mattheson showed clearly his preference for the newer style of secular music, and even went so far as to attack the time-honored methods of the Lutheran musicians. In every way the book was bound to be offensive to conservative musicians. Its appearance brought forth, several years later, a detailed critique by Johann Heinrich Buttstedt, organist of the *Predigerkirche* in Erfurt, and a man who was by several years Mattheson's senior. In his book, which was entitled *Ut, re, mi, fa, sol, la, tota Musica et Harmonia Aeterna,*[285] Buttstedt not only took issue with nearly all the con-

---

sern ehemaligen wehrtesten Mitgehülffen den Herrn M.-betreffen. Es hat erstlich geheissen: wozu es doch Nütze dass man eine aus den Englischen übersetzte gantze Abhandlung von Handschu[h]en eingerucket, solcher Kleinigkeit etliche Blätter gewidmet, wird nicht lieber sonst etwas vorgebracht habe? Ist es bissanhero nicht vorgeblich gewesen, wenn die gelehrtesten Leute von den Trachten der Alten Untersuchungen angestellet haben; so kann es eben so wenig getadelt werden, wenn von Handschu[h]en etwas neues, gründliches, und merckwürdiges ist beygebracht worden. . . ."

283. *Ehrenpforte*, p. 198: "Mattheson . . . fing nunmehro mit Macht an, *Musicam didactam & theoreticam* schrifftlich zu treiben. . . ."

284. Bibliography No. 27.

285. Cf. Bibliography No. 47.

tents of the *Orchestre,* but also devoted considerable space to a detailed defense of the traditional system of "solmization." This double-edged attack naturally spurred on the argumentative Mattheson. In 1717 he replied with a carefully documented enlargement of the contents of his first book and a crushing criticism of the irrationality of "Solmization"—a system which, he contended, could no longer satisfy any requirements of contemporary musical composition.[286]

A number of the statements made by Mattheson in the *Neu-Eröffnete Orchestre* were sufficiently revolutionary to require considerable amplification and justification. Some of these statements were based upon musical ideas and technical discoveries which by no means formed an established part of musical knowledge, and were, in fact, wholly misunderstood by many musicians. He introduced, for example, the concept of the differing tonal properties of the scales most frequently used in the early eighteenth century. The understanding of this aesthetic problem rested upon the tuning of keyboard instruments in such a way that all of the twenty-four major and minor scales could be sounded equally well. During Mattheson's lifetime various methods were worked out to achieve the desired result. In 1719 he published the *Exemplarische Organisten-Probe Im Artikel Vom General-Bass,*[287] in which he argued the importance of using and understanding all the twenty-four scales, and gave for the practical musician instruction and examples in the use of each, two years before Part One of Bach's *Wohltemperirtes Clavier* was completed. Twelve years later Mattheson published an enlarged and completely rewritten version of this book.[288] In 1721 he published the third of his *Orchestre* series, *Das Forschende Orchestre,*[289] in which he expanded his notions of the philosophical basis for the rational system of emotions which he had already (in 1713) declared of basic importance to musical theory and criticism. In this volume he showed himself opposed to the mathematical theory of music, which had so entirely dominated the musical criticism and thought of the older ecclesiastical musicians.

286. Bibliography No. 47.
287. Bibliography No. 62.
288. *Die Grosse General-Bass-Schule,* Bibliography No. 116.
289. Bibliography No. 73.

The implications of this philosophy of music—the justification
for which Mattheson found in the writings of contemporary philosophers such as John Locke—were far reaching. In order to pursue
the discussion of his ideas, Mattheson turned, in 1722, to a new type
of publication—a monthly journal entitled *Critica Musica*,[290]
which he continued to publish until September, 1725, and which
earned for him 200 reichsthaler.[291] The form of this periodical was
similar to that of such learned journals as the *Deutche Acta Eruditorum* and the *Present State of the Republic of Letters;* it included
original articles, translations of articles by other writers, letters
from readers of Mattheson's books, and news reports of music and
musicians from the various cities of Europe. Mattheson wrote eight
articles for it, which were continued from one issue to the next,[292]
and which provided an admirable opportunity for a more sponta-
neous and popular form of discussion of his opinions. The development of his belief in the importance of melody and its effect
upon the passions, and the exposition of the psychological principles which should control the setting of an oratorio text to music
exemplify the trend of his thought.[293]

It was two years later that Mattheson entered the lists on behalf
of dramatic church music with *Das Neue Göttingische . . .
EPHORUS.*[294] Heretofore his writings, while not ignoring the issues relating to the style and production of church music, had been
mainly concerned with other matters. The only really direct attack
he had made upon the "ignorant" opponents of church music had
been concealed in the Foreword to his Flute Sonatas published in
1720.[295] In *Der Musicalische Patriot*[296] of 1728, however, he was
openly fighting for a musical concept which, although it was disapproved of by ministers of the church themselves, lay at the root
of his innate Lutheran beliefs. This belief he stated at the outset
as follows:

290. Bibliography Nos. 77 and 91.
291. *Ehrenpforte*, p. 209: ". . . endigte hernach den zweeten Band seiner Critick am
28. Sept. mit einem reinen Gewinn, von 200 Reichsthl., eignen Verlage."
292. Cf. Bibliography Nos. 74 and 91 for the titles of these articles.
293. *Der Melodische Vorhof* and *Der Fragende Componist* are the two most important
articles in this connection.
294. Bibliography No. 100.
295. *Der Brauchbare VIRTUOSO*, Bibliography No. 69.
296. Bibliography No. 107.

All the efforts of our composers, singers, and instrumentalists will be of
not the least avail unless, without the slightest hypocrisy and with the true
earnestness of David himself, they aim directly or indirectly at the honor and
praise of the Lord. They may sing and play in Operas, they may explain and
compose as much as they want—in the end all must be fixed, immutably, in
the church.[297]

While he was defending his opinions on church music, he was also
defending the Hamburg Opera, which was at this period entering
upon its period of decline. It was perhaps for some such reason
that Mattheson chose for this second of his periodicals a title so
closely resembling that of *Der Patriot,* Hamburg's popular and
successful "moral weekly."

In 1728, Mattheson, having resigned from the Dom, was at
liberty to devote himself almost exclusively to the continuation of
his various musical-literary projects. By this time he had a very
clear idea not only as to what all these were, but what they ought
to be. At the conclusion of his *Musicalische Patriot,* he lists them
in careful detail.

The gentle reader will gather at a glance, as from an index, the following
facts: 1. in my dissertation on the *Divine demands* concerning the *musica
figuralis* [polyphonic, contrapuntal music] I have not treated even half the
material, because all the Prophets, all the Apocrypha, and all of the New
Testament remained untouched. 2. heretofore I have made no mention of
anything connected with the perfect *Kapellmeister;* 3. I have been more than
lenient to the enemies of music; when, however, I come to close quarters with
them they need expect little mercy; 4. the whole noble expanse of music has
been surveyed, quickly, for a moment only, and in suspense as it were,
while many a detail has had to be neglected; 5. there has been no time to
discuss the little *General-Bass-Schule;* 6. the erection of the harmonical
*Ehrenpforte* has not even been started, although some fifty loads of lime and
stones (by which I mean as many descriptions) have been drawn in; 7. the
*Klingende Fingersprache* that is to have many etchings, must also be counted
to the subjects still to be treated; 8. I have moreover, not touched upon anything in the field of the *Musica moralis*—when every day so many immorali-
ties occur that you could pick them off the floor with a skewer. . . .[298]

297. *Der Musicalische Patriot,* p. 9: "Alle Bemühungen unsrer Componisten, Sänger und
Instrumentisten ist von keiner Dauer; dafern sie nicht, ohne die geringste Heucheley, mit
Davidischen rechten Ernst, die Ehre und Lob GOttes zum Zweck hat: es sey nun mittel-
bahr, oder unmittelbahr. Singet und spielet in den Opern, infomirt und componirt so
lange, als ihr wollet, endlich muss doch die Kirche einen festen Sitz geben."
298. *Idem,* p. 357: "Der geneigte Leser wird hieraus, als aus einer Tabelle, in einem

In 1735 Mattheson made another attack on the "Music-Feinde" in his *Kleine General-Bass-Schule*.[299] The book was designed to give the rudimentary principles of thorough bass as a detailed supplement to his earlier books on the same subject. The introduction [300] dealt with the enemies of church music and their policy of slowly strangling it by not providing adequate financial support. The most violent of the passages that were leveled against the "Doctores, Pastores, Professores, Senatores" who were responsible for this opposition were quoted in the review of the book in the *Niedersächsische Nachrichten von Gelehrte Sachen*,[301] and were doubtless read by members of the Hamburger *Senat* and *Geistliches Ministerium*. The latter body drew up a letter enclosing the offensive issue of the magazine and sent it to the *Senat*, recommending a suitable reprimand to Mattheson.[302] Although the matter

Anblick ersehen, 1) dass ich von der Dissertation über die Göttlichen Gebote, wegen der Figural-Music, lange nicht die Helffte abgehandelt habe, indem alle Propheten, Apocryphische Bücher und das gantze N. T. noch unberührt geblieben: 2) dass ich von dem vollkommenen Capellmeister bissher kein Wort erwehnet: 3) dass die Music-Feinde im Vorübergehen angeredet sind, und ein gantz ander Facit herauskommen muss, wenn wir ihnen das Weisse im Auge betrachten wollen: 4) dass der ehrwürdige Schauplatz, mit Hindansetzung vieler besondern Dinge, nur gantz kurz und zur Probe, in äusserster Behutsamkeit, eröfnet worden: 5) dass von der kleinen General-Bass-Schule noch gar keine Zeit zu handeln gewesen: 6) dass der Bau der harmonischen Ehrenp-forte, obgleich etliche 50-Last Kalck und Steine (verstehe so viele Beschreibungen) dazu im Vorrath sind, noch keinen Anfang nehmen können: 7) dass die klingende Finger-Sprache, welche viele Kupffer erfordert, ebenfalls unter die zukünfftigen Sachen zu zehlen ist. Ich habe ferner und 8) die gantze *Musicam moralem* noch unbetastet vor mir, und es stossen täglich unsittliche Dinge genug auf, die man in die Spick-Nadel fassen kann. . . ."

299. Bibliography No. 127.

300. Inhalt: "I Der Vor-Bericht . . . handelt vom scheinheiligen Hass öffentlicher Spötter wieder die Göttliche Ton-Kunst, ihre hohe Wissenschafft und rechtmässige Uebung. . . ."

301. No. II, 7 Jan., 1735, p. 12: "Es giebt ja freilich unter den Predigern viel nasse Brüder. Es reimen sich auf die *humores*, sowohl auf Doctores, Pastores, Professores, Senatores, Legumlatores, als auf die armen Cantores. Und wenn sichs gleich nicht reimte, so ists doch wahr, dass es vor dem Altar sogenannte Diener des Göttlichen Worts giebt, die da, (GOTT vergebe es ihnen!) den Wein nicht ehre heiligen, als bis ihnen der Brandenwein die Zunge gelöset hat. . . . Zur Erhebung des Hertzens zu GOTT ist nicht allemahl eine ruhige Stille am bequemsten, sondern ein laut tönendes Sela . . . thut bey trägen Menschen offt eine bessere Wirckung als die schwägende Wehmuth einer schlummernden Predigt, darüber viele Zuhörer gar einschlafen. . . ."

302. *Ministerial Archiv III A19, CXXXLV*, p. 274. This letter was signed by twenty-five members of the *Geistliches Ministerium* and dated "d. 22. Mart. 1735." It was written by Johann Winckler, the Senior Pastor, and said in part: ". . . so habe nur hiemit beyliegende Piece ein Hoch u. wohlherausen communiciren u. uns videtur darüber mir aufbitten wollen. Mich dencket, dass wir es Amplissius Senatus so denunciren haben: dass

was considered by that august Assembly, and an order of confis-
cation of the issue drawn up in part, the projected action was not
carried through.[303]
Two years later, Mattheson published *Kern Melodischer Wissenschafft*[304] as a "precursor" of his *Vollkommene Capellmeister*. It
included the chief chapters of the later volume on melodic learning,
and earned for its author the most extravagant praise from the leading, learned journal in Hamburg,[305] and from Johann Scheibe,
whose *Critische Musikus* had been recently founded.[306] In placing

---

hatte ein zu überein [blot] Post Memoria zu dero Approbation hiebeÿ sende. Will anbey
er hoch-u. wohl Ehrwürdigen zu Gedancken gehen, ob mit anzuhangen sey, dass wir
E. Hochw. Rath [indecipherable phrase] ob derselbe sich bey den Herr. Envoye von
Wich über den Mattheson zu besprechen für dienlich wachbeten. . . ."
   303. *Ministerial Archiv III A19, CXXXIV*, p. 275. *Pro Memoria d. 1 April 1735.* "Wenn
nicht allein der Secretair u. Capellmeister Johann Matthesen in der Vorrede seiner ausser
Neue Jahr herausgegebenen Klein-General-Bass-Schule sich interessieren unterschiedliche
sehr gefällige u. ausschuldigende Reflexione auf das Predigerammt u. besonders . . . auf
Hiesiger Rev. Ministerium zur grössesten Verkleinerung desselben u. zum Ärgerniss aller
unparteyischen Leser zu machen; sondern auch der Concipient der in Felginerischen
Büchladen herauskommenden Niedersächsischen Nachrichten von gelehrten neuen Sachen
in No. 11 dieser Jahr mit Fleiss u. auch bittersten Gemüth gegen das öffentliche Lehr.
Ammt dieselbe Passagen *als die beträchtlichsten Stellen aus jenes Vorbericht* verbotenen
auszuführen Zur Lection von manchen desto bekannter zu machen, sich gelüsten. So
hat Rev. Ministerium solches bey E. Hochehrw. u. Hochewigen Rath unangezeiget nicht
besser, u. denselben zugleich Ergebnisse ersuchen wollen für das von vielen mehr als zu
viel gering geachtet Predigerammt u. für Rev. Ministerium besonders die Güte zu haben,
u. nicht allein obbermeldete Schrift des Mattheson so der büchführer Joh. Christoph Lisner
verleget, zu vermeten(?) sondern . . . auch die noch übrige Exemplarii dieser Piece bey
der weittere Felginers confisciren zu lassen. . . . Wir Sen. auch Rev. Ministerium bey
dieser Gelegenheit findet allen Büchführer u. Buchdrucker dieser Stadt, dass sie dergleichen
Bucher u. Schrifften, die mit vielen Missbrauch Göttlichen Worte u. Andere Verspottung
derselben u. des Predigammts dienenden Anmerckungen angefüllet sind, nicht vorlegen
noch nutzen," [here the document ends].
   304. Bibliography No. 134.
   305. *Staats u. Gelehrte Zeitung Des Hamburgischen unpartheyischen Correspondenten,*
1737, No. 181. 11 Nov. "Von neuen merckwürdigen gelehrten Sachen": "Der gelehrte
Herr Capellmeister Mattheson hat sich durch seine vernünftigen Schriften nicht wenig um
die Music verdient gemacht. Nicht wenige Wahrheiten sind von ihm darinn erfunden
und bestarcket worden. . . . Seine Geschicklichkeit und seine Arbeitsamkeit haben ihn
fähig gemacht, seine geprüften Sätze der Welt mitzutheilen, und er gehöret unter die
wenigen welche die wahre Eigenschaft der Music recht eingesehen."
   306. Scheibe wrote: "Wer kan wohl die glücklichen Früchte einer so ruhmlichen
Bemühung ohne ein erkenntliches Vergnügen bemercken? Wer siehet nicht den Nutzen,
welchen die Verbannung der abgeschmackten Solmisation mit sich bringet? Wer lieset
wohl, ohne Empfindung, die Vertheidigung des Gehörs, der Kirchen-Music und der
Schaubühne? Und wer hat wohl mit solcher Gedult, Standhafftigkeit und Sichbarkeit
die Verfolgungen, die Schmähungen, den Haas und die Unwissenheit seiner Feinde ertragen, und über sie den Sieg erhalten?"

his essential emphasis in the composition of music on melody, Mattheson disagreed fundamentally with Rameau and other musicians, as he took pains to state in the Foreword of this volume.[307] Scheibe, who was a friend and admirer of Gottsched, in his letter of approval to Mattheson, expatiated upon Mattheson's wisdom in recognizing melody as "natürlich," hence basically given in nature, and Harmony as "Künstlich," hence as an artificial product— citing the music of J. S. Bach as a tiresome example of the latter sort![308] In 1738 Mattheson published a pamphlet[309] in which he included this letter as a recommendation for his *Vollkommene Capellmeister,* which followed in 1739.[310] In this huge folio volume he included and expanded on much of the material contained in his earlier works, thus making it by far his most important single exposition of the theory and practice of the music of the Baroque period—it was, in short, his masterpiece.

The "building" of the "harmonische Ehren-Pforte" was finished in 1740. This project of publishing the lives of the most important German musicians of his time had been entertained by Mattheson longer than that of any of his other works. In 1714—a year after the appearance of his first *Orchestre*—he discussed, in the introduction to the German edition of his *Harmonisches Denckmahl,* the great need for some such biographical record.[311] Three years later, in the Foreword to *Das Beschützte Orchestre,* he formally announced his design for a "Neu zu errichtende Musicalische Ehren-

307. *Kern Melodischer Wissenschafft,* Vorbericht, p. 5: "[Ich] kann auch nicht begreiffen, warum man den deutlichen Unterschied zwischen der ein- und mehrfachen Harmonei . . . niemahls in gehörige Betrachtung ziehet, wenn, z.E. wieder alle Vernunft behauptet werden will: 'Dass die Melodie aus der Harmonie entspringe, aund alle Regeln der ersten von der andern hergenommen 'werden müssen, ja, dass es fast unmöglich sey, gewisse Regeln von der Melodie zu geben, weil das meiste auf den guten Geschmack ankomme.' "

308. "Die Harmonie ist . . . künstlich, die Melodie naturlich. Es ist auch über dieses des natürliche, im moralischen Verstande, offt weit schwerer, als das künstliche. Die Erreichung des natürlichen erfordert mehr Wissenschaft, mehr Kenntniss der Dinge, und überhaupt mehr Vernunfft. . . . *Bachische* Kirchen-Stücke sind allemahl künstlicher und mühsamer; keineswegs aber von solchen Nachdrucke. Überzeugung, und von solchem vernünfftigen Nachdencken, als die *Telemannischen* und *Graunischen Wercke.*"

309. *Gültige Zeugnisse . . . 1738,* Bibliography No. 137.

310. Bibliography No. 138.

311. Anrede: "Mein unmassgebliches *Project, Messieurs,* Wäre dieses: Dass man vorläufig einige persönliche Nachrichten *de Viris musica clarissimis* sammlete, und solche der *curieux* gelehrte Welt vor Augen legte. . . ."

Pforte," [312] and appealed to fourteen leading German musicians, including Fux, Händel, Keiser, Kuhnau, and Teleman, to aid him in doing honor to the Art of Music by providing him with the information he required.[313] In 1719 he continued his appeal in the "Vorbereitung" of his *Organisten-Probe* [314] and again in his *Grosse General-Bass-Schule* in 1731, in which he quoted the letter from Telemann that contained his autobiography.[315] When it was finally published in 1740, it included the "lives, works, merits &c." of one hundred and forty-eight of the "most excellent *Capellmeister, Componisten, Musikgelehrten, Tonkünstler &c.*" [316] in Germany and the rest of Europe, a most grandiloquent *Vorbericht*, remarks on the qualifications guiding his selection of musicians worthy of inclusion in this *Ehrenpforte*, and on the high esteem in which music was held by learned men.

# 4

## OLD AGE

The twenty-four years between the publishing of the *Ehrenpforte* and Mattheson's death in 1764 show little change in his way of life other than what may be laid at the door of his declining

312. "Der Titel davon dörffte ungefehr so ausfallen: Die / Neu zu errichtende / Musicalische / Ehrenpforte, / Daran / Der berühmtesten Teutschen, theils / vor mehr als hundert Jahren, theils annoch / blühenden Kayserlichen, Königlichen, Chur-/und Fürstlichen, wie auch verschiedener / Reichs- und Handel Städte, Hoch-/ansehnlicher, vortrefflicher / Herren Capell-Meister, / *Directorum, Intendanten, Com-/ponisten* und anderer hervor-/ragenden *Virtuosen* / Wohlgeführtes Leben, rühmli-/che und löbliche Verrichtungen, schöne / *Studia,* grosse *Dignitäten* und Einkommen,/(als ein zur gelehrten Historie von allen Dingen gehö-/riger bissher aber ermangelnder Theil) der Nach-Welt / zum Unterricht und zur Tugend-Folge, der heutigen / aber zur Auffmunterung und Anfrischung in be-/sondern Glantze zu erblicken seyn / werden, &c."

313. *Beschützte Orchestre,* [Dedication]. "Das Dritte [so ich bitten will] besteht darinn, dass ich den fünffen unter Ew. Hoch-Edl., die mir ihre *Curricula Vitae* würcklich eingesandt, oder doch bald senden werden, hiemit vors erste öffentlichen und vielen Danck abstatte, anbey die übrigen . . . Virtuosen inständigst ersuchet haben wil, zur Beförderung *Musicalischer* Ehren und meines, unter andern, vorhabenden Werckes, das ihrige grossgünstig zu *contribuiren.*"

314. *Theoretische Vorbereitung,* pp. 116 f.

315. *Vorbereitung zur Organisten-Probe* pp. 165 ff. He published the names of sixty musicians about whom he had information at this time (p. 167).

316. *Grundlage einer Ehren-Pforte.* . . . Bibliography No. 139.

strength. Although the published account of his life (which is contained in the above-mentioned work) ended with 1739, he did not cease to keep records of his activities until at least two years before his death.[317] With the help of these notes and biographical references in his later works and in those of his contemporaries written in these last years, it is possible to round out the narrative of his career.

In 1741, the year after the completion of the *Ehrenpforte,* which was his sixtieth, the even tenure of his secretarial existence was interrupted by the appointment of his employer, Sir Cyrill Wich, as "Envoye Extraordinary" to the Court of the Czar at Petersburg.[318] Wich, who was not in the least anxious to accept this position [319] would gladly have taken his secretary with him "if his infirmities would have permitted it." [320] Mattheson apparently felt that the occupation which he had always looked upon as being permanent was then at an end, for he wrote to a secretary of Harrington, who was at Hanover, as follows:

Sir,
  After a faithful and unreprovable Service of thirty-six years I am somewhat worn out and not in a condition to follow Sir Cyril Wich to Petersburg, especially, since by degrees a good Part of my Hearing has left me.
  Having therefore taken the Liberty to petition the King for a small Pension during His Pleasure, which Petition Sir Cyrill who sets out to morrow for Hanover has taken upon him to present himself to His Majesty, I beg and flatter myself, Sir, that you will be so generous, as to speak a favourable Word to my Lord Harrington, that his Lordship may be pleased to support

317. The record of the years 1741–58 (there is no record for the year 1740), entitled by Mattheson "Fortsetzung des Matthesonschen Lebenslaufs," is printed in the Anhang, pp. 13–38, of Max Schneider's 1910 edition of the *Ehrenpforte* (cf. Bibliography No. 139.) The record of the next four years, 1759–62 inclusive, I had the good fortune to unearth from the Mattheson manuscripts in the Hamburger Stadt-Bibliothek. The manuscript was headed "Weitere Fortsetzung des Matthesonichen Lebenslaufes," and is transcribed in the Appendix.
318. *Ehrenpforte,* Anhang, p. 18: "[Mattheson] lief desselben Jahres am 19. Jul. [1741] die unerwartete Nachricht ein, dass Hr. von Wich zum Nachfolger des Herrn Finch in Petersburg, als Königl. bevollmächtigter Abgesandter Sr. damahls in Hanover Hofhaltenden Grosbritannischen Maj. ernennet worden. . . ."
319. SP 82/62, Wich to [Weston(?)]. 15 July 1741.
320. *Ehrenpforte,* Anhang, p. 18: Mattheson quotes part of Wich's letter to him: "Si vos infirmités vous auroient permis d'entreprendre un si long et penible voyage, j'aurois été charmé de vous voir avec moi; mais le tout bien consideré, je comprens que cela ne se peut pas. . . ."

my humble Request for the sake of my ancienty [*sic*] and pretty narrow Circumstances.        Pardon this trouble and believe me to be with due regard and great gratitude

Sir
your most obedient
humble Servant
JMattheson

Hamburg, July 29. 1741.[321]

But Wich was delayed in his departure for a considerable time, and continued to use Mattheson as his secretary in the interim, and again after his return to Hamburg in 1744. Sir Cyrill also paid him half of the arrears of his salary, which apparently amounted to well over 5,000 florins.[322]

Before the arrival in Hamburg of Wich's successor, James Cope, and before he could know what his relationship with the new English Resident would be, Mattheson was notified of his appointment as "actuellen Legations-Secretaire" to the Duke of Schleswig-Holstein,[323] and was inducted into office a year later, in 1742, by Heinrich von Rohden, the Duke's minister to Hamburg.[324] In 1744 the Duke raised him to the rank of *Legations-Rath,* which, Mattheson noted with pride, gave him the title of "Wohlgebohren." [325]

321. No such petition can be traced in the Calendar of Treasury Papers.

322. *Ehrenpforte,* Anhang, p. 19: "Hr. Wich hergegen wartete . . . bis d. 18. Octr., nachdem er am *5ten* seinen Mattheson 1500 fl., u.d. 28. darauf noch 1161 fl. zusammen 2661 fl., als den Halbschied seines Rückstandes hatte zahlen lassen; wegen der andern Helffte aber eine Pfandschrifft zu 4. p. ct. von sich gestellet hatte, wovon auch die Zinsen erfolget sind. S. das 1746 wegen völliger Bezalung."

323. *Ibid.:* "Am 30. Octr. . . . erhielt Mattheson die Nachricht von dem Hn. *Envoie,* dass Ihro Königl. Hoheit der Hertzog von Holstein ihn Dero *actuellen* od. wircklichen *Legations-Secretaire* ernennen würden, welches auch 7. *Nov.* durch Ausfertigung des Patents in der That geschah."

Duke Carl Friedrich of Schleswig-Holstein, who had named Mattheson his Kapellmeister, had died in 1738. The present Duke, Carl Peter, married the daughter of Peter the Great in 1745, and thus became heir to the throne of Russia, which he ascended as Czar in 1762. Cf. Richard Lodge, *Great Britain and Prussia in the 18th century* (Oxford, 1923), p. 71.

324. *Ehrenpforte,* Anhang, p. 20: ". . . ertheilte der neuerwählte Hochfürstl. Holsteinische Minister und geheimer *Legations*-Rath, Heinrich von Rohden unserm Mattheson, wie die Ehren-Worte der Bestallung lauten, bekannter Geschicklichkeit und Verdienste halber, den *Caractère* und die Besoldung eines sonderbaren *Secretarii.*"

325. *Idem,* p. 21: "Und kurtz darauf [Ostern 1744] lief der Bestallung als Legations Rath Sr. Kaiserl. Hoh. des Grosfürsten, regierenden Hertzogs von Holstein, gantz unvermuthet und ungesuchet ein. (Note), Dieser Character hat das *praedicatum* Wohlgebohren und den Obristlieutenants-Rang."

It is extremely unlikely that these new posts involved any great amount of work for Mattheson, or rewarded him with much more than a title, after the fashion of his former post of Capellmeister to the late Duke.[326] He mentions his connection with the affairs of state of Schleswig-Holstein but once in the ensuing years, and then to protest apologetically that they were of no less moment to him than those of England.[327] For Cope seems to have retained Mattheson's services for at least occasional work. He employed Emanuel Matthias as his private secretary,[328] but reinstated Mattheson in his former "English *Element*" as first secretary in August, 1742, shortly after Mattheson had officially assumed his Schleswig-Holstein position.[329] From the biographical notes it appears that Mattheson's interest in foreign affairs was unflagging, but there are no indications of his having done more than make occasional copies of documents for Cope.[330] Mattheson's infirmities, to which Wich had alluded in his letter of 1741, were also spoken of by Cope in his letters to London. Undoubtedly they were increasingly noticeable, for he writes in 1751:

Mr. Mattheson, who has, during a long succession of Years, been Secretary to his Majesty's ministers at Hamburgh, and has continued so to me, is at present grown so infirm, as to be little capable of attending to Business; but my private Secretary, Mr. Matthias, shall under his Direction, have the honour to transmit to Your Grace's Office, from time to time, such Articles of Intelligence, as my Correspondents may supply him with during my Absence . . .[331]

In the following year Cope, again about to absent himself from

326. The Archives of the Duchy of Schleswig-Holstein at Kiel profess to have no documents from or concerning Mattheson in their possession.
327. *Ehrenpforte*, Anhang, p. 24 n.: "Weil die holsteineischen Staats-Sachen und ministerialische Vorfälle nicht weniger, als die Grossbritannischen in die Matthesonischen Angelegenheiten einschlagen, hat man sie summarische Weise anzuführen, nicht umhin gekönnt."
328. State Papers 82/64. After March 30, 1742, Cope's regular correspondence with Whitehall was written in Matthias' handwriting.
329. *Ehrenpforte*, Anhang, pp. 20–21: "Es blieb dabey noch nicht sondern am 14. Aug. 1742. folgte auch der königl. Grosbrit. Minister, Hr. *James Cope* diesem Beispiel, und setzte den Mattheson aufs neue in sein ehemaliges engländisches Element, indem er ihm gleichfalls, wie seine Vorfahren, Bestallung und Besoldung seines ersten *Secretarii* ertheilte, und zur Tafel zog."
330. *State Papers* 82/64–75, 1742–55, contain occasional documents in Mattheson's handwriting.
331. *State Papers* 82/73, June 25, 1751.

Hamburg, explains that his affairs will be taken care of by his own secretary, and adds:

The old Mr. Mattheson, who, thô worn in the Service of my Predecessors, I have continued to retain in mine at a small Salary, will be likewise aiding, so far as in him lies, (and as it is his Duty, that He should,) that his Majesty's Indulgence, in granting me a leave of Absence from my Post on account of my Health may not be attended with any Detriment to His Majesty's Service . . .[332]

After 1750 Mattheson himself writes of his physical ailments with increasing frequency;[333] he seems to have performed his last active services in 1755.[334]

Notwithstanding this decline in his routine duties, there is no indication of a falling off in Mattheson's intellectual pursuits for some years after 1741. Only one musical work from his pen was published, his *Odeon Morale, jucundum et vitale,* a collection of odes set to music in 1750,[335] but books and smaller pieces on his favorite musical interests continued to appear with little interruption. In 1744, he was defending the artistic form of the opera again in his *Untersuchung der Singspiele.*[336] The inspiration for this volume arose from the vehement attack upon the formal absurdities of the opera in a volume of poetry published in 1706[337] by the Italian writer Muratori, and translated and republished in part by Gottsched in his *Beyträge zur Critischen Historie.*[338] While admitting the faults of the Italian Opera, which, after the disap-

332. *State Papers* 82/73, March 7, 1752.
333. *Ehrenpforte,* Anhang, p. 27: "Im *Decr.* bekam Mattheson einen harten Anstoss von der *Colica nephrotica,* wobey ziemlich grosse Steine abgingen."
*Idem,* p. 28: "*Taylour,* der Augenartzt, wollte einen Ohrendoctor abgeben, und besuchte des Endes M. am 6. Jun. wegen seines Gehörs; getraute sich aber nicht die *operationem nervotomiae in temporibus* mit ihm vorzunehmen."
*Idem,* p. 32: ". . . als eben Mattheson am *Podagra, Chiragra* und *Coniagra* zu gleich starck u. lange laborirte. Eine hässliche dreyfache Schnurl die kein Artzt zerreissen kann. Gott allein that es."
334. *Ibid.:* ". . . da er [Cope] mir denn schriftlich auftrug, für dasjenige, was in seiner Abwesenheit vorfallen mögte, gehörige Sorge zu tragen, welches auch geschehen doch nicht erkannt ist." Cope died in the following year, 1756, and was succeeded by Philip Stanhope, whom Mattheson never mentions.
335. Bibliography No. 169.
336. Bibliography No. 146.
337. *Della perfetta poesia italiana* (Modena, 1706).
338. *Beyträge zur Critischen Historie Der Deutschen Sprache, Poesie, und Beredesamkeit* (1740), Stück 23, No. 10, pp. 485 f.

pearance of Hamburg's own operatic establishment in 1738, had won over that town as completely as it had the rest of Germany, Mattheson reiterated his belief in the essential splendor of this form of music. Several years later he must have read the painter Salvator Rosa's famous satire, which attacked music in general, and dramatic music in particular, as morally destructive.[339] In 1749 he published his reply to this satire, printing the original Italian text with his German translation, and a minute, pedantic criticism of its contents. This book was entitled *Mithridat wider den Gift einer Welschen Satyre*,[340] and was dedicated to Frederick the Great, who, Mattheson sorrowfully noted, never made or ordered to be made any acknowledgement of this honor.[341]

Mattheson also took frequent opportunities to give expression in essays and in briefer articles or notes to his opinions upon many of the musical questions which were interesting his contemporaries. In 1748 he published a short work on the scientific aspects of musical sound, entitled *Phthongologia Systematica*.[342] His shorter essays he collected and issued in four volumes between the years 1754 and 1757, under the general title of *Plus Ultra*.[343] These ranged in subject from such familiar topics as the importance of music in church services, and the question of the relation of melody and harmony (in the Foreword he welcomed the theories expressed by Rousseau in his *Lettre sur la Musique Française*) to the novel ideas such as the effect of music on animals.[334] He continued to contribute articles and notes to the various learned journals in Hamburg up to the year preceding his death—five of them appeared

339. *La Musica, La Poesia*, published first *circa* 1640. Mattheson speaks of an edition published in Amsterdam in 1719 in the Vorbericht to his *Mithridat*, Bibliography No. 163. Riemann's *Lexicon*, p. 1544, gives *ca.* 1664 as the date of the first Amsterdam edition.
340. Bibliography No. 163
341. *Ehrenpforte*, Anhang, p. 26: "Dieses Werck [*Mithridat*] . . . wurde dem Könige von Preussen zugeschrieben, der es allergnädigst aufgenommen haben soll, wie mir durch den H. Geheimen Cammerierer, Fredersdorff, der hernach in Ungnade gefallen, berichtet worden. Durch Quanz auch. Der grosse Königl. Held ohne Exempel ist seit dem mit so vielen unsterbl. Thaten beschäfftiget gewesen dass er des Mithridats vielleicht vergessen hat."
342. Bibliography No. 160.
343. Bibliography Nos. 176, 177, 178 and 179.
344. *Plus Ultra, erster Vorrath:* pp. 1–134: "Vom Klingenden Gottesdienst"; *Zweeter Vorrath*, pp. 141–165: "Von der Melodie und Harmonie"; pp. 165–213: "Von Wirckung der Musik bey dem Vieh."

in 1763 in the *Nachrichten aus dem Reiche der Gelehrsamkeit.*[345] He was also a contributor to Marpurg's *Historische Kritische Beyträge,* and to Lessing's *Beyträge zur Historie und Aufnahme des Theaters.*[346] The article published in the latter periodical was entitled "Nachricht von einem in Freyberg aufgeführten Schulschauspiele," and was occasioned by a dispute over the importance of music in general school education—a dispute which also drew forth the ire of Johann Sebastian Bach.[347] Rector Biedermann of the Freyberg Gymnasium had expressed his extreme disapproval of virtually any form of music in his school's curriculum immediately after a performance by the students of a *Singspiel* in 1748 to commemorate the anniversary of the Peace of Westphalia. Since this expression of opinion touched upon two of Mattheson's major musical tenets—a belief in the necessity both of education and of dramatic music—it inspired him, first to write this article, next to incorporate his views in two large supplements to his *Mithridat,*[348] and finally to publish a complete account of the whole matter as an appendix to his *Sieben Gespräche der Weisheit u. Musik* in 1751.[349]

Like many other writers in Germany in the first half of the eighteenth century, Mattheson was deeply interested in the improvement of the German language. His interest in the history and proper use of various musical terms is plainly discernible in the earliest of his books on music, and in some of his unpublished manuscripts.[350] In 1741, in an article in Gottsched's *Beyträge zur Critischen Historie,*[351] he took issue with the musical vocabulary used by Johann Scheibe in his *Critischer Musikus.* In 1752 he pub-

345. Bibliography No. 188.
346. Bibliography No. 166.
347. Cf. C. S. Terry, *Bach, a Biography,* pp. 261 f.; Spitta, *Johann Sebastian Bach,* III, 255–261.
348. *Panacea, erste Dosis,* 1750, and *Der Panacea, Zwote Dosis,* 1750. Bibliography Nos. 167 and 168.
349. Bibliography No. 170.
350. Bibliography Nos. 161 and 147 are examples of several similar manuscripts which are too fragmentary for inclusion in the bibliography.
351. Bibliography No. 141, Gottsched added at the end of this article a tribute to Mattheson's zeal: "Man muss es freilich Hn. *Mattheson* nachrühmen, dass er um die deutsche Sprache sich in seinen Schrifften sehr verdient gemacht, und seinen Nachfolgern, in musicalischen Sachen, den Weg zu einer guten Schreibart in diesen Materien gebahnet habe" (Vol. VII, Stück 25, p. 25).

lished a little volume, *Philologisches Tresespiel,* in which he recommended the rational reform of various word-forms.[352] Two years later, his friend, Michael Richey, Professor in Hamburg's Gymnasium, published a dictionary of words and expressions used in Hamburg and Nieder-Sachsen, entitled *Idioticon Hamburgense.*[353] From Richey's *Vorrede* it is clear that Mattheson's share in the compilation of this volume was considerable:

This perspicacious individual, who, for many years, made himself indispensible in Affairs of State, and who in musical art has acquired the name of a modern Aristoxenus, has likewise enlarged upon German linguistics on more than one occasion. Our friendship, which has endured since our youth . . . , would not permit him to view the work of his old friend with indifferent eyes, or without thinking of some kind of contribution. He sent me a quantity of words and phrases, and gave his generous permission for a selective inspection. . . .[354]

The tone of many of the reviews of his books during the last twenty years of his life indicates the eminence of Mattheson's position. In an age that was intensely absorbed in the problems of criticism, Mattheson's repute as a critic was very high. One of Hamburg's learned journals speaks of his untiring efforts in the dissemination of true musical learning,[355] another congratulates him on continuing to work for the art which had brought him success in his youth, instead of abandoning it, as so many others had done.[356] From further afield, no less a person than the Berlin mu-

352. Bibliography No. 172.
353. Bibliography No. 175.
354. *Idioticon Hamburgense,* Vorrede, pp. xxxviii–xxxix: "Dieser überall eindringende Geist, wie er sich vorlängst in Staats-Geschäfften nutzbar gemacht, und in der Ton-Kunst den Nahmen eines Aristoxeni unserer Zeiten erworben, also hat er sich auch bey mehr als einer Gelegenheit über die Teutsche Sprach-Kunde ausgebreitet. Unsere von Jugend auf gepflogene Freundschaft . . . erlaubten ihn nicht, die Arbeit seines Freundes mit glichgültigen Augen anzusehen, ohne auf einen möglichsten Beytrag zu dencken. Er schickte mir eine Menge Wörter und Redens-Arten zu, mit höflicher Erlaubniss einer beliebigen Ausmusterung. . . ."
355. *Hamburger Nachrichten aus dem Reich der Gelehrsamkeit* (1759), No. 30, p. 241: "Der unermüdete Hr. Legationsrath Mattheson, welcher noch itzo und immer, in seinem 78sten Jahr, auf das munterste fortfähret, seine Nebenstunden der wahren Musikalischen Gelehrsamkeit zu widmen. . . ."
356. *Staats- u. Gelehrte Zeitung des Hamburgischen Correspondenten,* 1749, Dec. 30: "Der Wohlgeborene Herr Verfasser scheinet gar nicht von der jenigen Art berühmter Männer zu seyn, welche die schönen Wissenschafften, dadurch sie ihr Glück in der Jugend gemacht haben, hernach mit Undank an den Nagel hängen, und solche gering, sich selbst aber viel zu vornehm dazu achten. . . ."

sical critic and composer, Friedrich Wilhelm Marpurg, dedicated his *Handbuch bey dem Generalbass* to the old man:

Pens more skillful than mine have recently vied with each other in singing the praises of your merits, and whoever thinks your name unworthy of admiration, has no true German heart beating in his breast. Even the remotest posterity will recognize how much it was to the glory of magnificent Hammonia [Hamburg] to have had living within her walls a man who combined the virtues of ten individuals: whose experience in the affairs of State was appreciated and rewarded by persons of the keenest judgment, at whose attainments the academies marvelled, and from whose thorough and admirable treatises the entire musical world drew the benefit of advantageous information for nearly half a century.[357]

When, however, the same writer, carried away by enthusiasm, spoke of the advisability of reprinting some of his works in 1761 without consulting the author, Mattheson took offense at the implied reference to the limitations of age, and issued a firmly worded announcement in the *Hamburger Nachrichten aus dem Reiche der Gelehrsamkeit,* in which he protested that he himself was perfectly competent to take care of any republication, should it prove necessary. He concluded with the following verse:

> Son coeur & son esprit, fort viogoureux (*sic*)
> Imiteront *Caleb* s'il plaît à Dieu!
> Il est encor, sans regarder la crise,
> Tout courageux, malgré, sa barbe grise![358]

357. "Geschicktere Federn als die meinige haben haben sich vorlängst um die Wette bemühet, *Deroselben* Verdienste zu besingen, und dem müsste in der That kein deutsches Herz in seinen Busen schlagen, dem IHR Nahme nicht verehrenswürdig seyn sollte. Noch bey der spätesten Nachwelt wird es der prächtigen Hammonia zum Vorzuge ihrer Zeit gereichen, in ihren Ringmauern einen Mann gehabt zu haben, der die Verdienste zehn einzelner Personen in der seinigen vereinigt, dessen Staatserfahrenheit die klugen Butter erkannt und belohnet, über dessen Gelehrsamkeit ganze Akademien erstaunen, und ausdessen gründlichen und vortreflichen Schriften die ganze musikalische Welt seit bey nahe einen halben Jahrhundert den vorteilhaftesten Unterricht ziehet. . . ."
358. *Hamburger Nachrichten aus dem Reiche der Gelehrsamkeit* (1761). No. 99, p. 768, Dec. 22. "Da Ihro wohlgeb. der Herr Legationsrath Mattheson mit Befremdung äusserlich vernommen, als ob man in Berlin bedacht sey, einige seiner Schriften, ohne dessen Beyfall und Geheiss, solchergestalt wieder aufzulegen, dass bloss diejenige Materie welche geradeswegs von der Musik handelt, hinein kommen, als übrige aber so eben nicht in jenen Kram dienlich herausgeworfen werden soll: So hat er hiemit wider ein solches eigenmächtiges ihm nachtheiliges Zergliedern und Zerstümmeln, als Verfasser, und auch von den meisten als Verleger sein unstreitiges Recht öffentlich behaupten, protestiren und erklären wollen, dass er es nimmermehr zugeben; . . . weil er selber ja Manns genug ist, zu einen neuen rechtmässigen Auflage das Seine beyzutagen, wenn sie für nöthig befunden werden sollte."

Despite the assurance of this self-portrait, one category of his writings—as yet unmentioned—reveals, in the twenty years preceding his death, a fundamental change in his psychological attitude. In 1728, he had spoken of his intention to record his ideas on what he called "musicam moralem."[359] He was, however, too absorbed by the prodigious number of his other activities to begin to do so until 1745, when the practical aspects of musical and moral philosophy apparently were no longer as interesting to him as the spiritual or theological ones. This change of emphasis in his interests may have been engendered by a conscious or unconscious realization of his own physical decline and the inexorable approach of old age. It is as significant as it is poignant to see that by the middle of the eighteenth century the condition of senescence so clearly visible in Mattheson's writings is likewise apparent in the life of his beloved Hamburg. Indeed, by the year 1750, many of the elements for which the city had been famous had completely disappeared or had sunk into desuetude. The Hamburg Opera, after a period of difficulty, had been discontinued in 1738, and the town had subsequently been supplied with its opera—be it said, entirely to its satisfaction—by visiting Italian companies. Furthermore, the disappearance of this famous old institution had, according to Mattheson, utterly failed to restore church music to its former preëminence, but had, indeed, caused its parallel decline, there being nothing left to attract and stimulate opera composers and musicians.[360] Another writer, Griesheim, complained that, although Telemann continued to add luster to the music of the town, the taste for music had totally vanished: people were, he said, more interested in educating their children to make money than to make or to appreciate music.[361] Literary activity came almost to a halt

359. Cf. text p. 86.
360. Mattheson, *Untersuchung der Singspiele* . . . , 1744 [Bibliography No. 146], p. 87: "Ohne solche wohlangelegte Pflanzgärten aber, als die Opern hier beschrieben werden, muss endlich die beste Musik, samt der ärgsten, ersterben und verderben, ja in den Kirchen selbst nicht länger eine bleibende Städte haben. Der Singbühne Verfall ziehet den Verfall des ganzen musikalischen Wesens nach sich: worunter Gottes Lob und Ehre denn auch leidet, welches viel wichtiger ist, als alles andre."
361. Griesheim, *Die Stadt Hamburg* . . . 1760, pp. 194–195: "Telemann ist zwar als ein grosser Capellmeister der kirchlichen Music in der Stadt, und auswärts berühmt; aber die Virtuosen in der Stadt, machen selten gross Glück; wenige Häuser wenden Geld darauf, ihrer Jugend die Music beybringen zu lassen. Sie glauben, dergleichen ziehe zu sehr von ernstlichen Geschäften ab mache mehr weltliche, als reiche Leute."

with the death of Hagedorn in 1754.[362] The decline of Hamburg's diplomatic importance was naturally deleterious to the social life of the city, which was further undermined by a serious decline in general prosperity and the frequency of highly unethical bankruptcies.[363]

In this atmosphere of change and decay, the venerable Mattheson lived on, regarded, apparently to his great annoyance,[364] as a marvel of longevity. It is not surprising, however, that his thoughts should have turned more frequently to spiritual and religious problems. By 1728 he had made a thorough study of the Psalms to justify his belief in the importance of church music,[365] and had already formed the habit of reading a chapter of the Bible and one Psalm every evening.[366] This he continued to do so faithfully that in 1748 he writes of beginning his thirteenth complete perusal of the Bible; as he continued to read, so he continued "to study it, and to make remarks of an edifying character upon it." [367]

In the year 1747, Mattheson published the first of his works which reflect his concern with spiritual matters. It was entitled *Inimici Mortis, verdächtiger Todes-Freund,* and was a simple statement of the Christian faith—a faith which, he asserted, "unlike that of the Aristotelians, Stoics, Deists, and modern philosophers," provided the only proper understanding of the experience of death.[368] His second book on this subject, while of an equally medi-

362. Reinke, *op. cit.*, p. 157.

363. Griesheim, *op. cit.*, p. 92: "Mancher macht einen betrügerischen Banquerot; er cedirt bonis, geht weg, kommt wieder, verstecket sich unter die Schürze der Frau, und bauet aus denen Trümmern seiner vorigen Handlung. . . ."

364. *Phthongologie Systematica, Vor-Erinnerung,* p. 3: "Jüngsthin aber schrieb mir ein grundredlicher Mann und braver Künstler folgende Worte: 'Gott sey gelobet, dass sie noch leben, sich gesund, auch sonst in guten Umständen befinden! . . . Seht! so gerne will man mir zu Leibe, und einen Pass schreiben. Wenn wird er sterben, heisst es, und sein Name vergehen?"

365. *Der Musicalische Patriot,* pp. 249–304, contains an exposition and analysis of references to music in the Psalms.

366. *Ehrenpforte,* p. 212: "Wie nun Matthesons Gewohnheit war, und noch ist, alle Abend ein Capitel aus der Bibel u. einen Psalm zu lesen. . . ."

367. *Ehrenpforte,* Anhang, p. 26: "Um dieselbe Zeit fing Mattheson an, die Bibel zum Dreyzehntmal durchzulesen, zu untersuchen, und Anmerkungen mit Erbaulichkeit darüber zu machen: denn ob er gleich von Jugend auf ein fleissiger Schüler und Betrachter des göttlichen Wortes gewesen, hat solchen seinen christlichen Eifer dennoch in den letzten Jahren mit mehrer Ordnung beständig getrieben. . . ."

368. Bibliography, No. 158.

tative character, was, however, primarily concerned with music, and was entitled *Behauptung der Himmlischen Musik aus den Gründen der Vernunft, Kirchen-Lehre und heiligen Schrift.*[369] In it Mattheson mingled a most literal interpretation of Biblical texts with a sort of rational mysticism, and proved that music was the occupation of the angels in Heaven, exactly as it ought to be for all the worshipers of God on earth. The contents of this volume were summarized in the *Hamburgische Berichte von den Neuesten Gelehrten Sachen,* and some doubt was cast upon the "reasonableness" of Mattheson's assertions.[370] This dissident opinion was sufficient to precipitate a lively controversy in this magazine,[371] and in letters to the author; the favorable ones, he published in his *Phthongologia Systematica.*

His constant study of the Bible evoked from Mattheson another expression of the importance of music in the Christian religion. In 1745 he published *Das Erläuterte Selah,*[372] in which he undertook to explain the meaning of the word *Selah:* he had found that of the eighty-three times it was used in the Psalms, all but nine had given it a definite musical connotation. From this arithmetic he deducted that *Selah* means "musical *Ritornell,"* that the writers of the Psalms are thus constantly referring to music, and that this is a virtually unanswerable argument for the use of music in the worship of God. He followed this same method of criticism in the two volumes entitled *Die neuangelegte Freuden-Akademie,* published

369. Bibliography, No. 157.
370. *Hamburgische Berichte* . . . , 1747, pp. 237–238: "Er glaubet, dass die Engel mit einem subtilen Leibe begabet seyn, und, nebst den Auserwehlten, ein grosses Concert den Vocal- und Instrumentalmusik im Himmel aufführen. . . . [Er] behauptet . . . dass also die Posaunen und Harfen der Engel wirkliche klingende Werkzeuge seyn müssten, ob wir gleich ihre eigentliche Beschaffenheit nicht bestimmen könten. Unsere Philosophen werden diese Abschnitte für keinen aus der Vernunft geführten Beweiss obigen Satzes halten."
371. *Idem,* pp. 502–504, 657–661, 664–667. The most enthusiastic approval of Mattheson's theory was L. F. Hudemann, who wrote a seventy-line poem in praise of the book (pp. 502–504, the first few lines of which read:
"Entzückt seh ich dir nach, da dich der Höhe Flug,
Gepriesner Mattheson, im edlen Geisteszug
Durch alle Himmel reist, in den volkommen Chören.
O süsse Frucht, der Müh! ein hohgethön zu hören,
Das dort weit herlicher, als hier, dem Herrn erklingt,
Wo unser Jubel noch mit tausend Mängeln ringt."
372. Bibliography No. 148.

102        *Johann Mattheson*

in 1751 and 1753,[373] in which he quotes certain verses from the Psalms and various other books of the Bible, which are concerned with the joyous adoration of the Heavenly Father. In remarks on each, he seeks to show that they represent the authorization for the presence of festal music in the life and religious thoughts of mankind. Indeed all his publications between 1745 and 1752 were concerned primarily with explaining and proving the spiritual significance and necessity of music; these concerns were, at the time, aptly termed the "investigation of a true musical theology"; about him it was written that "one might believe that the good man had nothing else to do than to incite the writing of laudatory divine services that were as consoling as they were passionate."[374]

Mattheson published no more works of this kind after 1753. On the eighth of February in that year his wife died, after an illness of three days.[375] Her funeral took place five days later, and she was interred in the burial lot Mattheson had purchased in the Marie Magdalenen Kloster.[376] In July of that year, he published in the *Hamburgische Berichte von den Neuesten Gelehrten Sachen,* along with a formal announcement of his bereavement, some verses written "in the very hour of her death"—a moving tribute to the mysterious and shadowy figure of his wife:

373. Bibliography Nos. 171 and 173.

374. *Gelehrte Neuigkeiten* (Hamburg, 1751), p. 70: "[*Die Freuden-Akademie*] enthält die löblichen Proben einer wahren musikalischen Theologie, einer ausnehmenden Doxologie, und einer gesunden Auslegungskunst . . . das den Vorschmack unbeschreiblicher Herrlichkeiten in jener Welt auf das Fröhlichste zu erkennen gibt, und denselben ungewöhnlicher massen erleuchtet. Kurz, das Werk hat, wie er selbst und sein übriges Bestreben, gar was eigenes und besonders an sich, und man solte glauben, der gute Mann hätte nichts anders zu thun, als die Schriften zum lobsingenden Gottesdienste, so tröstlich, als eifrig anzutreiben."

375. *Ehrenpforte,* Anhang, p. 30: "Ao. 1753. D. 8. Febr. früh um 7. Uhr, starb ihm seine unschätzbare Frau ab, an einer Engbrüstigkeit, nach einem dreytägigen Lager, etwa 75. Jahr alt."

376. *Der Marstall Rechnungs Buch Dec. 1750–Dec. 1755* (Hamburger Staats-Archiv). "Rödiger Mkt.

d. 13 Febr. / Matthison fr. / M. Magd. / Ja 4 Ferde
                    **Mk. 22. 18.**"
*Einnahm An Erd / Und Klocken Geld / Angefangen / Anno / 1734*
*Heiligen Geist und Maria Magdalenen Kloster* (Staats-Archiv):
"Febr. 14, No. 257, H. Legations Rath Mattheson seine Frau ins Grab. 7. Th."

Die wahre Krone theurer Frauen,
Die Got mich lies aus England schauen
   Schon über drei und vierzig Jahr;
Aufrichtig, redlich von Gemüthe,
Aus tapfrem brittischen Geblüte
   Liegt jetzt auf ihrer Todtenbahr.

Wer das Geschlecht von Jennings kennet,
Hat den berühmten Stam genennet;
   Doch ihre Tugend lange nicht;
Sie liebte mich von ganzen Herzen,
Ihr Abschied war auch ohne Schmerzen;
   Woran es mir doch nicht gebricht;

Sie lebt nach ihrem sanften Scheiden
In allerhöchsten Himmelsfreuden!
   Was ist es denn doch was mich kränkt?
In meinen muntern alten Tagen
Will ich noch frisch und frölich sagen:
   Mein Gott! du hast es wol gelenkt.

Sie kam aus England her zu mir.
Ich kom ins Engelland zu ihr.[377]

Soon after he became a widower, Mattheson was forced to re-
consider the disposal of his property, which, in his first will, had
been left to his wife.[378] Despite fairly serious losses arising from
the bankruptcies of various debtors—losses totaling 9,000 florins
and more between 1751 and 1750 [379]—Mattheson's wealth was con-

377. 1753, No. 58, 27 Juli, p. 462: "Der Herr Legations-Rath Mattheson [wollte an-
kündigen] dass er vor einigen Monaten, nemlich den 8. Febr. dieses Jahrs, sein geliebtes
Ehgemahl, eine gebohrne Engeländerin, mit welcher er in die vier und vierzig Jahre in
einem höchst vergnügten Ehestande gelebet hat durch den Tod verlohren hat. Zum ver-
dienten Andencken derselben wollen wir hier diejenigen poetischen Zeilen beifügen, welche
dem Hr. Mattheson in ebn der Stunde, da er von ihm Abschied genommen aus der Feder
geflossen sind."
378. Appendix, p. 221. "Er hatte Ao. 1729, d. 3. März, nehmlich vor 30 Jahren schon
ein Testamentum reciprocum mit seiner geliebten Ehegattin errichtet . . ."
379. Mattheson's references read as follows:
*Ehrenpforte,* Anhang, p. 29: "D. 20. Septr. [1751] erlitt M. eine beträchtlichere *banqueroute* als jemals, von 2800 fl. . . ."
P. 30: "D. 22. März [1752] kam ein schrifl. Vergleich mit den boldtischen Brüdern u.
matthesonischen Schuldnern zum Stande. Schlecht genug! noch schlechter gehalten. Doch

siderable, and so, two months after his bereavement, he wrote to
his lawyer concerning the feasibility of endowing a professorship
of music in the Hamburger Gymnasium:

À Monsieur,
> Monsieur Seitz
>> Docteur en Droit
>>> à
>>> Hambourg

Monsieur,
Comme je songe tout de bon à faire mon Testament, j'ose vous vous [*sic*]
prier, de vouloir bien vous informer auprès de vôtre digne ami, Monsieur le
Professeur Reimarus, "1) S'il approuve mon dessein, de léguer un certain
fonds, dont les interests pourroient servir à l'entretien d'un docte Professeur
de Musique, tant prattique que théorique? 2) Et si les vénérables Directeurs
du grand College public de cette Ville accepteroient et se chargéroient volon-
tiers, *à son avis,* de cet établissement nouveau, lorsque le cas existeroit?"
Vous, Monsieur, qui connoiseez toute la sincerité de ma façon de penser,
aurés la bonté d'appuyer ma proposition de vos meilleures raisons, et de me
croire au de là des expressions vulgaires
> Monsieur
>> Vôtre trés humble
>> et très obeissant
>> Serviteur

De chez moi,                                          Mattheson
le 26. d'Avril
1753.[380]

_____

endl. *accordirte* durch treuherzigen Vorschub des H. *Arch.* itzigen Syndici *Schuback* L.
eines ganzen Mannes."
  P. 31 [1775]: "*D. Zielinsky* stellte sich fleissig ein, u. hatte schon seit d. 19. *Dec. a. praet.*
die Boldtische Sache *proprio moto* übernommen, worin jedoch bisher nichts sonderliches
ausgerichtet worden. . . . der Verleger [des *Plus Ultra*] war nicht im Stande dem Drucker
zu *contentiren,* vielweniger dem Verfasser sein Anlehn vom Jahr 1750. ad. 1751. zu 3700
fl. wiederzugeben. . . ." (Note in the margin) "Im folgenden 1757sten Jahre machte dieser
Verleger, Martini banqueroute u. brachte Matteson um reine 1000 fl."
  P. 33 [1757]: "Ein abermalige Insolventz von 3700 fl., die der Buchhändler *Martini* ihm
machte, wurde mit Gedult ertragen."
  "*Weitere Fortsetzung des Matthesonischen Lebenslaufes,*" Appendix, p. 220 [1759]:
"Ubrigens war er mit Prozessen gegen seine bösen Schuldner wider seine Neigung noch
so stark geplaget, als die langsame Art des Gerichts . . . welches dem Recht zum Possen
nur gar zu oft geschlossen, immermehr leiden wollte, nachdem er fast 10,000 Mark durch
Verstorbner und Verdorbner Debitures eingebüsst . . . hatte."
  380. The manuscript of this letter is in the possession of Professor Heinrich Sieveking of
Hamburg, who has been good enough to permit me to make a copy of it.

Although a report of this project appeared in the *Hamburgische Berichte von den Neuesten Gelehrten Sachen* in July, 1753,[381] Mattheson had changed his mind a month or so earlier, and had decided to dispose of his money in another way. Three years previously, in 1750, the St. Michaelis Kirche in Hamburg had been struck by lightning and burned to the ground.[382] Soon after, the parish, which was the newest and wealthiest in Hamburg, determined to build its church anew. When completed, twelve years later, it was the largest and most magnificent in the entire city.[383] In shape it was a Celtic cross, and the style was an unusual combination of the grand, even severe, characteristics of northern baroque and the decorative detail of flamboyant rococo. In June, 1753, Mattheson made his second will, which left a sum necessary for the construction of a proper organ in this church (should he die before it was finished). The church in return agreed to provide for him and his late wife, a *"gemauertes Grab ad perpetuos dies,"* an "Epitaphium," and funeral-music.[384]

According to his records, Mattheson's chief concerns in the last ten years of his life were the ordering of his material affairs and the progress of the St. Michaelis organ.[385] It was to be built by Zacha-

381. *Hamburgische Berichte* . . . 1753, No. 58, 27 Juli, p. 462: ". . . Annitzo können wir die aus dessen eigenem Munde vernommene nähere Nachrichten ertheilen, dass er nicht nur bei diesem seinm lobenswürdigen Entschluss verharre, sondern auch wirklich damit umgehe, die Sache in Richtigkeit zu bringen. Solte dieses Werk, wie man hoffet und wünschet, zum Stande kommen, so würde es in der That eine der wichtigsten Umstände in der Lebensbeschreibung dieses berühmten Mannes abgeben."

382. *Ehrenpforte*, Anhang, p. 27: "1750. d. 10. März gerieth die grosse *Michael*-Kirche durch einen Donnerschlag in Brand, der sie grössesten Theils jä[m]erlich in die Asche legte; welches damals ein allgemeines Unglück war, darüber sich jedoch M. nach dreyen Jaren insbesonders mit dem Nachdruck erbarmte, wie weiter unten erhellen wird."

383. The present St. Michaelis Kirche in Hamburg is a modern replica of the eighteenth-century structure, which was destroyed by fire in 1906.

384. Since this will of Mattheson's has disappeared, one is forced to rely on subsequent events for this information, and on Mattheson's notes, which do not contain all the details, but read as follows: *Ehrenpforte*, Anhang, p. 30: "D. 23. Jun. [1753] machte er sein zwetes Testament in aller Form, legirte der neuen grossen Michaelis Kirche 40 fl. zur Orgel; dafür ihm die Kirche ein eigens gemauertes Grab *ad perpetuos dies*, samt seiner verstorbenen Eheliebsten, ein *Epitaphium*, laut Beylage *A.* u. eine Trauer-Musik versprach, mittelst ordentlichen schriflichen Vergleichs da er auch alle Bücher, deren Verfasser er ist, dem *NN.*—gewidmet hat, so gehört gegenwärtige Ehrenpforte mit dahin, und die Beylage *B.* bezeuget, mit welcher Gesinnung der *presidirende* Her Bürgermeister *Widow* dieses Werk aufgenommen hat. Wohl werth zum Andenken aufgehoben zu werden. *C.* enthält einen würdigen Traum."

385. Cf. Appendix, Mattheson makes one more reference in 1760 to his first and second

rias Hildebrandt, a pupil of Silbermann, and a famous organ-builder,[386] but following his death in 1757, his son was entrusted with the carrying out of the designs. Mattheson originally provided the princely sum of 40,000 Hamburg marks for the instrument, and gradually added 4,000 more with which to complete it.[387] Placed behind a colossal organ case, surmounted by a portrait of the donor, this extraordinary organ occupied the entire western end of the church. By far the most prominent feature in the building, it was an impressive tribute to Mattheson as well as to his beloved church music.[388] In 1762, the long-awaited consecration of the St. Michaelis Kirche took place. The old man was overjoyed to be able to attend the festivities, which he described as including a procession of the dignitaries of the town, music in the tower by trumpets and drums, a splendid oratorio before and after the sermon, and the ringing of the bells of the five *Hauptkirchen* for a full hour. Five thousand persons crowded into the church, and the collection was 5,470 florins.[389]

---

will, and his original gift to the St. Michaelis Kirche, which somewhat clarifies the existing information. Appendix, p. 221 "Er hatte Ao. 1729, d. 3. März, nehmlich vor 30 Jahren schon ein Testamentum reciprocum mit seiner geliebten Ehegattin errichtet, und als ihn aber dieselbe 1753, nach einer 44 jährigen unvergleichlich schönen Beywohnung, durch ihren tödtlichen Abschied zum ersten und letztenmal herzlich betrübte, macht er alsofort sein zweytes Testament in aller Form am Johannis Vorabend desselben Jahres und legierte darin wie bereits oben genant der abgebranten St. Michaelis Kirche, zu einem Orgelwerke, 40,000 fl. Hamb. cur., trug auch solche ganze Summe, nach und nach, bar und zum Voraus ab, indem er die letzten Posten davon am 7. Juni 1760. dem Hochansehnl. grossen Kirchencollegio einlieferte, auch darüber dessen Quitung gehörigermassen erhielt."

386. Jakob Adlung, *Musica Mechanica organoedi,* (two volumes, Berlin, 1768), I, 241.

387. Appendix, p. 221 (footnote): "Auf den 12. Juli desselben Jahres noch 3000 fl. und alda den 4. Febr. 1762 aberm. 1000 als Zugabe aus Konto damit 44000 fl. daraus würden."

388. A description of this enormous instrument is to be found in Adlung's *Musica Mechanica Organoedi,* I, 241. It contained sixty-four speaking stops, divided between three manuals and the pedal, and according to Emile Rupp's *Die Entwicklungsgeschichte der Orgelbaukunst,* 1929, p. 77, was a "Triumph der neueren Orgelbaukunst."

389. Appendix, pp. 224-225: "D. 19. Oct. [1762] erlebte M. in seinem 82sten Jahr die sonderbare Freude, dass an solchem Tag die feyerliche Einrichtung der Michaeliskirche vor sich ging und sowohl der ganze Rath als das Ministerium, die Obwalter, die Sechziger und Hunderachtziger sich in corpore Prozessionsweise in selbige verfügten, wobey Trompeten und Pauken vom Thurm erschallten ein vortreffliches Oratorium vor und nach der Predigt aufgeführet, sodann nach Auftrags auf beyden Glockenspielen zu St. Peter und Nikolai vom 3. bis 4. Uhr, und die ganze Feyerlichkeit mit Pauken und Trompeten von allen Thürmen der 5 Hauptkirchen zwischen 4 und 5 Uhr geendigt wurden. Glaubwürdigen Bericht nach, sind hierbey 5000 Personen in der Kirche und auch 5470 fl. in die angesetzten Becken gewesen. . . ."

Although Mattheson continued to write various short articles for learned journals, and even translated Mainwaring's life of Händel in 1761, he spent most of his time in reading the Bible, and in seeking "the true understanding of the Lord's words, morning and evening, to his special peace and pleasure." [390] The year before his death he presented all his books and manuscripts, totaling one hundred and twenty-eight volumes and *Convolute*, to the Hamburger Stadtbibliothek. [391]

Thus were spent the last few years of his life, and on April 17, 1764, in his eighty-third year the valiant old gentleman, "der wohlgebohrne Herr Legationsrath," died. [392] He was buried according to his wishes in the St. Michaelis Kirche five days later. [393] His epitaph, recently discovered in the church, bears the inscription:

Ruhe Kammer
für Herr
Johann Mattheson
weyland
Grosfürstlicher
Holsteinischer
Legations Raht
und dessen
Ehe Genossin
Zu ewigen Tagen. [394]

On April 25, a special service was held in the church in his honor, as a leading citizen of Hamburg. For two-and-a-half hours the bells of all the chief churches were tolled; the highest dignitaries of the town were invited to attend; and the town Cantor, Telemann, who had been born in the same year as Mattheson, conducted *Das fröliche Sterbelied, womit der numehro wolseelige Legations-Rath,*

390. *Idem*, p. 220: "Seine meiste Zeit wandte er hingegen auf das Bibellesen, und untersuchte, zu seiner besonderen Ruhe und Vergnügen den rechten Verstand des göttl. Wortes, Morgens und Abends. . . ."

391. C. Petersen, *Geschichte der Hamburgischen Stadtbibliothek* (Hamburg, 1838), p. 82.

392. *Staats und Gelehrte Zeitung des Hamburgischen unpartheyischen Correspondenten* (27 April, 1764), No. 67.

393. *Kirche St. Michaelis, Grab Buch* (Hamburger Staats-Archiv): "Ao. 1764 d. 23. April. ist H. Legations Rath Mattheson aus ein Kirchen Grab heraus genommen und hier eingesetzt, No. 62., irregularis Grab Suder Seite, zu ewigen Sorgen."

394. Heinrich Miesner, *Philipp Emanuel Bach in Hamburg,* "Beiträge zu seiner Biographie und zur Musikgeschichte seiner Zeit," Diss. (Berlin, 1929), p. 49, note 1, and p. 128. Miesner discovered this epitaph in 1925, together with that of C. Ph. E. Bach.

*Herr Johann Mattheson ihm selbst harmonisch und poetisch . . .
zu Grabe gesungen,*[395] which Mattheson had written four years
earlier for this occasion.[396] One of the many obituary notices that
appeared in the learned journals of Hamburg[397] remarked that
although Mattheson had earned many a distinction in his life, he
had gained yet another in his death—that of being the only person
"who had thus sung himself into his grave."[398]

395. J. Faulwasser, *De St. Michaelis Kirche in Hamburg*, pp. 107–108.
396. Bibliography No. 189.
397. *Nachrichten aus dem Reiche der Gelehrsamkeit* (Hamburg, 1 May, 1764), No. 34,
p. 268; *Staats und Gelehrte Zeitung des Hamburgischen unpartheyischen Correspondenten*
(April 1764), No. 67.
398. *Ibid.*, (*Hamb. Corresp.*): "Wir wissen, ausserdenen von des seiner grossen Verdienste wegen, unsterblichen ersten Bürgermeisters dieser Republik, An. Sillen, zur Trauer-
Musik hinterlassenen rührenden Worten, seit dem kein Beispiel, dass sich jemand selber
auf diese Art, zu Grabe gesungen habe."

*View of Hamburg in the Eighteenth Century*

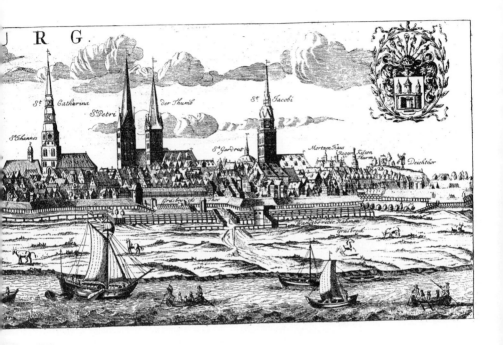

J R G.

St. Catharina     der Thumb     St. Jacobi

St. Petri

St. Johannes

St. Gardrut         Mortzen Haus       Kilzen
                        Rosen   Thurm
                                    Deichtror

Grasbrocks Thor

Plar der Rahm
Grasbrock

# III

## *The Enlightenment of the Musical Spectator*

THE greatest part of Johann Mattheson's active and prosperous life was passed within the limits of Lutheran Hamburg. In his security as diplomatic secretary, he could participate directly in the intellectual life of the city, and win local prominence in both music and letters. There is no indication that his reputation as a musician passed far beyond the borders of his own community, but it is clear that, as a writer on musical subjects, he was known throughout Germany. Although what he said often applied simply to local conditions, the critical ideas he expressed in his books nevertheless involved in most instances general issues common to the musical civilization of all early eighteenth-century Germany. Indeed, through most of his multifarious and disparate literary output it is possible to discern a single attitude of mind and to measure its importance in the development of music. He was a consistent champion of the "new" ideas, and in his chief critical works he attempted, by means of rational exposition and justification, to reconcile these with the "old." Since music was still an integral part of the conscious fabric of civilization, it was inevitable that the fundamental principles governing its form should be closely linked with the general currents of eighteenth-century culture—a culture which saw, particularly in the first half of the century, countless new and vital ideas meeting with established older ones to form the confusion discernible even in the critical standards of Mattheson and his contemporaries. But this conflict of ideas which was responsible for the criticism of a Mattheson did not arise suddenly or locally: to understand his writings, the background of European thought which contributed to the musical culture of his day must be carefully scrutinized.

Seventeenth-century Germany was composed of a mass of small states differing from each other in religious beliefs and political systems in which geographical proximity seemed to play a very small part. The states of the North were divided into four cities under Lutheran régimes, and into small kingdoms under Lutheran, Calvinist, and even Catholic princes, all of them showing completely heterogeneous political, social, and intellectual conditions. The states of the South, however, with the exception of such Protestant strongholds as Nürnberg and Ulm, were almost entirely Catholic kingdoms, whose close associations with Italy accounted for still further diversity of cultural influences. In general, however, it may be said that Lutheranism and Catholicism provided the most definite distinctions between northern and southern Germany. Reconstructed largely by the efforts of the Jesuits, the religious faith of the South bore a resemblance to that of the North in its marked emotionalism. But unlike that of Lutheranism, it seems to have found its chief expression in architecture and painting rather than in music, which had more the character of an essential accompaniment, a background, to the florid splendor of its sister arts. In the North, despite the theological controversies over the exact interpretation and definition of dogma,[1] the political philosophy and spiritual beliefs of Martin Luther were the basis for parallel religious and governmental organization, except where Calvinism flourished. As has been explained above, Hamburg in the seventeenth century may be taken as a typical example of a Lutheran community, particularly with respect to its musical life.

Outside the borders of the German Empire this same century witnessed the growth of a very different cultural and intellectual system. In France and in England no conflict equal in intensity to the Thirty Years' War interrupted the increasing importance and development of secular and individualistic forms in art and literature initiated by the Renaissance. In England, the reaction against the short-lived Puritan Revolution manifested itself strongly in the literature and theater of the Restoration. The disappearance of emotional inspiration in the face of rational theology and philosophy is also reflected by the poetry of this period and by the

1. These discussions of Lutheran dogma, in which the status of music seems not to have figured, are recounted in Otto Ritschl's *Dogmengeschichte des Protestantismus Grundlagen und Grundzüge der theologischen Gedanken- und Lehrbildung in den protestantischen Kirchen*, 4 vols. (Leipzig, 1908, 1912; Göttingen, 1926, 1927).

decline in the composition of native English music. In France, not-withstanding the existence of a strain of mysticism, represented in the Jansenist movement and the writings of Pascal, a thoroughly wordly culture, which reached a resplendent climax in the reign of Louis XIV, dominated the entire scene. The literature of the French classic drama, the philosophy of Descartes, and the archi-tecture of Versailles were all expressions of a materialistic rational-ism with which the predominantly religious thought of the seventeenth-century Germany had no relationship whatsoever. Louis XIV maintained a sumptuous musical establishment, which was designed partly to provide the necessary music for religious observances, but whose most important function under the great Lully was the presentation of concerts and theatrical spectacles. Although not a regular part of the Court establishment at Versailles, by far the most representative and flourishing musical form in France was the opera. Opera requires the manifestation of emotion, and awareness of this fact rapidly increased the potentialities of the newer forms of musical expression and—in accordance with the stylistic novelties through which the Italians made their operatic music the idiom of Europe—caused a revaluation and reinterpreta-tion of the older forms. The development of an instrumental mu-sic, depending for its existence on its own artistic merits, also enlarged the tonal medium. Because of the concerted use of dif-ferent instruments, the need for the standardization of pitch and tonal relations acted as a stimulus for scientific investigations of sound. All these developments resulted in a taste, a medium, and a purpose in French music with which the Lutheran music of Ger-many, still under ecclesiastical domination, had virtually nothing in common.

In Germany, throughout the reign of Louis XIV, French man-ners and thought progressively gained in importance. France was the most powerful and unified nation on the continent and, as re-gards Germany, her foreign policy was nothing more nor less than keeping alive the alarming political and religious anarchy which obtained within that country after the Thirty Years' War, in order to prevent interference with her own immediate aims else-where. The instruments of this policy were large subsidies presented to the various German princes, who, in this way, came to be more and more the political and, at the same time, cultural vassals of their western neighbor.

In the realm of music, the most general importation to have flourished at the petty courts of Germany consisted, obviously, of the forms of concert and of opera popular at Versailles. Its glorification of wordly splendor, though not unsuitable to the naturally theatrical tendencies latent in the culture of southern Germany, was basically opposed to the reverent and spiritual contemplation characteristic of Lutheran church music. Nevertheless, in its frank worldliness, it became increasingly popular with musicians, with princes, and with the rising middle class in the larger commercial centers. Because of the mutual identity of religious and secular musical organizations at many of the German courts, the modernization of ecclesiastical music was never brought to a satisfactory solution. The traditional institution of musical training, the Kantorei, which was linked up with the older form of church music, and the worldly, modern style, for which no musical schools existed, became more and more alienated. This contradictory situation is strikingly noticeable in Hamburg, where, as has been seen, the strongly intrenched musical organization of the seventeenth century did not yield to the opera and to theatrical church music without a struggle. In fact, there, as well as in Germany on the whole, the transition from the traditional choral institution to the modern orchestral organizations was rather abrupt; it had, at any rate, no intermediary phase in which opera expressed any real significance. For even in Hamburg, the opera enjoyed only temporary greatness and duration, and failed to establish any proper institution of operatic training either in singing or in composition.

The simultaneous existence of such opposite systems of thought was responsible for a most chaotic state of musical theory and knowledge, and, as might be supposed, the entire period from 1650 to 1750 is characterized by an enormous amount of critical and controversial writing upon all musical matters. The opinions upon these matters reflected, in general, the local experiences and beliefs of each individual writer. A balanced synthesis of ideas as divergent as these produced the music of Bach and the philosophy of Leibniz, both of which, however, were extraordinary exceptions, incomprehensible to their contemporaries—certainly at least, insofar as Bach was concerned. The slow rise of the newer "rationalistic" ideas in all realms of thought, known, in German intellectual history, as the "Aufklärung," gradually brought a new order out of this chaos. In music, as elsewhere, the generation of thinkers who are generally associated with this movement, equipped with the tools of rational analysis, attempted to overcome the "ignorance" which, they maintained, resulted from belief in the old system of theory and practice. The magnitude of such a task as a rational ordering of human knowledge demanded among many other things, not one but several encyclopedic codifications of facts and ideas and numerous "universal" treatises upon all subjects.

The majority of Mattheson's books were conceived with this end in view. They were written and published during a period of forty years which extended from the last phase of the Baroque epoch well into the period of the Enlightenment. They were the product of a cultural experience as greatly varied as that which might have been Mattheson's had he traveled more, for Hamburg contained within itself all those differing elements of civilization afforded by each one of the other cities of northern Germany.

Now, it is not only the very considerable dimensions of his voluminous treatises and the universality of his thinking which makes impossible any short summary of his whole work as musical critic, moralist, and philosopher, but the complex evolution of his thought. As volume followed volume—each, though not covering the same ground as the preceding ones, being in a way a supplement to the one before—his ideas and opinions changed and developed.[2] In large measure, it is true, this development went hand in hand with his constant wish to make accessible to his countrymen the work that was being done in France, England, and Italy, and consequently, with his attentive study of material that came in to him from foreign sources. It is, in any event, fortunate that in the first of all his books, possibly because it is intended as an introductory

2. Hugo Goldschmidt, *Die Musikästhetik des 18. Jahrhunderts* (Zurich and Leipzig, 1915), pp. 58–59. Goldschmidt suggested that Mattheson had gone through something of a retrogressive development; he assumes young Mattheson to have held æsthetic views that were close to those of our own time, but that as the years went by he put his faith more and more exclusively in eighteenth-century rationalism. This view is hardly justified, since he takes as the basis of his discussion the aspects of recent æsthetics.

treatise on the Art of Music, one can find the simpler outlines of his musical thought and the germs of the majority of the ideas he elaborated in greater detail in later works. Because of its tenor and its contents it also evoked, in the years after its publication, a more than usually comprehensive expression of opinion from other German musicians, which affords an indication of the contemporary significance of Mattheson's theories.

The title of this book, published in 1713, reads in part:

"Das Neu-Eröffnete *Orchestre,* Oder *Universelle* und grundliche Anleitung, Wie ein *Galant Homme* einen vollkommen Begriff von der Hoheit und Würde der edlen *MUSIC* erlangen, seinen *Gout* darnach *formiren* die *Terminos technicos* verstehen und geschicklich von dieser vortrefflichen Wissenschafft *raisonniren* möge . . . "[3]

The phraseology of this title contains a number of elements which become significant when one examines the author's own explanation of them. The inclusion of the somewhat frivolous French terms imply not only a fashionable conventionality, but even more a deliberate reaction from the learned, ponderously latinized style of important contemporary treatises. The word "Orchestre" was chosen because of the need of a term general enough to include dramatic, vocal, and instrumental music. To clarify this, Mattheson describes the position of the orchestra in a theater. Here are placed the symphonists, who provided the "force" and the "tutti" of the music, and here the leader of the entire musical company, upon whom all eyes are centered, takes his stand.[4] The use of this word and the explanation of it would not hitherto have been counte-

---

3. Bibliography No. 27.
4. *Das Neu-Eröffnete Orchestre,* p. 34: "Da denn, was den Titul des neu-eröffneten *Orchestres* betrifft, zu wünschen hätte sein können, dass ein *generalers* Wort, welches beides Kirchen- und *Theatral-* so wol *Vocal-* als *Instrumental-Music* begreiffen möchte, sich hätte wollen finden lassen; Allein so habe ich Abgang dessen, das *Orchestre* oder *Orqvestre* als eine noch nicht sehr gemeine und dabey *galante Expression* lieber setzen wollen. . . . Nachdem aber in den neuern Zeiten das *parterre* nicht mehr wir vor Alters der vornehmste Platz geblieben . . . so hat man den Ort, harte vors Theatre, wo die Herren *Symphonisten* ihre Stelle haben, mit dem Nahmen *Orchestre* oder Herren-Sitz beehren wollen, vermuthlich aus folgenden Ursachen, erstlich, weil die *force* und das *tutti* am meisten in der *Symphonie* oder *Instrumental-Music* stecket, zum andern und vornehmlich, weil daselbst das Haupt des gantzen Wesens *scilicet,* der Capelmeister . . . seinen bestandigen und gar *honorablen* Platz einnimmt, als auf dessen *mouvement* und Zeichen alle Augen gerichtet, und von dem so woll Sänger als *Symphonisten* gleichsam ihre *ordre* hohlen."

nanced because instrumental and dramatic music had not been recognized as part of the customary calling of the average musician. In fact the theoretical precepts of church music were alone thought worthy of serious discussion. Hence "Orchestre," with its suggestions of the opera, as the cognomen for a "universelle" introduction to music, implies 'a critical realism new to musical books at that time.[5]

The title further states that the contents of the book are intended for the "Galant Homme," which suggests that Mattheson was addressing only the fashionable society of a city such as Hamburg, where, during this period, "galant" was applied to everything that was *à la mode*.[6] In his *Vernünfftler,* published in the same year,[7] he recommended his *Orchestre* as a volume proper for the library of a lady of fashion. If this recommendation was all he meant by the word "galant," it might be taken for recognition of the growth of musical interest among the wealthy burghers of Hamburg and elsewhere. It is true that private and public presentations of concerts and serenatas were becoming more and more frequent [8] and interested listeners more numerous; indeed, from the record of Mattheson's life, it is apparent that lawyers and merchants regarded even active participation in music as a worthy accomplishment.[9] But, although this interest and activity among nonprofessional musicians may have influenced the writing of this treatise for the "galant homme," they do not account alone for the writing of a "popular" book; it is clear from his other use of the term that it had, rather, a broader connotation for him. In two instances he defines "galanterie" as a third element, along with melody and harmony, which is necessary in good musical composition, and which is acquired by "einen guten *Gout* und gesunden *Judicium.*" [10] Indeed, "galanterie" is so closely associated with the new

5. L. Meinardus, "Johann Mattheson und seine Verdienste um die deutsche Tonkunst," der Walderseeschen *Vortrage,* No. 8 (1879), pp. 244–245.

6. E. Finder, *Hamburgisches Bürgertum,* p. 76.

7. [Bibl. No. 29] No. 52, which is a translation of the *Spectator,* No. 39.

8. E. Preussner, *Die Bürgerliche Musikkultur,* pp. 15–16.

9. Cf. p. 45, n. 120, p. 155.

10. *Das Neu-Eröffnete Orchestre,* pp. 137–138: ". . . möchte noch überhaupt angemerckt werden, dass, da man sonst zu einer bereits verfertigten *Composition* nur die zwey Stücke, nemlich: *Melodicam & Harmoniam* erfordert, man bey jetzigen Zeiten sehr

musical style from France and Italy, that the "galant homme" must here be understood as the composer, or musician, who approves of this newer art, and who by reading this book may learn how to practice it. The term thus connotes all that is new, revolutionary, and foreign, all that is contrary to traditional German theory. This must have been perfectly clear to Mattheson's contemporaries. And it is in this sense that Mattheson takes Reinhard Keiser to be one of the best representatives of the "galant" style in music.

The short first section of the book, unlike the other three, is not designed to instruct, but to state quite definitely a would-be reformer's point of view on a number of problems facing the musical world of Germany. It is entitled "Introduction to the Decline of Music and its Cause," [11] and explains immediately that "since it is, now, through misuse and ignorance that the noble art of music, contrary to its very purpose, causes, alas!, more ill-humor than pleasure among many, that it is even held in utter disregard, it would not be unsuitable to investigate briefly the reasons for this disaster. . . ." [12] The first of the five reasons Mattheson gives for the decline of music is the reactionary attitude of a large group of musicians toward whatever was fresh or new. These musicians considered themselves, and were considered by many others, as the foremost exponents of their art; their idolatry of antiquity was consequently a very perilous thing.

For they are persuaded that this beautiful and perfect creation, which a beneficent God has given us men for our pleasure, and likewise as a model of the eternal, harmonious Splendor, depends solely upon deep learning and laborious knowledge. To prove this, they dispense their philosophical rules and scholarly vagaries, not only with great authority, but likewise with such obscurity that one has a rightful aversion for the stuff, and would rather remain in permanent ignorance than to go through such *horrenda*.[13]

---

schlecht bestehen würde, wofern man nicht das dritte Stück, nemlich die *Galanterie* hinzu fügte, welche . . . durch einen guten *gout* und gesunden *Judicium acquiriret* wird." See also p. 202.

11. "Einleitung, Vom Verfall der *MUSIC* Und Dessen Ursachen."

12. *Idem*, p. 1: "Da es an dem, dass die edle Music, ihrem rechten Endzweck zu wider mehr Verdruss, leider! als Ergetzen bey vielen verursachen will, und fast in die äusserste Geringachtung gerathen ist, es sey nun der Missbrauch oder die Unwissenheit schuld daran; so wird es nicht undienlich seyn, mit wenigen die Ursachen solches Unheils zu untersuchen. . . ."

13. *Idem*, pp. 2–3: "So ist nun höchstens zu verwundern, dass diejenigen, so in der Welt

Music, he asserts, requires no rules on its own account and for its own sake; it is man who needs them because of his frailties and limitations. Without rules, he would hardly be able to form any earthly idea of this heavenly art at all, "since the proper origin of all knowledge rises not alone from the senses themselves, *nam nihil est in Intellectu, quod non fuit in sensu.*" In other words, in the art of music all rules are made by and for man. But also there is no rule so stable as never to suffer change and even decay. Mattheson saw this matter with extraordinary clarity, and with the eyes of a true "historian." For he realized that artistic rules are, taken together, the outgrowth of temporary circumstances and manners, which latter, when applied to music, are as variable as are "the constellations in the sky." [14] Thus Mattheson, in observing the relative duration of any set of values, gives expression to the concept of style in art. To be sure, he was familiar with previous discussions of the nature of styles, since he recognized many connotations of stylistic terms used in the seventeenth century. He was acquainted with the terminology of Athanasius Kircher, and apparently with the treatise on composition by Christoph Bernhard, one of Hamburg's leading musicians in the preceding century. Furthermore, it is clear that Mattheson is groping for formulas in which to express his feeling for the importance of the senses—a concept

vor die grössesten Meister dieser Wissenschafft kurtzum haben angesehen seyn wollen, auch eben diejenigen, so zur itzigen Zeit von vielen Liebhabern der *Antiqvität* blindlings davor gehalten werden, den ersten und wichtigsten Anlass gegeben haben und noch geben, dass das unvergleichliche Geschencke des Allmächtigen Schöpffers so in Verfall gerathen ist. . . . Denn da überreden sie sich, dass die wunderschöne und vollkommene Geschöpffe, welches der gütige GOtt uns Menschen zur Lust, und gleichsam zum Vorbild der ewigen *harmonischen* Herrlichkeit gegeben, eintzig und allein von einer tieffen Gelehrsamkeit und arbeitsamen Wissenschaft *dependire,* geben zu dem Ende ihre *philosophische* Regeln und gelehrte Grillen, nicht allein mit grosser *Autoritat,* sondern zugleich mit solcher *Obscurität* heraus, dass einem vor dem Zeuge recht grauet, und man dahero lieber in steter Unwissenheit bleiben, als solche *horrenda* durchgehen. . . ."

14. *Idem,* pp. 3–4: "Sie möchten sich aber bescheiden . . . dass die *Music* an ihr selbst keiner Regeln bedürffe, sondern dass wir vielmehr, unsers Unvermögens wegen derselbigen benöthiget sind, um einiger massen einen irrdischen Begriff von diesem himmlischen Wesen zu erlangen, und dass dannenhero alle die unzehlige Reguln sich nach der Zeit, darinnen wir leben, auch nach den Umständen und *Manieren* die in der *Music* eben so veränderlich als die *Constellationes* am Himmel sind, ändern und *accomodiren* müssen, weil nicht allein in den Sinnen selbst der eigentliche Ursprung aller Wissenschafft steckt, *nam etc.* sondern weil *auch* keine Regul noch *Thesis* in der Welt so beschaffen, die sich nicht, zu Folge der ohandenen *Conjuncturen* und *Circumstantien,* woraus sie eigentlich fliesset, richten, ändern und Abfälle leiden müsse."

which could have come to him from no other source than John Locke. He cites a few illustrations of the most exaggerated musical pedantry, and declares that according to all reasonable considerations this time-honored *"Musica Practica"* has in the past been—in contrast to the achievements of his own day—a "simple, wretched, and naked creature" whom no one would now like to imitate.[15] Mattheson begs his readers not to think of him as an enemy of "musical erudition and a pure critical naturalist."[16] He states his case outright: the belief that as soon as one has attained a certain foundation, one should exert all his strength to reach his aim by practice itself, and to have a "healthy idea of music, purified of all unnecessary school-dust."[17]

Mattheson gives as his second reason for the decline of music the ignorance and false pretenses of performers and musicians. He typifies the latter as those who, if they have but a "suffisance" of knowledge, will smear in one day a dozen sheets of paper with "noisy notes"—as if no more were needed to enter the "book of immortality." If these so-called composers would take the opportunity and have the patience to examine their "weak note-architecture, founded on quick-sand," if they would learn and admit that they are fallible, some good might finally come from this "docility," but far too many are incorrigible and cannot bear the slightest discipline.[18]

15. *Idem*, p. 8: "Allen vernünfftigen Betrachtungen nach, stehet zu glauben, dass diese uralte *Musica Practica* . . . gegen der heutigen zu rechnen ein *simples* elendes und kahles Wesen begriffen habe, . . . und so leicht niemand *ad imitationem* verführen würde."

16. *Idem*, pp. 8–9: "Bisshero wird der Leser dencken, ich sey ein sonderlicher Feind der *musicalischen Erudition,* und etwann so ein *purer critisirender Naturaliste;* allein, er übereile sich nicht, und warte nur ein wenig, so wird er schon finden dass ich . . . kein Kunst-Feind sey. . . ."

17. *Idem*, p. 10: ". . . alle Kräfte anspannen, so bald man nur einen gewissen Grund hat, zum Ziel selbsten *per praxin* zu gelangen und eine gesunde von allem unnöthigen Schul-Staub gesauberte *Ideam* von der *Music* zu haben. . . ."

18. *Idem*, p. 11: "Die da meynen, wenn sie nur die *Suffisance* haben und mit unverschämter Stirn, in einem Tage, ein dutzend Bögen mit lauter *Noten* beschmieren können, so sey es schon genug sie dem Buche der Unsterblichkeit ein zu verleiben. . . . Wenn solche Sorte *praetendirter Compositeurs* etwas *favorisiret* wird, und nebst der Gedult, Gelegenheit hat, ihr auf Trieb-Sand gegründetes, selten über die erste *etage* ausgeführtes schwaches *Noten*-Gebäude wol zu betrachten, sich daraus zu *informiren* und mit keiner *infallibilité* zu *flattiren,* so kan noch endlich was gutes durch ihre *docilité* daraus werden; jene aber sind *incorrigibiles,* und können nicht die allergeringste Einwendung vertragen,

The third cause of the corruption of music, Mattheson declares, shames him to report, since it concerns "true craftsmen, brother-members and masters" of the art: it is that many of them are at fault in regarding the pursuit of music not as a matter of "honor" or "finesse," but only as a matter of "gross profit." [19] An example of this evil is the youth of musical talent—which talent is boxed and beaten out of him by the brutality of a training designed only to give him sufficient proficiency to earn an adequate liveli-hood.[20]

It is of particular interest to see Mattheson aggressively challeng-ing the educational principles of the Guild. The open revolt of other artists against the system of guilds that furnished their edu-cation, seems to have broken out considerably later; the painters, for example, did not come forward with complaints against the system until about the second half of the eighteenth century. Ac-cording to established tradition, the apprentice in the guild of painters was occupied with grinding colors and carrying paint-pots through the streets, as Anton Graff did, or with serving as coach-man for his master as Carstens was requested to do. In like manner the apprentice in the guild of fifers or other musicians spent more than half his time running errands and doing all sorts of house-work instead of devoting himself to the study of his art. Since Mattheson holds this absurd kind of "artistic" training to be directly responsible for a decline in musical craftsmanship, he certainly can claim to be an early and valuable critic of the system.

For the three faults already mentioned Mattheson holds as re-

welches ein gar gewisses Kenn-Zeichen grober und halsstarriger Unwissenheit zu seyn Pfleget."

19. *Idem*, pp. 13–14: "Von der dritten Art der *Music*-Verderber schäme mich fast etwas zu melden, weil es rechte Handwercks-Jungen, Gesellen und Meister unter ihnen giebt, deren *propos* weder Ehre noch *Finesse*, sondern bloss allein der grobe *Profit* ist, die froh sind, wenn das Geld nur verdienet, es habe geklungen oder geklappet."

20. *Idem*, pp. 14–15: "Es betrachte mir nur ein vernünfftiger Mensch, wenn ein Knabe, der die so genannte Pfeiffer-Kunst erlernen soll, in einer schweren schändlichen Dienst-barkeit gewisse Jahre aushalten, Mägde-Arbeit, ja davor sich Mägde schamen, verrichten, mit Prügeln und Ohrfeigen, mit *Injurien* vom Morgen biss in den Abend, an statt Essen und Trinckens vorlieb nehmen muss, und noch kein Wort dawieder reden darff, ob nicht ein solcher, wenn er auch das allerbeste *naturel* in der gantzen Welt hätte, nothwendig verderben muss; eine viehische Lebens-Art an sich nimmt, grob, tölpisch und unbescheiden wird, und am Ende seiner Lehr-Jahre, die er in der grösten *Poenitenz* zugebracht, eben so ein *Idiote* bleibt wie er im Anfange gewesen?"

sponsible the musicians themselves. And he adds two more with which the musician is, in turn, forced to contend. The first of these is the ignorance of the audience, which to a good composer is as unavoidable as it is unbearable. For how is it possible, he asks, that an entire auditorium should have the same taste for, not to say the same knowledge of, music? To compensate for this painful fact there is no better comfort than this: that the favorable judgment of one or more intelligent persons must counterbalance the ill humor produced by the lack of favor of the unexperienced.[21] The second fault is that the art of music is in no way encouraged; neither is the work of truly good masters brought before the public, nor is ingenious and "galant" work paid for according to its worth:

> Der Liebhaber giebt es die Menge;
> Die Beutel aber sind enge.[22]

What then, he asks, is to be done? If a true "virtuoso" does not wish to end his days in obscurity he must leave the country and seek an "asylum," where "he can put his talent to better profit"[23]— and Mattheson gives as an example of the treatment proper to a great composer the honor and popularity meted out to artistic talent at the court of France.[24] His introduction concludes with a peroration on the merits of music, the high esteem in which it was held by Luther and others, and its supremacy among the arts since even its

21. "Einleitung, Vom Verfall der *MUSIC* Und Dessen Ursachen," p. 16: "Was sonst die Unwissenheit der Zuhörer betrifft, so ist solche einem guten *Componisten* oder *Musico* so unvermeidlich als unerträglich. Denn wie kan es möglich seyn, dass ein gantzes *Auditorium* gleichen *gout*, will nicht sagen, gleiche Wissenschafft von der *Music* haben solle? wider dieses schmertzliche Unglück ist kein besserer Trost, als dieser, dass das gute Urtheil eines oder weniger verständiger, dem Verdruss abhelffen müsse, welchen vieler unerfahrnen wiedriges *Sentiment* verursachet."

22. *Idem*, p. 18: "Eine wichtige Ursache des Verfalls dere *Music* ist auch, dass dieselbe bey uns auf keinerley Weisse *encouragiret* wird; *veritable* grosse Meister werden nicht hervorgezogen; Künstliche und *galante* Arbeit wird nicht nach Würden bezahlet; der Liebhaber etc."

23. *Idem*, p. 19: "Wass ist denn zu thun? Will ein rechtschaffner *Virtuoso* nicht *crepiren*, oder in *Obscuro* seine Tage zu bringen, so muss er seinen Stab weiter setzen und ein *azylum* suchen, da man seyn *Talent* besser auf Wucher legen kann."

24. *Idem*, p. 21: ". . . sondern es machen, wie die Herren Frantzosen zur Zeit *Lully*, dessen Andencken bey allen unpartheyischen in Ehren, von denen *St. Evremont* so schreibet: *C'est Louigi, c'est Cavallo, c'est Cesti qui se presentent à l'imagination; & onne scauroit nier, qu'aux Representations du Palais Royal on ne songe cent fois plus à Baptiste qu'à Thesée ni à Cadmus. . . .*"

secular element is given by God to man as a special "recreation." [25]
Mattheson's five reasons for the "decline" of music are clearly
not of equal significance or importance. The first and the last of
them, however, are extremely illuminating criticisms of the general musical situation in Germany at the time they were written,
and the others may be considered as the vigorous expression of
Mattheson's idealistic attitude towards his beloved art. The confusion and verbosity of his statement of the first reason, however,
obscures the real intellectual problem he recognized as existing.
In criticizing contemporary German musicians for being smothered
by their respect for the past he was not condemning the practice
of justifying one's opinions by an appeal to the ancients; he was,
rather, voicing his disapproval of the supremacy and dominance
of traditional musical practice and theory in school and church.
For the young German musician there was no formal system of
musical education or advancement outside of these Lutheran institutions. A newer spirit, represented by Pietism, natural science,
and philosophy, was animating the universities into becoming the
intellectual rivals of the Lutheran Gymnasium, but music had no
official place in their curricula.[26] Mattheson advocates the senses as
paramount in the creation of music, as opposed to the elaborately
conventionalized intellectualism of the past; to support his tenet,
he is forced to call upon "practice" to justify his musical opinions.
By "practice," Mattheson was undoubtedly thinking of the writing
of operatic or other secular music which had not been codified,
and whose only laws were taste, the "judgment of the senses," and
the realization of the concept of the "galant." He and his contemporaries in Germany were not consciously influenced, as yet,
by the psychological doctrines of John Locke and those of his
school; but it is clear, in all this, that Mattheson, however un-
consciously, was already basing his theories on ideas that ran parallel with those of Locke. He was perhaps the only musical thinker
so to do at this time, and therefore it is not surprising that, eight

25. *Idem*, pp. 23–33, p. 25: "Da auch die *Music*, so fern sie weltlich heissen mag, unter
allen Künsten von GOtt den Menschen zur sonderlichen *Recreation* gegeben ist, und das
rechte *dulce* fast allein in sich halt. . . ."
26. Georg Schünemann, *Geschichte der Deutschen Schulmusik* (Leipzig, 1928), p. 159.

years later, he actually rested his own musical esthetic, of which this work was the beginning, upon Locke's teaching.[27]

The second most important of Mattheson's grievances is merely another aspect of the quarrel between the two intellectual systems in power at this time; it was manifested in the opposition of the secular princes, as they increased in wealth and prestige, to the Lutheran-controlled municipalities. It was in fact the aristocracy which supported the new music, gave it life, representative opportunities, allowed it expression, and supplied the enthusiasm and intelligent appreciation which the musician naturally welcomed. The question of whether to become a town cantor or the Kapellmeister to a prince was one which corresponded with the dichotomy existing in the musical world. The leading musicians of Mattheson's generation acted upon this problem in different ways: Bach's profound faith and love for traditional forms of church-music was probably the deciding factor in his desertion of the secular post of his earlier life for the cantorship in Leipzig; Händel, on the other hand, "sought an asylum" in intellectually emancipated England rather than in the narrower freedom of a small German court; Telemann, after Händel the most famous German composer of his day, although thoroughly conversant with French society and music, found the Hamburg cantorship satisfactory because of the unusual variety and freedom of musical life there;[28] Keiser, Hasse, and Graun, however, all remained as Kapellmeister at German courts. Mattheson's disapproval of the municipal musical organizations was increased by his recognition of the inadequacy of musicians who had gained positions of importance in them. Some years later he was to use the example of corruption which caused Bach's defeat as candidate for the post of organist

27. *Das Forschende Orchestre,* 1721. Bibliography No. 73.

28. Telemann wrote to Uffenbach (July 31, 1723) concerning the musical life of Hamburg in part as follows: ". . . ich glaube nicht, dass irgendwo ein solcher Ort als Hamburg zu finden, der den Geist eines in dieser Wissenschaft [Music] arbeitenden mehr aufmuntern kann. Hierzu trägt ein grosses bey, dass ausser den anwesenden viele Standes-Personen auch die ersten Männer der Stadt ja das ganze Raths-Kollegium sich den öffentlichen Concerts nicht entziehen; item die vernünftigen Urtheile so vieler Kenner und kluger Leute geben Gelegenheit dazu; nicht weniger die Opera, welche itzo in höchster Flor ist; und endlich der *nervus rerum gerendarum,* der hier bey den Liebhabern nicht fest angewachsen ist." Quoted from Preussner, *Die bürgerliche Musikkultur,* p. 29.

in the Jacobikirche in Hamburg as another reason for the decline of church music.[29]

In Mattheson's own career this same conflict is again evident. His musical experience was almost entirely acquired at the Opera. Motivated in all probability by the very sentiments in regard to church music that he expressed in the introduction to his first book, he refused several advantageous offers made to him by various churches. Yet his innate beliefs made him throughout his life the defender of the traditional place of music in the Lutheran church. His criticism was designed to correct the weaknesses in the system rather than to destroy it. The introduction to *Das Neu-Eröffnete Orchestre* provides, it is true, the critical background for the dogmatic contents of the book, but, what is more important, it also reveals his fundamental aim to initiate a musical enlightenment.

The book proper divides the field of musical study into three sections: *"Pars Prima Designatoria,* oder Von den Dingen und Zeichen die zu einer *Musicalischen Composition* gehören"; *"Pars Secunda Compositoria,* oder von der *Musicalischen Composition* und dem Contrapunct an sich selbst"; *"Pars Tertia Judicatoria,* oder Wie eins und anders in der Music zu beurtheilen."* Within these three sections, in a brief and untechnical style, the general principles of music are defined somewhat as they would be in a dictionary.[30] Since the discussion of all controversial matters of theory is ignored, as are all references to the opinions of other writers, the result is the first example of a popular compendium of musical knowledge written in Germany. Indeed, Mattheson seems to have held to the tenets of the introduction, in defining music in terms of his own experience, so consistently that the "galant homme" who read Bayle's *Dictionnaire* with pleasure might gain equal enjoyment from a perusal of Mattheson's work. No matter how uncontroversial much of his information might be, he nevertheless treats of certain technical questions upon which musicians of the old and the new schools of thought were in sharp disagreement. It will

---

29. *Der Musicalische Patriot*, pp. 315 f. Cf. C. S. Terry, *Bach, a Biography*, pp. 130–134.
30. Mattheson was familiar with Sébastien de Brossard's *Dictionnaire de musique contenant une explication des termes grecs, italiens et français les plus usites dans la musique* etc. (Paris, 1703); he first refers to it on p. 101 in *Das Neu-Eröffnete Orchestre*.

be sufficient to examine only the chief of these in order to understand Mattheson's position.

The first problem which Mattheson touches upon is the question of the proper status of the harmonic interval of the fourth. Whether it should be treated as a consonance or a dissonance had for long been the subject of controversy among theoreticians. According to the medieval mathematical interpretation of musical intervals it was held to be a consonance because of its relation to the other intervals in the scale. In his chart of harmonic intervals, Mattheson, however, calls it both a consonance and a dissonance,[31] and in the second section, on composition,[32] he defends this view by arguments which undermine those of his predecessors. That the fourth is a consonance, being based on the mathematical division of the octave, is ridiculous, he declares, since

numbers in music do not govern but merely instruct; the Hearing is the only channel through which their force is communicated to the inner soul of the attentive listener . . . the true aim of music is not its appeal to the eye, nor yet altogether to the so-called "reason," but only to the Hearing, which communicates pleasure, as it is experienced, to the Soul and the "reason." Hence if the testimony of the ear is followed, it will be discovered that in its relation to the surrounding sounds and harmony, the fourth will be either consonant or dissonant.[33]

By this rational explanation, Mattheson reconciles musical theory both with practice and with the harmonic concepts of the new music. By elevating an organ of sense above abstract mathematical

31. *Das Neu-Eröffnete Orchestre*, pp. 54–55: "Man wird allhier bemercken, dass da die *Quarta* mit unter die *Consonantien* gesetzet, dieselbe zugleich mit einer *Marqve* bezeichnet worden, um dadurch anzudeuten, dass sie ihr Bürger-Recht noch lange nicht daselbst gewonnen, auch dass unmöglich eine eintzige *proportion* zugleich *dis*- und *consonans* seyn könne. Der Streit aber, den man über das *intervallum* der *Quartae* führet, ob es nehmlich *Consonans* oder *dissonans* sey, ist noch nicht recht erörtert. Etliche halten es vor *consonans* aus der Ursach, *quia Quarta dividit Octavam arithmeticè;* allein andere die nicht so wol die Zahlen, als den Gebrauch des *intervalli* erwegen und untersuchen . . . geben vor, es sey bissweilen *con*- bissweilen auch *dissonans*."

32. *Idem*, Part II, Cap. III, pp. 122 f.

33. *Idem*, pp. 126–127: ". . . dass die Zahlen in der *Music* nicht *decidiren*, sondern nur *instruiren;* Das Gehör aber allein der *Canal* sey, durch welchen ihre Krafft in das innerste der Seelen eines aufmercksamen Zuhörers eindringet . . . dass der Zweck der *Music* nicht das Gesicht, noch der eigentlich so genandte Verstand ist, sondern eintzig und allein das Gehör, welches der Seelen und dem Verstande, die Ergetzung, so es empfindet, mittheilet. . . ."

reasoning he is likewise putting to actual use the precepts of the new philosophy.

In the first section of the book, Mattheson also commits himself to the then modern conception of tonality, which was dependent upon the tempering of the scale—a difficulty which had at that time been by no means solved. The course of musical evolution had brought about an increasingly complex use of a chromatically enlarged means of expression, which, because of the requirements demanded by the *stylus luxurians* of the music-drama, made use of unusual tonalities and modulations. At the same time, the practice of thorough bass was forcing music to become increasingly dependent upon keyboard instruments, which had to be tuned permanently according to a fixed scheme. The problem of evolving a system of equal temperament which would resolve at once both of the problems had occupied theorists and mathematicians such as Zarlino and Keppler since the sixteenth century. In 1691, Andreas Werckmeister had actually outlined a system whereby all the intervals of the scale could be tuned equally,[34] and thereafter various other methods and improvements gradually made the requirements of modern harmonies attainable. Until two years before the appearance of Mattheson's book, there had been no systematic attempt to distinguish clearly between the use and identity of the different major and minor keys.[35] German traditionalists in music, because of their inherited learning and the old-fashioned construction of organs, held to the ancient system of eight ecclesiastical modes. Their method of instruction in these was still the solmization of Guido d'Arezzo, which was built upon the order of hexachords and thus used only six of the seven intervals of the natural scale. Here then was another gulf between the old and the new music.

In his realistic way Mattheson at first tries to effect a compromise. He cites the names and lettered intervals of the twelve original

34. *Musicalische Temperatur, oder deutlicher und wahrer mathematischer Unterricht, wie man durch Anweisung des Monochords ein Clavier, sonderlich die Orgelwerke, Positive, Regale, Spinetten und dergl. wohltemperiert stimmen könne* . . . 1691.

35. In 1711 Heinichen published his *Neu erfundene und gründliche Anweisung wie ein Musikliebender auf gewisse vortheilhaftige Art könne zu vollkommener Erlernung des General-Basses . . . gelangen* (Hamburg, 1711).

Greek modes and the eight medieval scales—the ecclesiastical modes.[36] He then passes on to consider the new system, saying that the "Italians and modern composers make use of still another system to 'differentiate' their modulations," [37] and proceeds to list the twenty-four major and minor scales.[38] The notation of each is illustrated in tables in the front of the book. While admitting the novelty and fashionable use of the more remote keys, and the limitations of practical tempering, he declares that he had, from sheer curiosity, tried out the system by setting musical pieces to each of the last eight keys, which had made a tolerable "Effect." [39]

In a later section of this book, his treatment of the scales from a different point of view lacks all such compromise and apology. Here he is concerned with an aspect of the problem which had engrossed many musical writers in the preceding century.[40] In his own words, it is an examination of the "particular characteristics of musical scales and their power to affect the Passions" ("Von der *Musicalischen* Tohne Eigenschafft und Würckung in Ausdrückung der *Affecten.*" [41]) In the succeeding section he declares that all those who maintain that the basic differentiation of scales lies in the major and minor third, and who "will have it that all minors are necessarily sad, but all majors joyous," have in general warped the facts not too grossly. The difficulty is, however, that they have not carried their investigations sufficiently far.[42] For this reason Mattheson undertakes to explain his own experience with the

36. *Das Neu-Eröffnete Orchestre*, pp. 58–59.
37. *Idem*, p. 60: "Die Italiäner und heutigen *Componisten* gebrauchen sich einer noch andern Art ihre *modulationes* zu unterscheiden. . . ."
38. *Idem*, pp. 61–63.
39. *Idem*, p. 64: "Wahr ist es zwar, dass unterschiedliche dieser *Modorum* sind, daraus man sehr selten, auch wol schier niehmals ein *Musicalisches* Stück setzet. . . . Ich habe es *probiret*, und aus dergleichen *Tonen* wie die letzten 8. sind, etwas gesetzt, welches zur *Curiosité* schon einen ziemlichen *Effect* gethan hat. . . ." It is interesting to note, however, that his instrumental compositions are almost without exception written in the most conventional keys.
40. Cf. Irmgard Otto, "Deutsche Musikanschauung im 17. Jahrhundert," Dissertation (Berlin, 1937). "Von der Wurckung und von sonderbahrer Krafft der Music," pp. 74 f.
41. *Das Neu-Eröffnete Orchestre*, p. 231.
42. *Idem*, p. 232: "Diejenigen, die da meinen, es stecke das gantze Geheimniss in der *Tertia minore* oder *majore*, und darthun wollen, dass alle *molle* Tohne, *in genere* davon zu reden, nothwendig traurig sind, hergegen aber, dass all *dure* Tohne gemeiniglich eine lustige Eigenschafft hegen, haben zwar nicht in allen gar zu grosses Unrecht, sie sind aber in der Untersuchung noch nicht weit gekommen."

"affective" differences of the first sixteen scales.[43] His description of the most common scales is drawn in part from the writings of the theoreticians Athanasius Kircher and Seth Calvisius.[44] His analyses of the properties of the less common scales, however, are more original and interesting. Of F-sharp minor he writes: " . . . it is a key characterized by sadness, but a sadness more pensive and lovelorn than tragic and gloomy; it is a key that has about it a certain loneliness, an individuality, a misanthropy." [45] This bizarre wording leaves a casual reader somewhat bewildered and perhaps a trifle unconvinced. To see it as more than verbiage, to feel that, in reality, it represents a feeling about this particular key which may be realized through notes, one has only to turn to the world's greatest practical demonstration of the different "particular characteristics" of keys, J. S. Bach's forty-eight Preludes and Fugues in the two volumes of the *Wohltemperiertes Clavier.* There he will find a striking similarity between this mood which Johann Mattheson was attempting to describe in words, and that which the Preludes and Fugues in F-sharp minor describe in music. This becomes only the more striking when one finds other instances of a parallel between interpretations by the two men. Mattheson did not, at this time, however, present in its entirety his belief in the importance of an understanding of the connection between the "Affection" and tonality; it is only in his later works that he supported this youthful, experimental attitude by a clearly defined, inclusive, and systematic theory. In fact, he eventually became the most prominent representative of the Cartesian doctrine of "affections" in music.

Mattheson's obvious desire to clarify and define in a rational manner all the confused elements of musical knowledge is discernible throughout the entire volume. In his exposition of the different kinds of composition [46] he is again in sharp conflict with the opposing musical system then rife in Germany. He states that

43. *Idem,* pp. 236–253.
44. Athanasius Kircher: *Musurgia universalis sive ars magna consoni et dissoni, etc.,* 1650. Sethus Calvisius: *Exercitatio musicae tertia,* 1611.
45. *Das Neu-Eröffnete Orchestre,* p. 251: ". . . ob er gleich zu einer grossen Betrübniss leitet, ist dieselbe doch mehr *languissant* und verliebet als *lethal;* es hat sonst dieser Tohn etwas *abandonirtes, singulieres* und *misanthropisches* an sich."
46. *Idem,* pp. 138 f.: "Von der *Composition* unterschiedenen Arten und Sorten."

there are three general styles in all music: Ecclesiastical, Theoretical, and Chamber, the first being the most worthy of esteem since it is used in Divine Worship.[47] To separate the basic styles in this way was strictly in accord with existing conditions in composition. But, in making all three equal in scope and in treating all three alike, Mattheson rode roughshod over traditional teachings, which divided the ecclesiastical style into many subdivisions and then, through exhaustive definitions of each of these, made them seem far to outweigh in theoretical importance the two secular styles put together. Mattheson's first exposition of all three is brief, for, he admits, a complete discussion of each paragraph, not to say sentence, might occupy a whole book, or at least a whole chapter.[48] Nevertheless in a succeeding section he discusses the changes in contemporary church music which conventional theoreticians would have preferred to overlook.

What one finds on further examination of church music [he writes], is the fact that at the present time the composer is allowed more freedom, so that it is no longer a fault to compose *Canto & Basso solo;* Arias, Recitatives and the like may be set without scruple, as, for example, in Passions, Oratorios etc. where they are customary and pleasing.

But he qualifies this statement by adding that

it would be just as well if greater restraint were sometimes showed in these pieces, and if they and their *Accompagnement,* even when using Arias and Recitatives, were composed altogether with more seriousness and *solidité* than is necessary in chamber or theatrical music.[49]

47. *Idem,* p. 139: "Gleichwie *inter Stylos Musicos,* nemlich *Ecclesiae, Theatri & Camerae,* der erste den Platz und Rang hat, so stehet auch unter den vielfältigen Arten der *Composition* der *Choral* . . . wol billig oben an, theils weil dadurch die Ehre Gottes, als des Allmächtigen Schöpffers so wol dieser als anderer Creaturen, schuldigster massen erhoben, theils auch, weil zu solcher *Choral-Composition* schwerlich, ausser erleuchteten und geist-reichen Männern, jemand recht geschickt seyn wird."

48. *Idem,* p. 154: ". . . da sonst eine voll kommene *Discussion* eines jeden *Paragraphi,* will nicht sagen *Periodi,* wol ein gantzes Buch oder doch ein gantzes Capitel erfordern würde."

49. *Idem,* p. 155: "Was nun ferner die in der Ordnung zu *examinirenden* noch übrigen Kirchen-Sachen betrifft, so hat man sich darinnen bey diesen neuern Zeiten grösserer Freyheit bedienet, als vorhin, so dass man sich nicht mehr eine *Faute* daraus machet, wie *Olims* Zeiten, *Canto & Basso solo* zu *componiren* . . . Man setzet *Arien, Recitativ* und dergleichen . . . ohne einigen *Scrupel,* wie nemlich in *Passionen, Oratoriis &c.* gar gebräuchlich und gefällig. Es könte aber nicht schaden, wenn man sich jezuweilen ein wenig *modester* in diesem Stücke bezeigete, und, obgleich *Arien* und *Recitativ* gebraucht würden, doch selbige und ihr *Accompagnement* allezeit mit mehrerem Ernste und *solidité* ausarbeitete, als etwan in einer Cammer- oder *Theatral-Music* nöthig ist."

This statement seems to reveal a desire on Mattheson's part to remain moderate and not too openly to ally himself with one side or the other in the church-music conflict which had broken out openly in Hamburg three years earlier.[50] In contrast to this restrained criticism of ecclesiastical music his description of theatrical music is rapturously enthusiastic, and shows what musical style ranked truly foremost in his estimation. In the opera one meets a "confluxum" of all musical beauties:

There the composer has the grand opportunity to give free rein to his invention. With many surprises and with much grace he there can, most naturally and diversely, portray love, jealousy, hatred, gentleness, impatience, lust, indifference, fear, vengeance, fortitude, timidity, magnanimity, horror, dignity, baseness, splendor, indigence, pride, humility, joy, laughter, weeping, mirth, pain, happiness, despair, storm, tranquillity, even heaven and earth, sea and hell, together with all the actions in which men participate.[51]

His enthusiasm for the medium knows no bounds.

Through the skill of composer and singer each and every *Affectus* can be expressed beautifully and naturally better than in an Oratorio, better than in painting or sculpture, for not only are Operas expressed in words, but they are helped along by appropriate actions and above all interpreted by heart-moving music . . .[52]

After this ecstatic prelude there follows a description of each of the instrumental and vocal forms of secular music with their outstanding formal and emotional characteristics.[53] Thus, although he avoids a deliberate critical comparison between ecclesiastical and secular music, his true convictions are more than obvious. In championing the opera he assumes that the prime function of music

50. Preussner, *Die bürgerliche Musikkultur*, p. 12; cf. p. 15.
51. *Das Neu-Eröffnete Orchestre*, pp. 160–161: "Da hat ein *Componist* rechte Gelegenheit seinen *Inventionibus* den Zügel schiessen zu lassen! da kan er auff unzehlige Art Liebe, Eifersucht, Hass, Sanfftmuth, Ungedult, Begierde, Gleichgültigkeit, Furcht, Rache, Tapferkeit, Zagheit, Grosmuth, Entsetzen, Hoheit, Niedrigkeit, Pracht, Dürfftigkeit, Stoltz, Demuth, Freude, Lachen, Weinen, Lust, Schmertzen, Glückseeligkeit, Verzweiflung, Sturm, Stille, ja Himmel, Erde, Meer, Hölle, und all darinn vorkommende Verrichtungen . . . mit tausenderley Verwunderungen und Anmuth sehr natürlich abbilden."
52. *Idem*, pp. 167–168: ". . . da durch des *Componisten* und der Sänger Geschicklichkeit alle und jede *Affectus* besser als in der *Oratorio*, besser als in der Mahlerey, besser als in der *Sculpture*, nicht allein vivâ voce schlecht weg, sondern mit Zuthun einer *convenablen Action*, und hauptsächlich vermittelst Hertz-bewegender *Music*, gar schön und natürlich mögen *exprimiret* werden."
53. *Idem*, pp. 169–199.

is to move the passions by means of expressive devices which strictly-composed church music does not make use of. Read in conjunction with the Introduction, this section of the book is clearly an attempt to show the author's compatriots that the psychology and philosophy of the new music must be understood and adopted by ecclesiastical composers if the decline of music in Germany is to be checked.

This fundamental idea comes to light in one other interesting passage, which presents an examination of the difference between the various national styles in music.[54] Mattheson includes this section because of his profound concern with the state of music in his own country. His analysis of the merits of foreign styles arises from a wish not only to enlighten his contemporaries, but to stimulate them to compose in a more modern manner. He first states the following principles:

> Whoever would like to set down a general and sound judgment, free from all *Praejudiciis,* on Italian, French, English, and German music, must not confuse but must carefully distinguish the composition and execution of such national styles.[55]

The general characteristics and musical capacities of the four "nations" of Europe are then enumerated. The Italians Mattheson regards as preëminent because of "the accomplished beauty of their works, and, partly, their polished and *insinuante* artistic ideas." [56] "It is certain—he continues—that all Nations who have desired to be distinguished in music have borrowed nearly everything from the Italians, and have imitated them completely in all things." [57] As to the French, there is no doubt that their eminence is due not so much to their "composition" as to their "execution," which does

54. *Idem,* pp. 200 f.: "Vom Unterschied der heutigen Italiänischen, Frantzösischen, Englischen und Teutschen *Music."*
55. *Idem,* p. 200: "Wer von der heutigen Italiänischen, Frantzösischen, Englischen und Teutschen *Music* ein *generales,* von allen *Praejudiciis* gesaubertes, und gesundes Urtheil fällen wil, der muss die *Composition* und *Execution* solcher *National-Music* . . . nicht mit einander *confundiren,* sondern nothwendig und sehr genau *distinguiren."*
56. *Idem,* pp. 202–203: "Die Italiäner . . . theils durch die wesentliche Schönheit ihrer Wercke, theils auch durch die übertünchte und *insinuante* Kûnst-Griffe in der *Composition,* den Preiss vor allen andern *Nationen* davon zu tragen scheinen. . . ."
57. *Idem,* p. 205: "Es ist dieses so gewiss, dass auch alle übrige *Nationes,* die sich in der *Music* jehmals haben *distinguiren* wollen, den Italiänern fast alles abgeborget, und sie schier in allen Stücken nachgeäffet haben. . . ."

not yield in much to the Italians. Of instrumental, especially dance, music, the French are, however, the unmistakable masters, "und werden überall, ohne mitiret zu werden, imitiret."[58] The English at present "flat-footedly imitate the Italian style," and run up great expenses for accomplished virtuosi of whom they have a pretty select crowd.[59]

This discussion of the disproportionate shares that various nations contributed to the artistic style in music reflects the actual, historical situation of the baroque age. By its very nature style in all the arts seems to group different countries into what may be called central and peripheral spheres. For about 150 years Italy was the center of the baroque style in music. Mattheson recognized this fact, and also the fact that France, England, and Germany were during the period in a peripheral position. No matter what great genius it produced no country as a whole ever succeeded in freeing itself from this inequality in musical style. When the dominant or central style was at its climax, or entering its last phase—and by 1713 the Italian baroque was close to the point of its most powerful expansion—musicians living in the peripheral countries often began to voice their dissatisfaction, or even to break into open revolt; and sometimes they spoke what appears to be a "nationalistic" language. Such expressions had, however, nothing to do with political nationalism, but were indicative of a purely artistic phenomenon related to style. At the end of every stylistic period, a very natural reaction of native forces in the peripheral countries becomes apparent. Mattheson recognized this stylistic peculiarity, but understood neither its implications nor the regularity of its appearance in history. He wished, nevertheless, to remedy the situation; and he speaks in the patriotic language familiar to all peripheral nations.

Having described the separate merits of all these countries

58. *Idem*, pp. 207–208: "Man streitet hierbey nicht, dass nicht so wol die Frantzösische *Composition* als *Execution*, in ihrer Art ihr eigenes Lob verdiene, und vielleicht der Italiänischen nicht viel nachgiebet. . . . So viel muss man gerne gestehen: In der *Instrumental*, insonderheit aber in der *Choraischen* oder *Tantze-Music* sind die Frantzosen Meister, und werden überall. . . ." etc.

59. *Idem*, pp. 210–211: "Itziger Zeit *imitirt* diese *Nation* platterdings den Italiänischen *Stylum*, wendet grosse Spesen auff tüchtige *Virtuosen*, hat derselben auch einen ziemlichen auserlesenen *Confluxum*. . . ."

Mattheson is then at pains to point out the paucity of German music.

Among the educated Germans [he writes] the *Estime* for music has never been really small or thoroughly prosperous either. In fact, this noble art . . . has come to be treated somewhat sleepily and indifferently; hence the great revolution in musical affairs has not come to my countrymen as it has to those in other lands. . . .[60] Our German virtuosi, who are—to speak dispassionately—altogether worthy to bear such a title with honor, are much more deserving of esteem than whole bands of foreigners. . . . But a contemptible custom affecting these matters has come to pass; we prefer anything that is foreign, not necessarily because of its beauty and value, but merely because it is foreign, to our own people and things, which are not bad or simple in themselves, but merely suffer the odium of being native.[61]

The result of this is that, although the Germans have all the work, the "Italians make all the money and then go home."[62] The injustice of this situation, which clearly he attributes to the Germans' ignorance of musical matters, causes him to burst forth in nationalistic pride—a sad anomaly, since, for artistic reasons, he cannot help but pay full tribute to the predominance of the Italian style.[63] As the personification of German ability, Mattheson cites the composer, Reinhard Keiser, the "premier homme du monde," who has written in addition to a number of "Church pieces, Cantatas, Suites, &c., with his own hand and from his own brain forty or

60. *Idem*, pp. 211–212: "Unter den redlichen Teutschen ist die *Estime* von der *Music* nimmer gantz geringe, auch nimmer recht hoch gediehen, sondern diese edle Kunst ist von den *Fautoribus*, durchgehens davon zu reden, bey uns jederzeit etwas schläfrich und gleichgültig *tractiret* worden; dahero denn unter meinen Lands-Leuten solche denckwürdige *Revolutiones in rebus Musicis* nicht vorgefallen sind, als in andern Ländern. . . ."
61. *Idem*, pp. 212–213: "Die jenigen teutschen *Virtuosen*, die solchen Nahmen mit Recht und Ehren führen, sind würcklich, und ohne *Passion* zu sagen, viel höher zu achten, als gantze Banden Ausländer. . . . Es ist gewiss bey uns in allen Sachen fast ein recht schimpfliches Wesen eingerissen, dass wir alles, was aus der Frembde kommt, nicht darum allezeit, weil es schön und gut, sondern bloss weil es frembd ist, unsern einheimischen Personen und Dingen, nicht weil sie etwan schlecht und recht, sondern eintzig und allein, weil sie bey uns zu Hause gehören."
62. *Idem*, pp. 214–215: "Da hat nun in solchen Fällen der ehrliche Teutsche die Arbeit; der Italiäner aber nimmt das Geld und geht davon."
63. *Idem*, p. 216: "Wolan! man *vindicire* denn, recht wie sichs gebühret, die gedruckte teutsche Ehre, gegen und wieder solch unnützes Völckchen, dessen sich so wol das hönische Frankreich, als das ausbündige Italien billig selbst schämet; man lege der unpartheyischen Welt vor Augen, was ein geschickter Teutscher vor andern *Nationen* in vielen Sachen (vornemlich in der *Music*) vermöge seines natürlichen Triebes voraus habe."

fifty entire Operas." [64] And Mattheson concludes with a catalogue of Keiser's achievements in the entire field of music.

Despite the confused reasoning in this section, its significance and purpose are not hard to grasp. Mattheson was not the only musician in Germany at this time who witnessed with fury the inroads of foreign musicians in German musical life.[65] He clearly felt that the readers of his book should be inspired to action in order to meet this challenge by musical enlightenment of their own. In 1713 Keiser was the only German musician who not only understood these new prominent forms of music but excelled in their composition. To Mattheson he was the model for all that German composers should be, particularly since he did not waste his ability upon outmoded forms.

From the foregoing survey of the most outstanding sections of the *Neu-Eröffnetes Orchestre* several deductions may be made about the state of German music in 1713 and about Mattheson's musical theories. It is clear to him, at least, that the monopoly of the outmoded Lutheran musical organization of the seventeenth century is sharply challenged by the influx of new principles of style. The two systems of thought do not agree, and the older one cannot survive without coming to terms with the newer. As a believer in the faith which had inspired German music in the past, Mattheson feels that the greatest menace to it arises from ignorance and contempt, and his book is clearly an attempt to remedy this situation. He is unable to realize that the triumph of the new secular, individualistic theory of music actually signalizes the downfall and disappearance of the musical heritage of the Middle Ages. Nor is it likely that the implications of his musical "revolution" seemed actually so far reaching to him and to his contemporaries.

64. *Idem*, pp. 216–217: "Es trete mir der *Componiste* auff in allen übrigen Theilen *Europae*, der benebenst einer zahlreichen Menge Kirchen-Sachen, *Cantaten, Suiten &c.* mit eigener Hand und aus eignem Gehirn . . . 40. biss 50. gantze *Opern* hervorgebracht habe, wie der *premier homme du monde*, der in aller Welt berühmte Capell-Meister, Herr Reinhard Keiser gethan, und dadurch verdienet hat, dass er die Ehre Teutschlandes mag genennet werden?" Mattheson is, of course, mistaken. Almost every Italian composer of renown could have shown him an even longer list of operas. Alessandro Scarlatti, for instance, at the time of his *Telemacco* (1718) had nearly doubled the figure Mattheson mentions for Keiser's operas.

65. Johann Kuhnau wrote *Der Musikalische Quacksalber* (1700) as a satire upon the Italian style of music in Germany.

The best indication of the contemporary significance of this book is to be found in its reception among German musicians, the first of which is to be found at the conclusion of the *Neu-Eröffnetes Orchestre*. It is an enthusiastic recommendation of its contents by Reinhard Keiser, the acknowledged master of the Hamburg Opera: [66]

. . . I find myself forced to testify publicly that I have met in perusing [this book] an extraordinary and unusually laborious industry, a truly laudable and praiseworthy *Intention*, a *fundamentale* knowledge, a *Raisonnement* grounded on experimentation and the *Praxin* which distinguishes the present from the *antiquen Musique.* . . .[67] I praise it as the founding of a solid theory and the banishment of ancient practice. I recommend it to the Reasonable Man and the Perfect . . . And too, I encourage already renowned *Virtuosen* to read it through, for they may find in it one thing or another that has perhaps escaped them.[68]

The book was thus launched with the intelligent approval of a composer who, although older than Mattheson, was one of the first Germans to distinguish himself in the new style.

No trace can be found of contemporary reactions to Mattheson's ideas for several years after the publication of his first "sample," as he himself termed it.[69] It found at least one bitter opponent, however, who between 1715 and 1717 issued a treatise to confute Mattheson's teachings. Johann Heinrich Buttstedt, the organist of the Predigerkirche in Erfurt, was the author of this pedantic tome, which he called: *"UT, MI, SOL, RE, FA, LA, TOTA MUSICA ET HARMONIA AETERNA* Oder Neu-eröffnetes, altes wahres,

66. *Das Neu-Eröffnete Orchestre*, pp. 330 f.: "Kurtze Anmerckungen, Über den *Musicalischen Tractat*, Das Neu-Eröffnete *Orchestre* genandt."
67. *Idem*, p. 336: ". . . [ich] finde mich gemüssiget, *publiquement* zu *contestiren*, dass durchgehends nichts al einen ungemeinen und überaus mühsamen Fleiss, eine recht löbliche, und rühmliche *Intention*, eine *fundamentale* Wissenschafft, ein auf die *Experientz* und beste *Praxin* gegründetes *Raisonnement*, so die jetzige, von der *antiquen Musique* distinguiret . . . angetroffen."
68. *Idem*, p. 337: "Ich habe es denen Anfängern, zur Legund einer *soliden Theorie* und zur Anweisung einer geschickten *Praxis*. Ich rühme es denen Verständigern und *Perfectern*. . . . Ich *encouragire* die auch schon' *renommirten Virtuosen*, es durch-zulesen, weil sie darinn noch eins und das andere antreffen möchten, so ihnen vielleicht sonst *echappiret*."
69. *Ehrenpforte*, p. 198: "Mattheson . . . fing nunmehro mit Macht an, *Musicam didacticam & theoreticam* schrifftlich zu treiben, wovon im *Junio* eine Probe erschien. . . ."

eintziges, und ewiges *FUNDAMENTUM MUSICES,* entgegen gesetzt Dem neu-eröffneten *Orchestre,* und in Zweene *Partes,* eingetheilet. In welchen, und zwar im ersten Theile, des Herrn *Authoris* des *Orchestre* irrige Meynungen, *in Specie de Tonis seu Modis Musicis* wiederleget. Im andern Theile aber das rechte *Fundamentum Musices* gezeiget, *Solmisatio Gvidonica* nicht allein *defendiret,* sondern auch solcher Nutzen bey Einführung eines *Comitis* gewiesen, dann auch behauptet wird, dass man dereinst im Himmel mit eben den *Sonis,* welche hier in der Welt gebräuchlich *musiciren* werde. . . ." In 1717 Buttstedt was a man of fifty-one, and, as may be surmised from the above title, was thoroughly satisfied with the musical precepts in which he had been educated. The second half of his volume is one of the last expositions of the ideas of Guido d'Arezzo, and hence a landmark in the history of musical solmization.[70] The first half, however, with its point-by-point analysis of the *Orchestre* is a perfect example of the very theory Mattheson was attacking. A few excerpts will therefore be sufficient to demonstrate the difference in the beliefs of these two writers.

At first sight Buttstedt seems to agree with Mattheson on the decline of music for what appear to be similar reasons; but his interpretation of these reasons is completely the opposite of his antagonist's. The inadequate remuneration of musicians and the contempt for music originate, he says, in the fact that music is now considered "Spielmanns-Wesen" and not true study, although no study is more admirable than that of musical theory.[71] So great is the ignorance of true musical theory that he is forced to exclaim:

How many musicians will one find today who have real knowledge?—most of them do not even know how many styles and modes there are and what music is suitable for ecclesiastical or motet styles. The knowledge of such styles is almost entirely lost. . . . Why? [This music] is hard to understand

70. The solmization controversy has been thoroughly presented by Ludwig Meinardus in his article, No. 8, in the Walderseeschen *Vorträge* (1879), entitled "Johann Mattheson und seine Verdienste um die deutsche Tonkunst."

71. *Ut, Re, Mi* . . . , p. 11: "Demnach ist 1 die Haupt-Ursach des Verfalls der *Music,* dass solche nur für ein Spielmanns-Wesen und nich für ein *Studium* gehalten wird, da sie doch das *admirableste* ist, und in keinem *Studio* solche *Curiosa* vorkommen als in dem *Studio Musico Theoretico.*"

and not well paid for. And so, instead of correct knowledge mere *Galanterie* suffices, just as the finery of ladies once consisted of pearls and golden chains but now of mere ribbons and laces. . . .[72] Dr. Luther would have no patience with the *Drödelwerck* (which belongs rightfully in *stylo phantastico & Choraico* and in *Galanterie*) as used today in the Theatre, in the *privat Collegiis* and also in church music. He would instead approve the authorized, correct knowledge of musical theory . . . which comprises all in itself and of which Dr. Luther had so keen an understanding.[73]

The following definition of musical theory which Buttstedt then gives is quoted verbatim from Werckmeister's translation, made in 1699, of Agostino Steffani's treatise on music: *Quanta certezza habbia da suoi principii la musica* (Amsterdam, 1695). In its verbosity, its obscurity of language, its pedantic reasoning, and its assumption of the mathematical basis of music it perfectly represents the traditionalism which Mattheson scorned:

Wir wollen mit wenigen hinzuthun, wie die *Music* ihre *Principia* aus der *Arithmetica* und *Mathematica* habe, und wodurch sie grosse Kräffte und Bewegungen nehme. *Mathematica* ist entweder *pura* oder *mixta: Mathematica pura* ist, die *quantitat* oder grösse *abstractè* ohne *Materi* betrachtet, die wird auch *subalternans* genennet: und wird wieder *in Arithmeticam* und *Geometricam* getheilet, da diese *in quantitate continua*, das ist in Abmessung der Linien, Flächen und Cörperlichen Dingen beschäfftiget ist: Jene aber die *Arithmetica* handelt nur von den Zahlen, oder *de quantitate discreta* . . . *Mathematica mixta* ist, welche die *quantität* in einem gewissen *subjecto*, und einer vernehmlichen *Materie* betrachtet, entweder *in sono,* daher die *Musica,* oder im Lichte oder Gesichte, daher die *Optica* . . . diese alle werden *Disciplinae Mathematicae inferiores* genennet, weil sie ohne Hülffe der Rechnung und Abmessung nicht bestehen können. . . . *Musica est scientia Mathematica circa numerum in sono, ad efficiendam Cantilenam.* So ist demnach die *Musica* eine *scientia,* weil die Ursachen der *Musicalischen intervall:* durch die Zahlen *proportiones* und *quantitaten* auf dem *Monochordo*

72. *Idem,* p. 9: "Alleine wie viel findet man heut zu tage solche *Musicos* welche dergleichen Wissenschafft haben, die meisten wissen nicht einmahl wie viel *Styli,* wie viel *Toni vel Modi in Musicis* sind, und welcher *Musicus* thut etwas *in stylo Ecclesiastico?* Wo bleibt der *Stylus Motecticus?* Dieser ist ja fast gar verloschen. . . . Warum? es geht schwer ein, und wird nicht bezahlet. Daher kommt es dass man sich statt des rechten Wesens nur mit *Galanterien* behilfft, wie des Frauenzimmers Schmuck, welcher vor Alters in Perlen und güldenen Ketten bestanden, heut zu tage aber Bänder und Spitzen sind."

73. *Idem,* p. 6: "Alleine D. *Luther* hat nicht das Drödelwerck so *in Musicis* heut zu tage so wohl auf dem *Theatro* als sonst in *privat Collegiis,* auch in Kirchen-*Musicken* gebraucht wird, als welches nur *in stylo phantastico & Choraico* und in *Galanterien* bestehet, wohl aber das rechte Wesen *in Musicâ Theoreticâ* . . . als welcher alles in sich begreiffet, D. *Luther* auch solchen sonderlich wohl verstanden hat, gemeinet."

als *corpore sonoro* gezeuget werden . . . und dieserwegen ist die *Musica* auch eine *scientia Mathematica subalternata.*[74]

Since this definition represents Buttstedt's idea of what musical knowledge should be and therefore his idea of the basis of musical instruction, it is apparent that his educational remedy was the exact opposite of Mattheson's. Whereas the latter sought an enlightened realism for music, Buttstedt conceived of music as the handmaiden of theological teaching and as the mirror and picture of true knowledge, "since all pure combinations of sound come from pure Unison and Unity, and ultimately from God."[75] The high purpose of music, its correct application and interpretation are self-evident in the story of God's creation of the world, since all the elements of music are symbolized therein.[76] His musical esthetic is directed against the very practices which Mattheson was seeking to recognize and justify.

An examination of Buttstedt's reaction to other important tenets of Mattheson's treatises serves to demonstrate further the fundamental disagreement of the two men. To Mattheson's advocacy of musical practice as opposed to the knowledge of theory he replies, quoting Werckmeister again:

How can a present-day *Tyro*, much less a mere music-lover and *galant homme*, correct the basic rules which have been used for a hundred or more years not only *ad Theoriam* but also *ad praxin Musices*, and in this way learn *Music*, or attain for himself a thorough idea of it?"[77]

Mattheson's division of musical styles he finds incorrect, because

74. *Idem*, pp. 6–8. It is to be noted that only the essential parts of this definition have been quoted here.
75. *Idem*, p. 23: Buttstedt quotes from Werckmeister's *Musicae mathematicae Hodegus curiosus, oder ichtiger musicalischer Weg-Weiser* . . . (1687), chapter I: "Den alle reine Zusammenstimmung kommet aus dem reinen *Unisono* und *Unität.*"
76. *Idem*, pp. 24–26 (chapter II): "Erstlich wenn wir die Tage der Erschaffung mit der *Music* vergleichen, so sehen wir, das GOtt am Anfange oder ersten Tage, Himmel und Erden erschaffen habe; dieser Anfang ist die *Unitas* oder *Unisonus*, aus welchen alle *Consonantien* und *Dissonantien* herfliessen, ja GOtt selbst ist die *Unitat*, ein Anfang ohne Anfang oder Ende. Das Licht bildet auch vor denselben *Unisonum*, welcher mit dem *Sensu* kan begriffen werden. . . ." etc.
77. *Idem*, pp. 56–57: "Wie kan sich dann ein heutiger *Tyro*, vielweniger ein blosser Liebhaber und *galant homme* noch denen vor hundert und mehr Jahren gebräuchlichen nur *ad Theoriam* nicht aber so sehr *ad praxin Musices* gehörigen Grund-Sätzen richten, und daraus die *Music* erlernen, oder sich davon einen völligen Begriff machen?"

of its false emphasis on worldly music and its omission of a full exposition of the many traditional church styles.[78] His reading of this section prompted the following significant observation:

> When I read [it] through for the first time . . . I nearly died of wonderment. For I could not, and at this moment do not yet, believe, that a musician will be found who will thus throw away, yes, even slander the ancient *Principia*, axioms, inherited rules such as the twelve Greek modes as they are called *in stylo Ecclesiastico.* . . . This one [section] overthrows the entire *Orchestre.* . . ." [79]

To Mattheson's statement regarding the importance of the ear in judging the status of the interval of the fourth, Buttstedt suggests innumerable objections, which show that he misunderstands the implications of the problem completely, since to him the question can be solved only on theoretical grounds.[80] He expresses doubt as to the ability of Mattheson or anyone else to criticize the different national styles.[81] He disapproves of Mattheson's analysis of the "effective" qualities of the different tonalities.[82] In short, all of Mattheson's remedies to set up a rational, practical system of modern musical learning are found inadequate and unnecessary.

Buttstedt's book constituted a public challenge to Mattheson's progressive doctrines. What is more, it drew the attention of musicians throughout Germany to these doctrines as is apparent from laudatory verses published by Mattheson in his next book.[83] What was more natural, then, than that Mattheson should publish in 1717 a detailed defense of his position?

This he did in *Das Beschützte Orchestre.*[84] By contrast with *Das Neu-Eröffnete Orchestre,* the first part of this volume contains dis-

78. *Idem,* pp. 61–64.

79. *Idem,* pp. 83–84: "Als ich diesen § zum ersten mahl durchlesen, hätte ich mich . . . schier zu tode wundern mögen. Indem nicht begreiffen kunte, auch bis diese Stunde noch nicht, dass ein *Musicus* gefunden wird, welcher die alten *Principia,* Grund-Sätze, gegebene Kunst-Regeln die 12. Griechischen *Modos vel Tonos* wie sie *in stylo Ecclesiastico* genennet werden, so gar verwirfft, ja gleichsam darauf lästert. . . . Dieser § wirfft das gantze *Orchestré* über einen Hauffen."

80. *Idem,* pp. 71–75.

81. *Idem,* pp. 89–91.

82. *Idem,* pp. 92–98.

83. *Das Beschützte Orchestre* (1717), pp. [13]–[20]. Also *Exemplarische Organisten-Probe* (1719), pp. [7]–[14].

84. Bibliography No. 47.

cussions of the doctrines of many theoreticians, including those of Buttstedt, while the second half is specifically devoted to an exposition of the faults of the old system of solmization. In general, Mattheson did not add much to the stature of his ideas, but he did add considerable fuel to the controversy by appealing, in the dedication of the book, to a number of leading musicians for an "entirely impartial, free, and candid opinion" of his writings.[85] The thirteen personages thus addressed all responded with letters of varying size and length, which Mattheson published in the second part of his *Critica Musica* in 1724–25.[86] Since there is no better evidence of the reaction of the German musical world to his efforts at musical reform than these letters, a brief examination of their contents will not be out of place.

The most important of these letters were written by Händel in London, Telemann in Frankfort, Fux, the venerable and much honored Kapellmeister of the imperial Court in Vienna, Kuhnau, Bach's predecessor in the Leipzig cantorship, Theile, the composer of the first Hamburg opera, and Heinichen, the Kapellmeister at Weissenfels. The opinions, both favorable and unfavorable, of many of the most important German musicians are thus represented. Fux, who was the author of *Gradus ad Parnassum,* was the most critical of all, as could be expected, and Mattheson quotes not only his original letter but the subsequent correspondence which passed between them.

In his first letter, Fux takes issue with three of Mattheson's major principles. Of Mattheson's attack on the traditional solmization he writes that he:

was greatly astonished to find, that poor Guido d'Arezzo, who can never be praised sufficiently because musical practice owes more to him than to any other author in the world, has been so atrociously ridiculed; I must confess that I was not a little irritated: for it is certain that music, especially the vocal

85. *Das Beschützte Orchestre,* p. [12]: "Das vierdte und letzte, aber wichtigste Stück meines Anliegens, Hochansehnliche Herren, ist, dass Ew. Wohlgeb. u. Hoch-Edl., als vollenkommene und unverwerffliche *Judices competentes,* mir ein gantz unpartheyisches freyes und auffrichtiges Urtheil über den, meinem *Orchestre* unverschuldeter Weise, erregte Streit angedeyen lassen. . . ."

86. Bibliography No. 91. The title of this section is: "Die Orchester-Kanzeley, oder: Gutachten, Briefe, Ausspruche, Untersuchungen &c. der ehmaligen Scheides-Männer beym Orchester-Process."

art, would never have become what it is had Guido's method never been invented.[87]

The significance of the "galant homme" he also fails to comprehend:

In my opinion, even a man who has studied music on the basis of ut, re, mi, fa, sol, la, can nevertheless be a *Galant-Homme*. I am not at all a blind worshipper of superstitious antiquity; but until something better has been invented, I shall venerate in every way what through so many centuries the noblest masters have held to be good and proper.[88]

As for the modern system of tonality, Fux finds no foundation for the twenty-four new "modi," since there is no necessity for the development of modulation! [89] The skeptical tone of the entire letter, which caused Mattheson to comment rudely: "La colere & la prevention derangent terriblement la Dialectique" [90] also inspired him to write a long and argumentive retort.[91] Fux, however, replied by declaring the unshakableness of his views and his disinclination to continue the correspondence.[92]

The only other antagonistic letter among the thirteen came from Johann Christoph Schmidt, the senior Kapellmeister at the Saxon Court.[93] He was of the generation of Buttstedt and Fux, having been born in 1664, and his disapproval might therefore have been foreseen. He admits that he had found the plans, "accurate alle-

87. *Critica Musica* II, 185: ". . . aber wohl mich höchst verwundern, dass der arme, doch niehmallen sattsamb geprissene *Guido Aretinus*, als deme *Musica practica* mehr schuldig als keinem *Authori* in der Welt, so lästerlich durch die Hächl gezogen wirdt, ich muss bekhennen, das ich mich hürüber nit ein wenig geörgert habe: indeme gewiss ist, das, was diese *methode* niehmallen erfunden worden wäre, die *Musique*, aufs wenigst die Singkunst, mit nichten so weit hätte können gebracht werden."

88. *Idem*, p. 186: "Kan also meiner Mainung nach auch einer, der die *Musique* durch das ut, re, mi, fa, sol, la, erlernet hat, gleichwohl ein *Galant-homme* sein. Ich bin gar Kein Anbetter der *superstitieusen Antiquitet*, doch was durch so ville *saecula* von vornehmbsten Maistern für gutt und recht behalten worden, biss nit wass bessers erfunden wirdt, *venerire* ich auf alle weiss."

89. *Ibid.*: "Die 24. meue *Modi* haben auch gar keinen Grundt, dann weillen *Tonus* oder *modus* nichts ist, als eine *circolirende modulation intra limites octavae*, als folgt notwendig, das so uill *toni* und nit mehr sein können, als offt gedachte *modulation* vermög dess *Semitonii* kan verändert werden, welches nur 6. mahl geschehen kan."

90. *Idem*, p. 187.

91. *Idem*, pp. 188–197.

92. *Idem*, pp. 197–200: "Bey diesen, meine Meinung anbelangend, soll es seine Bewandnüss haben, dann ich weder Zeit weder *humor*, noch *inclination* zu dergleichen strittigen Schreib-Art habe" (p. 200).

93. *Idem*, pp. 266–268.

gata," and "fertigen und galanten Stylum" to admire, but cannot agree with the propositions concerning solmization, the new tonality, or the interval of the fourth.[94] Mattheson again took pains to correct his statement in a detailed letter to which he apparently received no reply.[95]

The opinions of the other more important composers are favorable, and vary considerably in their completeness and in their recognition of the implications of the controversial issues. For Händel the whole question was purely a practical one:

. . . je ne puis me dispenser de declarer, que mon opinion se trouve generalement conforme à ce que vous avez si bien deduit & prouvé dans votre livre touchant la Solmisation & les Modes Grecs. La question ce me semble se reduit à ceci: Si l'on doit preferer une Methode aisée & des plus parfaites à une autre qui est accompagnée de grandes difficultés, capables non seulement de degouter les eleves dans la Musique, mais aussi de leur faire consumer un tems pretieux, qu'on peut employer mieux à approfondir cet art & à cultiver son genie? . . . Leur [Les Modes Grecs] connoissance est sans doute necessaire à ceux qui veulent pratiquer & executer la Musique ancienne, qui a eté composée suivant ces Modes; mais come on s'est affranchi des bornes etroites de l'ancienne Musique, je ne vois pas de quelle utilité les Modes Grecs puissent être pour la Musique moderne . . .[96]

Heinichen gives two very good reasons for his approval, the second of which shows a recognition of the fundamental distinction Mattheson made between the old and the new music. To him, it seems clear that those musical antiquarians who seek to revive the fallen *"rudera antiquitatis"* must have passed their entire youth, or even their whole life, absorbed in such "whims." [97]

All will be sheer Greek to those steeped in prejudices when nowadays they hear that a moving music composed for the ears requires even more subtle and skilful rules—to say nothing of lengthy practice—than the heavily oppressive music composed for the eyes which the cantors of even the tiniest towns maltreat on innocent paper according to all the venerable rules of

94. *Idem*, p. 266: ". . . indem ich nicht nur dessen gute Absichten, sondern auch dessen geschickte Ordnung, *accurate allegata*, und fertigen und *galanten Stylum* darinnen zu *admiriren* gefunden. Was aber die Haupt-*Controvers* von dem Ut re &c. und den 12. *Modis graecorum* anlanget. . . ."

95. *Idem*, pp. 268–276.

96. *Idem*, pp. 210–211.

97. *Idem*, pp. 212–213: ". . . denn erstlich haben solche musicalischen Herren Antiquarii ihre gantze Jugend, oder vielmehr ihre gantze Lebens Zeit mit solchen Grillen zugebracht, und das wollen sie bey Leibe nicht umsonst gelernet haben."

counterpoint . . . And we Germans alone are such fools as to jog on in the old groove and, absurdly and ridiculously, to make the appearance of the composition on paper, rather than the hearing of it, the aim of music.[98]

Of the older generation of musicians, Johann Philip Krieger expresses his approval briefly,[99] while his younger brother, Johann, writes a most detailed and approving critique of Mattheson's ideas.[100] Johann Theile, living in retirement in his old age in Naumburg, declares that he greatly admires Mattheson's labor and learning, and adds that he has recommended the second volume to his son for careful perusal.[101] Johann Kuhnau is also most enthusiastic:

The work itself glorifies its master. You have shown yourself to be not only a musician profoundly learned both in practice and in theory, but also a veritable polyhistorian. As regards the great controversy that the gentleman of Erfurt has brought upon you, I do not believe that, save for him, anyone will disapprove of your *Orchestra*. This is especially true of your point of view in matters of the solmisation and the old ecclesiastical modes; for you wrote your *Orchestre* for a *galant-homme* who, being no professional musician, has not the least interest in amusing himself with innumerable old freaks which are usually outmoded at best and worth—virtually nothing.[102]

Of all the writers of these letters Telemann seems to have appreciated the import of Mattheson's writings most thoroughly. It

98. *Idem,* p. 213: ". . . so scheinen es solchen in *praejudiciis* steckenden Leuthen lauter Böhmischen Dörffer zu seyn, wenn man heute zu Tage saget, dass zu einer *touchanten* Ohren-Music vielmehr subtile und geschickte Regeln, nebst einer langwierigen *Praxi,* gehören, als zu einer Herz-druckenden Augen-Music, welche auf dem unschuldigen Papier, nach allen *venerablen Contrapuncten* der Herren Cantors in den allerkleinsten Städtlein, durchmartirisiret worden. . . . Und wir Teutschen allein seynd solche Narren, dass wir, in vielen abgeschmackten Dingen, lieber bey dem alten Schlendrian bleiben, und lächerlicher weise mehr die Augen auf dem Papier, als die Ohren zum *objecto* der Music machen wollen."
99. *Idem,* p. 215.
100. *Idem,* pp. 216–229.
101. *Idem,* pp. 282–283: "Ich muss gestehen, dass mir dessen wohl ausgearbeitetes und sehr gelehrtes, auch den Kunst-begierigen sehr nützliches Buch, sehr wohl gefällt, wie ich denn solches schon bestens, und sonderlich meinem Sohn, dem Organisten in Naumburg sehr hoch recommendiret habe, solches fleissig zu studiren und ihm zu Nutz zu machen."
102. *Idem,* p. 230: "Das Werck lobet seinen Meister, und haben sie sich darinne nicht nur als einen so wohl in *Praxi,* als *Theorie,* gründlich-gelehrten *Musicum,* sondern auch als einen so *veritablen Polyhistorem,* erzeiget. Was nun die Haupt-*Controverse* anbelanget, welche ihnen der Erfurter *moviret* hat, so glaube ich nicht, dass jemand anders, als dieser, ihr *Orchestre,* das sie vor einen *galant-homme,* der kein *Musicus ex professo,* vielweniger sich mit vielen, und meistentheils alten unnützen, Grillen *amusiren* will, geschrieben, vornehmlich *in puncto Solmisationis & veterum Modorum musicorum, improbiren* werde."

is perhaps significant that the most popular and in many respects the most conventional of Mattheson's contemporaries should have written in the following terms:

. . . C'est plutôt la beauté de vos oeuvres, qui m'oblige, de vous rendre justice, & de vous dire sans affectation, que vous meritez l'estime de toute la Republique musicale. Pour moi j'ai lû & relû quelques fois votre Orchestre avec la derniere Satisfaction. Je ne puis qu'approver vos deux dessoins, dont le premier est, de decouvrir la faux brillant des Anciens, & de chatier la caprice de ceux, qui les idolatrent & meprisent le siecle d'aujourdhui. Et le second, de montrer un droit chemin, pour parvenir facilement à la connoissance de la Musique. Enfin votre sujet est juste, la proposition vive, le stile coulant, & l'on voit par tout un discernement fin & une lecture tres extraordinaire. Au reste je vous prie, Monsieur, de vouloir bien continuer vos travaux pour la gloire de notre nation & de votre nom, & pour instruire le prochain par le riche talent que le bon Dieu vous a accordé. Ce louable exemple eveillera sans doute des gens, qui suivront vos pas, & feront de plus en plus revaloir notre agreable science . . .[103]

The significance of these letters, when considered in conjunction with the contents of *Das Neu-Eröffnete Orchestre,* is undoubtedly very great. The existence of what appears to have been an overwhelming majority of members of the "Republic of Music" who approved of Mattheson's philosophy indicates that he can scarcely be considered an originator of heretofore unknown ideas. In fact, an examination of much of the music which was being written in the first decades of the eighteenth century shows that many of the theoretical principles he advocated were already in practical use. It cannot therefore be said that his doctrines were responsible for this new style or practice. They merely took cognizance of it, and attempted to justify it according to rational principles. The essential conflict between the thinking of a Mattheson and that of a Buttstedt is discernible in both the letters and books analyzed here. If the old system of musical thought, as defended by Buttstedt, Fux, and Schmidt is clearly outmoded in the light of Mattheson's rationalism, the strength of this well-entrenched habit of thought and belief is also apparent. Few if any of the "modern" musicians, Mattheson included, appear to have been willing to discard the strict contrapuntal style, or the rules that governed it as a mode

103. *Idem*, pp. 277–278.

of expression. Yet they seem to have felt the necessity for the re-interpretation of it in terms of the new dramatic, individualistic feeling and philosophy which are implicit in the opera—the single most important art-form to which the Baroque gave birth. All the controversial issues contained in *Das Neu-Eröffnete Orchestre* are the result of the clash of the mutually antagonistic systems of musical thinking of the Baroque, the Renaissance, and the Middle Ages which still faced each other in the Germany of 1700. Mattheson, by reason of natural predilection, and keen insight into the musical and cultural tenor of his time, became cognizant of the thought and philosophy of many seventeenth- and eighteenth-century writers outside of Germany. Possessed of a naturally philosophical turn of mind, he could not fail to appreciate the connection of the rationalism of a Locke, a Descartes, an Abbé Gênet, or a La Mothe le Vayer with the psychological observations and reasoning of the seventeenth-century musical doctrines of the *Affektenlehre*. The dramatic music of Reinhard Keiser of Hamburg, whom he so admired, exemplified these theories. Of all the issues which this controversy brought to light, the correct evaluation of the status of the interval of the fourth became for Mattheson the most significant: the fourth volume to come from his pen, *Das Forschende Orchestre*,[104] is devoted entirely to its philosophical, and hence musical implications.

Mattheson's first book can then be best regarded as an "introduction" to the formalization of the musical esthetic spreading through Germany in the first half of the eighteenth century. In Mattheson's subsequent works, as might be expected from so great an admirer of the opera, his interpretation of this esthetic amounts to the universal application of the principles of dramatic melody. Through the expression of the emotional implications of a text, the human voice provides the most direct method of affecting the passions. A sound understanding of this technique thus will afford the most satisfactory preparation for the composition of all musical forms of an "affective" nature. With the publication of his *Vollkommene Capellmeister,* twenty-six years after that of his first volume,

104. Bibliography No. 73.

Mattheson may be said to have synthesized and systematized more completely than any other of the musical thinkers contemporary with him the musical principles which he undertook to champion in *Das Neu-Eröffnete Orchestre.*

# IV

## Critical Bibliography of the Works of Johann Mattheson

## NOTE

THE purpose of this bibliography is to describe in as compact and accurate a form as possible the various products of Johann Mattheson's pen. Incomplete lists of his works are to be found in the *Hamburger Nachrichten aus dem Reich der Gelehrsamkeit*, 1759, Stück 93, pp. 744 f., *Eitner's Biographisch-Bibliographisches Quellen-Lexikon der Musiker und Musik-Gelehrten*, VI, 385–389, Schröder's *Lexikon der Hamburgischen Schriftsteller*, V, 69–80, as well as in certain of Mattheson's own books. This bibliography is not a supplement to these, but is based upon independent investigation. Nor does it refer to any of them in a critical capacity. Since it is primarily concerned with the recording of the actual fact of each of Mattheson's works, it does not contain references to all the versions or even all the editions of certain works, unless they represent particular work on Mattheson's part.

The specific aims of the bibliography are two: the first is to provide a means of presenting information regarding the complete titles and contents of works, which, for reasons of space, have been referred to only in abbreviated form in the text; the second is to present clearly the extraordinary variety and mixture of Mattheson's intellectual interests. Because of this second consideration, the bibliography is planned chronologically, presenting a cross-section, so to speak, of his manifold efforts during a single year of his life. Within the limits of each year, his different works are listed under suitable categories, such as: "books," which includes all original published volumes; "music," which includes all published music; "pamphlets," which includes miscellaneous smaller published works; "published translations"; "manuscript books," etc.

Unless specifically stated otherwise, all the items mentioned are in the possession of the Hamburger Stadt-Bibliothek, although Mattheson's chief musical treatises are in the Lowell Mason Collection in the Library of the Yale School of Music.

In the case of musical manuscripts written to printed texts, such as operas, oratorios, serenatas, etc., the title as given in print is quoted herein, unless otherwise stated, and also the number of pages of both the text and the musical manuscript.

Since many of the titles are so long and so comprehensive that they give a summary of the contents of a specific item, the critical comment does not summarize them again. Nor does the comment contain all the possible information about each work, or all the references to it. The title and comment together are intended to give the reader a general idea of the contents and importance of each item. And by means of the bibliography as a whole, it is hoped that some conception of the enormous amount of Mattheson's labors, and the versatility of his interests—so typical of the man as a historical personality—will be obtained.

## 1699

### MUSICAL MANUSCRIPT

1 Die / PLEJADES / Oder das / Sieben-Gestirne, / In einem / Sing-Spiele vorgestellet / Im Jahr 1694. / HAMBURG. / Gedruckt bey Conrad Neumann, E. Edlen / und Hochw. Raths Buchdrucker. /
Text 62 pp.

The text of this opera,[1] which was written by Bressand, the Court Poet at Braunschweig,[2] is based on the Pleiades myth. Only one aria for contralto,[3] with orchestral ritornelli remains extant from Mattheson's score, in the Preussische Staatsbibliothek, Mus. Ms. 13902.

## 1702

### MUSICAL MANUSCRIPTS

2 Porsenna. /
MS. Score 135 pp.

The score of this opera is dated by Mattheson "Anno 1702 d. 2. Jan. aet. 20." The text,[4] also written by Bressand, deals with the complicated love affairs of three couples. Matthe-

1. Mattheson, *Musicalische Patriot,* p. 183. No. 78. In the list of operas produced in Hamburg.
2. Chrysander, *Georg Friedrich Händel* (Leipzig, 1919), I, 115.
3. "So lang mein Hertze lebt, so lang mein Anthem lebt. . . ."
4. Mattheson, *Musicalische Patriot,* p. 184. No. 94.

son's musical setting has no striking characteristics. It is overladen with lengthy recitative; the arias, which are all written in the rhythms of the gigue, rigaudon and minuet, are short and vocally simple; choruses begin and end the entire opera; there is but one ballet;— Autograph, except the overture.

3  Der Tod / Des / Grossen Pans: / und / Das Frühzeitige Abster-ben / des / Hoch-Edlen, Hoch-Weisen, und Hoch-/Bekehrten Herrn / GERHARD / Schotten, *J.U.L.* / Und Hoch-Verdienten Raths- und / Land-Herrn der Stadt Hamburg / Beklagete mit dieser / Traur- *MU-SIC.* / Das von Ihm gestifftete, und in die 30. Jahr unterhaltene / *OPERN-THEATHRUM* / in *HAMBURG.* / Gedruckt bey Conrad Neumann / G. Edl. und Hochw. Raths Buchdr. / Text (16) pp.

The title explains the occasion for this work.[5] The text was written by Hinsche, the pastor at the Hamburg Krankenhofe.[6] No vestige of the score remains. It was composed officially by Bronner, the organist of the Heiligen-Geist Kirche in Hamburg,[7] but Mattheson considered it virtually his own because of the large part he took in its composition.[8]

4  *VICTOR* / Hertzog der Normannen / OPERA. / Text (70) pp.

The text, also by Hinsche, is based on the Norman Conquest, and concludes with "Victor" triumphant upon the throne of "Albion." The score has perished. Mattheson wrote only the music for Act II, the two other acts being composed respectively by Schiefferdecker,[9] and Bronner.[10]

1704

MUSICAL MANUSCRIPT

5  *Cleopatra* / *Drama per musica* / MS. Score (141) pp. Dated "Den 28. März (?) 1704"

The text of this opera [11] was written by Feustking, who became rector at Tolk in Schleswig in 1706.[12] It recounts the romance and tragedy of "Antonius" and "Cleo-patra." The tone is highly moral, Antonius' long death being accompanied by a ballet of satanic spirits, some of whom are to dance and "einige der von ihm erschlagener nahen sich zu Anton. ihn zu quählen." After Cleopatra's death there is a long scene in

5. *Idem*, p. 185, No. 100.
6. Schröder, *Lexicon der Hamburgischen Schriftsteller*, III, pp. 267–8.
7. Hugo Riemanns, *Musik Lexikon* (elfte Auflage, Berlin, 1929), p. 233.
8. *Ehrenpforte*, p. 190: "Hierher gehört noch ein Trauerspiel, Tod des grossen Pans genannt . . . an dessen Composition Mattheson viel Theil genommen."
9. Riemanns, *Musiklexicon*, p. 1615.
10. Mattheson, *Musicalische Patriot*, p. 185, No. 96. Also *Ehrenpforte*, p. 190: "Seine . . . vierte theatralische Arbeit war eine Handlung aus der Opera, Victor, davon zween andre Componisten die beiden übrigen Actus sich nahmen, und also mit ihm gleichsam um den Preis stritten."
11. Mattheson, *Musicalische Patriot*, p. 186, No. 108.
12. Schröder, *Lexicon der Hamburgischen Schriftsteller*, II, 294–295.

which the remaining characters sing appropriate moral sentiments. Mattheson's score was so hurriedly written and revised that it is almost illegible. The overture and several other pages are missing. The arias are much more prominent than those in *Porsenna*, being much further developed both musically and dramatically.

## 1705
## MUSICAL MANUSCRIPTS

6 *Le retour du Siecle d'Or.*

Neither text nor score of this operetta is extant. In his autobiography Mattheson writes of it: "Unter währender Messe componirte der miemahls-müssige Mattheson ein frantzösisches Operetgen, welches auf Befehl des königsmarckischen Hauses, nach seiner Wiederkunfft von Braunschweig, auf Dero Gütern, Nempt und Bordöhl, im Holsteinischen bey Plön belegen, köstlich aufgeführet, und in allen Stücken von ihm angeordnet wurde. Die Gräfinn Löwenhaupt, auch eine Königsmarckinn von Geburth, und Schwester der Aurora, hatte die edle Poesie selbst dazu verfertiget . . ." [13]

7 *Sonate à due Cembali* per il Signore Cyrillo Wich gran Virtuoso. MS. (2) pp. for each *cembalo.*

The date of this composition and of No. 8 is doubtful. Since, however, Mattheson was tutor to Cyril Wich in 1705 before he undertook the duties of secretary to the elder Wich,[14] it seems reasonable to date them in this year. This "Sonata," written in G-minor in one long movement, is very brilliant in style. Its form is somewhat similar to the "concerto" form of that period, with a main theme as the "tutti" appearing in different related keys, and separated by episodes of contrasting rapidity and virtuosity.

8 (*Suite for Two Cembali.*) MS. (8) pp. for each *cembalo.*

This suite, written in G-minor, consists of four short sections: "Allemande," "'Courante," "Sarabande," and "Gigue."

9 *Ouverture. / avec Sa Suite, pour les Hautbois / de Mr. le General de Schoulenbourg. /* Score (6) pp.

The date of this suite is also uncertain, as it has not been possible to ascertain the identity or whereabouts of a General de Schoulenbourg. It is written in the key of F-major for 2 "cornetti," 3 "hautbois," and "basso." It has six sections: "Ouverture," in the usual two sections, (a "Grave" and a "Gigue") "Marche," "Angloise," "Polonaise" "Aria," and "Menuet."

## 1707
## PAMPHLET

10 *DEPORTATIS NUPER / LONDINI / IN MAGNO ET JUSTO TRIUMPHO / TROPHAEO, / OB RES / ANGLORUM / DOMI, FORISQUE; / ARTE ET MARTE; / CONSILIO MANUQUE; /*

13. *Ehrenpforte*, p. 194.
14. *Ehrenpforte*, p. 195.

*Prudenter / Fortiter / Feliciter / CESTAS / Hannce arjecit acclamatiun-
culum / Quidam, virtute populi Anglicani adductas / ad / Concelebranda
Bleintheim, Ramelliesque / ANNO MDCCVII. /*
(4) pp.

This congratulatory address and ode are ascribed to Mattheson by the Hamburger
Stadtbibliothek in the absence of any other likely author.[15]

## 1708

## MUSIC

11   *XII SONATES / à Deux & Trois Flutes sans Basse / Composées par /
MONSIEUR J. MATTHESON / Premier Ouvrage / Edition Corrigée
tres exactement sur la Partition par Estienne Roger / A AMSTERDAM /
Chez Estienne Roger Marchand Libraire / Qui vend la Musique du Monde
la plus correcte & qui s'engage / de la donner à meilleur marché que qui
que ce soit, quand / même il devroit la donner pour rien. /*
Flauto Primo 17 pp., Flauto Secundo 16 pp., Flauto Terzo 10 pp.

These "sonatas" are written only in the most usual keys. They might properly be
called suites, since their different sections are almost entirely based upon the typical dance
forms of the time. There is considerable variety in them as to the number of sections,
the forms used, and the resultant emotional content. The writing is more consistently
contrapuntal, perhaps because of the medium, than that in any of Mattheson's other
instrumental compositions.

## PUBLISHED TRANSLATION

12   Die / Vermittelst eines Künstlich eingerichteten und / gantz *accuraten
AUTOMATONS,* oder / von selbst-gehenden Uhrwercke zu findende /
*LONGITUDO,* / Dadurch man wissen kan, wie weit dieser oder jener
Ort, / wo man sich, es sey zur See oder zu Lande, befindet, / von einem
andern entlegen; / In 4. Theile, / Derer Erster etwas von der Gestalt der
Erden, nebst etlichen Beweiss-Gründen ihre Runde betreffend, und einem
Kupferstiche, dieselbe / zu *demonstriren,* in sich begreifft: / Der Andere
enthält das Hauptsächlichste, nemlich *Methodum / Practicam,* oder
einen ordentlichen und würklich zu machenden Ver-/such, wie die
Entlegenheit eines Ortes von dem andern, durch Hülffe des / *Auto-
motans,* möge entdeckt werden, durch verschiedene Capittul und Auff-
/gaben, gleichsam als in einer Reise rund umb die gantze Welt dargelegt,
und / mit den Nord- und Südlichen Hemisphaer-Charten erläutert: / Die
dritte Eintheilung handelt von dem Alterthum der / Uhrwecken, und
gibt eine Beschreibung verschiedener ausbündiger Schlag-/und anderer
Uhren, erzehlet anbey wie sie gestrigen, und nach und nach zu der itzigen
Richtigkeit gebracht worden sey: / Im vierdten Stücke wird von etlichen

15. It is not listed in the article on Mattheson and his works in Schröder's *Lexikon
der Hamburgischen Schriftsteller.*

*Experimentis* des *Compasses* geredet, dabey die benöthigte Anmerckungen auch ein Kupfer mit dem Copernischen *Systemate* ertheilet werden. / Durch / *JOHN CARTE,* / Uhrmacher aus *London,* wie auch Ihro Czaarischen Majestät *Geographi*schen / Uhrmacher, an der Ecke des Nesses in Hamburg zu erfragen. (12), 56 pp.

At the end of this title, Mattheson added, "Ins Teutsch und in Ordnung gebracht von Mattheson 1708." Nothing is known about John Carte, the author of the English original.[16] That he had been practicing the trade of watchmaker in London in 1701 may be surmised from the title of a huge calendar-chart by him now in the British Museum.[17] Little need be added concerning the contents of the book, since they are so fully catalogued in the title. Only parts I and II were published, however, since, as a note explains, Mattheson never received parts III and IV. There is a foreword by Mattheson recommending the contents, which is concluded by a long laudatory poem, entitled, "On Longitude Found Out by Mr. John Carte," in English, with a German translation on the opposite pages by the translator.[18]

## MUSICAL MANUSCRIPTS

13  *Sei Cantate / 3. con 3. sensa Stromenti / OPERA SECONDA. / 1708.* MS. Score (56) pp.

From the title-page of this set of cantatas, it appears that a first collection had already been written. Although attributed to Mattheson by the Hamburger Stadtbibliothek, they may well have been written by Cyril Wich, who is known to have composed several arias in much the same style in an opera of Mattheson's several years later.[19] All the cantatas are written for soprano, the verses being in Italian. Each consists of two arias and one or two recitatives. The first, third, and fifth are written for voice and continuo alone; the others, for voice, continuo, and violins. They are typical examples of the conventional, secular, Italian cantata of the period.

14  *Cantata Voce Sola con Violini Soli Del Sigr. Mattheson. /* MS. Score (2) pp.

This cantata is undated, but because of similarity in style and handwriting appears to date from the same general period as No. 13. Likewise it is written for soprano, and consists of two arias separated by a short recitative.

## PAMPHLETS

15  Matthesons Glückwunschungs Rede / an Graf Schönborn / 4 Juni 1708 / 8 pp.

16. Schröder, *Lexikon der Hamburgischen Schriftsteller,* I, 509: "Ein Engländer, der als Uhrmacher erst in London, u. 1713 in Hamburg lebte, aber sonst unbekannt ist."
17. *The Frontispiece of a curiouse Clock which will inform Gentelmen and others in all the useful things / contained in Almanacks for the year 1701 besides other curiosities for Ever. / Invented by John Carte Watchmaker near ye Fountain in ye Temple, London. /*
18. Cf. p. 71 of this text, where this poem is quoted.
19. Cf. No. 20, *Die geheimen Begebenheiten Henrico IV. . . . .*

The occasion for this speech of welcome to Graf Schönborn was the arrival in Hamburg of the Imperial Commission which was to resolve dispute between the Hamburger Rath and the dissatisfied burgers, mentioned in Chapter I, p. 37. Mattheson noted on the outside of the manuscript: "Dergleichen Andrede hat Mattheson noch vielmehr gehalten an Kaiserl. u. Königl. Minister bey deren Ankunft und anderer Gelegenheit."

16 Der / grundrichtige / Tonmeister, / in verschiedenen zu dieser Meister- / schaft gehörigen und beantworteten / Fragen, / (Neudruckt) herausgegeben / von . . . [the paper is cut off].
9 pp.

This manuscript is undated as well as unfinished. Six questions are posed and answered concerning the moral status of the opera. We list it here because of the relation to the opera, although it may have been written later.

## 1709

## MUSICAL MANUSCRIPTS

17 SEI CANTATE / Tre con etre Senza Stromenti / OPERA TERZA. / MS. Score (54) pp.

This collection of six cantatas forms an identical companion piece to No. 13. It is dated on the last page, "April 18, 1709."

18 Bey dehm / Von / GOTT in Ruhe / Verliehenen, / und von des / Käys. Herren Bottschaffters / Hochgrafl. *Excellence,* / durch Persöhnliche Hohe Gegenwarth, / Verherrlichten / Eines Edlen und Hochweissen Rathes / Der Stadt *Hamburg* / Gewöhnlichen / Ehren- und Freuden-Wahl / Auf *Matthias* / *Anno* 1709. / Wolte / Mit einem *Musicali*schen *Concert,* unter nachfolgenden / Zeilen, seinen tieffen *Respect* derlegen, / *Johan Matthiesson,* / *S.B.R.E.D.R.S.* /
Text 8 pp.

The text for this composition [20] was written by Lucas von Bostel, the lawyer, author and later Burgermeister of Hamburg.[21] Mattheson's score has perished. The occasion for the composition was the annual holiday of the Hamburger Rath, an event of considerable local importance. In addition to the honor of composing the music, Mattheson received a gold medal worth 12 ducats.[22]

## 1710

## MUSICAL MANUSCRIPT

19 BORIS GODENOW / DRAMA per MUSICA. / 1710. / MS. Score (3), 131 pp.

20. *Ehrenpforte*, p. 197.
21. Schröder, *Lexikon der Hamburgischen Schriftsteller*, I, 352–354.
22. *Ehrenpforte*, p. 197.

This opera bears the subtitle: "Boris *GOUDENOW* / oder / der / durch Verschlagen-heit / Erlangte Trohn. /" Mattheson wrote both the text and the music.[23] It was never performed, presumably because of intrigues in the opera company.[24] The plot concerns the death of "Theodorus Ivanowitz, Gross Fürst in Moscou," the succession of Boris, his success in opposing the rebellious factions headed by Irina, Theodorus' sister, and the triumph of love which ultimately brings about the happy union of Boris and Irina. The score is an interesting example of the rapid development of Mattheson's musical ability. There are many choruses of dramatic importance, and numerous dances. Many of the arias are in Italian, according to the vogue then becoming popular in Hamburg. The most noteworthy feature is the triumphant, concluding finale which consists of an extended Chaconne in seventeen sections. This form allows great variation in the treatment of the soloists, the chorus, and the orchestra of which Mattheson takes full advantage.

## 1711

### MUSICAL MANUSCRIPT

20  Die geheimen Begebenheiten / *HENRICO IV.* / Königs von Castilien und Leon / Oder: / Die getheilte Liebe, / In einer *OPERA* / Auff dem grossen *HAMBURGI*schen / Schau-Platz / Vorgestellet / Im Jahr 1711 im Monath Februarius. / Hamburg, gedruckt bey Friderich Conrad Greßinger. /
Text (12), 48 pp.
MS. Score 202 pp.
Dated: "Jan. 12, 1711," Representata "gli nove di Februaro 1711."

The text of this opera, Mattheson's last, was written by Johann Joachim Hoë, a little-known poet living in Hamburg at this time.[25] It concerns the love affairs of three couples, who, although already in love with each other, because of a whim of the king, exchange partners and rings, thereby binding themselves to the loving service of these new pairs. The resultant complications, which nearly approach tragedy, are straightened out at the end by the wisdom of King Henry. Because the plot seems to approach the level of comedy, Mattheson wrote a long foreword to the text explaining his views on the relation of drama and music, which are such as to preclude any association of true music and comedy. The scenic requirements of the opera were on the lavish scale customary at this time in Hamburg. They included twelve distinct changes of scene, one of these being a representation of a bull-fight. Mattheson's music for this scene is highly dramatic. His score is chiefly notable for the large number of charming arias, about half of them being sung to Italian verse.

### MUSIC

21  *Arie Scelte / dell' / Opera / d' / Henrico IV. Re di Castiglia / dedicate / All Illustrissimo Signore / il Signor / Cyrillo Wich, / Nobile Scudier Inglese, / da / Giovanno Mattheson, / Segretario dell Excellentissimo*

23. *Ibid.*
24. *Ibid.*: ". . . selbige ('Boris') aber, aus gewissen Ursachen, dem Theatro zu überlassen Bedencken trug. Sie ist also nicht aufgeführet worden."
25. Schröder, *Lexikon der Hamburgischen Schriftsteller,* III, 284–285.

*Signore Inviato Straordinario | de la Gran Bretagna. | Hamburgo, | Apresso l'Autore, 1711. |* Full score (7), 87 pp.; Parte Prima 23 pp.; Parte Secunda 10 pp.; Parte Terza 7 pp.; Bassono overro Violoncello 28 pp.

This collection includes forty-four arias—duets and solos, in Italian and German [26]— from the opera, *Henrico IV*. The instrumental accompaniments are written out in full in four parts, according to the original requirements of the opera. In Mattheson's long dedication to Cyril Wich, written both in Italian and English, the reason for this lavish edition is made apparent.[27] His music had not received a fair hearing when produced, due to the enmity of members of the opera, and this edition was prepared in order to show its true merits.

## PUBLISHED TRANSLATION

22   Herrn / *JOHANN ROBINSONS,* / Der Heiligen Schrifft *Doctoris,* / Vormahls / Ihr. Königl. Maj. von Gross-/Brittannien Hochansehnlichen *Extraordin.* / Abgestandten an Ihr. Kön. Maj. von Schweden &c. / Nunmehro aber (S. T.) / Hochwürdigsten *Lord* Bischoffs von *Bristol* / Predigt, / So er em Donnerstag den 8. Martii des 1711ten Jahrs, / Als an dem Jahrs-Tage / Ihr. Königlichen Gross-Brit-/tan. Maj. glücklichster Gelangung zum Trohne / vor / Deroselben und den Ober-Hause / gehalten; / Aus dem Englischen ins Teutsche übersetzet von / Johann Mattheson, / *E.D.A.E.S.R.M.M.B.* / Secretario. / Hamburg, Gedruckt bey Johan Niclas Gennagel. /
(6), 31 pp.
*Translated from:* A / SERMON / PREACH'D / At St. *JAMES'S,* / on *Thursday, March* 8, 1710. / Being the ANNIVERSARY / Of Her MAJESTY'S / *Happy Accession to the* Throne. / By the Right Reverend Father in GOD, / JOHN Lord Bishop of *Bristol.* / *Publish'd by Her Majesty's Special Command.* / LONDON. / Printed for Sam. Crouch, at the Cor-/ner of *Popes-head Ally* in *Cornhill,* 1711. / [28]
24 pp.

Mattheson's Foreword to his translation expresses admiration for the author [29] and the sentiments in his sermon. He makes no allusion to his personal acquaintance with Robinson.[30]

## 1712

## PUBLISHED TRANSLATION

23   Die / Ausbündig-schönen / Eigenschafften / Der / In Heilung allerhand Kranck-/heiten und zur Erhaltung beständi-/ger Gesundheit be-

26. In the Dedication, Mattheson explains that several arias were written by Cyril Wich.
27. Cf. p. 32 of this text.
28. British Museum.
29. *D.N.B.* XLIX, 23–26.
30. He had known Robinson since the latter's diplomatic mission to Hamburg in 1707. *Ehrenpforte,* p. 196.

währt und / heilsam befundenen / *AMERICAN*Ischen / Tobacks-Pflantzen; / Den / Höchst-schädlichen / *QUALITAETEN* / Des Inden Nordischen Ländern / wachsenden / Tobacks / entgegen gesetzet. / *HAMBURG*, gedruckt bey Frid. Conr. Greflingern, 1712. / (24) pp.

I have not been able to identify the English original of this little pamphlet. It is dedicated to Garlieb Sillem, who was in charge of the measures being taken to control the plague which was attacking Hamburg and its environs at that time.[31] Mattheson explains in the dedication that Bishop Robinson.[32] had suggested the translation on the grounds that the Hamburgers should know of the beneficial effect of tobacco in combating the infection.[33] Undoubtedly the original pamphlet dates back to the great plague in London, when tobacco was the most popular, if the most ineffective, of all the remedies tried.[34] Mattheson wrote of the labor involved in this translation: "Die Sache verlohnte sich der Mühe sehr wohl," [35] which indicates, perhaps, that Hamburg also succumbed to the charms of this patent remedy.

## MUSICAL MANUSCRIPTS

24  Die / Nach Verdienst Erhobene Jugend / Als der / Hoch-Edle, Vest-und Hoch-Gelahrte Herr, / Herr, / *JOHANN ANTHON* / Winckler, / *J. V. D.* / Zu eines Hoch-Edlen Und Hoch-Weisen Rahts / der *Republique HAMBURG*, / Hochbetrautem *SYNDICO* / Im Jahr Christi 1712, den 21 Octobr. erwählet wurde, / In einer *SERENATA* vorgestellet. / *HAMBURG*, Gedruckt bey Conrad Neumann, E. E. Hoch-Weisen Rahts-Buchdrucker. / Text (14) pp.

The score of this serenata is lost. In his copy of the text, Mattheson wrote, "La Musica di Mattheson Poesia di Neudorff." [36] The title makes plain the occasion for which the piece was composed. According to the text it was performed "in einer nahgelegenen Wohnung an dem Neuen Tempel St. Michaëlis." Winckler, to whom Mattheson taught the art of thoroughbass a year later,[37] was a prominent lawyer in Hamburg.[38]

25  *Amors* / Unnothige *Intriguen* / An / Dem erfreulichen Geburths-Tage / Des wohlgebohren Fräuleins, / FRAULEINS / Anna Christina / von

31. Schröder, *Lexikon der Hamburgischen Schriftsteller*, VII, 185.

32. Cf. No. 22.

33. The Dedication reads in part as follows: (his reason for translation) "ist die Ubsicht nichts anders gewesen, als meine nie aus den Augen gesetzte schuldige Pflicht gegen dem lieben Vaterlande, zu mahlen bey itzigen Kranckheit drauende hanfften, auch öffentlich hiermit einigermassen zu bezeugen, der Hofnung, dass vielleicht eine oder andere darinn enthaltene *Thesis* dem *Publico* zur heilsamen Nachricht gereichen möchte."

34. W. G. Bell, *The Great Plague in London, in 1665*, (London, 1924), pp. 155–156.

35. *Ehrenpforte*, p. 198.

36. Schröder, *Lexikon der Hamburgischen Schriftsteller*, V, 489, calls Neudorff a native of Hamburg, born 169–?, died 1752, having been Corrector of the Johanneum since 1719.

37. *Ehrenpforte*, p. 200.

38. Schröder, *Lexikon der Hamburgischen Schriftsteller*, VIII, 75.

Wedderkop, / In einer / *SERENATA* / vorgestellet, / Hamburg den 6. Januar. / 1712. / Gedruckt, bey Philipp Ludwig Stromer./ Text (4) pp.

The score of this serenata is no longer extant. Christina von Wedderkop, in whose honor it was performed, was the daughter of the wealthy Bürgermeister of Lübeck who had invited Mattheson to that town in 1703 as a possible successor to the famous organist, Buxtehude.[39] Several years later Fräulein von Wedderkop became the wife of Cyril Wich, who probably commissioned the serenata.[40]

## 1713

### BOOKS

26  Die unermeszliche Vorsorge / der / durch Göttliche Allmacht wirck-kenden / gütigsten Natur. / Mittelst welcher / Ein, anitzo auf hiesiger Rheede angekommener, Gross Brittannischer / Schiffs-*Capitaine* / Ge-nannt: / *Alexander Salkirk,* / Vier gantzer Jahr und vier Monaht, gantz allein / auf einer, in der Süder-See belegenen, unbe-/wohnten Insul, Nahmens *Juan Fernandez,* sein / Leben wundenbahr un nohtdursttiglich er-/halten: / Davon dieser wahrhaffte / Bericht, / Theils aus seiner eigenen Munde, theils, und ab-/sonderlich, aus einem wohlbeglaubten See-Jour-/nal, so allerdings mit bemeldten *Capitains* Erzeh-/lung überein stimet, mit Fleiss zusamen getra-/gen ist, und *curieusen* Ge-mühtern hiemit *com-/municiret* wird, / Auf *expressen* Befehl Se. *Excel-lentz* / des Königl. Gross-Brittannischen *Extra-/ordinair Envoye* hieselbst, / von *Mattheson.* / *Hamburg* / Gedruckt bey Seel. Thomas von Wierings Erben im güldnen A.B.C. 1713. / MS. 19 pp.

The above title is taken from Mattheson's MS. in the Hamburger Stadtbibliothek, the published title being almost exactly identical. In an article published in 1886, "Alexander Selkirk in Hamburg . . . ,"[41] the author, Otto Rüdiger, discusses the historical back-ground of this interesting booklet. His conclusions are that Alexander Selkirk, whose exploit had been already described by Woodes Rogers in 1712,[42] definitely came to Hamburg as Captain of a ship in 1713, as implied in the above title. Wich had perhaps read this former account, and the presence of Selkirk in Hamburg presumably prompted him to have Mattheson prepare this short account in German.[43] By comparing the text

39. *Ehrenpforte*, p. 94. Cf. p. 28 of this text.
40. Cf. No. 32.
41. *Aus Hamburgs Vergangenheit, Kulturhistorische Bilder aus verschiedenen Jahr-hunderten.* Herausgegeben von Karl Koppman (Hamburg und Leipzig, 1886), pp. 185–208: "Alexander Selkirk in Hamburg. (Nach einer Flugschrift vom Jahre 1713)," by Otto Rüdiger.
42. *Voyage to the South Seas and Round the World 1708–1711,* (London, 1712).
43. Rüdiger suggests that the lack of a regular news-organ in Hamburg at this time prompted Wich to have this pamphlet written. (*Aus Hamburgs Vergangenheit*, p. 188.)

of Mattheson's version [44] with that of Rogers, Rüdiger points out enough similarities to establish Rogers as the main source of this text.[45]

27 Das / Neu-Eröffnete / *Orchestre*, / Oder / *Universelle* und gründliche Anleitung, / Wie ein *Galant Homme* ei-/nen vollkommen Begriff von / der Hoheit und Würde der edlen / *MUSIC* / erlangen, seinen *Gout* darnach formi-/ren, die *Terminos technicos* verstehen / und geschicklich von dieser vortreffli-/chen Wissenschafft raisonni-/ren möge. / Durch / *J. Mattheson, Secr.* / Mit beygefügten Anmerckungen / Herrn Capell-Meister *Keisers.* / *HAMBURG*, bey *Benjamin Schillers* Witt-/we im Thum 1713. / (30), 338, (11) pp.

This book is the first of Mattheson's treatises on music. It is indeed a "universal and fundamental introduction" to music, written in terms comprehensible to the educated person of the time. Its contents are divided into three parts, the first dealing with the terminology of music, the second with the rules and principles of composition, and the third with analytical criticism. The book is dedicated to Aurora von Königsmarck, the famous mistress of Augustus the Strong of Saxony, and a prominent musical amateur and patron.[46]

## MUSIC

28 SONATE POUR LE CLAVECIN—*composée par I. MATTHESON. SECR. et dediée à QUI LA JOUERA LE MIEUX.* /
Second title: SONATE vors CLAVIER—verfertiget durch J. MATTHESON. SECR. und derjenigen Persohn gewidmet, DIE AM BESTEN SPIELEN KAN.
1 large broadside.

In Mattheson's own lists of his works, this piece is described as "Sonate . . . in Form einer Land Charte," probably because of the unusual format in which it was issued. Mattheson himself engraved it on one side of a large sheet of paper, its fantastic size being, therefore, its chief resemblance to a map. It is written in G-major, and its form is a combination of the operatic *da capo* and the instrumental concerto. In 1723 twenty more copies were struck off from the original copper plate, apparently because of its popularity.[47]

## PUBLISHED TRANSLATION

29 Die / Vernünfftler. / Das ist: / ein teutscher Auszug / Aus dem Engeländischen *Moral*-Schrifften / Des / TATLER / und / SPECTATOR,

44. Mattheson's pamphlet is completely reprinted by Rüdiger, pp. 195–208.
45. It is interesting to note in this connection that the first translation of Defoe's *Robinson Crusoe* was made and published by M. Vischer in Hamburg in 1720. (*University of California Publications*, IX [1920], p. 175.)
46. Cf. pp. 116–133 of this text for further details concerning the contents of this book.
47. *Niedersächsische Neue Zeitungen von Gelehrten Sachen*, 1729, No. 19.

vormahls verfertiget; / Mit etlichen Zugaben versehen, / Und auf Ort und Zeit gerichtet / von / JOANNE MATTHESON, / *Secretario* des Königl. Gross-Brittannischen *Ministri* im Nieder-/Sächsischen Kreise; Hoch-Fürstl. Schleswig-Holsteinischen Capellmeister; / des Hamburgischen Stiffts-*Canonico min. und Directori / Musices.* / Hamburg, 1721. / 386 pp.

This title is taken from that of the 1721 collection. Although the first number is undated, the fourth bears the date of June 21, 1713. The numbers, totaling in all one hundred, were issued irregularly on the average of twice a week up to May 26, 1714. With the exception of numbers 14, 15, 21, 22, 24, 75, and 76, which are the product of Mattheson's own pen, all are translations or adaptations from the *Tatler* and *Spectator*. This *Vernünfftler* was the first imitation of the English journals in Germany.[48] In his letter to Steele,[49] Mattheson explains the origin of the publication, and his own experience with it. His free method of adapting various situations of the originals to the local scene in Hamburg certainly reproduces much of their vitality.[50] The results were convincing enough, apparently, to draw forth the ire of certain local citizens who interpreted the contents as impertinent allusions to themselves.[51] That it was literally censored out of existence on this account, as asserted a few years later by Bodmer,[52] appears to be an overstatement, which Mattheson took great pains to deny.[53]

## 1714

## MUSIC

30  *PIECES DE CLAVECIN / en Deux Volumes / Consistant des / Ouvertures, Preludes, Fugues, Allemandes, / Courentes, Sarabandes, Gigues, et Aires. / Composees / par / J. Mattheson, / Secr. / 1714 / London Printed for I. D. Fletcher, and Sold at most Musick Shops. / Entered in the Hall Book according to Act of Parliament. /* (9), 47 pp.
*Second Title, German Edition:* MATTHESONS / Harmonisches Denckmahl, / Aus / Zwölf erwählten Clavier-Suiten, / Bestehend in Ouver*tur*en, *Symphonien, Fugen, Boutaden, Praeludien, Allemanden, Couranten, Sarabanden, Giguen, Arien* und / *Menuetten*, nebst ihren *Doublen* oder Variantionen, / Von / Arbeitsamer und ungemeiner STRUCTUR / errichtet, / Auch mit einer etwas unständlichen doch wolgemeinten / Vor-

48. Ferdinand Krome, *Anfänge des Musicalischen Journalismus in Deutschland* (Leipzig, 1896), p. 5.
49. Cf. pp. 76–78 of this text.
50. Karl Jacoby, *Die ersten moralischen Wochenschriften Hamburgs am Anfange des achtzehnten Jahrhunderts* (Hamburg, 1888), which contains an analysis of this journal.
51. Notes at the conclusions of both Nos. 10 and 14 speak of the appearance of "Gegen Vernünfftler" pamphlets.
52. Johann Jakob Bodmer, *Anklagung Des Verderbten Geschmackes Oder Critische Anmerkungen Über Den Hamburgischen Patrioten, Und die Hallischen Tadlerinnen* (Frankfurt and Leipzig, 1728).
53. *Ehrenpforte,* p. 199.

oder Anrede / An die heutige berühmte COMPOSITEURS / *loco Frontispicii* versehen. / 1714. / London Printed for I. D. Fletcher etc. (as above).
(12), 47 pp.

It should be noted that this is but one collection with two titles printed on the same fundamental frontispiece, one being for the German and the other for the English trade. The former contains the publisher Fletcher's brief recommendation by way of a foreword, while the German edition contains an announcement of Mattheson's project ot a "Musikalische Ehrenpforte." The German title summarizes the contents thoroughly. The suites, all of which are in the most usual keys, vary as to number and form of the pieces mentioned above.

## MUSICAL MANUSCRIPTS

31 Die / Frohlockende Themse, / Auf das / Höchsterfreulichster / Krönungs-Fest / Des / Aller-Durchlauchtigsten, Grossmächtigsten / Königs und Herrn, / HERRN / Georg Ludewigs, / Königs von Gross-Brittannien, Frankreich / und Irrland, Beschützers des Glaubens &c. &c. / Hertzogs zu Braunschweig und Lüneburg &c. / Des Heil. Reichs Ertz-Schatzmeisters / und Chur-Fürstens, / Bey einem / Von dem hiesigen Gross-Brittannischen Residenten / Herrn von Wich, / Dessfalls allhier angestellten Freuden-Fest, und einer dar-/auf zielenden *Illumination,* unter währender Tafel / In einer SERENATA / Allerunterthänigst aufgeführt. / HAMBURG, gedruckt bey Friderich Conrad Greflingen, an der Ellern-Brückern. / Text (16) pp.

On the inner page is written: "Die *Music* ward gesetzt durch Herrn *Mattheson,* Englischen Secr. Die Poësie ist von Monsr. König." [54] Mattheson's score is unfortunately lost. The musical part of this celebration seems, however, to have been of considerable importance. Each of the four "Personen, Die Themse, Der Ocean, Hybernia, Das Glücke" in the text sings one solo aria and one aria with her attendant chorus. These are respectively "Die Fluss-Nymphen, Die Tritonen, Die Land-Nymphen, Die Lustbarkeiten." The Illumination, which is described in magnificent detail in the text, followed.

32 Die / Vermählung der Kluhheit / mit der Tugend, / Bey Gelegenheit eines *solennen Festeins,* / Welche / Der Gross-Britannische RESIDENT / Herr von *Wich,* / Auf Die Königl. Gross-Britannische / Krönung / angestellt, / Wegen Seiner eigenen / Glücklichen Vermählung / mit der / Hochgebohrnen Fräulein / von Wedderkopp. / In einer CANTATA / zu Bezeugung seines gehorsamen *Respects* / Vorgestellet / von / König / Hamburg, gedruckt bey Friedrich Conrad Greflingen, 1714. / Text (8) pp.

54. Johann Ulrich König (1688–1744), writer of much prose and poetry, resided in Hamburg until 1719, when he became court poet and secretary to the King of Saxony (August I) at Dresden. Schröder, *Lexikon der Hamburgischen Schriftsteller,* IV, 121–126.

Mattheson's score for this wedding cantata is no longer in existence. Apparently Wich celebrated the coronation of George I by his own marriage. Although this cantata and the serenata, No. 31 were associated together in composition and the juxtaposition of two simultaneous celebrations, this one was conceived on a suitably smaller scale.

## 1715
### PAMPHLET

33   Dem Hoch-Wohlgebohrnen Herrn, / Herr / CYRILLO von WICH, / Ihro Königl. Majestät von Gross-Britannien, &c. &c. / an die Hansee-Städte des Nieder-Sächsischen Krayses / accreditirten MINISTRO, beyder Carolinen Land-Grafen, &c. &c. / Zu Ehren Wolte ein alter Diener poetisiren, / und wurde / Dis Wenige / Auff den am 9. Julius einfallenden / Cyrullus-Tag / Ersonnen / von / Ehre. / 1 broadside.

The inspiration for this fourteen line sonnet is made clear by the title. It is dated 1715 at the conclusion of the verse.

### MUSICAL MANUSCRIPTS

34   Den verewigten Ruhm und Rahmen / Des / Durchl. Fürstl. Hauses / Gagarin / Wolte / In Gegenwart / Ihre Hoheit / des Printzen / GA-GARIN, / Seines Gnädigsten Herrn, / In einer SERENATA / und / ILLUMINATION / Zu Contestirung seiner tiefsten Ergebenheit und Erkändt-/lichkeit genossener Hoher Gnade / Allerunter-thanigst in Eil vorstellen / J.H.I.L.P.C. / HAMBURG, gedruckt bey Friederich Conrad Greflingern, 1715. / Text (12) pp. MS. Score (7), 44 pp.

The author of the text is unknown. Seven characters, including "Der Praeses der Götter," "Ruthenia," "Fama," and "Die Ewigkeit" recount in bombastic style the prestige of the House of Gagarin in their particular provinces. Mattheson's score is not notable in any way except for the length and monotony of the recitatives, for which he was not entirely to blame. A short overture commences the piece. From the notations in the score it is clear that the leading singers at the Opera were the soloists in this serenata, as in many others by Mattheson.

35   Keusche Liebe, / Bey dem / Viet- / Und Mohrmannischen / Hochzeit-Feste, / In einer / SERENATA / Vorgestellt / Von / König. / Hamburg, gedruckt bey Friderich Conrad Greflingern, / Im Jahr 1715., den 2 September. / Text (8) pp. MS. Score 27 pp.

König's [55] text, written for four soloists and chorus, calls for five arias and five choruses, set off by recitatives. Mattheson entitled his score: "Die / Wiedtische SERE-

55. Cf. No. 31.

NATA / componirt in Zwölf Stünden / von / Mattheson / d. 2. Sept. 1715." All of the pieces are short, but several of the arias have remarkably good melodies.

36  Die vergnügte Treue / Bey der / Kraus- / und Kählerischen / Trauung / In einer / CANTATA / *musical*isch auffgeführet. / Hamburg. den 17 Junii 1715. / Text (8) pp. MS. Score 19 pp.

The author of the text is unknown. Although written only for two solo voices, bass and contralto, with five arias, it is scored for the usual strings and two *Cornette di Caccia.*

37  Die Heilsame Geburt / Und / Menschwerdung / Unsers Herrn und Heylandes / Jesu Christi, / Nach den / Evangelisten *LUCAS,* / In einer / Kirchen-*MUSIQUE* / aufgefuhret / *ANNO* 1705 / *HAMBURG,* / Gedruckt bey Conrad Neumann, E. Edl. Hochw. Rahts. Buchdrucker. / Text (8) pp. MS. Score 32 pp.

This is the first of Mattheson's oratorios written and performed while he was Director of Music in the Domkirche. The erroneous date of the text (1705) is corrected in the title of the MS. score, which, while corresponding to the first part of the above title, concludes: "nach dem Evangelisten Lucas / in der / Hamburgischen Alter Stiffts-Kirche / Musicalisch aufgeführet / Anno 1715 dec. 27. / Von / J. Mattheson / Vicario. /" [56] It is scored for strings, 2 *clarinos* and *timpano.* As is generally customary, the tenor sings the narrative part of the evangelist. The opening chorus is severely contrapuntal, making use of the traditional chorale, *Von Himmel Hoch,* as a *cantus firmus.* The music is written in a somewhat less florid or operatic style than the majority of Mattheson's oratorios.

## 1716

## PUBLISHED TRANSLATIONS

38  Königlicher / Gross-Britannischer / Gnaden-Brieff. / gegeben / im dritten Jahr / Der Regierung / *GEORG I* / Königs von Gross-Britannien, / Frankreich und Irrland. / Bey versamleten Parlament, so zu Westmin-ster ange-/fangen und gehalten worden, am siebzehnten *Martii,* im Jahr / Christi 1714. im ersten Jahr der Regierung unsers *souverainen* / Königs und Herren, *GEORG I* von Gottes Gnaden, Kö/nig von Gross-Britannien, Frankreich und Irr-/land, Beschützer des Glaubens &c. / Und von der Zeit an fortgesetzet, mittelst verschiedener Aufscheibungen und Verlangerungen, bis auf den Zwanzigsten Februarii 1716. da die / zweyte Sitzung des gegen wärtigen Parlaments gehalten worden. / Aus dem *Original* ins Teutsche gebracht von / *MATTHESON.* / Hamburg, gedruckt und zu bekommen bey seel. *Thomas* von *Wierings* Erben bey der Börse. im güldnen A. B. C. / 20 pp.

56. *Ehrenpforte,* p. 201.

The "original" Mattheson speaks of was most probably the accounts in the English newspapers. These speeches were presumably of interest in Hamburg because of their declaration of general European policy.

39   EXTRACT / Der Zeitungen / aus / Gross-Britannien, / So der hiesige / Königliche *Ministre,* Herr von *Wich.* mit gestriger Post erhalten, / und hiemit auff dessen Befehl *publicirt* werden. / *HAMBURG.* / Gedruckt bey seel. Thomas von Wierings Erben, / bey der Börse, im güldnen A. B. C. 1716. /
(8) pp.

The contents of this pamphlet are reports on the movements of the rebels and the victorious troops of the government in England. According to the text, they are based upon a report in the "Post Comptoir zu Edenburg" of February 3, a second report in another nameless newspaper, dated Whitehall, February 10, and from "einem besondern Hand-Schreiben von obigen Dato."

40   Anrede, / des *Lord* Gross-Meisters, / Bey / Verurtheilung / *James,* Grafen von *Derwentwater,* / *William, Lord Widdington, Wil-/liam,* Grafen von *Nithisdale, Robert,* Grafen von *Cornwath, William,* Burggrafen *Kenmure,* und / *William, Lord Nairn.* / HAMBURG, / Gedruckt bey seel. Thomas von Wierings Erben / bey der Börse, im güldnen A. B. C. /
(8) pp.

Mattheson may have found this speech reported in the *Political State* for the month of January, 1716.[57] The trial of these unfortunate Jacobites attracted much attention at the time. This speech of the Lord Steward may be found in Howell's *State Trials,* XV, 795–801.

## MUSICAL MANUSCRIPTS

41   Die / Gnädige Sendung / Gottes / des / Heiligen Geistes, / Zur Erwickung / Christlicher Andacht, / Am / Dritten heiligen Pfingst-Tage / in hiesiger Stiffts-Kirche / auffgeführet / Von / *Mattheson HAMBURG.* /
Text (8) pp.
MS. Score 53 pp.

The author of the text is unknown. The score is dated 1716. In this, Mattheson's second oratorio, all the soloists and the chorus are dramatic representations of characters, such as "Jesus," "Petrus," "Der Heilige Geist," "Chor der Jünge," etc. The most dramatic and interesting music is a dialogue, in the form of a chorale, between the chorus and "Jesus," who sometimes sings with the chorus and sometimes in the interludes between the phrases of the chorale.

57. An excerpt is quoted in the *St. James Evening Post,* No. 118, London, March 1, and described as being condensed from the *Political State* for the month of January. The complete account is to be found in Howell's *State Trials,* XV, 762 f.

42   CHERA, / Oder / Die Leidtragende und getröstete / Wittwe zu Nain. / Am XVI Sonntage nach Trinitatis / auffgeführet / Von / *MATTHE-SON.* / Hoch-Fürstl. Schleswig-Holst. Capellmeister. / Text (10) pp.
MS. Score 47 pp.

The text recounts the story of Christ's raising of the dead son of the Widow of Nain,[58] and adds the contemplative figures of "Der Glaube" and "Die Andacht" to interpret its religious significance. Mattheson's score takes full advantage of the dramatic implications of the text.[59] The production of this oratorio was signalized by the appearance of opera singers as soloists.[60]

43   Der / Verlangte / Und / Erlangte Heiland, / Zur Bezeugung Gott-gewidmeter / Weynachts-Freude, / Sammt angehängtene / Zwey-Chörichten / *MAGNIFICAT,* / Oder / Lob-Gessang Mariä, / Musica-lisch gesetzet / Und / Aufgeführet / Von / MATTHESON. / HAM-BURG. / Text (6) pp.
MS. Score oratorio 36 pp.
MS. Score Magnificat (23) pp.; cf. No. 44.

From the text it appears that this oratorio and Magnificat were sung together. Since the score of the Magnificat is dated 1716, it seems probable that both were composed for the Christmas service of that year. The score of the oratorio contains no noteworthy characteristics. Mattheson noted on its last page that its performance takes "eine halbe Stünde oder just 30 Minuten."

44   *Magnificat:* / *A Due Cori.* / Text, cf. above No. 43.
MS. Score (23) pp.

This score shows signs of considerable use.[61] It is the only one of Mattheson's written for double chorus. All three choruses in the score (the first is repeated at the end) are unusually contrapuntal and make good use of antiphonal effects.

45   ORATORIUM, / Auff die / (Tit.) / Trummer-/Und / (Tit.) / Lonauische / Verehligung, / Als selbige den 18. Nov. 1716. / Durch Priesterliche Hand vollzogen / wurde, / Verfertiget / Von / MATTHE-SON. / HAMBURG, / Gedruckt bey Friderich Conrad Greflingern. / Text (8) pp.

58. Luke VII. 11–18.
59. Cf. pp. 50–52 of this text.
60. Their names are noted in the MS. score by Mattheson. In the *Ehrenpforte*, p. 203, he wrote of this event: "Den 17. Sept. hielt er Musik im Dom, und führte Madame Kayser aufs Chor, welches, ausser obigem Exempel, zuvor in keiner hamburgischen Kirche ge-schehen war, dass ein Frauenzimmer mit musiciret hätte."
61. On feastdays it was customary at this time in many Lutheran churches to sing the Magnificat (Luke I. 46–55) in the evening. Schweitzer, *J. S. Bach,* II, 166.

The score of this wedding oratorio is lost. Mattheson speaks of its performance in his autobiography.[62]

46  Das / *Mercurialis*che Opffer, / Bey dem / Trummer- / und / Lonaischen / Hochzeit-Feste, / In einer / *SERENATA* / vorgestellet / von / *MATTHESON.* / *HAMBURG,* / Gedruckt bey Friderich Conrad Greflingern, 1716. / Text (8) pp.

The score of this wedding serenata, the secular companion-piece to No. 45 is likewise lost. Three soloists are required for both. In the first they represent the Christian forces of "Liebe," "Andacht," "Segen"; in the second, the pagan deities of "Amor, der Gott der Liebe," "Mercurius, der Gott des Handels," and "Conavia, Eine Nymphe der Elbe." According to the text the performance of this serenata took place "im Tempel des *Mercurii,* welcher mit vielen Facheln zum Opffer-Fest erleuchtet ist."

1717

BOOKS [63]

47  Das / Beschützte / *Orchestre,* / oder desselben / Zweyte Eröffnung. / Worinn / Nicht nur einem würkl-/chen *galant-homme,* der eben kein / Professions-Verwandter, sondern auch man-/chen *Musico* selbst die alleraufrichtigste und deutlich-/ste Vorstellung *musicali*scher Wissenschafften, wie sich / dieselbe vom Schulstaub tüchtig gesäubert, eigentlich / und wahrhafftig verhalten, ertheilet; aller wiedrigen / Auslegung und gedungenen Aufbürdung aber völliger / und truckener Bescheid gegeben; so dann endlich / des lange verbennet gewesenen / *Ut Mi Sol* / *Re Fa La* / Todte (nicht *tota*) Musica / Unter ansehnlicher Begleitung der zwölff Grie-/chischen *Modorum,* als ehrbahrer Verwandten und Trauer-/Leute, zu Grabe gebracht und mit einem *Monument,* / zum ewigen Andencken,

62. *Ehrenpforte,* p. 203: "Im November machte er eine starcke Hochzeit-Musick, welche den 18. aufgeführet wurde."

63. Mattheson edited this year Christopher Raupach's *VERITOPHILI Deutliche Beweis-Gründe, Worauf der rechte Gebrauch der MUSIC, beydes in den Kirchen als ausser denselben, beruht; Aus der heil. Schrifft, denen Zeugnüssen der heil. Fäter und aus der* Theorie *der Music selbst, mit alt- und neuen, sowol geistals weltlichen Exempeln, nebst der müglichen Pflicht eines jeden Christen im Gebrauch dieser Göttl. Gabe erörtert, Und Mit ungemeinen bisher verstecket-gewesenen doch nöthigen Erinnerungen, Samt einer Vorrede, heraus gegeben Von* MATTHESON. *HAMBURG, Bey sel. Benjamin Schillers Erben im Dohm, 1717.* (12), 56 pp.
Also the third part of Friederich Erhard Niedt's *Handleitung zur Variationen, wie man die General-Bass und darüber gesetzte Zahlen variiren, artige Inventiones machen und aus einen schlechten General-Bass Praeludia, Ciaconen, Allemanden, Sarabanden, Menueten, Giquen und dergleichen leichtlich verfertigen können.* . . . Hamburg 1706. This part "handelt vom Contra-Punct, Canon, Motteten, Choral, Recitativ-Style und Cavaten. . . ." (Robert Eitner, *Biographisch-Bibliographisches Quellen-Lexikon* [Leipzig 1900–1904], VII, 200).

beehret wird / von / *MATTHESON.* / HAMBURG, zu finden im Dom, im Schillerischen / Buchladen, 1717. / (22), 561, (1) pp.

As the title suggests, this volume is a defense and enlargement of Mattheson's musical opinions expressed in *Das Neu-eröffnete Orchestre.*[64] It was inspired directly by Johann Heinrich Buttstedt's *Ut, Mi, Sol, Re, Fa, La Tota Musica, et Harmonia Aeterna, oder Neu-eröffnetes, altes, wahres, eintziges und ewiges Fundamentum Musices entgegen gesetzt Dem Neu-eroffneten Orchestre*, etc., which appeared in the years 1714–16.[65] The first half answers each of Buttstedt's objections specifically; the second changes its tone to an attack upon the old, outmoded system of solmisation advocated by Buttstedt.[66]

## PUBLISHED TRANSLATIONS

48   Das / in allen Rechten / fest-gründete / Verfahren / mit den / Königl. Schwedis. Bestandten / in / Engelland und Holland, / betreffend / Die jüngste-obhanden-gewesene / und / entdeckete *Rebellion*. / In einem Parisis. Briefe vom 19 Mart. 1717 / dargestellet / und / Aus dem *Original* übersetzet / durch / MATTHESON. Hamburg, gedruckt im April, 1717. /
20 pp.

I have not been able to discover the original of this pamphlet. It deals, as do the next two of Mattheson's translations, with the scandalous Swedish-Jacobite Conspiracy, which was a product of the Northern War.[67] The unusual legal procedure resorted to in this case, namely the arrest of Count Gyllenborg, the Swedish Ambassador in London, aroused a storm of excitement in diplomatic and legal circles. This pamphlet describes the actual proceedings, and is regarded by Wolfgang Michael [68] as a typical defense of the English government's action.

49   Brieffe / So zwischen / Dem Graff Gyllenborg, dem Freyherrn von / Görtz, Sparre und andern gewechselt / worden, / Betreffend den / Auschlag / Einer Anzustifftenden / *REBELLION,* / In / Ihro Königl. Majest. von Gross-Britan-/nien Reichen und Landen, / Unterstützt durch / Schwedische Macht. / Aus dem mit Königl. Gross-Britannischer Autoritaet in Engelland publi-/cirten, *Original* ins Teutsche übersetzet, / von / Mattheson. / Hamburg, *Anno* 1717. /
(64) pp.

64. Cf. No. 27.
65. J. H. Buttstedt (1666–1725), organist at the Predigerkirche in Erfurt. Riemanns *Musiklexikon*, p. 258.
66. Graf von Waldersee's *Sammlung Musikalischer Vorträge*, No. 8, 1789: "Johann Mattheson und seine Verdienste um die deutsche Tonkunst." This article is an excellent account of the solmisation controversy.
67. Wolfgang Michael, *Englische Geschichte im achtzehnten Jahrhundert* (4 vols. Leipzig, 1896–1937), I, 737 f., contains a full account of this conspiracy, in which the chief protagonists were Count Gyllenborg in London and the Barons Görtz and Sperre on the continent.
68. *Idem*, p. 741.

*Translated from:* Letters which passed between Count G., the barons Gortz, Sparre, and others, relating to the design of raising a rebellion in his Majesty's dominions, to be supported by a force from Sweden. Published by Authority. London 1717.

Some of these letters had been laid before the House of Commons by Stanhope. They produced such a sensation that the collection was added to and published as the above pamphlet.[69] The interest this affair aroused in London as well as Hamburg, in view of the Northern War and the position of George I, must have been very great.[70]

50    Anmerckungen / über die auffgefangene / Briefe, / des Grafen von / Gyllenburg, / und der Frey-Herrn von / Görtz und Sparr. / Aus dem Englischen übersetzet. / Gedruckt im Martio 1717. / (8) pp.

I have not been able to discover the original of this pamphlet.[71] It appears to have been written to defend the Swedish forces from the calumny of wishing to destroy the freedom of the English people.[72]

## MUSICAL MANUSCRIPTS

51    Das /über die Güte Gottes / Erfreute / ZION, / Wurde, / Da / Der Hoch-Ehr-würdige und Hoch-gelahrte Herr, / HERR / DANIEL Sass zum / Probst der Graffschafft Pinnenberg / und / Haupt-*Pastor* der Stadt Altona, / am / Grünen-Donnerstage des 1717ten Jahrs, *introduci*ret wurde; / In einer / CANTATA / aufgeführet / von / MATTHESON. / ALTONA, gedruckt bey Bernard Simon Dreyer. / Text (8) pp.
MS. Score 11 pp.

The score of this piece is entitled *Cantata per Chiesa*. It consists of three arias divided by recitatives for tenor solo, accompanied by strings, oboe, and continuo. The simplicity of the score suggests the presence of less experienced performers than Mattheson usually had at his disposal in Hamburg.

52    Der / Altonaische / Hirten-Segen, / Nebst / einer Passions-Andacht / uber den / verlassenen JESUM, / Bey Priesterlicher Einweihung / Der Hoch-Wohl-Ehr-würdigen Herren, / HERREN / Ernst Hinrich Schultz, / Compastoris, / und / Joachim Conrad Victor, / Frühpredigers, / Bey der Lutherischen Gemeine Gottes daselbst; / Am Stillen-Freytage dieses 1717ten Jahrs, / In einem ORATORIUM / aufgefuhrt / von / MATTHE-SON. /
Text (8) pp.
MS. Score 10, 16 pp.

69. *Ibid.*, and note.
70. This pamphlet was also translated into French.
71. This translation is not signed by Mattheson, but since a copy is bound up with the other miscellaneous products of his pen (*Miscellania Matthesoniana I*, Hamburg Stadtbibliothek), it is natural to attribute it to him.
72. Michael, *Englische Geschichte*, I, 743 and note.

This oratorio is divided into two quite separate parts to be sung before and after the sermon. The score for the first is entitled "DIALOGO / Vor der Predigt / am Stillen-Freytag." It is written for bass (Jesus) and soprano (der Seele), accompanied by violins in unison and continuo, and is very simple. With the second part the meditative quality, appropriate to Good Friday, is discarded. Oboes and remaining strings are added to the accompanying forces; another soloist and chorus also join in.

53  Das / Hamburgische / Tempel-Fest, / Wurde / Wie ein Hoch-Ehrwürdiges / Dom-Capitul / Daselbst *Anno* 1717 den 17. *Junii* / Dero Jährliches / Ehren-Mahl / feyerlichst begieng, / Musicalisch entworffen / Von *Mattheson,* / *Vicar.* / *HAMBURG, MDCCXVII.* / Text (8) pp.
MS. Score 30 pp.

The text for this piece, which was written for the holiday of a Christian, if secular, church corporation, betrays in an interesting manner the dualistic nature of the Domkapitel. The characters the four soloists are supposed to portray are a combination of Christian and distinctly heathen deities, for example: "Hammon, Der Schuz-GOtt des Tempels," "Eusebia, Oder die Gottesfurcht," etc. Mattheson's music leaves no doubt as to the secular aspect of this festivity. The choruses and arias are all dance-like in character, and particularly florid in style.

54  ORATORIO, / Bey der Trauung, / Des Hoch-Ehrwürdigen und Hochgelahrten Herrn, / HERRN / Balthaser Mentzer, / Wohlverdiensten *Pastoris* der Evangelisch-Lu-/therischen Gemeine zur H. Drey-Einigkeit in *LONDON,* / Wie solche, / Mit der / Hoch-Edlen, Hoch-Ehr-und Tugendreichen Jungfer, / JUNGFER / Johanna Hedwig / Winckler, / *R. Min. Hamb. Sen.* / Eheleiblichen Jungfer Tochter, / Durch Priesterliche Hand, / den 12. Aug. 1717 vollzogen wurde, / Musicalisch gesetzt und aufgeführet von / *MATTHESON.* / Hamburg, gedruckt mit sel. Friederich Conrad Greflingers Schrifften. / Text (8) pp.

The score of this wedding oratorio is lost. The text was written by a candidate for the ministry, named Glauche.[73] Johanna Winckler was the sister of the Johann Anton Winckler of No. 24, and a member of one of Hamburg's most distinguished families.[74]

55  Die / Über die Entfernung / Triumphirende Beständigkeit, / Bey dem Mentzer- / Und / Wincklerischen / Hochzeit-Feste, / In einer / SERENATA, / zu Bezeugung seiner ergebesten Hochachtung / Glückwünschend verfertiget und vorgestellet / Von / MATTHESON. / Hamburg, gedruckt mit sel. Friederich Conrad Greflingers Schrifften, / In Jahr 1717, den 12. Augusti. / Text (12) pp.
MS. Score 41 pp.

73. Text-book, p. 2. Schröder's *Lexikon* contains no mention of such a writer.
74. Cf. Schröder *Lexikon,* VIII, 65–91, where considerable space is devoted to the lives and works of nine Wincklers, sons or grandsons of the original Johann (1642–1705).

The text was written by the poet König "und, auf Begehren, von Dresden übersandt." [75] It is written for four soloists, who represent "Phoebus, Vorsteher der Wissenschafften," "Euterpe, die Muse der öffentlichen Lustbarkeiten," "Terpsichore, Vorsteherin der Music," and "Momus, bestellter Richter auf dem Parnass." The chorus represented in turn "Die öffentlichen Lustbarkeiten," "Die Musen an der Elbe," and "Der an dem Elbe-Strohm sich aufhaltende Themse-Schäfer." This particularly elaborate serenata Mattheson wrote for an orchestra which, beside the usual strings, included two flutes and two trombas. The score is notable because it contains a formal overture and arias of far greater elaboration than those of his other serenatas.

56 Der / Siegende Gideon / wurde, wegen des / durch / Ihro Röm. Kay serl. Majestät / KARL des VI. / glückliche Waffen, / unter tapfferer Auführung / des / Durchlauchtigen Printzen *EUGENII,* / wider den Erb-Feind am 16 *Aug.* 1717. / befochtenen herrlichen / Sieges / Und darauff erfolgten übergabe der / Haupt-Vestung / Belgrad, / bey feyerlichster Begehung des am XVIII. *post Trinitatis* / als den 26. Sept. verordneten / Hamburgischen Danck-Festes / in dasiger Stiffts-Kirche / auffgeführet von / *Mattheson.* / HAMBURG, *ANNO* 1717. / Text (12) pp. MS. Score 53 pp.

The text of this festival oratorio was written by Glauche, the author of the text of No. 54. The reference to Gideon is the only biblical aspect of the text, which is a long paean of praise to Jehovah.[76] As befitting the joyousness of the occasion trombas play an important part in choruses and arias. Mattheson's score contains seven full choruses and twelve full arias.

57 Der / reformirende / JOHANNES, / an dem / durch die Gnade Gottes erlebten / Zweyten / Jubel-Feste / der / Evangelisch-Lutherischen / Kirche / nach der heilsamen Reformation / des seel. Lutheri / als dasselbe / zu / Hamburg / den 31. Octobr. Anno 1717. / als am XXIII nach Trinitatis, hochfeyerlich begangen wurde, / in der Dom-Kirche daselbst musicalisch aufgefuhrt / von / Mattheson. / Hamburg, gedruckt im Jahr 1717. / Text (16) pp. MS. Score 106 pp.

The author of this text is anonymous. It recounts the story of Luther's coming and of his crusade against church abuses in terms of the story of John the Baptist. The narrative is entirely presented by the "Lutheraner," while the other characters, "Johannes," "Glaube," "Liebe," "Hoffnung," and "Messias" are introduced in the same manner as the many characters in the Passion music of the time. Inevitably the music is written for full, festival orchestra. Although, according to his own notation, Mattheson wrote the music in four days, the score is unquestionably one of his best, and betrays no indication of hurry.[77]

75. Cf. No. 31. König had not yet left Hamburg permanently.
76. Cf. p. 53 of this text.
77. Cf. p. 53 of this text.

## 1718

## MUSICAL MANUSCRIPTS

58  Der / Für die Sünde der Welt / Gemartete und Sterbende / JESUS. / Musicalisch gesetzt, und / in hiesiger Stiffts-Kirche / aufgeführet / Von / *JOANNE MATTHESON.* / Canonico min. & Directore Musices / Cathedralis. / HAMBURG. /
Text (18) pp.
MS. Score 131 pp.

This text was written by Hamburg's most famous poet of the time, Heinrich Brockes.[78] It had already been set to music by Keiser in 1712 and by Telemann and Händel in 1716, which is evidence enough of its popularity.[79] Mattheson's score contains many fine passages.[80] It was produced on Palm Sunday, "mit dem Beifall vieler tausend Zuhörer." [81]

59  Der / aller-erfreulichste / TRIUMPH / in einem *ORATORIO* / vorgestellet / und / Zu Gottes Ehren, auch mehrer Auffnahm und / Beförderung der Music, / am dritten H. Oster-Tage / in hiesiger / Cathedral-Kirche / auffgeführet / von / Mattheson. / Direct. / HAMBURG. /
Text (8) pp.
MS. Score 48 pp.

The story of the Resurrection as recounted in this text seems to be based on elements from all four of the Gospels. Its form is a series of scenes rather than a narrative. Mattheson's music is written for a large orchestra, and naturally takes advantage of the dramatic directness of the text.

60  Die / glücklic-streitende / Kirche, / auf / den achten Sonntag nach/ Trinitatis / gerichtet / und componirt / von / *Mattheson.* / In Hamburg. /
Text (8) pp.
MS. Score 56 pp.

This oratorio is divided, as usual, into two parts. The first is a dialogue between the Soul, beset by weakness and doubt, and Jesus, Devotion, and the Church, who seek to strengthen the Soul's convictions. In the second half the Soul is set upon by the Three False Prophets. Despite their temptations and their derision, the Soul remains undefiled, and is united with Jesus at the end. This text naturally offers admirable excellent opportunities for the expression of Mattheson's musical-dramatic ideas. Although the style of the

78. 1688–1747. He became a member of the Hamburg Senat in 1720. His chief literary work was nine volumes of verse, entitled *Irrdisches Vergnügen in Gott,* 1721–48. Alois Brandl, *B. H. Brockes,* etc.

79. Schweitzer, *J. S. Bach,* I, 94. The text of Bach's St. John's Passion is based upon this one.

80. Karl von Winterfeld, *Evangelische Kirchengesang und sein Verhältnis zur Kunst des Tonsatzes* (Leipzig, 1843–47), III, 177–85, contains an analysis of this work.

81. *Ehrenpforte,* p. 204.

music is extremely operatic, the frequent use of chorale melodies in the choruses and as obbligati to the arias emphasizes the religious significance of the piece.[82]

61   Die / Göttliche Vorsorge / über / Alle Creaturen, / in einem / ORA-TORIO / auff den / Funfzehnten Sonntag nach / Trinitatis / vorge-stellet und componiret / von *Mattheson.* / Hamburg. / Text (8) pp. MS. Score 50 pp.

The text is also from the pen of König.[83] It is a dramatization of the conflict between the Vices and Virtues. The score is signed and dated Sept. 4, 1718. Apparently it was not performed until 1722.[84] The text provides dramatic contrasts of a most sudden and striking nature, to which Mattheson does justice.

## 1719

## BOOK

62   Exemplarische / Organisten-Probe / Im Artikel / Vom /GENERAL-BASS. / Welche mittelst 24. leichter, und eben so viel etwas schwerer Exempel, / aus allen Tonen, des Endes anzustellen ist, dass einer, der / Diese 48 Prob-Stücke / Rein trifft, und das darinn Enthaltene wohl an-bringt, sich vor / andern rühmen möge: / Er sey ein Meister im accom-pagniren. / Alles zum unentbehrlichen Unberricht und Behuf, nicht-nur einiger / Herren Organisten und Clavicembalisten *ex professo,* sondern / Aller Liebhaber der Music, / Zuförderst derer, die der Haupt-Wissen-schafft des Claviers, des Ge-/neral-Basses, und des geschickten, manier-lichen *Accompagnements* / fleissig obliegen, / Mit den nothwendigsten Er-läuterungen und Anmerckungen, bey jedem Exempel, / und mit einer ausführlichen, zur Probe dienenden / Theoretischen Vorbereitung, / Uber verschiedene musicalische Merckwürdigkeiten, / versehen von / MAT-THESON. / *Longum iter est per praecepta; breve & officax.per exempla.* / *Seneca, Epist.* 6. / HAMBURG, im Schiller-und Kissnerischen Buch-Laden, 1719. / (14), 128, 276 pp.

This very full title offers an excellent indication of the contents of the book.[85] It is prefaced by a series of nine complimentary poems addressed to Mattheson by friends

82. The score is dated 1718.
83. Cf, No. 27.
84. *Ehrenpforte,* p. 207: ". . . verfertigte er auch noch das dritte neue Oratorium von diesem Jahr, dessen Poesie der berühmte König einsandte, und den Nahmen der göttlichen Vorsorge führte." The apparent discrepancy in dates implied by the use of the word "verfertigte" in this context seems to suggest forgetfulness on Mattheson's part. Since he was in the habit of signing his oratorio scores as well as noting the time employed in their composition, it seems more reasonable to rely upon this evidence than upon that of the *Ehrenpforte.*
85. E. T. Arnold *The Art of Accompaniment from a Thorough-Bass as Practised in the*

and admirers. The lengthy Foreword deals for the most part with the general musical ideas of Mattheson, which have little to do with the specific problem of thoroughbass.

## MUSICAL MANUSCRIPTS

63 Das / Betrübte Schweden / Wurde, / Als in hiesiges / Hoch-Ehrwürdiges Dom-Capitel / Ihro in Gott ruhenden / Königl. Maj. von Schweden &c. / *CAROLO XII.* / Am 26 Febr. 1719. / In der Stiffts-Kirche / Die schuldigsten *PARENTALIA* / feyerlich halten liess, / In einer / Trauer-Music / aufgeführet / von / *J. MATTHESON.* / *Canon. min. & Direct. Chori-Cathedr.* / HAMBURG. /
Text (8) pp.
MS. Score 32 pp.

The author of the text, as noted in the score, was Gustav Willhelm Hero.[86] The allegorical figures, all of whom bemoan the death of the king, include "Fama," "Das Verhängnis," "Das betrübte Schweden," "Das bethränte Elb-Fluss," and "Das tröstende Himmel." Mattheson's score, though composed, according to his notation, in twenty-four hours, is certainly one of his best.[87]

64 Die / Frucht des Geistes / In einem / *ORATORIO* / auf Pfingsten / musicalisch vorgestellet / Von / MATTHESON. /
Text (8) pp.
MS. Score 52 pp.

The text was written by Erdmann Neumeister, pastor of the St. Jacobi-Kirche in Hamburg, a strong advocate of the Hamburg Opera, and the author of many texts of J. S. Bach's Cantatas.[88] The inspiration for this text is to be found in St. Paul's Epistle to the Galatians V. 22–23. The nine Christian virtues mentioned therein are allegorically personified in this text. Mattheson's score is dated May 26, 1719. The undramatic form and hence music of this oratorio are almost unique amongst Mattheson's church music.

65 Christi / Wunder-Wercke / Bey den / Schwach-gläubigen. / In die Music gebracht / und / Am fünfften Sonntage / nach *Trinitatis* / aufgeführet / von / *MATTHESON.* / Hochfürstl. Schleswig-Holsteinischem Capellmeister. /
Text (8) pp.
MS. Score 62 pp.

According to Mattheson's notation, the text was written by H. D. Hoesst.[89] The biblical basis for it is the weakness of Simon Peter as exemplified in the scene of Christ's meeting with him by the Sea of Galilee.[90] Mattheson noted on this score: "Commencé le 10 fini

---

*17th and 18th Centuries* (London, 1931), contains a critique of this book and Nos. 116 and 127.
86. I have been unable to discover further details concerning this writer.
87. Cf. *Ehrenpforte*, pp. 204–5, and pp. 56–57 of this text.
88. An account of the life and a list of the numerous works of Neumeister are to be found in Schröder, *Lexikon*, V, 494–512.
89. I have been unable to discover any other reference to this writer.
90. Mark I. 16, 17.

le 18 Juni 1719." This score and that for No. 64 contain choruses of much greater force and content than any of the other oratorios up to this time.

66  Der / Verlohrne und wiedergefundene / AMOR. / Dem Durchlauch-tigsten Fürsten und / HERRN, / Herrn CAROLO / FRIDERICO, / Erben zu Norwegen, Hertzogen zu Schleswig, Hol-/stein Stormarn und der Dittmarsen, Gräfin zu Olden-/burg und Delmenhorst, &c. / Als / Ihro Königl. Hoheit / Dem / Hecklau-Roepstorffischen / Vermählungs-Feste / gnädigst beywohnten, / In einer / SERENATA / unterhänigst vorgestellet / von / *J. MATTHESON,* / Hoch-Fürstl. Schleswig-Holsteinischen Capellmeistern. / Hamburg, den 8 October. 1719. / Text (8) pp.
MS. Score 28 pp.

The text presents the Gods and Goddesses sorrowing over the loss of Cupid, and their happiness at his return. The tone of Mattheson's score is typically secular.[91]

67  Als / In hoher Gegenwart / Des Durchlauchtigsten Fürsten und / HERRN, / Herrn *CAROLI* / *FRIDERICI,* / Erben zu Norwegen, Hert-zogen zu Schleswig, / Holstein, Stormarn und der Dittmarsen; Grafen zu / Oldenburg und Delmenhorst, &c. &c. / Die / *RICH-THIBOU*ische / Vermählung vollzogen wurde, / Hat Ihro Königl. Hoheit, / Auf Dero gnädigsten Befehl, / Mit einer / *SERENATA,* / Die vergnügte Nacht / betitelt, / auffwarten sollen / J. MATTHESON. / Hoch-Fürstl. Capell-meister /
Text (12) pp.
MS. Score 46 pp.

Mattheson wrote in the text: "Erfindung, Worte u. Music sind von Mattheson." The textbook also states: "Der Auftritt geschiebet in einem illuminirten Sahl des Furstlichen Pallastes." It contains no plot, but instead isolated verses for such personages as "Die Nacht," "Die Treue," and accompanying choruses. Most of the text is in Italian. The music is scored for large orchestra, and several of the arias are notable for their interesting orchestration.

1720

## BOOK

68  *REFLEXIONS* / *sur* / *L'ECLAIRCISSEMENT* / *d'un* / *Probleme de Musique* / *pratique,* / *Dediées* / *A SON EXCELLENCE* / *Monsieur de Wich,* / *Ministre de Sa Majesté le Roi de Grand-/Bretagne au Cercle de la Basse Saxe,* / *Landgrave des deux Carolines,* / *Seigneur de Tang-stede, &c. &c.* / *par* / *Son tres-humble et tres-obeissant* / *Serviteur* / *JEAN MATTHESON.* / *Etiam in tenui labor.* / *HAMBURG, 1720.* / *Aux depens de l'Auteur.* /
(8), 33 pp.

91. Cf. p. 63 of this text.

These are "reflections" upon a short article in the *Memoires de Trevoux*,[92] entitled "Eclaircissement d'un problême de Musique pratique, pourquoi l'on employe quelquefois dans la composition, les tons ou modes transposez preferablement aux tons ou modes naturels?" Mattheson's intention in publishing these reflections "n'est pas de refuter l'Auteur de l'Eclaircissement, ni de faire tort à qui que soit; mais le seul but, . . . est la recherche de la verité." In actual fact, he discusses each one of the author's propositions to support his suggestion, showing them to be the product of ignorance, inasmuch as it is essential to the beauty of melodies that they should by their very nature require the unique qualities of each different tonality.

## MUSIC

69  Der / Brauchbare / VIRTUOSO, / Welcher sich / (Nach beliebiger Überlesung der Vorrede) / Mit / Zwölff neuen / Kammer-Sonaten, / Auf der / *Flute Traversiere*, / Der / Violine / Und dem / Claviere, / Bey Gelegenheit hören lassen mag; / Als wozu ihm / hiemit völlige Erlaubniss gibt / *JOANNES MATTHESON*, / Hoch-Fürstl.-Schleswig-Holsteinischer Capellmeister, des Königl. Gross-Britannischen / *Ministri* im Nieder-Sächsischen Kreise *Secretarius*, des Hamburgische Stiffts *Canonicus* / *minor, Chori musici Dirictor &c.* / [Quotation from Sallust.] / HAMBURG, / Im Schiller- und Kissnerischen Buch-Laden, 1720. / (6), 14, 65 pp.

Mattheson's long Foreword to this volume of music is an attack upon the enemies of music, and a defense of his own ideas of the good musician and music lover.[93] The first he characterizes as "unbrauchbare," and the second, "brauchbare Virtuosi," which is the explanation of the title. The sonatas are written for solo and figured bass. Like his other instrumental works, they are written in the most usual keys. There is considerable variation in the number of sections in each sonata as well as the form of each. Some of the sonatas might better be called suites, but, on the other hand, the last ones display a much greater unity and more serious content than the first.[94]

## PUBLISHED TRANSLATION

70  Betrachtung / des Neuen / Finanz-Wercks. / Allwo der Schade angezeiget wird, / welcher aus Errichtung der / *COMPAGNIEN* / entstehet. / Alles auff die Erfahrung und vernünff-/tige Folge gegründet. / Nebst / Angehängtem *Project,* wie nem-/lich ein Staat, zur Bezahlung seiner / Schulden, anders wo solcher gestalt / Geld finden könne: dass die Unterthanen da-/durch eine Erleichterung au Auflagen, und ei-/nen

92. *Memoires pour L'Histoire Des Sciences & des beaux Arts. Recueillis par l'Ordre de son Altesse Serenissime Monseigneur Prince Souverain de Dombes.* Aout 1718, Article XXII, pp. 310–319.

93. Cf. p. 65 of this text.

94. The music, without the Foreword, was republished in 1923 under the title: *Zwölf Kammer-Sonaten für Flöte und Klavier Johannes Mattheson (1720) In freier Bearbeitung zum ersten Male herausgegeben von Ary Van Leeuwen* in two volumes, published by Wilhelm Zimmerman, Leipzig.

Zuwachs an Gütern erhalten; Dass *commer-/cium* nicht unterbrochen; sondern die noth-/wendige Gleichheit wohl beobachtet war-/den möge. / Aus dem Frantzösischen ubersetzet. / 1720. / Hamburg, Gedruckt, bey seel. Thomas von / Wierings Erben bey der Börse, im güldnen A. B. C. /

(39) pp.

Mattheson's dedication of this pamphlet to the Hamburg Rath, is explained by him as follows: "Der Holländische Bidermann, welcher seinem Vaterlande durch diese Schrifft zu rathen gedacht, hat mich ermuntert, dem meinigen ebenfalls durch die Ubersetzung an die Hand zu gehen. Und ob gleich nicht alles, so wird doch das meiste auch hiesiges Ortes *applicable* seyn." I have not succeeded in discovering the original pamphlet. It amounts to a general attack upon unsound methods of raising municipal funds, as illustrated by the difficulties of the South Sea Company and the collapse of the financial system of John Law.

## MUSICAL MANUSCRIPTS

71  Die / durch / Christi Auferstehung / bestätigte / Auferstehung aller / Todten, / Musicalisch gesetzet / und / am Heil. Oster-Feste / aufgeführet / von / *J. MATTHESON,* / Hoch-Fürstl. Schleswig-Holsteinischen Capellmeister. /

Text (16) pp.

MS. Score 90 pp.

The text of this oratorio was written by C. F. Weichmann, one of Hamburg's leading poets.[95] The text is prefaced by a short defense by Mattheson of his own much-criticized church music. The first half of the oratorio depicts the doubt and despair of the period immediately before Christ's Resurrection, with "Rache" and "Furcht" prevailing over "Glaube" and "Hoffnung." The second half shows the joy and triumph of the Easter celebration. The text is well adapted to Mattheson's dramatic principles, and the work is one of the most elaborate and successful he ever undertook.

72  Das / Gröste Kind, / In einem / ORATORIO / auf Weynacht / musicalisch vorgestellet / von / *MATTHESON,* / Hoch-Fürstl. Schleswig-Holsteinischem Capellmeister, / wie auch *Directore* der Music im Dom zu / Hamburg. / Psal. 97, 6. / Es stehet herrlich und prächtig vor Ihm, und gehet gewal-/tig und löblich zu in seinem Heiligthum. /

Text (9) pp.

MS. Score 76 pp.

The text, the author of which is unknown, is a particularly joyous one. From his notation it appears that Mattheson was able to assemble a particularly distinguished group of soloists for the occasion.[96] To the customary persons attending upon the birth of Christ are added "Christi Braut," "Die Andacht," and "Die Nachdencken." The music is

95. He was a member of the Teutsch-übenden Gesellschaft, a founder of the Patriotische Gesellschaft, and the editor of the *Poesie der Niedersachsen,* Hamburg, 1721–38. (Schröder, *Lexikon,* VII, 592–3.)

96. According to Mattheson's score, they included Madame Keiser, Mr. Arnoldi, Mr. Möhring and Mr. Riemschneider.

scored for strings, two clarini, two oboes, two cornetti, and timpani. The general style of the music is so florid, with arias requiring extraordinarily great range of voice, the choruses are so dance-like and gay, that of all Mattheson's oratorios this is much the most operatic.

## 1721 [97]

## BOOK

73   Das / Forschende / *Orchestre,* / oder desselben / Dritte Eröffnung, / Darinn / *SENSUS VINDICIAE / ET / QUARTAE BLANDITIAE,* / D. i. / Der beschirmte Sinnen-Rang / Und der / Schmeichelnde *quarten-*Klang, / Allen unpartheyischen *Syntechnitis* / zum Nutzen und Nachdenken; keinem Menschen / aber zum Nachtheil, *sana ratione & autoritate* un-/tersuchet, und vermuhtlich in ihr rechtes / Licht gestellet werden / von / *JOANNE MATTHESON,* / Hoch-Fürstl. Schleswig-Hollsteinischem Capellmeister. / Ich denke des Nachts an mein Säiten-Spiel, / mein Geist muss forschen. *Ps. LXXVII, 7.* / Hamburg, bey Benjamin Schillers Wittwe, und / Joh. Christoph Kissner im Dom, 1721. / (46), 789, (75) pp.

Although this book is the continuation, in a sense, of the first two *Orchestres,*[98] its first half is an examination of an aspect of music hitherto only briefly referred to by Mattheson. This is the effect of music upon the senses. In the course of this treatise, Mattheson justifies his own theories by the psychological ideas of John Locke and others. The book is thus of particular importance to the course and development of his own system of musical philosophy and æsthetics. The second half is devoted to an examination of the theories concerning the harmonic interval of the fourth, in which Mattheson's own attitude is that of a modern rationalist.[99]

## MUSICAL MANUSCRIPTS

74   Der / Blut-rünstige / Kelter-Treter / Und / Von der Erden erhöhete / Menschen-Sohn, / Zur Fasten-Zeit / In Melodien / gebracht / Von / *MATTHESON.* / Ihro Königl. Hoheit, des regierenden Hertzogs zu Schleswig-Holstein &c. / Capellmeister, auch *Directore* der Music in der Hamburgischen / Stiffts-Kirche. / Text (24) pp.

97. Mattheson also edited in this year the following: *Friederich Erhard Niedtens Musicalische Handleitung, zur VARIATIONEN Des General-Basses, Samt einer Anweisung, Wie man aus einen schlechten General-Bass allerley Sachen, als Praeludia, Ciaconen, Allemanden, &c. erfinden könne. Die Zweyte Auflage, Verbessert, vermehret, mit verschiedenen Grund-richtigen Anmerckungen, und einem Anhang von mehr als 60. Orgel-Wercken versehen durch J. Mattheson, Hoch-Fürstl. Schleswig-Holsteinischen Capellmeister. HAMBURG Bey Benjamin Schillers Wittwe und Joh. Christoph Kissner im Dom, 1721.* (12), 204 pp.

98. No. 27 and 47.

99. Cf. pp. 124–125 of this text.

The author of the text of this Passion music is unknown, and Mattheson's music is unhappily lost. The form of the text is most unorthodox and advanced. Most noticeable is the absence of a narrator, and the complete lack of biblical quotations or references, and traditional chorales. As in No. 71, Mattheson wrote a preface to "Mein Lieber Zuhörer" for this text. His belief in the complete supremacy of "lauter Melodien" is its keynote. Because of the highly dramatic character of the text, "Die Chöre haben mir in diesem Werke keine Gelegenheit zu Fugen und doppelten *Contrapunctis* geben wollen." He also gives his principles governing the writing of a good recitative. For this reason, the loss of the score, which must have been a particularly elaborate one, is much to be regretted.

75   Das / irrende / und / wieder zu recht gebrachte / Sünden-Schaaf, / am / Dritten Sonntage, / nach / *Trinitatis* / in einem / *ORATORIO* / vorgestellst / von / *MATTHESON*. / Hochfürstl. Schleswig-Hollsteinischem Capellmeister, auch *Directore* / der Music im Dom zu Hamburg. / Hamburg.
Text (8) pp.
MS. Score 61 pp.

The score is signed "Mattheson, Juin 9, 1721." The text whose author is unknown, presents the conflict between "Weltlust" and "Gottesfurcht" for supremacy over "Das Sünden-Schaaf." It is only by the intense pleading of Jesus that "Weltlust" is at length overcome. The most interesting element in Mattheson's score is the musical differentiation between the two conflicting emotions herein personified.

76   Die / Freuden-reiche / Geburt / und Menschwerdung / unsers / Herrn und Heilandes / Jesu Christi, / nach dem Evangelisten Lucas. / Musicalisch gesetzt, und aufgeführet / von / MATTHESON. / Text (6) pp.

The score of this oratorio is lost. The text, which is undated, is an expansion of *Die Heilsame Geburth,* No. 37. In his autobiography,[100] Mattheson speaks of composing an oratorio for Christmas. Since there is no evidence of any other of his oratorios being the one here referred to, it is reasonable to date this one by the reference in the *Ehrenpforte.*

## 1722

## PERIODICAL

77   *CRITICA MUSICA*. / d. i. / Grundrichtige / Untersuch-/und Beurtheilung, / Vieler, theils vorgefassten, theils einfältigen / Meinungen, Argumenten und Einwürffe, so in / alten und neue, gedruckten und ungedruckten, / Musicalischen Schrifften / zu finden. / Zur müglichsten Ausräutung aller groben Irrthü-/mer, und zur Beförderung eines bessern Wachsthums der / reinen harmonischen Wissenschaft, in verschiedene / Theile abgefasset, / Und Stück-weise heraus gegeben / Von / *Mattheson.*

100. *Ehrenpforte,* p. 208: "Endlich verfertigte er auf Weihnacht das vierte Oratorium dieses Jahrs. . . ."

# Critical Bibliography 177

/ Erstes Stück. / (Latin Quotation) / Hamburg, in May. 1722. / Auf Unkosten des *Autoris.* /
368, (17) pp.

This is the first musical periodical to be issued in Germany.[101] The title gives an indication of its general contents and aims. It appeared in twenty-four numbers, at irregular intervals during the years 1722–25, and was then collected in two volumes of twelve numbers each.[102] Each number contained at its conclusion, a section, usually under the heading, "Musicalische Merkwürdigkeiten," which contained news of practical and scientific musical interest from various European cities, and correspondence. Mattheson confined his attention to but eight general topics throughout, dividing the whole series, thereby, into eight parts. In form it thus corresponds with many a learned journal of the period.[103]

Part One, including the first three numbers, is entitled "Die Melopoetische Licht-Scheere. Zum Dienst der jämmerlichen Schmader-Katze, auf der sogenennten hohen *Compositions-Schule* zu U. L. Fr. in München . . ." It is a continuation of the general controversies initiated by the three *Orchestres.* In particular it is an attack upon Francis Xavier Mürschhauser's *Academica Musico-Poetica bipartita,*[104] which was in turn a violent protest against Mattheson's theories.[105]

Part Two (Numbers 4–6) is entitled "Die Parallele, Das ist: Eine Vergleichung zwischen den Italiänern und Franzosen, betreffend die Music und Opern." [106] In parallel columns of the original French version and Mattheson's German translation, it contains the Abbé Raguenet's *Parallele des Italiens & des François, en ce qui regarde la musique et les operas* (Paris, 1702).

Part Three, "Der Französische Anwald . . ." (Numbers 7 and 8), contains the reply to Raguenet by the Sieur de Vieuville, *Comparaison de la Musique Françoise & Italienne* (Paris, 1712).

Part Four (Numbers 9–12) is entitled "Die Canonische Anatomie. Oder Untersuchung derjenigen Kunst-Stücke, und ihres Nutzens, welche bey den *Musicis CANONES* genennet, und, als was sonderbahres, angesehen werden." It is a discussion on the relative merits of contrapuntal and melodic learning, occasioned by a letter from Heinrich Bokemeyer,[107] Cantor at the court of Wolfenbüttel.[108]

101. F. Krome, *Die Anfange des musicalischen Journalismus in Deutschland* (Leipzig, 1896), p. 9.

102. For Volume III see No. 91.

103. *Deutsche Acta Eruditorum* in Germany and *The Present State of the Republic of Letters* in England, for example.

104. Mattheson quotes the entire title in a note on page 5 of the *Critica Musica.*

105. Mürschhauser (1663?1738) was Capellmeister to the Elector of Bavaria. Riemanns *Musiklexikon,* p. 1232.

106. It is a continuation and enlargement of the same topic as presented in the *Neu-Eröffnete Orchestre* No. 27, Pars Tertia, Cap. I. "Vom Unterschied der heutigen Italianischen, Frantzosischen, Englischen und Teutsch Music."

107. Bokemeyer, according to Walthers *Musikalisches Lexikon* (pp. 102–103), had become Cantor at Wolfenbüttel in 1720.

108. A number of anonymous pamphlets were written by Mattheson and Christopher Weichmann, the poet, concerning an article on Telemann's opera, *Gensericus, oder der siegenden Schönheit.* The text had been written by the poet Postel, and was a favorite in Hamburg, having already been set twice before by Conradi and Cousser. Weichmann had made some changes in it for Telemann, which Mattheson ventured to comment upon in the first volume of his *Critica Musica,* pp. 87–88. Weichmann misinterpreted his criti-

## PAMPHLET

78  *Prologo / per il / Sacro / del / Rè Christianissimo / LUDOVICO. XV. / da rappresentarsi / al Famosissimo Teatro / d'HAMBURGO / gli 26 d'Ottobre / 1722. /*
(8) pp.

Mattheson noted on the title-page of his copy of the text "La Parole sono ordinate del Sigr. Mattheson." The music was by an Italian, Viocca. As the title suggests, the prologue is of the conventional, complimentary nature.

## PUBLISHED TRANSLATIONS

79  *Zenobia* / oder Was Muster rechtschaffener / Ehelichen Liebe, / in einer / *OPERA* / Auf dem Hamburgischen / Schau-Platz / vorgestellet, / Im Jahr 1722. / Gedruckt bey Caspar Jakhel. /
(39) pp.

This is the translation of the text of an opera by Händel.[109] Although Mattheson lists its production in Hamburg for the year 1721,[110] the date of publication of the text and his own lists of his published works invariably give the date 1722.

80  Der / Ehrsüchtige / *ARSACES.* / In einer / *OPERA* / Auf dem / Hamburgischen Schauplatz / vorgestellet / Im Jahr M DCC XXII. / Gedruckt bey Caspar Jakhel. /
(48) pp.

Mattheson translated the text for the production of this opera in Hamburg, as in the case of No. 78. The music was by Orlandini and Amadei.[111]

## MUSICAL MANUSCRIPTS

81  Der / Unter den Todten gesuchte, / Und / Unter den lebendigen gefundene / Sieges-Fürst, / Am / Oster-Feste, / In einem / *ORATORIO* / Aufgeführet / Von / *MATTHESON.* /
Text (8) pp.

Mattheson's score for this Easter oratorio is lost.

---

cism as personal slander. The resultant battle of pamphlets has been described in the *Denkmäler Der Deutschen Tonkunst,* Vol. XXVIII, in the introduction to Telemann's Life, p. xlv.

109. This opera was written and produced by Händel in 1720 under the name of *Radamisto,* by which it is generally known. *Library of Congress Catalogue of Opera Librettos printed before 1800,* p. 914.

110. Mattheson, *Musicalische Patriot,* p. 190, No. 170, in the list of operas produced in Hamburg.

111. *Musicalische Patriot,* p. 191, No. 171.

82   Das / Grosse in dem Kleinen / Oder / GOTT / In den Herzen / eines glaübigen Christen, / Am heil. Pfingst-Feste / in einem *ORATORIO* / vorgestellst / von / *Mattheson.* /
Text (8) pp.
MS. Score 59 pp.

The score is signed "Mattheson. Mai 13. 1722." The first half of the oratorio describes the sorrow of "Das christliche Herz" over the fate of Christ. The second describes the revelation of Christ, ascended, with God the Father to the Christian Heart. The score shows signs of considerable work and revision by Mattheson. Although the arias are secular in spirit throughout, the choruses are of a severely ecclesiastical nature.

1723

PAMPHLET

83   Besondere, / Neue / Gross-Britannische / Denkwürdigkeiten. Erstes
Stuck. / Anno 1723 vom 22 bis 27 Septembris. /
(18) pp.

This publication (two numbers alone are extant, the second being for the first week in October) is presumably by Mattheson.[112] In the brief Foreword, the author explains that the publication was prompted by his curiosity to know of other peoples' activities. The contents of the two numbers, probably culled from English newspapers in Hamburg, describe the activities of the foot-guards in Hyde Park, numerous recent robberies, the paintings in Lord Harley's chapel which are now ready for inspection, etc.

PUBLISHED TRANSLATIONS

84   Die Neu-Entdeckte / Gross-Britannische / Haupt-Verrätherey, / nach dem umständlichen / Bericht / der Herren Deputirten, / welche das / Hochlöblichen Unter-Hauss des Parlaments, / zur Befragung des bekannten Christopher Layer / und andrer, ernennen wollen, / wie solcher / Den / Mertz 1722–3 alten Styls / durch / Ihro Hochwohlgebornen / den Herrn / Wilhelm Pulteney, / Presidenten besagter Deputation, / abgestattet, / und anitzo / aus dem Engländischen Original verteutschet worden, / durch / *Mattheson.* / HAMBURG, gedruckt und zu bekommen bey seel. Thomas von Wierings Erben, bey / der Börse, im güldnen A. B. C. 1723. /
136 pp.

I have not been able to discover the original of this translation. In his Foreword to it, Mattheson discusses the work involved in making a translation. He gives no indication as to his source. The report of Christopher Layer's extraordinary plot, as uncovered in

112. It is bound up in Volume I of the *Miscellanea Matthesoniana* in the Hamburger Stadtbibliothek.

his trial, occupies two hundred and twenty-eight pages in Howell's *A Complete Collection of State Trials.*[113]

85 *MOLL FLANDERS.* / Das ist: / einer, also genennten, Engländerinn / Erstaunens-wehrte / Glücks-/ und / Unglücks-Fälle, / Die sie, in 60 Jahren, und darüber, mit unaussprechlichen / Veränderungen erlebet, und endlich selber beschrieben hat. / Nach der vierten Auflage aus dem Englandischen verteutschet / durch / *Mattheson.* / HAMBURG, / Gedruckt und verlegt von seel. *Thomas* von Wierings Erben, bey der Borse im güldnen A. B. C. 1723. / (14), 478 pp.

Although the title-page states that this translation is from the fourth English edition, Mr. Theodore Hatfield[114] has demonstrated by comparison of texts that Mattheson must have used both the third edition of 1722 and (J. Reed's) *The Life and Action of Moll Flanders* (July 6, 1723). In the Foreword Mattheson devotes some space to his principles of translation. Mr. Hatfield points out that the translation is excellent, because of its freedom and the natural literary taste it displays. It appears that the work enjoyed no popularity, as there are no references to it in the literary works of the time, and as the next translation did not appear until 1903.

86 *NERO* / in einem / Sing-Spiele / auf dem / Hamburgischen / Schau-Platze / vorgestellt / im Jahr 1723 / Gedruckt bey Caspar Jakhel, auf dem Doms Kirchhofe. / (48) pp.

This opera text was not the same one Händel had set to music in 1705.[115] The composer, in this case, was Orlandini. In addition to translating the original Italian text, Mattheson added considerable original musical material. Of it he wrote, ". . . er verschiedene neue Anordnungen der Arien mochte, den gantzen Recitativ setzte, und viele Stücke von seiner Composition, auf Begehren hinzufügte.[116]

## MUSICAL MANUSCRIPTS

87 Das / Lied des Lammes / zur / Fasten-Zeit / angestimmt / von *Mattheson.* / Psallentibus Dignanter / Admisceri Sancti Angeli Solent. / S. Bernh. Serm. 7. Cantica. / Text (8) pp. / MS. Score 80 pp.

The score is headed "Das Lied des Lammes / i. e. / J. *MATTHESONII* / in / *PASSIONEM CHRISTI* / *MELOS.* / *M.DCC.XXIII.* /." This is Mattheson's third Passion oratorio. The score is perhaps his most interesting one because of its own merits, and

113. XVI, 94–322.
114. Theodore M. Hatfield, "Moll Flanders in Germany." in *Journal of English and German Philology,* Vol. XXXII, 1933.
115. *Musicalische Patriot,* p. 186, No. 110. *Ehrenpforte,* p. 193.
116. *Ehrenpforte,* p. 208. See also *Musicalische Patriot,* p. 191, No. 180, where Mattheson writes, "Mattheson setzte einige Arien hinzu, weil ihrer zu wenin waren, und er verteutschte auch das gantze Wercklein aus dem Italiänischen."

because of the fact that Händel had set the text, which is by Christian Postel,[117] as his first oratorio in 1704,[118] when it was performed in Hamburg.[119] The fifth part of Mattheson's *Critica Musica*,[120] published presumably in the following year,[121] entitled "Des Fragenden Componisten," is a critical dialogue upon the method of setting this particular Passion text to music.[122] In apparent ignorance of the existence of Mattheson's setting, Chrysander, the great Händel scholar, interpreted this critique merely as an attempt to demonstrate the weakness of Händel's score.[123] Actually a comparison of Mattheson's own score and the principles in his critique reveals mutual agreement, and at the same time general disapproval of Händel's youthful effort.[124] While Mattheson may, as Chrysander suggests, have been jealous of Händel's musical success, in view of his other pronouncements on the proper method of setting text to music,[125] it seems unreasonable to ascribe such a paltry motive for the writing of such a significant document. Mattheson's score, in connection with his general musical treatises and this critique, deserves a thorough analysis, which is beyond the present limits of this bibliography.

88   Der / Liebreiche und gedultige / *DAVID* / in ein *ORATORIO* / gebracht / auf den / XVIII. Trinitatis Sonntag / gerichtet, gesetzt und aufgeführt / von *MATTHESON.* /
Text (12) pp.
MS. Score 59 pp.

The score is signed by Mattheson and dated "Aug. 10. 1723." The text, by an unknown author, is inspired by the revolt of Absalom. After several dialogues between "David" and "Meditatio" as to the wisest course of action, the order is given to attack. His army, singing *Ein Feste Burg,* is just ready to go into battle when a messenger brings the news of Absalom's unhappy fate. The oratorio is concluded by a moving lament sung by "David," and a joyous chorus. The music for the lament, written in the usual chromatic harmonies of the period, is one of Mattheson's most beautiful productions.

## 1724

## PUBLISHED TRANSLATIONS

89   Bischof Burnets / Geschichte, / die er selbst erlebet hat. / Erster Band. / Von der /Wieder-Herstellung König Carls II. / Biss zur / Erhöhung König Wilhelms und der Kö-/ginn Maria auf den Gross-Britannischen Thron. / Mit vorhergehenden / Summerischen Bericht der Kirchen- und Staats-Sa-/chen, so, von König Jacobs I. Zeiten an, biss zu gedachter, / im Jahr 1660 geschehenen, Herstellung, vorgefal-/len sind. / Aus dem

117. F. Chrysander, *Georg Friedrich Händel,* I, 88.
118. The title as given in Vol. IX of the *Händel Gesellschaft* is "Passion nach dem Evan. Johannes von Georg Friedrich Händel."
119. F. Chrysander, *Georg Friedrich Händel,* I, 88.
120. II, 1–64. See below, No. 91.
121. F. Krome, *Die Anfänge des musikalischen Journalismus in Deutschland,* p. 10.
122. Friederich Marpurg wrote of it in his *Kritische Briefe über die Tonkunst* (1760), I, 56: "Es ist vielleicht die erste gute Kritik, die über Singsachen gemachet worden. . . ."
123. F. Chrysander, *Georg Friedrich Händel,* I, 88–102. The more recent Händel authority, Hugo Leichtentritt, falls into the same error.
124. It will be recalled that Händel was but nineteen at that time.
125. Cf. Nos. 74 and 86.

Engländischen übersetzet von / *Mattheson.* / Mit Königlichen Pohlnischen und Churfürstl. Sachsischen / allergnädigsten *PRIVILEGIO.* / Hamburg und Leipzig, bey Philip Herteln. 1724. / Gedruckt bey seel. Thomas von Wierings Erben, bey der Börse im / güldnen A.B.C. und auch bey derselben zu bekommen. /
(20), 936, (16) pp.
Translated from: Bishop *BURNET'S* / HISTORY / OF / His Own Time. / VOL. I. / LONDON 1724. /

This is a complete and unaltered translation of the first volume of the English edition, which was published in the same year. Mattheson speaks with unconcealed pride of the feat of this enormous translation in the Dedication of the book, and in his autobiography,[126] stating that he translated the entire work in "69 Tagen, Sonntage und Posttage blieben ohne dergleichen Arbeit. . . ."

## MUSICAL MANUSCRIPT

90  Der / überwindende / Immanuel, / in einem / *ORATORIO* / auf Ostern / vorgestellet / von *Mattheson.* /
Text (8) pp.

The score of this oratorio is lost. As the text, with the exception of the title, is identical with that of "Der Aller-Erfreulichste Triumph," No. 59, it is probable that Mattheson wrote no new music for it.

### 1725

### BOOK

91  *CRITICAE MUSICAE* / *Tomus Secundus.* / d. i. / Zweyter Band / der Grund-richtigen / Untersuch-/ und Beurtheilung / vieler, theils guten, theils bösen, Meynungen, / Argumenten, und Einwürffe, so in alten und neuen, / gedruckten und ungedruckten / Musicalischen Schrifften / befindlich: / zur Ansräutung grober Irrthümer, und zur Be-/förderung bessern Wachsthums der reinen Harmonischen / Wissenschafft, in verschiedene Theile verfasset, / und Stückweise herausgegeben / von / *Mattheson.* / Dreyzehntes Stück. / *Non Criticos verborum, sed rerum, amo.* Giov. in Germ. Prin. / HAMBURG, gedruckt und zu bekommen bey seel. Thomas von *Wierings* Erben, bey der Börse im Güldnen *A. B. C.* 1725. / (16), 380, (20) pp.

This is a continuation and conclusion of No. 77. It was published in periodical form presumably in 1724–25,[127] and collected as Volume Two at its termination in 1725. Its format is in all respects similar to that of Volume One.
The first of the four topics of this volume, Part V, which takes up the first two numbers, is entitled "Des fragenden Componisten," for notice of which, see No. 87.

126. *Ehrenpforte*, p. 209.
127. F. Krome, *Die Anfänge des Musikalischen Journalismus in Deutschland*, p. 9.

Part VI is entitled "Die Lehr-reiche Meister-Schule. / oder: / Freundlicher Unterricht für solche, die, ohne zu-/länglicher musicalischen Gelehrsamkeit, den Meister / spielen wollen." / It is continued in the succeeding two numbers, and is a survey and criticism of the chief contemporary theoretical and practical works on music.

Part VII is entitled "Die Orchester-Kanzeley. / oder: / Gutachten, Briefe, Aussprüche, / Untersuchungen &c. der ehemaligen Schei-/ des-Männer beyn Orchester-Process." / This article contains the letters of thirteen musicians to Mattheson—Händel, Fux, Telemann, Kuhnau, and nine other less well known—expressing their respective opinions on the contents of the first two *Orchestres*, Nos. 27 and 47. With brief commentaries by Mattheson and several of his replies, this part occupies three numbers.

Part VIII is entitled "Der Melodische Vorhof. / Das ist: / Herrn Heinrich Bokemeyers, / *Cantoris* der Fürstl. Schule in Wolffenbüt-/tel, Versuch von der Melodica." / As in Part IV in the first volume, Mattheson discusses in these two remaining numbers the melodic theories of Bokemeyer, as a basis for the presentation of his own.

## PUBLISHED TRANSLATION

92  Erlesener / Davidischen Trost / In Noth und Tod. / Aus dem Italiäni-schen übersetzet, / und, / nach der berühmten / Marcellischen Composi-tion, / aufgeführet / von / MATTHESON. / (8) pp.

Mattheson translated this text for his musical presentation of the Marcello composition in the Hamburger Dom on the sixteenth Sunday after Trinity.[128] The text, which is a free adaptation of Psalms XXIII, and XXV, and the music form part of the composer Marcello's famous work.[129]

## LITERARY MANUSCRIPTS

93  *Predigt-Gedancken* / oder / Vertheidigung / des / Singens, Lesens und Betens / wieder die Verächte solche heilig Übungen / die von nichts, als versämten Predigen & Predig hören wollen. / Wir werden hier nicht von dem Heiligen Amte; sondern nur von des Unheiligen Mis-brauche. / MS. 24 pp.

This manuscript, written in thirty-four sections, probably about 1725, is another defense of Mattheson's ideas concerning the efficacy and proper use of music in the church.

94  Adverseria / ad Mentem / Lockii / disposita / inchoata in fine Septem-bris. 1725 / Hamburgi. / MS. 60 pp.

This curiously entitled manuscript is a notebook containing epigrammatic definitions of various words and terms, culled from the works of such diverse writers as Shaftesbury, Locke, Voltaire, Thomas Brown, La Mothe le Vayer, Middleton, Cleaveland and others. It is an interesting example of Mattheson's methods of acquiring data to be used in the writing of his books.

128. *Ehrenpforte*, p. 209.
129. Riemanns *Musiklexikon*, p. 1111.

184 *Johann Mattheson*

## MUSICAL MANUSCRIPTS

95 Der / Aus dem Löwen-Graben / befreyte, himmlische / DANIEL. / Bey / Heiliger Oster-Feyer / In einem / ORATORIO / Aufgeführet / Von / MATTHESON. / Text (8) pp. MS. Score 36 pp.

The score of this oratorio is dated by Mattheson "Mars 15, 1725." The text, which is of mediocre quality, was written by Tobias Heinrich Schubert, who was at that time rector of the Neuenkirche in Lande Hadeln, and who three years later became rector of the Michaeliskirche in Hamburg.[130] Mattheson's score is undistinguished, with the exception of the first chorus, in which his use of periods of complete silence is very effective.

96 Das / Gottseelige / Geheimniss, / in einer / Weihnacht-Music / vorgestellet / von / *MATTHESON* / Text (8) pp.

The score of this oratorio is lost. Mattheson wrote of it in his autobiography for the year 1725,[131] "Auf Weihnacht erfolgte abermahl ein neues Oratorium, dessen Poesie Hr. Pastor Neumeister wiederum verfertigte, und mit dem Titel des gottseligen Geheimnisses belegte."

### 1726

### PUBLISHED TRANSLATIONS

97 Merckwürdige / Danck-Schrifften, / So dem / Könige von Gross-Britannien / von / Beyden Parlaments-Häusern / Im Februario 1726. / Übergeben worden; / Nebst der / Von Seiner Majestät / Darauf ertheilten Allergnädigsten / Antwort: / Aus dem Engländischen Original übersetzet. / Hamburg. / (8) pp.

This translation can with some safety be attributed to Mattheson, since a copy of the pamphlet is bound up with his other works.[132] The originals were presumably found in English newspapers or dispatches from the Foreign Office. The speeches took place at the conclusion of the Houses' debates upon the Treaties of Hanover and Vienna.[133]

98 Die / Geschichte / von dem / Leben und von der Regierung / *MARIAE,* / Königinn der Schotten / und / Wittwen von Frankreich. / Aus Urkunden und glaudwürdigen / Scribenten zusammen gezogen, / und / aus dem Engländischen übesetzt / von / *Mattheson.* / HAMBURG, / Gedruckt und verlegt von seel. *Thomas* von *Wierings* Erben, / bey der Börse, im

130. Schröder, *Lexikon*, VII, 58 f.
131. *Ehrenpforte*, p. 210.
132. It is bound up in Volume I of the *Miscellanea Matthesoniana* in the Hamburger Stadtbibliothek.
133. Cobbett, *Parliamentary History of England*, 36 vols. (London, 1806–20), VIII, 502–512.

güldnen *A. B. C.* 1726. / Ist auch bey Philip Herteln in Leipzig zu bekommen. /

(14), 400 pp.

Translated from: THE / LIFE / OF / *MARY STEWART,* QUEEN / OF *Scotland* and *France.* / WRITTEN / Originally in FRENCH, / AND / *Now done into ENGLISH.* / WITH / NOTES *illustrating* and *confirming* the most / *material Passages* of this HISTORY, collected / from *Contemporary,* and other *Authors* / of the Grea-/test *Character* and *Reputation.* / By JAMES FREEBAIRN. / (Quotation) / *EDINBURGH:* / Printed for the AUTHOR, and are to be sold by / most of the Booksellers in Town. MDCCXXV. /

60, 328 pp.

Mattheson's translation includes all the miscellaneous documents included in the original. It is dedicated to Freyherr von Löwendal, "Ihro Königl. Majest. von Pohlen und Churfl. Durchl. zu Sachsen hochbestelltem Obristen über ein Regiment zu Fuss," and his wife.

## MUSICAL MANUSCRIPT

99  Der / Undanckbare / JEROBEAM / Auf / Den vierzehnten Sonntag nach dem Feste der / Heiligen Dreyfaltigkeit / gedeutet, / Und in einem / *ORATORIO* / vorgestellet / Von / *MATTHESON.* /

Text (8) pp.

Both the text and the music (which is lost) of this oratorio were by Mattheson. It was produced September 22, 1726.[184] In the text, the story of Jeroboam is narrated briefly by "Sacra Scriptorum." The moral precepts of the arias are paraphrases of verses from the Psalms. There appears to have been but one chorus, and that at the conclusion.

## 1727

## BOOK

100  Der Neue Göttingische / Aber / Viel schlechter, als / Die alten Lacedämonischen, / urtheilende / *EPHORUS,* / wegen der / Kirchen-Music / eines andern belehret / Von / *IO. MATTHESON.* / nebst dessen angehängtem, merckwürdigen / Lauten-Memorial. / (Quotation) / HAMBURG, 1727. / In Verlag des Verfassers, und zu bekommen bey Joh. Christoph / Kissnern im Dom daselbst, und zu Leipzig bey / Jacob Schustern. /

(4), 124 pp.

This pamphlet was written as a defense of dramatic church music, in response to a sober attack upon the same, entitled: *Unvorgreiffliche Gedancken über die Neulich eingerissene Theatralische Kirchen-MUSIC und Denen darinen bishero ublich gewordenen*

134. *Ehrenpforte,* p. 210. "Den 22. Sept. führte Mattheson wiederum ein neues Oratorium in besagter Kirche auf, und zwar den undankbaren Jerobeam, davon er auch die Worte selbst gesetzet hatte."

*CANTATEN mit Vergleichung Der Music voriger Zeiten zur Verbesserung der Unsrigen vorgestellet J. M. D. Anno MDCCXXVI.* (70) pp. This pamphlet was written by Joachim Meyer, Doctor of Laws, and Professor at the University of Göttingen. Mattheson's reply overwhelms the somewhat inadequate reasoning and careless literary style of Meyer in his customarily violent, not to say rude, manner. Meyer replied in the following year with a book of greater length,[135] in which he attacked many of Mattheson's books and the doctrines therein. Heinrich Philipp Guden also took sides with Meyer [136] and these two last documents were attacked in turn by the Berlin music critic, Martin Heinrich Fuhrmann.[137] Mattheson, likewise, aired his views in a much more thorough manner in his new periodical, *Der Musicalische Patriot.*[138]

The supplement (*Lauten-Memorial*) was written as a response to controversial assertions made by E. G. Baron in his *Untersuchung des Instruments der Lauten* (Nürnberg 1727), which took issue with statements of Mattheson regarding the lute in his first musical treatise.[139]

## PUBLISHED TRANSLATIONS

101   Untersuchung / der / Ursachen, / welche / Gross-Britannien / zu der / itzigen Aufführung / bewogen haben: / in so weit selbige den gegenwärtigen Zustand / von / Europa / betrifft. / Aus dem Engländischen übersetzet / von / Mattheson. / Hamburg / Gedruckt im Februario 1727. /

71 pp.

Translated from: An / Enquiry / into the / Reasons / of the / Conduct of Great Britain, / with Relation to the / Present State of Affairs / in Ed-

---

135. *Der anmassliche Hamburgische CRITICUS SINE CRISI Entgegen gesetzet dem so genannten Göttingischen EPHORO JOH. MATTHESON, Und dessen vermeyntlicher Belehrungs Ungrund in Vertheidigung der Theatralischen Kirchen-Music gewiesen Von Joachim Meyer, J.V. Doctore und Professore des Königl. Gross-Britan. Gymnasii in Göttingen . . . Anno 1728.* (180 pp).

136. He was a colleague of Meyer's at Göttingen (*Jöchers allgemeines Gelehrten-Lexicon, Fortsetzung und Ergänzungen* II, 1650), but the pamphlet with which he joined in this controversy is unknown.

137. *Gerechte Wag-Schal, Darin Tit, Herrn JOACHIM MEYERS, J.U. DOCTORIS &c. so genannter Anmasslich Hamburgischer CRITICUS SINE CRISI, Und dessen Suffragatoris, Tit. Herrn HEINR. PHILIPP. GUDEN, S. THEOL. DOCTORIS &c. Superlativ Suffragium, Und Tit. Herrn JOH. MATTHESON. &c. Hoch-Fürstl. Schleswig-Holstein. Capellmeisters Göttingischer Ephorus, richtig aufgezogen, genau abgewogen, und darauf der Calculus gezogen: Dass der Capell-Meister die 2. Doctores überwogen, Und diese beyde in die Lufft geflogen, Und weniger dem nichts gewogen, und dass dis nicht erlogen, Haben erwiesen in diesen 3. Bogen die 2 Colloquenten LAURENTIUS und INNOCENTIUS. Gedruckt zu Altona.* (48 pp.) The anonymous pamphlet listed in Eitner's *Quellen Lexikon,* VI, 387, is still another expression of the opinion of Meyer's Partisans: *Der Abgewürdigte Wagemeister oder der fälschlich genannte Wagschale nun verkapten und wohlbekannten Innocentii Frankenbergs auf dem Parnasse erkandte Unrechtigkeit u. Betrug . . . von einem dankbaren Discipient des fälschlich aufgezogenen Joach. Meyers. Anno 1729.*

138. No. 107.

139. *Das Neu-eröffnete Orchestre,* No. 27.

rope. / London: / Printed and sold by James Roberts in War-/wick-Lane. M.DCC.XXVII. /
112 pp.

This pamphlet, written by the prominent Whig, Low-Churchman, and controversialist, Bishop Hoadly,[140] criticizes the secret treaty of Vienna, 1725, and defends the action of England and the other powers, which had responded by the Alliance of Hañover, 1725.

102  Die / Augenscheinliche / Herannäherung / eines / Krieges; / dabey etwas, / Von der / Nothwendigkeit desselben, / zur / Erhaltung des Friedens und zum / Flor der Handlung, / erwehnet wird. / *Pax quaeritur Bello* / Mit beygefügtem genauen Grund-Riss, auch einer um-/ständlichen Beschreibung des Meerbusems und der Stadt / Gibraltar. / Aus dem Engländischen mit Fleiss verteutschet 1727. /
68 pp.
Translated from: THE EVIDENT APPROACH OF A WAR: And Something of the NECESSITY of It, In Order to Establish PEACE, and Preserve TRADE. *Pax Quaeritur Bello.* To which is Added, An Exact Plan and Description of the Bay and City of Gibraltar. London, 1727.
63 pp.

This pamphlet, which is attributed to Daniel Defoe,[141] discusses the merits of a war with Spain, and the effect of such a conflict upon the trade and commerce of Great Britain.

## MUSICAL MANUSCRIPTS

103  Auf das /Absterben des / Königs von Grossbritannien / Georg I. / Erbe von Hanover /
MS. Score 48 pp.

This oratorio, which was written for the service commemorating the death of George I, is signed by Mattheson and dated "Jul. 1727." Mattheson also added: "Wend hat dir wohlgemacht." [142] The text and score possess no unusual characteristics. The funeral service and performance of the oratorio apparently never took place, for Mattheson wrote in his autobiography: [143] "Dem gottseeligen Könige, als Bischofen der bremisch-hamburgischen Kirche, sollte die Begängniss im Dom allhier gehalten werden; Mattheson setzte zu solchem Ende ein starckes Epicedium, und liess es ausschreiben; allein das hanöversche Ministerium verbat alles gepränge instandigst, weil es mit der Beerdigung selbst in gorsser Stille zugegangen war."

104  Der / gegen seine Brüder barmherzige / *JOSEPH,* / Am / vierten

140. *Dictionary of National Biography*, XXVII, 16–21.
141. *Dictionary of Anonymous and Pseudonymous English Literature*, II, 224.
142. C. G. Wend was a poet and teacher, living in Hamburg from 1725 to 1745. Schröder, *Lexikon*, VII, 603–604.
143. *Ehrenpforte*, p. 211.

Sonntage / nach dem Feste der Heil. Dreieinigkeit / auffgeführet / von
/ MATTHESON. /
Text (8) pp.
MS. Score 60 pp.

In the account of his activities in the year 1727, Mattheson records the composition
and performance of this oratorio.[144] The text, which was written by T. H. Schubert,[145]
is one of the most dramatic and musically appropriate of all of Mattheson's oratorios.
In recounting the story and moral of young Joseph's life, a number of different literary
forms are used, thus providing the basis for varied musical treatment. The score is,
therefore, one of Mattheson's best.

105  Das / durch die Fleischwerdung / des ewigen Wortes / erfüllte /
Wort / der / Verheissung, / in die Music gebracht / und / am heiligen
Weinacht-Fest / aufgeführet / von / *Mattheson.* /
Text (12) pp.

The score of this oratorio, the text of which was written by C. G. Wend,[146] is unfortunately lost. Mattheson mentions its composition in his account of the year 1727.[147]

1728

PAMPHLET

106  *ODE* / Auf des *S. T. Hrn.* / Capellmeister Heinichen / schönes neues
Werck / Von / *GENERAL-BASS.* /
(4) pp.

This congratulatory poem on Heinichen's new book,[148] which was one of the best
and most important eighteenth-century treatises on thorough bass, consists of eleven ten-
line stanzas, and is dated, "Hamburg, den 1 May, 1728."

BOOK

107  Der Musicalische / Patriot, / welcher seine gründliche / Betrachtungen,
/ über / Geist- und Weltl. Harmonien, / samt dem, was durchgehende /
davon abhänget, / In angenehmer Abwechslung / zu solchem Ende mittheilet, / dass / GOttes Ehre, das Gemeine Beste, / und eines jeden Lesers

144. *Ibid.*
145. Cf. No. 95.
146. Cf. No. 103.
147. *Ehrenpforte,* p. 211.
148. *Der GENERAL-BASS in der COMPOSITION, Oder: Neue und gründliche Anweisung, Wie ein Music-Liebender mit besonderm Vortheil, durch die Principia der
Composition, nicht allein den General-Bass im Kirchen- Cammer- und Theatralischen
Stylo vollkommen, & in altiori Graden erlernen; sondern auch zu gleicher Zeit in der
Composition selbst, wichtige Profectus machen könne. . . . In Dresden bey dem Autore
zu finden. 1728.*

besondere Erbauung / dadurch befördert werde. / Ans licht gestellst / von / *Mattheson.* / HAMBURG, im Jahr 1728. / 376 pp.

The title of this work was directly inspired by that of the weekly, *Der Patriot* (1724–28), published and written by the Hamburger Patriotische Gesellschaft. Although the "Betrachtungen" are undated, it appears that they were actually issued by the week.[149] Considered as a book, it is a complete dissertation upon the biblical and philosophical justification of "theatralisch" church music, the inadequate support and understanding of church music in towns such as Hamburg, the theoretical, moral, and artistic excellence of the opera, with the Hamburg opera used as an illustration,[150] and finally, the proper attitude of the "patriotic" musician toward the entire problem of dramatic music.[151]

## PUBLISHED TRANSLATIONS

108   Des / Ritters Ramsay / Reisender / CYRUS, / welcher / die höchste Weissheit seiner Zeiten, /sowol in Staats-Sachen, als Philoso-/phischen und übernatürlichen Dingen, / erforschet. / Dem beigefüget eine Abhand-lung / von der / Gotts-Gelahrtheit und / Dicht-Kunde der Alten. / Aus dem Engländischen verteutschet / durch / *Mattheson.* / HAMBURG, Ge-druckt und verlegt von seel. Thomas von Wierings Erben, / im güldnen *A. B. C.* bey der Börse. 1728. / Ist auch in Leipzig bey Philip Hertel zu bekommen. / (24), 416 pp.
Translated from: The / Travels / of / Cyrus. / In Two Volumes. / To which is annex'd, / A Discourse / upon the / Theology and Mythology / of the Ancients. / By the Chevalier Ramsay. / (Third Edition) / Lon-don, / M:DCC.XXVIII. /

Mattheson's translation is probably from the third English edition of this very popu-lar book of travels. It is dedicated to "Herrn Friedrich, Hertzoge zu Sachsen, Jülich, Cleve und Berg," and is prefaced by a discussion of the problems involved in making a good translation.

109   *AESOPUS* bey Hofe, / in einem / Sing-Spiele / auf dem / Hamburgi-schen / Schau-Platze / vorgestellet. / Im Jahr 1729. / Gedruckt mit Stro-merischen Schrifften. / (62) pp.

---

149. F. Krome, *Die Anfänge des Musikalischen Journalismus in Deutschland*, p. 17; pp. 18–22 contain a summary of the contents of this journal.

150. Betrachtungen, pp. 22–24, contain a list of operas performed in Hamburg in the years 1678–28.

151. Mattheson wrote of this publication (*Ehrenpforte*, p. 211, note): "Er hat bisher, die Verlags-Kosten abgerechnet, 454 Mark 3ss, eingebracht, und es ist nur noch ein eintziges Exemplar übrig."

Mattheson writes of this translation in his account of the year 1728:[152] "Er machte sich so dann über die Oper, Aesopus her: wozu die Verse von ihm; die Noten aber von Telemann sind. Jene aus dem welschen; diese aus eigenem Erfindungs-Kasten."

## LITERARY MANUSCRIPT

110   *Adversarium Lockii* / Gespräche im Reiche der Musicanten, / Erster Zusam. / *Kürtzkopff, Hochbein, Ferndavon.* / (4) pp.

This article is a satirical sketch of the three above-named personages, and was apparently inspired by criticism of *Der Musicalische Patriot*, No. 107. It is dated 1728.

### 1729

## PUBLISHED TRANSLATIONS

111   Die / Wichtigkeit / des / Gross-Britannischen / Reichthums / und / Gewerbes, / gründlich betrachtet, / und / aus dem Engländischen ins Teutsche versetzst / von / *Mattheson*. / HAMBURG, / Gedruckt und zu bekommen beu seel. Thomas von Wierings Er-/ben bey der Börse, im guldnen *A. B. C.* 1729. / 11 pp.

Translated from: The Wealth and Commerce of / *Great-Britain* consider'd. / 8 pp.

Mattheson's translation is complete, and includes the table of figures on British commerce that was printed at the end of the original pamphlet.

112   Anmerckungen / uber die / Aufführung / abseiten / Gross-Brittanniens, / in Absicht / auf die Friedens-Handlung, und / andre Staats-Geschäffte, / ausserhalb Landes. / Aus dem Engländischen verteutschet / durch / *Mattheson*. / Gedruckt im *Februario* 1729. / 40 pp.

Translated from: Observations / on the / Conduct / of / Great-Britain, / with / Regard to the Negociations and / other Transactions Abroad. / London, / Printed: And Sold by J. Roberts near the Oxford / Arms in Warwick-Lane. 1729. / 61 pp.

This pamphlet contains a description of the Spanish outrages on British shipping, a table of ships, captains, their voyages, the value of their cargoes, etc., since the Treaty of Hanover in 1725.

### 1730

## PUBLISHED TRANSLATIONS

113   Anmerckungen / über den, / zwischen / Gross-Britannien, Franck-/ reich und Spanien, / zu Sevilien / den neunten November im Jahr 1729.

152. *Ehrenpforte*, p. 212.

N. St. / geschlossenen / Tractat, / darin sich drey Kronen zum Frieden, zur Vereinigung, zur / Freundschafft, und einander zu vertheidigen anheissig machen / (Quotation) / Aus dem Engländischen übersetzet / von / Mattheson. / HAMBURG, / Gedruckt im Februario, / 1730. / 15 pp.

Translated from: OBSERVATIONS / UPON THE / TREATY / Between the Crowns of / *Great-Britain, France,* and *Spain,* / Concluded at *SEVILLE* on the Ninth / of *November,* 1729, N. S. / (Quotation) / *LONDON:* / Printed, and Sold by *J. Roberts,* near the *Ox-/ford-Arms* in Warwick-Lane. 1729. Price 1 s. / 29 pp.

The authorship of this pamphlet, which Mattheson translated complete, is attributed to Robert Walpole, first Earl of Orford.[153]

114   M. H. J. Sivers / Gelehrter Cantor, / Bey Gelegenheit einer zu Rostock gehaltenen / Hohe-Schul-Uebung, / in Zwantzig, / Aus den Geschichten der Gelehrsamkeit ausgesuchten / Exempeln, / zur Probe, Vertheidigung und Nachfolge / vorgestellet, / Sodann, / wegen der Seltenheit des Inhalts, aus dem Lateinischen / übersetzet. / Auch / mit einigen kurtzen Anmerckungen / versehen / von *Mattheson.* / Hamburg, gedruckt und verlegt von Seel. *Thomas* von Wierings Erben im güldnen / *A. B. C.* bey der Börse. 1730. / 30, (2) pp.

Translated from: *DISSERTATION EX HISTORIA / LITTERARIA, / SISTENS / CANTORUM / DECADES DUAS, / QUAM, / SUB UMBONE ALTISSIMI, / AMPLISS. FACULTATIS PHILOSOPH. CONSENSU, / IN ACADEMIAE VARNIACAE AUDITORIO MAXIMO / D. XI. MAJI MDCCXXIX. / PUBLIO CLARISSIMORUM COMMILTONUM / COLLOQVIO EXHIBITURI SUNT / PRAESES / M / HEINRICUS JACOBUS / SIVERS. / LUBECENSIS. / ET / RESPONDENS / SINON CROLL. / CICENSIS MISMICUS, / Philosoph. & J. U. Studiosus. / ROSTOCHII, / Typus 10. LAC. ADLERI. SERENISS. PRINC. & ACAD. / Typographi /* 22 pp.

The author of this pamphlet, H. J. Sivers, was "Mag. der Phil. und Com Pastor bey der Deutschen Gemeinde zu Norköpfing in Schweden, auch Mitglied der Kön. Preuss. Akademie der Wissenschafte, geb. zu Lübeck . . ."[154] Mattheson not only translated the original text, but supplemented it, made numerous corrections, and added the correct authorities, or his own opinions.

153. *Y.U.L. College Pamphlets,* No. 361.
154. E. L. Gerber, *Historisch-Biographisches Lexikon der Tonkünstler* (Leipzig, 1790–92), p. 526.

## LITERARY MANUSCRIPT

115  Collectanea / ad Conficiiendum Historiam Musicam / 1730. / Mense Novembris. /
35 pp.

This notebook contains quotations from books Mattheson had been reading which he here collected for the purpose of using them later in his musical writings.

### 1731

## BOOK

116  Johann Matthesons / Grosse / General-Bass-Schule. / Oder: / Der exemplarischen / Organisten-Probe / Zweite verbesserte und vermehrte Auflage, / Bestehend in / Dreien Classen, / Als: / In einer gründlichen Verbereitung, / In 24 leichten Exempeln, / In 24. schwerern Prob-Stücken: / Solcher Gestalt eingerichtet, / Dass, wer die erste wol verstehet; und in den beiden andern Classen / alles rein trifft; so dann das darin enthaltene gut anzubringen weiss; derselbe / ein Meister im General-Bass heissen konne. / Hamburg, / Zu finden in Johann Christoph Kissners Buchladen. / 1731. /
(40), 484 pp.

Although this volume is essentially the same as *Der exemplarische Organisten-Probe*,[155] the entire contents have been so thoroughly rewritten and so greatly expanded in many instances, that it can scarcely be considered as merely a new edition.

## PERIODICAL ARTICLES

117  Contributions to the: Niedersächsische Nachrichten / von / Gelehrte Sachen. / (1731–33).

This learned journal had been founded two years previously by Christian Leisner.[156] Each issue, consisting of ten or more pages, appeared twice a week, on Mondays and Thursdays. The articles, which are on miscellaneous matters, are all unsigned, but it is possible by referring to the Foreword to the collected issues of the year 1731, published in 1732, to throw some light upon Mattheson's activities in this venture. Among the contributors, he is the first to be mentioned: "Unter denselben verdient der beruhmte Herr Capell-Meister und Secretar Mattheson vor allen andern ein öffentliches Lob. Von dem kommen die Auszüge des Englischen Present State, wie auch die übrigen Nachrichten London, und das jenige, so von der Music und Theatralischen Sachen handelt, her. Ihm haben die Leser den ordentlichen, vollständigen, und gründlichen Bericht der in England vorgefallenen neuen zur Gelehrsamkeit gehörenden Sachen zu dancken . . . Man gesteht es gerne, dass sein Beytrag einen grossen und wichtigen Theil der Neiders. Nachr. ausmacht." The majority of articles which may be considered as coming from Mattheson's pen are reports of the latest books published in England, in the style typical of the learned journals of the period. There are also entire articles translated from journals such as

155. No. 62.
156. Schröder, *Lexikon*, IV, 415.

The *Craftsman,* The *Bee,* and The *Present State of the Republic of Letters.* It was because of criticism of the translation of an article from the latter [157] that Mattheson
terminated his contributions to the magazine in 1733.[158]

## PUBLISHED TRANSLATION

118  Betrachtungen / über den / Gegenwärtigen Zustand / der / Europäischen / Staats-Geschäffte, / absonderlich / In Ansehung der in Gross-
Britanni-/schem Sold stehenden Krieges-Völcker / und ihrer Anzahl. Aus
dem Engländischen / übersetzt / Von / *Mattheson.* / Anno 1731. /
31 pp.
Translated from: Considerations / on the / Present State / of / Affairs /
in Europe, / and particularly with Regard to the Num-/ber of Forces in
the Pay of *Great-Britain.* / London: / Printed for *J. Roberts* in Warwick-
Lane. / 1730. /
53 pp.

This tract, the author of which is unknown,[159] reviews European affairs since the
Treaty of Vienna. In particular it deals with the increasing size of European armaments
as the justification for England's hiring of Hessian troops. It examines both arguments
concerning this latter question, defending this action of England.

### 1732

## PAMPHLET

119  *DE / ERUDITIONE / MUSICA, / Ad / Virum plurimem Reveren-
dum. Amplissimum / atque Doctissimum, / JOANNEM CHRISTO-
PHORUM / KRUSIKE, / Artium Magistrum & Oratorem Sacrum
apud / Hamburgenses disertissimum, / SCHEDIASMA EPISTOLICUM
/ JOANNIS MATTHESONII. / Accedunt ejusdem literae / ad V. C. /
CHRISTOPHORUM FRIEDERICUM / LEISNERUM / de eodem
argumento scriptae. / HAMBRUGI, apud Felgineri Viduam. 1732. /*
16 pp.

This pamphlet was written in reply to a question raised by J. C. Krüsike, the pastor
of the Petri-Kirche,[160] concerning the existence of any musical authorities upon musical
learning.[161] Mattheson gives a short disquisition upon the great importance accorded

157. Vol. X, October 1732, Article XII, pp. 289–302, "A Dissertation on *Gloves*
shewing their Antiquity and Use in the Several Ages of the World." Mattheson's translation, "Abhandlung von Handschuhen," began in Number 46, 15 June, 1733, and was
continued in the succeeding four numbers.
158. Cf. p. 82.
159. This pamphlet is not listed in Halkett and Laing's *Dictionary of Anonymous and
Pseudonymous English Authors.*
160. Schröder, *Lexikon,* IV, 224–227.
161. Krüsike, a theologian and a Latinist, had published in this same year, 1731,
a treatise on scholarly learning: *Vindemiarum literarium Specimen III, de varia eruditione. Hamb. 1731.*

to musical learning by the ancients, and the equally high estimation it should enjoy in the present, with references to famous scholars who have discoursed upon music. A second edition of the pamphlet appeared in Freiberg in 1751 with the same title-page.

## 1733
### UNPUBLISHED TRANSLATION

120 Bewährtes Mittel, einem Scepticum zu machen / Ubersetzet von Aristoxenus. /
Translated from: Proper Ingredients to make a Sceptic.

The translation of this verse by the extraordinary poet, Stephen Duck,[162] is dated "22 Aug. 1733." It is an example of a number of casual literary efforts on the part of Mattheson, and in and of itself is of no importance. Both in this year and the preceding one, he was undoubtedly chiefly occupied with his contributions to the *Niedersächsische Nachrichten von Gelehrte Sachen*, No. 117. He probably found this poem in the literary journal entitled *The Bee*.[163]

## 1734
### PUBLISHED TRANSLATION

121 Freundschafft / im / Tode, / durch / Zwantzig Briefe / von den Verstorbenen an die Le-/bendigen vorgestellet. / Aus dem Engländischen ubersetzt / von / *Mattheson*. / (Quotation) / HAMBURG, / Gedruckt und verlegt von seel. Thomas von Wierings / Erben. 1734. / (8), 92 pp.
Translated from: Friendship in Death: In Twenty Letters from the Dead to the Living. London 1728 (by Elizabeth Rowe).

From the Foreword to Mattheson's translation of these letters it is clear how important he felt them to be, for he writes: "Ob nun die tüchtigsten Bücher voller christlicher und moralischer Proben davon zu finden sind, hat doch 'ein gewisser Englander' dafür gehalten, dass man kein Mittel unversucht lassen müsse, dem Umglaube zu steuern." He dedicated the volume to the "preiswürdigen Orden des guten Geschmacks," a literary group which numbered himself, the poet Hagedorn, and others in its membership, but whose proceedings are entirely unknown.[164] It was the first of many of Elizabeth Rowe's devotional writings to be translated into German in the eighteenth century.[165]

162. *Poems on Several Occasions*, 1736, p. 144.
163. Cf. Bibliography No. 122, note.
164. In the *Hamburger Nachrichten aus dem Reiche der Gelehrsamkeit*, 1759, p. 704, there is a list of Mattheson's literary efforts, the following title occurs: "Tagebuch des Ordens von guten Geschmeck, gestiftet durch M. von Hagedorn ein Mitglied gewesen, Drey Bänder in einem. Hamb. 1733 & 34. 4to Maj. mit vielen merckwürdigen Beylagen." Unfortunately the Hamburger Stadtbibliothek has no record of its existence.
165. Louise Wolf, "Elizabeth Rowe in Deutschland, ein Beytrag zur Literatur Geschichte des 18. Jahrhundert," Dissertation (Heidelberg, 1910).

## LITERARY MANUSCRIPTS

**122 Des Menschen Eitelkeit /**
**4 pp.**

This manuscript contains notes on Pascal's *Pensées*. Although undated, this evidence of Mattheson's interest in Pascal is borne out in some of his later works. The present manuscript and the succeeding ones listed for the year 1734 are undoubtedly the literary efforts Mattheson mentioned as possibilities for a publication to be entitled *Der Kalten Küche.*[166]

**123 Der Toback. / Non indecoro pulvere sordidos. / Hor. II Od. 1. /**

This verse of ten lines is written in praise of tobacco:

> Du Pflantzen-Königin! den alten unbewusst;
> Der gantzen neuen Welt Vergnügen, Heilung, Lust:
> Was dem Studenten hilfst, den Staatsmann (blot) gewogen,
> Ist deines Uhles Krafft, durch Höheren eingezogen;
> So bald man aber dich zu feinem Pulver reibt,
> Fühlts Märcius im Hirn, (wo Hirn noch' in ihm bleibt)
> Jetzt wird er Trauerspiel, und nachmahls Oden machen,
> Bald Hochzeit-Carmina, nebst Opern, Kirchen-Sachen:
> Der feineste Geschmack behält in dir den Sitz,
> Voll Weisheit ist dein Rauch, dein Schnupfen voller Witz.

**124 Fabel / Vom Sperber, Grünspecht, der Drosel, / darin du Leser: / Sehr begehret, / mehr vermehrt / enthalten. /**
**2 large pages in MS.**

This poem is clearly an imitation of the fables of La Fontaine, as are also Nos. 144 and 155.

**125 Gedult-Büchlein / aus dem Welchen des Zarlino übersetzt von M. / (44) pp.**

I have not been able to discover the original of this translation: a book by the sixteenth-century musical theorist, Gioseffo Zarlino.

**126 Kurtzer Begriff / der vornehmsten Heilsamen Tugenden / und / Eigenschaften / der Pyrmont Brunnen-Wasser, / ausgezogen und übersetzet / aus dem fünften Capitel einer von Dr. Johann Philipp Seix, / Rath und Leibartzt des Fürsten von Waldeck, / zu Pyrmont herausgegebenen. /**
**4 pp.**

I have not been able to discover the volume from which this interesting fragment was extracted.

166. *Ehrenpforte*, p. 215. "Im Jahr 1734. übersetzte er für sich, Zarlins Werck von der Gedult, samt einigen Stücken der Wochenschrifft, *Bee, die Biene;* die, nebst vielen andern Beiträgen (note: Diese Beiträge konnten dareinst wohl, unter dem Nahmen der kalten Küche, das Licht sehen, und sind sehr sonderbar . . .) in der Ordens-Versammlung verlesen wurden."

1735

## BOOKS

127   Johann Matthesons, / Hoch-Fürstl. Schleswig-Hollsteinischen Capell-
Meisters, und Königl. Gross. Britan-/nischen Gestandten-Secretars im
Nieder-Sächsischen Kreise, / Kleine / General-Bass-Schule. / Worin /
Nicht nur ʟernende, sondern vornehmlich Lehrende. / Aus / Den al-
lerersten Anfangs-Gründen des Clavier-Spielens, / überhaupt und besonders, / Durch / Verschiedene Glassen u. Ordnungen der Accords / Stuffen-
weise, / Mittelst / Gewisser Lectionen oder stundlicher Aufgaben, / Zu
/ Mehrer Vollkommenheit in dieser Wissenschafft, / Rightig, getreulich,
und auf die deutlichste Lehr-Art, / kurtzlich angeführet werden. / *Utilis,
non subtilia.* / Hamburg, bey Joh. Christoph Kissner, 1735. /
(14), 253, (12) pp.

This volume contains the harmonic and contrapuntal principles necessary to the
knowledge of thorough bass and composition. Its numerous examples are of a more
elementary nature than those in Mattheson's other volumes on the same subject. In the
Dedication he takes opportunity to mention seven fundamental principles of Rameau,
found in his *Traité sur l'Harmonie,* which he considers false. In his first chapter he
attacks the niggardly policies of municipalities such as Hamburg toward the church-music
organization. The volume was reviewed in the *Niedersächsische Nachrichten von Gelehrte
Sachen* in March, 1734,[167] and considerable prominence was given to the contents of
the first chapter, entire excerpts being quoted. Mattheson's disrespectful attitude aroused
the ire of the Geistliches Ministerium, which discussed the possibilities of banning the
volume.

128   A / Complete Treatise / of / THOROUGH BASS / Containing the
true Rules / with a TABLE of all the Figures & their proper Ac-Company-
ments / To which is added / Several Examples of each Figure / By /
JOHN MATTHESON / Britisch Consul at Hamburgh. / Price 7:6 /
NB: The first Line is proper as it is in each Example. / The second two
Lines the Complete Chord as it is to be Played. / London. printed for
P. Hodson Maiden Lane Covt. Garden / Where may be had every Ar-
ticel in the Musical way. /
32 pp. (folio).

This undated volume contains the simple musical illustrations to be found in Mattheson's *Kleine General-Bass-Schule,* No. 127. As Mattheson makes no allusion to it, it may
have been a pirated edition of which he knew nothing. It is in no sense a complete
translation or even adaptation of the original, but is merely a sort of popular handbook
for the simplest problems in thorough bass.

## MUSIC

129   Die / wol-klingende / Finger-Sprache, / in / Zwölff Fugen, / mit
/ zwey biss drey Subjecten, / entworffen; / und dem / Hoch-Edel-

167. 8. Märtz No. 19, pp. 153 f.

Gebohrnen, Hochgelahrten und / Weltberühmten Herrn, / Herrn Georg Friedrich Händel, / Königl. Gross-Br. und Churfürstl. Braunschw. Lüneb. / Capellmeister, / als ein Merckmal sonderbarer Ehrbezeigung, / zugeeignet / von / Mattheson. / Erster Theil. / HAMBURG, 1735. im Verlage des Verfassers. /

(2), 14 pp.

This is the first half of a set of twelve fugues published by Mattheson, the second half appearing two years later.[168] The first four fugues have but one subject, and No. 4 is followed by an Allemande, Corrente, and Gavotta, whose themes are variants of the fugue subject. No. 5 contains but one subject also, but No. 6 is in two parts, the first of which is a long treatment of two subjects, and the second a sort of Fughetta refrain.[169]

## PUBLISHED TRANSLATION

130   Bischof Burnets / Geschichte, / die er selbst erlebet hat. / Zweiter Band. / Von der / *REVOLUTION* / Biss zum / Schluss des Utrechtischen Friedens, / unter / Der Königinn Anna / Regierung: / Mit beigefügtem Lebens-Lauff des Verfassers, / von dem Herausgeber beschrieben. / Aus dem Engländischen übersetzet, / und mit einigen Anmerckungen versehen / von / *Mattheson.* / HAMBURG, / Gedruckt und verlegt von seel. Thomas von Wierings Erben, bey der / Börse, im Güldnen *A. B. C.* 1736. / Ist auch in Leipzig bey Philip Hertel zu bekommen. / (8), 760, 136 pp.

Translated from: Bishop *BURNET'S* / HISTORY / OF / His Own Time. / VOL. II / . . . To which is added, / The AUTHOR'S LIFE, by the Editor. / London: 1734. 765 pp.

Like his translation of the first volume of Burnet's *History*, No. 89, this is a complete, literal translation of the second volume, which had been published in the preceding year. According to Mattheson the translation, which he began in April, 1734, took him nineteen weeks to complete.[170]

168. Bibliography No. 135.
169. The autograph manuscript of the entire set of twelve fugues is in the Preussische Staatsbibliothek, Mus. MS. 13906. A second edition of the set appeared in 1749 (*Ehrenpforte,* Anhang, p. 27) under the titles: *Les Doits Parlants en Douze Fugues Doubles à deux et trois Sujets Pour le Clavessin, ár Monsieur de Mattheson, Conseiller des Ambassades de S. A. J. Monseigneur le Grand-Duc de toutes les Russies, Duc de Holstein etc. Seconde Edition. A Nuremberg, aux dépens de Jean Ulric Haffner Maitre du Lut.*
170. *Ehrenpforte,* p. 215. "Nachdem am 3. April die Uebersetzung des zweeten Bandes burnetscher Geschichte angefangen worden, . . . Den 12. Aug. kam der andere burnetsche Band zum Stande, innerhalb 19 Wochen 113 Bogen, Cicero-Schrifft."

## LITERARY MANUSCRIPT (TRANSLATION)

131   Abhandlung / von der / Seeligkeit Esaus / aus dem Lateinischen / übersetzet / von / Mattheson. / Hamburg im October / 1735. / 68 pp.

I have not been able to identify the original of this little theological work.

## LITERARY MANUSCRIPTS

132   Mattheson's Schutz-Wehr / Regium est: *bene* facere; et male audire.— Alex. Magn. / 21 pp.

This manuscript and the following one, No. 133, are both written as defenses against the article in the *Niedersächsische Nachrichten* [171] which had summarized the contents of the Foreword of Mattheson's *Kleine General-Bass-Schule*.[172] It was in this volume that he attacked the policy of the Hamburg government toward the municipal church music organization. The tone of both manuscripts is so violently scurrilous that one would like to know if either had been published.

133   Das wolgetroffene Urbild der Falschheit, und Kleine, doch nach / dem Leben entworffen von ihn selbst, und in einer Psalm (?) gefasset von M. / 5 pp.

For an account of this see above. It is dated 1735.

## 1737

## BOOK

134   Kern / Melodischer / Wissenschafft, / bestehend / in den auserlesensten / Haupt- und Grund-Lehren / der musicalischen / Setz-Kunst oder Composition, / als ein vorläuffer des / Vollkommenen Capellmeisters, / ausgearbeitet von / *MATTHESON*. / Hamburg, / Verlegts Christian Herold. / MDCCXXXVII. / (18), 182, (8) pp.

As the title suggests, this volume contains Mattheson's theory and analysis of melodic learning. With the exception of the Foreword, the entire contents were incorporated in his most complete treatise on musical composition and theory, *Der Vollkommene Capellmeister,* which was published two years later.[173] In this Foreword Mattheson defends his belief in the importance of learning and understanding the art of melody as the fundamental principle underlying all composition. In assuming this position, he is disagreeing with the other most distinguished musical theorist of his time, J. P. Rameau,

171. No. 31, 1735.
172. Bibliography No. 127.
173. Bibliography No. 138.

whose system of musical theory was based upon the fundamental importance of harmonic learning. The body of the volume contains Mattheson's complete principles with regard to the proper writing of all variety of melodies.

## MUSIC

135 Der / wolklingenden / Finger-Sprache / Zweyter Theil / Hamburg 1737. im Verlag des / Verfassers. / (12) pp.

This set of harpsichord pieces is the second and concluding part of No. 129. The six fugues of this part are larger and more complex in form than those of the first part.

## PUBLISHED TRANSLATION

136 Historische / Anmerckungen / über / Burnets Geschichte, / Die er selbst erlebet hat, / Als ein / Unentbehrlicher Anhang / zum gantzen Werck, / Auf vieler Verlangen / übersetzet, / und mit einigen Erläuterungen versehen / von / Mattheson. / HAMBURG, / Gedruckt bey seel. Thomas von Wierings Erben im Guldenen / A. B. C. bey der Börse, 1737. / (8), 72, (2) pp.
Translated from: Historical and Critical Remarks on Bishop Burnet's History of his own Time. 1725 (by Bevil Higgons).

This volume was reissued in 1736, but Mattheson states that he began the translation immediately after finishing the last volume of Burnet's *History* in 1734.[174]

## 1738

## PAMPHLET

137 Gültige / Zeugnisse / über die jüngste / Matthesonisch-Musicalische / Kern-Schrifft, / Als ein / Füglicher Anhang derselben, / zum Druck befordert / von / Aristoxen, dem jüngern. / (Quotation) / Hamburg, 1738. / 14 pp.

The "testimonials" mentioned in the title are three letters to Mattheson concerning his *Kern Melodischer Wissenschafft*, No. 134. The first is conventional thanks from an anonymous underling of the Duke of Schleswig-Holstein for the dedication of the volume. The second is a short letter of approval from J. P. Kuntzen, a Lübeck musician.[175] The third and longest is from Johann Adolph Scheibe, the musical disciple of Gottsched, and author of the important periodical, *Der Critische Musicus* (1737–40). His enthusiasm for Mattheson's book appears to have been unbounded. This is the first occasion Mattheson signed himself "Aristoxenus"—a name he chose in recognition of

174. *Ehrenpforte*, p. 215. "Er machte sich über die *Remarks on Burnet.*"
175. Kuntzen's biography is to be found in the *Ehrenpforte*, pp. 158–165.

that early theoretician's musical doctrines—which were opposed to the Pythagorean theory of harmony.[176]

## 1739

## BOOK

138   Der / Vollkommene / Capellmeister / das ist / Gründliche Anzeige / aller derjenigen Sachen, / die einer wissen, können, und vollkommen inne haben muss, / der eine Capelle / mit Ehren und Nutzen vorstehen will: / Zum Versuch entworffen / von / MATTHESON. / Hamburg, / Verlegts Christian Herold, 1739. / 28, (4), 484, (20) pp.

As the title suggests, this huge treatise, of encyclopedic proportions, contains the practical, theoretical, and æsthetic precepts which the eighteenth-century Capellmeister needs to know as director of a secular and ecclesiastical music organization. It is thus the product of all of Mattheson's earlier works on music, and it does include much that is to be found in them. It is divided into three sections and an introduction. In the latter are stated two fundamental musical beliefs of Mattheson, about which he had written much in the past. These are his belief in the importance of church music as a means of worshiping God, and his belief in melody as the basis for all musical learning and composition, which he sums up briefly: "Alles muss gehörig singen." In the first of the three sections are presented many different facts of musical knowledge, such as: "Vom Klange an sich selbst, und von der musikalischen Natur-Lehre"; "Vom Matthematischen Verhalt oder klingenden Intervalle"; "Von der Geberden-Kunst", etc. The second section is entirely devoted to the elements of melodic learning,[177] under the general heading: "Von der wirklichen Verfertigung einer Melodie, oder die einstimmigen Gesänge samt deren Unstände und Eigenschafften." Having outlined the method and principles of writing a single melody, Mattheson turns in the third section to the principles governing more complex problems in composition; the section is entitled: "Von der Zusammensetzung verschiedener Melodien, oder von der vollstimmigen Setzkunst, so man eigentlich Harmonie heisst." This naturally includes the traditional rules of counterpoint, which are represented with numerous illustrations. At the conclusion, three chapters deal with such practical considerations as the construction of instruments, "die Spielkunst," "Die Regierung An- Auf- und Ausführung einer Musik."

## 1740

## BOOK

139   Grundlage / einer / Ehren-Pforte, / woran der / Tüchtigsten Capellmeister, / Componisten, Musikgelehrten, / Tonkünstler &c. / Leben,

176. H. S. Macran, *The Harmonics of Aristoxenus* (Oxford, 1902), p. 89. "The conception, then, of a science of music which will accept its materials from the ear, and carry its analysis no further than the ear can follow; and the conception of a system of sound functions, . . . are the two great contributions of Aristoxenus to the philosophy of music." To Mattheson he was the champion of the senses, and opposed to the scientific rationalism of the Pythagoreans.

177. The greater part of the contents of this section were published in 1737 in *Kern melodischer Wissenschaft,* No. 134.

Werke, Verdienste &c. / erscheinen sollen. / Zum fernern Ausbau ange-
geben / von / Mattheson. / *HAMBURG* 1740. / In Verlegung des
Verfassers /
xliv, 428, (16) pp.

This volume contains the lives of one hundred and forty-eight of the most "excellent"
musicians who qualified for Mattheson's critical standards set forth in the Foreword.[178]
The general outlines of this work had been first announced in the Foreword to the
German edition of his *Harmonisches Denckmahl* in 1714.[179] Three years later, in
*Das Beschützte Orchestre*,[180] it was described in greater detail, and Mattheson appealed
to fourteen leading musicians for aid in acquiring the information. The materials for the
biographies were ultimately drawn from books, the accounts of the musicians themselves, and Mattheson's own investigations. J. S. Bach is the only important German
musician of the time who did not acknowledge Mattheson's request for information,
and to whom there is therefore no reference. The amount and, in some instances, the
accuracy of detail in this book have made it a more important volume of source material than the two other similar eighteenth-century biographical dictionaries issued in
Germany: Johann Walther's *Musicalisches Lexicon*, 1732, and Ernst Ludwig Gerber's
*Historisch-Biographisches Lexikon der Tonkünstler*, 1791–92. The entire work was republished in 1910 by Max Schneider, in a typographical facsimile edition, with some
references to modern secondary sources in the margins, and an "Anhang," containing
Mattheson's notes in his copy in the Hamburger Stadtbibliothek, and in particular the
"Fortsetzung des Matthesonischen Lebenslaufs." [181] This account carries his autobiography up to the year 1758. A continuation of it entitled "Weitere Fortsetzung des Matthesonischen Lebenslaufes," I discovered among his manuscripts in Hamburg, and it is
reproduced for the first time as an Appendix to this volume.

## PAMPHLET

140  Etwas Neues unter der Sonnen! / oder / Das Unterirrdische / Klippen-
Concert / in Norwegen, / aus glaubwürdigen Urkunden / auf Begehren
angezeiget, / von / *Mattheson*. / Felsenlied unsichtbarer Geschöpffe. /
(Musical Quotation) / HAMBURG, im Brachmonath, 1740. / Gedruckt
bey seel. Thomas Wierings Erben, im güldnen A. B. C. /
(8) pp.

This pamphlet contains two letters sent to Mattheson by his friend, General Bertouch,
which give accounts of ghostly singing that had been heard issuing from under some
cliffs in Norway. The tune which both witnesses heard is quoted also. Mattheson concludes with observations on the amazing phenomena that are to be met with in the
world at large.

## 1741

## ARTICLE

141  Contribution to: (Gottsched's) Beyträge zur Critischen Historie der
Deutschen Sprache, Poesie und Beredsamkeit . . . Leipzig, 1741. Mat-

178. *Vorbericht*, pp. xxviii–xxix.
179. Bibliography No. 30.
180. Bibliography No. 47.
181. "Anhang," pp. 18–33.

theson Gedancken über ein paar Artikel des drey und zwanzigsten Stücke der Beyträge zur C. H. d. D. S. P. u. B.

Vol. VII, St. 25, pp. 8–25.

Mattheson's article is a critique of an essay printed in 1740 in this same journal (St. 23, pp. 453 f.), which was a review of *Der Critische Musikus, herausgegeben von Johann Adolph Scheibe . . . Hamburg 1738*. Mattheson takes issue with certain statements of Scheibe, and quoted by Gottsched, on the question of good writing on musical subjects in Germany.

## 1742

## PUBLISHED TRANSLATION

142  Pamela / oder die belohnte Tugend / eines armen, / doch wunderschönen / Dienst-Mädgens, / aus ihren eignen, / auf Wahrheit und Natur / gegründten, Briefen / entdecket, / ans Licht gestellet, / und, nach der dritten Auflage, aus dem Engländischen übersetzet / von / M. /Erster Band. / HAMBURG, gedruckt und verlegt durch seel. Thomas von / Wierings Erben im güldnen A. B. C. 1742. /

(22), 40, 454 pp.

Translated from: PAMELA: / OR, / VIRTUE Rewarded. / In a SERIES of / FAMILIAR LETTERS / FROM A / Beautiful Young DAMSEL, / To her PARENTS. / Now first Published / In order to cultivate the Principles of VIRTUE / and RELIGION in the Minds of the YOUTH / of BOTH SEXES. / A Narrative which has its Foundation in TRUTH . . . / In TWO VOLUMES / THE THIRD EDITION / To which are prefixed EXTRACTS from several curious / LETTERS written to the *Editor* on the Subject. / VOL. I. / LONDON: Printed for C. RIVINGTON, in St. Paul's Church / Yard; and J. OSBORN, in Pater-noster Row. / MDCCXLI. /

Vol. I, xxxviii, 296 pp.

Vol. II (with same title), (2), 396 pp.

This is the first German translation of *Pamela,* the second, by Jacob Schuster, appeared a year later in Leipzig.[182] The second volume of the translation also appeared in this year: *Pamela, / oder / die belohnte Tugend. / Zweiter Band. / Vierter Theil. / Aus dem Engländischen übersetzt / von / M. HAMBURG. / gedruckt und verlegt von seel. Thomas von Wierings / Erben, im güldnen A. B. C. bey der Börse. / 1742. /* 654 pp. These two together are complete translations of the first two volumes of the third English edition. Mattheson published the remainder in a third volume in 1743 (Bibliography No. 143).

182. L. M. Price, *The Reception of English Literature in Germany* (Berkeley, Cal., 1932), p. 190.

### 1743

### PUBLISHED TRANSLATION

143  Pamela, / oder / die belohnte Tugend, / in einem / kurtzen Beriff / des / Dritten und Vierten Bandes, / als ein / Siebender und Letzter Theil, / aus dem Engländischen ubersetzet / von / M. / HAMBURG. / Gedruckt und verlegt von seel. Thomas von Wierings / Erben im güldnen A.B.C. bey der Börse. 1743. /

14, 359, 8 pp.

Translated from: *PAMELA:* / OR, / VIRTUE Rewarded. / In a SERIES of / FAMILIAR LETTERS / From a Beautiful / Young DAMSEL to her PARENTS: / And afterwards, / In her EXALTED CONDITION, / BETWEEN / HER, and Persons of *Figure* and Quality, / UPON THE / most Important and Entertaining SUBJECTS, / In FOUR VOLUMES: / . . . / THE THIRD EDITION, corrected. / LONDON . . . / MDCCXLII. /

Vol. III, (2), iv, 419 pp.

Vol. IV, (with same title), (2), 471 pp.

Matthesonʼs translation of these two supplementary volumes is much condensed, a treatment which he explains and justifies in his Foreword.[188]

### LITERARY MANUSCRIPTS

144  Sur le livre de Kellner 3*e* edition / Aôut 30. 1743. / 1 page

I have been unable to identify the book which inspired this verse, which is as follows:

> "Lʼignorant vend bon marché
> Les bijoux quʼil a volé.
> Un pauvre plagiare,
> Stupide et temeraire,
> Ne peut jamais briller
> Quʼà force de piller;
> Et on lui fait beaucoup de bien
> Lorsque son larcin
> Ne dit rien.
>
> Mattheson le benin."

145  Schöne Gelegenheit / für / unerbetene Rathgeber / bey der / Firn-haber-/ und / Wincklerischen / Hochzeit. / M. / 1743. / 4 pp.

This manuscript contains a number of irregular congratulatory stanzas in French and German.

183. Cf. pp. 80–81.

## 1744

### BOOK

146  Die neueste / Untersuchung / der / Singspiele, / nebst beygefügter / musikalischen / Geschmacksprobe, / liefert hiemit / Aristoxenus, / der jüngere. / (Quotation) / Hamburg, / verlegts Christian Herold. / 1744. /
(8), 168 pp.

This volume is an examination of the opera on the basis of its moral and artistic value as an art form. It was inspired by the criticism made of the opera by the Italian writer, Muratori, in his volume entitled *Della perfetta poesia italiana,* published in Modena in 1706, and translated and published in part by Gottsched in his *Beyträge zur Critischen Historie der Deutschen Sprache, Poesie und Beredsamkeit,* 1740, St. 23, no. 10, pp. 485 f. Mattheson appended to this work an essay entitled "Die Musikalische Geschmacksprobe, worin die heutigen allergalantesten Mittel und Wege zur Niedlichkeit des Gesanges und Klanges nachdrücklichst anpreiset Aristoxenus, der jüngere."

### LITERARY MANUSCRIPT

147  Fontenelle / Gespräche von mehr als einer Welt, / verdolmetschet / von / *Gottsched* / Anmerckungen über das anstössige, so sich mir in demselben gefunden, und dem Verstande hinderlich gefallen. /
8 pp.

Mattheson wrote at the end of this manuscript the date "5 Jul. 1744," and the word "Amusement." It is an analysis of various phrases in Gottsched's translation of Fontenelle's *Entretiens sur la Pluralité des Mondes,* 1686. [184]

## 1745

### BOOKS

148  A. Das / Erläuterte Selah, / nebst einigen andern nützlichen / Anmerckungen / und / erbaulichen Gedanken, / über / Lob und Liebe, / von / M. / als eine Fortsetzung / seiner vermischten Werke. / Hamburg, / verlegts Christian Herold / 1745. /
(20), 164 pp.

The above title applies to the first of the three essays in this volume, pp. 1–58, which is an examination of the word *Selah;* Mattheson interprets it as meaning a musical *Ritornell.* Working on this basis he analyzes the use of this word in the Psalms.

B. Etliche hundert / erkohrner / Schrifft-Stellen, / die sich ausdrücklich

184. I have been unable to discover Gottsched's translation; his translation entitled *Bernhard von Fontenelle Historie der Heydnischen Orakel . . . aus dem Französischen übersetzt . . . von J. C. Gottscheden, (Leipzig 1730)* (Catalogue of the British Museum) is the only one listed in available works of reference.

auf die / Tonkunst / beziehen, / und / zur bessern Aufnahme derselben / gesammlet sind. /
(57) pp. (pp. 59–116 in Volume No. 146).

This is a list of seven hundred quotations, all of which refer to music, taken from the Old and New Testaments.

C. Versuch / einiger / Oden, / über die / Gebote GOttes. / Wohl dem, der den HErrn fürchtet, der / grosse Lust hat zu seinen Geboten. / Ps. CXII. 1. /
(47) pp. (pp. 117–164 in Volume No. 146).

This is a collection of ten religious odes by Mattheson, and his own remarks upon them.

149  *REMÈDES / CHRETIENS ET PHILOSOPHIQUES / contre la Medisance, / sur tout / CONTRE LES EXCES / des / ECRITS SATYRIQUES. / par / J. MATTHESON, / Conseiller d' Ambassade / de S. A. I. Monseigneur le Grand-Prince / de Toutes les Russies, Duc Regnant / de Sleswic-Holstein &c. / Peu de Paroles, beaucoup de verités. / A HAMBOURG / chez. C. HEROLD. / MDCCXLV. /*
(14), 55 pp.

This volume is dedicated to Heinrich de Rohden, the Minister to Hamburg from Schleswig-Holstein.[185] It contains a condemnation of slanders and moralistic recommendations as to the proper means of meeting and treating them.

150  Contributions to: Freie Urtheile u. Nachrichten zum Aufnehmen der Wissenschaften und der Historie überhaupt. Hamburg, 1745. Stück 72, pp. 591–594; St. 73, pp. 599–603; St. 74, pp. 607–609.

These are all continuations of one article which denies the statement in the *Hamburgische Berichte von den neuesten Gelehrten Sachen*, Aug. 24, 1745: "Dass die gelehrtesten und vornehmsten Musikverständigen darinn übereinstimmen, dass alle Annehmlichkeit in der Harmonie aus der öfteren Vereinigung der Vibrationen unterschiedener Töne herrühre."

## LITERARY MANUSCRIPTS

151  Das Buch / oder / Versuch / einer Abhandlung / vom / Bücherschreiben. /
27 pp.

This manuscript, which is dated 1745, is divided into ten sections, with such headings as: "Wie weit die Furcht beym Bücherschreiben gehen soll?" "Warum doch gewisse würdige Schrifftsteller für mittelmässig gehalten werden?" etc.[186]

185. He appears to have been instrumental in acquiring for Mattheson the title of "Legationsrath" to the Duke of Schleswig-Holstein. Cf. p. 92.
186. An earlier version of this essay also exists, dated 1744, and entitled *Versuch einer Abhandlung vom Bücherschreiben* (16 pp.).

152    Sentimens Chrétiens / et Casuels / sur / L'EXAMEN DE LA RE-LIGION. / Faciunt intelligendo ut nihil intelligant. Ternt. / 8 pp.

This pamphlet was directed against the atheistic doctrines in the book entitled, according to Mattheson's explanation on the first page,[187] *Examen de la Religion dont on cherche l'eclaircissement de bonne foi, attribué à Mr. de St. Evremont,* [sic] *à Trevoux, aux depens des Pères de la Societé de Jesus 1745."*

## 1746

## LITERARY MANUSCRIPTS

153    *Correspondence Caracterisée / de deux voyageurs amoreux. /* 32 pp.

From the evidence of the handwriting, this manuscript, though undated, appears to have been written at the same time as No. 154. The two "correspondents," *Craton* and *Eupheme,* write five letters apiece on polite subjects, such as "La distinction qu'il faut faire en matiere de galanterie," with anecdotes and epigrammatic verses as illustrations.

154    *A Mr. E. M. / L'Incommode de bonne humeur / EPIGRAMME /*

This twelve-line verse is signed and dated, "J. M. Punster, Fevr. 19. 1746."

155    *Imitation d'une Fable de Mr. de la Fontaine. /*

One large sheet of paper, dated "Sept. 24. 1746." The poem, which is well over sixty lines long, is written in German, the first lines being:

> "Ein Mann war in sich selbst verliebt,
> Von Nebenbuhlern nie betrübt;
> Er dachte fest in seinem Sinn;
> Ich weiss, dass ich der schönste bin . . ."

156    Rémarques / Sur / L'Orgue oculaire, / et sur / La Traduction de cette pièce. / oder / überhaupt: / Die Thorheit der Augenorgel. / Hamburg. / 1746. / 34 pp.

This manuscript is written in four parallel columns. The texts of each of these are respectively: an original short article from the *Mercure de France* on the idea of a color organ; exhaustive remarks upon this by Mattheson; Telemann's translation; and Mattheson's translation, which is designed to correct Telemann's errors. The manuscript was mentioned as ready for publication in the list of Mattheson's works published in *Hamburger Nachrichten aus dem Reiche der Gelehrsamkeit,* 1759, no. 93, p. 744.

187. A later version of this article, of which only the first few pages remain, ascribes the original pamphlet to a "Lieutenant de la Serre," who "fut éxecuté à Mastricht le 10 d'avril 1748, pour plusieurs crimes, et y fit, avant sa mort, une Rétraction formelle de tous ses écrits scandaleux."

1747

BOOKS

157 Behauptung / der / Himmlischen Musik / aus den Gründen / der / Vernunft, Kirchen-Lehre und / heiligen Schrift. / (Quotation) / Hamburg, / zu finden bey Christian Herold. / 1747. / (8), 144, (8) pp.

Matutheson analyzes in this volume various statements in the Bible and other works regarding the existence of music in Heaven. He concludes that music is made by the angels for the purpose of worshiping God, an example which he recommends to the attention of mortals.

158 *INIMICI MORTIS* / verdächtiger / Todes-Freund. / Sie halten den Tod für Freund. / B. der Weish. 1,16. / verlegts der Verfasser. 1747. / (16), 48 pp.

This little volume, which Mattheson mentions as going to press on September 23, 1747,[188] contains his thought on the experience of death. It reviews the attitudes of the Ancients, of the Deists, and of the rational philosophers toward death, and concludes that Christian teaching alone provides the proper precepts and directions for facing this event.

LITERARY MANUSCRIPT

159 *Reflexions sur l'indifference a l'egard de la Mort.* / 8 pp.

The contents of this manuscript may well have been the basis for No. 158. They are for the most part random notes and quotations on the subject of death taken from the Bible, and conclude with ten reasons for disagreeing with "ceux qui disent: Bonne vie et courte."

1748

BOOK

160 *Aristoxeni* / *iunior.* / *Phthongologia* / *Systematica.* / *Versuch* / einer systematischen / Klang-Lahre / wider / die irrigen Begriffe / von diesem geistigen Wesen, / von dessen Geschlechten, / Ton-Arten, Dreyklängen, / und auch / vom mathematischen Musikanten, / nebst einer / Vor-Erinnerung / wegen der / behaupteten himmlischen Musik. / (Quotation) / Hamburg, / In Commission bey Joh, Adolph Martini. 1748. / 167 pp.

This book attempts to define in scientific and philosophical terms the nature of sound. It is based almost entirely upon the books of earlier writers than Mattheson. The

188. *Ehrenpforte, Anhang,* p. 25. "D. 23. Septr. kam der sogenannte Vordächtige Todesfreund auf die Michaelis-Messe, aus der Presse 8° in eignem Verlage."

supplement contains letters to Mattheson and his own comments upon the controversy over his *Behauptung der himmlischen Musik,* No. 157.

## LITERARY MANUSCRIPTS

161 Quelques Remarques sur la traduction de N(euen) T(estamentes). / par H. /
4 pp.

This manuscript, dated "Oct. 30 1748," contains Mattheson's opinions on the *Deutsche Übersetzung des Neuen Testamentes,* Hanover, 1748, by Christoph August Heumann, Doctor and Professor of Theology in Göttingen.[189]

162 *Animadversiones / ad / S.S. / inter legendum collectae / M. /*
44 pp.

This notebook contains a number of quotations from various books of the Bible, with Mattheson's remarks upon them. It is undoubtedly one of the pursuits he referred to in the following passage upon his life in 1748: "Um dieselbe Zeit fing Mattheson an, die Bibel zum Dreyzehntmal durchzulesen, zu untersuchen, und Anmerckungen mit Erbaulichkeit darüber zu machen . . ."[190]

## 1749

## BOOKS

163 Matthesons / Mithridat / wider / den Gift einer welschen / Satyre, / genannt, / *LA MUSICA.* / (Quotation) / Hamburg, MDCCXLIX, / Im Verlage des Verfassers, / und zu finden bey Carl Samuel Geissler. / (16), LXI, 340, (20) pp.

Mattheson dedicated this volume to Frederick the Great. It opens with the text of Salvator Rosa's poem, *La Musica, Satira I,*[191] in the original Italian, with Mattheson's German translation underneath. The rest of the book is devoted to a refutation of Rosa's satirical attack on music, and particularly dramatic music, as being morally evil.

164 Abhandlung / von den / Pantomimen, / historisch und critisch ausgeführt. / Hamburg, bey Carl Samuel Geissler, 1749. / (12), 81 pp.

This anonymous booklet is ascribed to Mattheson by the Hamburger Stadtbibliothek and by the Holzmann and Bohatta *Deutsches Anonymen Lexikon,* (Weimar, 1910), VI, 6, no. 157.[192] Since Mattheson devoted some space to an exposition of the pantomime or

189. *Fortsetzung und Ergänzungen zu C. G. Jöchers allgemeinem Gelehrten-Lexico* (Leipzig, 1787), II, 1978.

190. *Ehrenpforte,* "Anhang," p. 26.

191. *La Musica, La Poesia,* published first *circa* 1640. Mattheson speaks of an edition published in Amsterdam in 1719 in the "Vorbericht" to this volume, but *Riemann's Lexikon,* p. 1554, dates the Amsterdam edition *ca.* 1664.

192. The 1928 Supplement (Vol. VII) to this *Anonymen Lexikon,* p. 3, no. 70, ascribes this pamphlet to Johann Christoph Strodtmann, apparently correcting its earlier state-

"Geberdenkunst" in his *Vollkommene Capellmeister,*[193] it is surprising that he did not acknowledge the authorship of this work in any way. The two parts of the book deal with the pantomime in history, especially in ancient Rome, and with the particular characteristics of the pantomime as a form.

## LITERARY MANUSCRIPT

165  *Raisons Chretiennes et Morales / contre les Duels. /*
12 pp.

This manuscript is dated "le 22. Nov. 1749," and signed by Mattheson. After critical definitions of "Duels," "Honeur," and Courage," Mattheson coucludes that it is wrong to fight duels because the combatants ". . . loin d'employer leurs passions au service de la vie, ces heros pervers consument la vie au service des passions dominantes. . . ." The manuscript is concluded by a list of thirty-one books on duels, and by the following poetical sentiment:

> "The Hard words, *Jealousies and Tears*
> Set Folks together by the Ears,
> And make them fight, like mad or drunk,
> For this and that, and for a Punk."

## 1750

## LITERARY ARTICLE

166  Contribution to: (Lessing's) Beyträge zur Historie und Aufnahme des Theaters, viertes Stück. Stuttgart, 1750, pp. 596–606. Nachricht / von einem in Freyberg / aufgeführten / Schulschauspiele. / [194]

The controversy which was aroused by this "Schulschauspiel" and by the disapproval of the rector of the school, was the basis for a number of expressions of opinion on Mattheson's part on the excellence of music in the curriculum of schools.[195]

## BOOKS

167  Matthesons / bewährte / Panacea, / als eine Zugabe / zu seinem musikalischen / Mithridat, / überaus heilsam / wider die leidige Kacherie / irriger Lehrer, schwermüthiger Verächter / und gottloser

---

ment. According to Schröder's*Lexikon,* VII, 334, Strodtmann was a "Candidat des Hamburgischen Ministeriums" in 1742, but had no further connection with that city.

193. (Der erste Theil), Cap. 6, "von der Geberden-Kunst," pp. 33–41.

194. The collected edition of Lessing's works (*Gotthold Ephraim Lessing's Sämtliche Schriften herausgegeben von Karl Lachmann,* Stuttgart G. A. Göschen'sche Verlagshandlung, 1889. Vierter Band, p. 193) ascribes this article to Mylius. Mattheson, however, inserted his own initials in his copy of the journal.

195. Cantor Doles, the director of this "Schulschauspiel," was a pupil of J. S. Bach, who uttered some violent opinions upon this subject. Cf. C. S. Terry, *Bach, a Biography,* pp. 261 f., and Spitta, *Johann Sebastian Bach,* III, 255–261.

Schänder / der Tonkunst. / Erste Dosis. / (Quotation) / Hamburg 1750. / (2), 84, (2) pp.

This volume seems to have been inspired directly by the derogatory remarks on music uttered by Rector Biedermann of the Freyburg Gymnasium upon the performance of the "Schulschauspiel" mentioned in No. 166. Mattheson gives a number of reasons why music should and would be a beneficial part of the curriculum of every school.

168 Joh. Matthesons / Grossfürstl. Holsteinischen Legations-Raths etc. / Wahrer Begriff / des / Harmonischen / Lebens. Der Panacea / Zwote Dosis. / Mit beygefügter Beantwortung dreyer / Einwürffe wider die Behauptung der / himmlischen Musik. / (Quotation) / Hamburg, / bey Johann Adolph Martini, 1750. / 119, (5) pp.

This volume is a continuation of the ideas expressed in No. 166. By arguing against as well as with the opinions of a number of different writers Mattheson attempts to give further proof of the beneficial effects of music.

## 1751

### MUSIC

169 *ODEON / MORALE, IUCUNDUM, ET VITALE.* / Sittliche Gesänge, angenehme Klänge, / gut zur Lebenslänge. / Text und Ton / von / Mattheson. / Mit vorgesetzten sonderbaren, / nach dem neuesten Geschmack eingerichteten, / VII Andreden. / (Musical Quotation) / Nürnberg / verlegts Johann Ulrich Haffner, / Lautenist. / 1751. / (6), 19 pp.

Fourteen odes for solo voice or chorus and continuo are here collected. In Mattheson's "Anrede," he discusses the taste for such musical forms, and the moral sentiments contained in each of the odes. The collection is an excellent example of hundreds of similar ones published in Germany in the middle of the eighteenth century, but, strangely enough, was not included by Marpurg in his "Verzeichniss deutscher Odensammlungen mit Melodien" in the *Kritische Briefe über die Tonkunst* (Berlin, 1760), Vol. I.

### BOOKS

170 Sieben / Gespräche / der / Weisheit und Musik / samt zwo Beylagen; als / die dritte Dosis der Panacea, / mitgetheilet / von / Mattheson. / (Quotation) / Hamburg, / bey Johann Adolph Martini, / 1751. / (30), 207, (1) pp.

In this book Mattheson continues to discuss his sentiments on the moral goodness and uses of music, together with its spiritual importance, especially with respect to musical forms, such as odes. The two "Beylagen" are also continuations of the controversy over music in Heaven, initiated by No. 157.

171 Die / neuangelegte / Freuden-Akademie, / zum lehrreichen Vorschmack / unbeschreiblicher Herrlichkeit / in der / besten göttlichen

Macht. / Angepriesen /von / Johann Mattheson, / Grossfürstl. Legations-Rath. / (Quotation) / Hamburg, / verlegts Johann Adolph Martini. / 1751. /
(4), 302, (22) pp.

Various quotations from the Bible concerning the joyous worship of God make up the contents of this volume. In his accompanying remarks, Mattheson interprets them as a proper philosophy of life.

## 1752

## BOOK

172 Matthesons / Philologisches / Tresespiel, / als ein / kleiner Beytrag / zur kritischen Geschichte der deutschen / Sprache. / vornehmlich aber, / mittelst gescheuter Anwendung, in der / Tonwissenschaft nützlich zu gebrauchen. / (Quotation) / Hamburg, / bey Johann Adolph Martini. 1752.
(32), 133, (10) pp.

This volume contains a number of random remarks on the form and history of various German words. On pages 3–4 Mattheson explains the title as an epigrammatic allusion to the thirteen sections of the book which might correspond with the drawing of thirteen cards in the game of "Bassette."

## 1753

## BOOK

173 Johann Matthesons / Grossfürstl. Legations-Raths &c. / neuangelegter / Freuden-Akademie / zweyter Band / mit /vorgesetzter Abhandlung / betreffend / alle Freudenstörer / und / Todwünscher. / (Quotation) / Hamburg, / verlegts Johann Adolph Martini. / 1753. /
(74), 322, (17) pp.

This volume is a continuation and conclusion of No. 171.

## ARTICLE

174 Contribution to: Die Hamburgischen Berichte von den neuesten Gelehrten Sachen, Hamburg, 1753, p. 463.

In this article Mattheson makes a brief announcement of the death of his wife, and adds to it some verses written in her memory.[196]

## 1754

175 *IDIOTICON / HAMBURGENSE* / oder / Wörter-Buch, / Zur Erklärung / der eigenen, / in und um Hamburg gebräuchlichen, Nieder-

196. Cf. p. 103, where the verses are quoted in full.

Sächsischen / Mund-Art. / Jetzt vielfältig vermehret, / und mit / Anmerckungen und Zusätzen / Zweener berühmten Männer, / nebst einem Vierfachen Anhange, / ausgefertiget / von / Michael Richey, P.P. / Hamburg, / verlegt von Conrad König, 1754. / (10), LII, 480 pp.

Michael Richey, Professor of Literature in the Hamburg Gymnasium, was chiefly responsible for this dictionary of words and expressions used locally in Hamburg and the neighboring territory of Lower Saxony. The two contributors mentioned in the title were, as Richey explains in the *Vorrede,* Joannes Grammius, Justiz-Rath to the King of Denmark, and Johann Mattheson. Mattheson's contributions were marked throughout the book with the initial *M.,* and he seems to have provided about a fifth of the contents.

176 Matthesonii / PLVS VLTRA, / ein /Stückwert / von neuer und mancherley Art. / Erster Vorrath / dazu. / Unser Wissen ist Stückwerk. / 1 Kor. 13, 9. / Hamburg, verlegts Johann Adolph Martini. / 1754. / 134 pp.

This is a collection of essays on various musical subjects in which Mattheson had long been interested. The collection was continued in a similar volume published in the next two years, under the same title, with sub-titles of "zweeter," "dritter," and "vierter Vorrath." The first volume contains one essay entitled, "Vom klingenden Gottesdienste."

## 1755

## BOOKS

177 *Matthesonii / PLVS VLTRA* / ein / Stückwerk / von / neuer und mancherley / Art. / Zweeter Vorrath / dazu. / Unser Wissen ist Stückwerk, / 1 Kor. 13, 9. / Hamburg, verlegts Johann Adolph Martini. / 1755. / 135–382. (16) pp.

This is a continuation of No. 176, the pagination being likewise sequential. The volume contains a short "Vorredchen" and three essays: "Von der Melodie und Harmonie," "Von Wirkung der Musik bey dem Vieh," and "Von der singenden Messkunst."

178 *Matthesonii / PLVS VLTRA,* / ein /Stückwerk / von neuer und mancherley Art. / Dritter Vorrath. / Unser Wissen ist Stückwerk. / 1 Kor. 13, 9. / und dabey bleibt es. / Hamburg, verlegts Joh. Ad. Martini. 1755. / 383–606 pp.

This volume is the third in the "Plus Ultra" series. It contains four essays: "Grosser Vorzug der Tonkunst" (which is the conclusion to the last essay in the preceding volume), "Erzehlung unglaublicher Dinge," and "Die Neue Zahl-Theorie. 1739."

## 1756

## BOOK

179 *Matthesonii / PLVS VLTRA,* / oder Des Stückwerks Vierter Vorrath. / Hamburg, verlegts Johann Adolph Martini. 1756. / 607–786 pp.

With this volume the "Plus Ultra" series comes to a conclusion. It contains two essays, of which the first is a continuation of the first essay in the "Dritter Vorrath," being entitled: "Fortsetzung des Artikels von der Annehmlichkeit in der Neuen Zahl-Theorie." The title of the second is "Betrachtung musikalischer Unwahrheiten."

## 1759

## ARTICLES

180  Contributions to: Die Hamburger Nachrichten aus dem Reiche der Gelehrsamkeit, Hamburg, 1759.
a. Cogitata Quaedam Matthesonii de Dissertaione eximia Noeltingii jun. St. XLIII, 8 Juni, pp. 340–342.

This is a short note correcting the use of words in an article which I have not been able to identify.

b. Verlangte Ursachen warum die Worte des 69sten Psalms v.
4. *Laboravi clamans; Raucae factae sunt fauces meae* &c. sich zu keiner vielstimmigen Fuge schicken?
St. LXII, 28 Sept., pp. 593–596.

Mattheson here makes a brief critique of the elements in the text of this Psalm which would make the setting of it to a fugue inappropriate.

## 1760

## ARTICLES

181  Contributions to: Die Hamburger Nachrichten aus dem Reiche der Gelehrsamkeit, Hamburg, 1760.
a. Sonderbare neue Zeitung aus dem kritischen Parnass.
St. XLII, 6 Juni, pp. 329–332.

This article consists of random notes upon the use of certain words by the Hamburgers.

b. 8 Gründe und Vortheile, aus welchen, und um welchen, wir Deutschen die letzten seyn sollten, den Reim aus unsern Gedichten zu verweisen, oder wenigstens Anstand nehmen müssten, ihn als unnutzlich, ja als einem guten Gedichte schädlich zu verdammen:
St. LXXVIII, 10 Oct., pp. 621–622.
Continued: St. LCIII, 2 Dec., pp. 741–744.

Mattheson's reasons are based upon the importance of rhymed verse for musical purposes.

c. Einige Biographische Anmerkungen.
St. LXXX, 17 Oct., pp. 639–640.

These "remarks" were designed to call attention to the omission of some details concerning Mattheson's life in an earlier article in an unnamed literary journal.

d. Unsäglicher Reichthum der Musik, in kurzem Begriff, dergleichen wol keine andere Wissenschaft aufweisen kan.
St. LXXXVII, 11. Nov., pp. 694–696.
This article recites briefly the "learned" virtues of music.

182   Contribution to: Kritische Briefe über die Tonkunst . . . von einer musikalischen Gesellschaft in Berlin, 1760–1762. XLV Brief an die Gesellschaft, Berlin der 26 April, 1760.
pp. 351–355.

Mattheson is here replying to the "XXXIII Brief, an den Herrn Legationsrath Mattheson, Berlin den 2 Februar, 1760," pp. 255–261, continued pp. 263–270, and pp. 271–277, which asked for his opinion of the writer's criticism of fugal writing as exemplified by the "zweyte aus dem ersten Stücke der Marpurgischen Fugensammlung." [197]

1761

PUBLISHED TRANSLATION

183   George Friedrich Händels / Lebensbeschreibung, / nebst einem / Verzeichnisse seiner Ausübungswerke / und / deren Beurtheilung; übersetzet, / auch mit einigen Anmerkungen, / absonderlich über den hamburgischen Artikel, / versehen / vom / Legations-Rath *Mattheson*. / (Quotation) / Hamburg, / Auf Kosten des übersetzers. 1761.
(10), 156, (8) pp.
Translated from: MEMOIRS / OF THE LIFE / OF THE LATE / GEORGE FREDERIC HANDEL. / To which is added, / A CATA-LOGUE of his WORKS, / AND / OBSERVATIONS UPON THEM. / (Quotation) / *LONDON:* Printed for R. and J. Dodsley, in *Pall-Mall.* / M.DCC.LX. /
(2), 208 pp.

Mattheson's last translation was, appropriately enough, the biography of Händel by Mainwaring. It is complete, and contains valuable supplementary notes and corrections by the translator.

ARTICLE

184.   Contribution to: Die Hamburger Nachrichten aus dem Reiche der Gelehrsamkeit, Hamburg, 1761.
*In Mortem Richeii*
St. LII, 14 Julii, p. 424.

This is an epigram on the death of Mattheson's friend, Michael Richey, which reads as follows:

197. The work referred to is probably the one listed in Eitner's *Quellen-Lexikon,* VI, 342: *Fugensammlung, Berlin 1758, Lange, gedruckt in Leipzig bey Breitkopf.*"

"Schweigt still! Poeten, Schweigt, Geschichte!
Verstummet!—daran thut ihr Recht:
Den alle Ruhm- und Lob-Gedichte
Sind meinem Richey viel zu schlecht.
Maxima laude Major?
Mattheson."

## LITERARY MANUSCRIPT

185   *Eloquentia Verticordia / Sonora. / i.e. /* Herzbekehrende Wohlreden-
heit / im Singen und Klingen. / mittelst / verschiedener Abhandlungen
/ betracht. untersucht / und gegen schädliche Einwürffe / vertheidiget
/ von / Mattheson / Pour le bien comprendre / Il faut bien entendre.

Mattheson states that he was working on this manuscript in 1761 for publication in
the following year.[198] As it stands, the manuscript is laid out with carefully transcribed
footnotes as if in its final form. The contents are divided into three sections, forming essays similar to those in his *Plus Ultra.* The title of the first is "Vorstellung einer recht-
schaffenen exemplarischen *Opern-Moral,"* that of the second is "Gedancken, Zusätze und
Fragstücke zum Vollkommenen Kapellmeister," and that of the third is "Fragstücke aus
der Tonkunst."

1762

## ARTICLE

186   Contribution to: Die Hamburger Nachrichten aus dem Reiche der Ge-
lehrsamkeit, Hamburg, 1762.
*Deux Epigrammes.*
St. XCVII, 3 Dec., p. 796

The first of these epigrams is entitled: "Contre les opinions vulgaires," the second:
"Surlebel Air: Da waren Gnad und Zorn vereint &c."

## MUSICAL MANUSCRIPT

187   Aria aus der Einweyhungs Musik zu St. Michaelis, / welche unbillig
ein Oratorium heisst, / weil sich keine Personen darin Unterreden. /
(6) pp.

This single aria is scored for two oboes, strings, and baritone. From the title it appears
that Mattheson composed it for his own pleasure; there is no mention of any music by
him being used for the consecration of the St. Michaelis Kirche.[199]

198. Appendix, p. 223. ". . . erhielt auch ein anderes Werk, mit dem Titel eloquentia
verticordia sonora für Einrichtung, des Vorsatzes dasselbe den folgenden Winter über
mit Gottes Hülfe zum Standrecht bringen."
199. Appendix, pp. 224–225.

1763

ARTICLES

188  Contributions to: Die Hamburgischen Nachrichten aus dem Reiche der Gelehrsamkeit, Hamburg, 1763.
a. Anecdote zu den Kirchenliedern, zum Beweise, dass auch weltlich genante Noten zur geistlichen Andact dienen können. St. XV. 22 Feb., p. 119.

This is a short note pointing out that the tunes of chorales are often based upon secular melodies.

b. (Anmerckungen)
St. XXIII, 22 Märtz, pp. 177–179.

Mattheson gave no title to this article. It outlines his intention to publish a volume containing his remarks on Martin Luther's attitude toward music which will be his "89stes Impressum."

c. 3 Gründe worauf die deutsche Rechtschreibung fusset.
St. XXIV, 25 Märtz, pp. 191–192.

The burden of this article is contained in the statement: "Alles Schreiben und Buchstabiren muss sich also vorzüglich nach der besten, natürlichen, reinen Aussprache richten."

d. *Ratio Status Monarchiae Sonorae type considerata.*
St. XLV, 7 Junii, p. 360.

This article is a tabulation of Mattheson's system of the hierarchy of musical forms.

e. *Non est harmonice compositus, qui Harmonia non delectatur.*
St. 56, 15 Julii, pp. 443–447.

In this article Mattheson affirms his belief in God as the source of all harmony.

1764

MUSICAL MANUSCRIPT

189  Das / fröhliche Sterbelied, / womit der / nunmehreo wolseelige / Legations-Rath, / Herr / Johann Mattheson, / ihm selbst, / harmonisch und poetisch, im 83sten Jahre seines Alters, / zu Grabe gesungen. / Herr, nun lässt Du deinen Diener im Friede fahren! / Luk. 2. 29. / Hamburg, den 25sten April 1764. / Wenns zum Sterben komt, so stirbt Johannes, Petrus, Paulus dahin; aber / ein Christ stirbt nicht. Luth. I. Adv. / Gedruckt bey Dieterich Anton Harmsen. /
Text (8) pp.
6 mutilated pages of the score remain.

Mattheson composed the music for this funeral oratorio, to a text of his own composition, in 1760.[200] It was sung at his funeral service in the St. Michaelis Kirche.[201] The text, the copies of which were bound in silver paper, is made up of Mattheson's versions of quotations from the Bible, the source for each being carefully given in footnotes. He added a subtitle on the first page: "Matthesonii Melos exsquisiale, per voces S.S., Sanctissimi Sanctorum; S.I., Sanctorum Iobi; S.P., Saucti Pauli; S.B., Sancti Bernhardi; S.O., Sanctorum Omnium, et ipsius; Theotini decantantem." The arias and choruses were separated by numerous chorales from the *Neu- vermehrtes Hamburgisches Gesang-Buch,* published in the preceding year. The parts of the score which remain show that the music was scored for full orchestra, a quartet of soloists, and chorus. Its style is much simpler and less florid than that of Mattheson's earlier oratorios.

## NOTE

A number of odd sections of manuscripts, literary and musical, in a state of such ruin that the contents can scarcely be made out, exist among the rest of Mattheson's "Nachlass" in the Hamburger Stadtbibliothek. After sufficient examination of these I have concluded them to be of too little use or significance for inclusion in any form in this Bibliography.

200. Appendix p. 220. ". . . entwarf auch, ein andern zur Andacht gehörigen Beschäftigungen, sein eignes Epicedium, mit folgender Aufschrift: *Das fröhliche Sterbelied. . . .*"
201. Cf. pp. 107–108.

# APPENDIX

THE manuscript transcribed in this appendix is to be found in the disorganized collection of his manuscripts left to the Hamburger Stadtbibliothek by Mattheson before he died. It consists of eight pages, numbered 247–253, and is the continuation of the *Fortsetzung des Matthesonischen Lebenslaufs,* published in the "Anhang" (p. 18–33) of the modern edition of Mattheson's *Grundlage einer Ehrenpforte,* edited by Max Schneider and published in 1910. It is regrettable that Schneider overlooked these pages when compiling his own edition, for they carry on Mattheson's own account of his life to within less than two years of his death on April 17, 1764. These eight pages contain no startling disclosures in regard to these, his last years, but, ending with his account of the consecration of the St. Michaelis Kirche in his eighty-first year, provide a satisfactory conclusion to his autobiography. For this reason, this manuscript has been included herein as an appendix.

The manuscript, like many others of Mattheson's, displays numerous revisions in the form of crossed-out words, phrases, and whole sections, as well as marginal and interlinear emendations. Because of this fact, certain sections and words have resisted all attempts at deciphering. In order that the entire manuscript might be as faithfully and at the same time as clearly transcribed as possible, the following method has been used: Mattheson's footnotes (usually added in the margins in the manuscript) have been placed at the bottom of the pages in the customary manner; his marginal notes have been inserted in the text according to his indications, and enclosed in parentheses, thus ( ); words or phrases which have been crossed out are enclosed in brackets, thus [ ], when still legible; words or phrases, which, because of the actual script, are indecipherable, are indicated thus . . . . . ; words or phrases which have been crossed out and are indecipherable are indicated thus [. . . . .].

1759            WEITERE FORTSETZUNG DES
                MATTHESONISCHEN LEBENSLAUFES

*Mit Gott von Nutz*
DIE Durchlesung der Bibel sum zweiundzwanzigstenmal angefangen. Nunmehr war man mit dem Bau der neuen grossen St. Michaely-Kirch soweit gekommen, dass auf die Anlegung eines beträchtlichen Orgelwerkes gedacht werden konnte. Es fanden sich daher bey dem Legations Rath Mattheson am 25. Jenner zu dem Ende die Herren Sonnen, als Baumeister, und

Alssen, als Organist u. Protokollist mit ihren Rissen ein, und conferirten über verschiedene Umstände, die zu dieser Sache gehören.

Ubrigens war er mit Prozessen gegen seine bösen Schuldner wider seine Neigung noch so stark geplaget, als es die langsame Art des Gerichts (und die schädliche Falliten Ordnung) welches dem Rechte zum Possen nur gar zu oft geschlossen, immermehr leiden wollte, nachdem er fast [5 à 6] 10.000 Mark durch Verstorbner und Verdorbner [banqueroutiers] Debitures eingebüsst (und doch Gott Lob kein Mangel sondern sein Lab und übriges) hatte.

Dem ungeachtet fuhr er fort der Kirche noch am 15. Febr. ein gutes Kapitel auf Abschlag seines (Legates) Vermächtnisses Zuschüsse zu lassen, und seine Gedanken mehr auf den klingenden Gottesdienst, als auf Staats– und Kriegs-Händel zu richten. Vielmehr stellte er forthin den bisherigen weitläufigen Briefwechsel fast gänzlich ein u. forschte in der Schrift und erbaulichen Auslegern nach dem Zustande des ewigen Lebens, in Erwartung eines neuen Himmels und einer neuen Erde, da Gerechtigkeit wohnen wird, und dahin unsere Werke gewisslich nachfolgen müssen. Ein jeder . . . . . . sichs . . . . . . . .

Er [fuhr] ging mit Abtragung seiner grossen Legati am Ende des Jahres dermassen frisch fort, dass die Kirche nunmehro im November bereits 38062 fl. baar erhalten hatte: befiel aber in eben diesem Monat mit [einem] der Podagra und dessen Anhang so stark, dass es ihm im Lager nun beynabe 4 Monate kostete. Gott erhielt ihn aber lebendig; da ander in die Hölle fuhren, und im März kam er wieder auf die Beine. *Acht Stücke* von seiner 1760     Arbeit sind nach und nach in den Hamburgischen Nachrichten aus dem Reiche der Gelehrsamkeit * beygetragen worden, mit der Berlinischen Gesellschaft *kritischer Briefe über die Tonkunst* gerieth er in einen gedruckten Briefwechsel. Indessen entzog er sich doch, nach und nach, den herrschenden Staatsgeschäften, wiewol dieselben nicht gänzlich auf einmal wieder ruhiger waren. Seine meiste Zeit wandte er hingegen auf das Bibellesen, und untersuchte, zu seiner besonderen Ruhe und Vergnügen den rechten Verstand des göttl. Wortes, Morgends und Abends, entwarf auch, unter andern zur Andacht gehörigen Beschäftigungen, sein eignes Epicedium, unter das mit folgender Aufschrift: *Das fröhliche Sterbelied, womit der Legations-Rath, Johann Mattheson, ihm selbst harmonisch und poetisch bey herannahenden achtzigsten Jahre seines Alters, zu Grabe gesungen.* Die hiezu erforderliche musikalische Ausarbeitung aber verschob er mit Fleiss nach einer kleinen vergönnten Weile, aus Beysorge sie mögte, vor der Aufführung, einigermassen aus der Mode kommen, weil doch hierin ein Tag den andern zu lehren pflegt. Der Special Titel lautet so: Matthesonii Melos

---

* In derselben . . . ein ziemlich vollständiges Catalogus seiner Schriften enthält, deren gedruckte sich auf 87—u. die MSS. auf 18 werden, doch lange nicht alles erschöpfen. Sie sind heute angeschlossen, nämlich die Verzeichnisse.

exsquisiale, pervoces S.S. SI. SP. SB. SO. Th.i.e. Sancti Sanctorum, Sancti Iobi, Sancti Pauli, Sancti Bernhardi, Santorum omnium et ipsius Theotini. In Erinnerung aber des Horazianischen Linquenda tellus ex domus traf er d. 13. Jun. einen ziemlich wichtigen und vorteilhaften Verkauf, der von ihm, durch Gottes Gnade, vor 45 Jahren erbaut, und ebenso lange glücklich bewohnten 4 Häuser und Gärten, deren grösstes über 20, die andern aber 9 und weniger Zimmer oder Absonderungen enthalten, mit ein Paar Ober-wohnungen oder sogenannte Salon.* Er hatte Ao 1729, d. 3. März, nehmlich vor 30 Jahren schon ein Testamentum reciprocum mit seiner geliebten Ehegattin errichtet, und als ihn aber dieselbe 1753, nach einer 44 jährigen unvergleichlich schönen Beywohnung, durch ihren tödtlichen Abschied zum ersten und letztenmal herzlich betrübte, machte er alsofort sein zweytes Testament in aller Form am Johannis Vorabend desselben Jahres und legierte darin wie bereits oben genannt der abgebrannten St. Michaelis Kirche, zu einem Orgelwerke, 40.000 fl. Hamb. cur., trug auch solche ganze Summe, nach und nach, bar und zum Voraus ab, indem er die letzten Posten davon am 7. Juni 1760. dem hochansehnl. grossen Kirchencollegio einlieferte, auch darüber dessen dankbare Quitung gehörigermassen erhielt.† Weil nun das letzte Testament . . . . . . . . . . ebenfalls abolirt [. . .] . . . keine Leiberser-ben, sondern bloss einige Seitenverwandte vorhanden waren, so wurde, allem Zwist vorsubeugen, die dritte Art einer letztwilligen Erklärung, nehmlich ein Kodicill zu Stande gebracht, und [wurden] darin nicht nur die Nach-kömmlinge entfernter Freunde und Vettern, aus freyen Stücken von wohlge-wonnenen Gutern gewisse legata beschieden, sondern auch [die Ham-burgischen . . . . . . . . . . . . . . . . . . . . . . . . . . . . Häusern] andern . . . . . . . . . . . . . . . . . . ihr Theil bestimmet, [. . . . . . . .] vornehm-lich aber [aufs Neue vorbesagte Kirche selbst mit einer anshnlichen Zugabe von 3000 fl. bedacht, und zwar [. . . . . . . . . . in der Eigenschaft eines Universal Erbens und Eigenthümers] solchergestalt, dass diese abermalige Vermächtnis Summe aus dem Kaufschilling der Häuser, aus den hinterlas-senen Mobilien, Büchern etc. zu Theil schon zugegen ist. Dereinst aber weiter gehoben werden soll. Das heisst rechtschaffen testieren.]

Wer vergnügt zu leben gedenkt,
Nehme hieran ein Beyspiel ab;
Brauche die Mittel, die Gott ihm geschenket,
Und baue sich ein Sorgengrab:
Denn es ist doch nichts so gut,

* Es ist kein Haus in . . . . . . , das nicht . . . . . . oder einen endern . . . [hat] werden muss. Warum sollte ich erst eine . . . und [der] alda . . . andern über-lassen.
† Auf den 12. Juli desselben Jahres noch 3000 fl. und alda den 4. Feb. 1762 aberm. 100 [. . .] als Zugabe aus Konto damit 44000 fl. daraus wurden.

Von allem was der Mensch treibet und thut,
Als frölich und freudig in Arbeit seyn;
Dieses bleibet sein Theil allein.
Keinen wird es doch gelingen,
Und niemand wird es dahin bringen,
Dass er ersehe
Was nach ihm geschehe.

*Kohelet 3,22*

Doch auch diese Verordnung ging nicht ohne Einwürfe ab: Denn bei einer jeden göttlichen Kirche baut der Satan gleich seine Hölle daneben. Die Häuser stunden im Stadtbuche auf Bürgers Namen, gegen Revers: [weil] in dem ein Fremder (oder in fremder Herrn Dienste stehender Mann) in Hamburg keine liegende Gründe besitzen kann. Einer von diesen Bürgern oder vielleicht dessen ungerathener Erbe, machte also Chickane wegendes Namens und impugnirte [den Verkauf] [Handel] die Zuschreibung; allein die Käuffer waren schon im Besitz und der Verkäufer ein Jurymann. Das fiel im Augusto vor.

[Den 8. Sep. erhielt er von der grossen Kirchen Collegio eine gesamte Quitung, wegen bezahlter 43000 fl. und belegte seit dem 8. August bey derselben Kirche noch 2000 fl. mehr zu 4 procent ordinair Rente mit Vorbehalt des Kapitals für weitläufige Verwandte und Arme. Bei seinem Eintritt ins 80. Jahr d. 28. Septr. befand er sich nicht zum Besten, wegen eines Falles in seiner Stube. Liess aber dem ungeachtet sein Codicill, [nachdem das Testament abolirt war,] desselben Tages durch 5 Zeugen unterschreiben.]

Den 25. [Sept.] Octr. starb King George II im 77t. Jahre. D. 26. wurde Georg III proklamirt.

D. 20. Nov. bezog er damit er nicht weit wandern durfte zur Miete ein nah gelegenes Haus zu [. . . . .] das er vormals selbst erbaut und mit den andern verkauft hatte und beschloss das Jahr in ziemlicher Gesundheit.

1761 im Januar arbeitete er an seinen Denkwürdigkeiten und an Ubersetzung des Händelschen Lebenslaufes. correspondirt darüber mit Marquez und andern, doch auf [. . . . . . .] eingehende Art. im März gab er besagte Händelsche Lebensbeschreibung mit neuem Kupferstich, Vorrede, Anmerkung und Register auf eigne Kosten heraus. [Im selbigen Monath belegte er abermal 1000 fl. bey der St. Michaeli Kirche zu 4 pct. freyer Rente, und errichtete zugleich ein neues Kodicill, worin die Verwandten und Armenhäuser mit vergrösserten legatis bedacht wurden, in Erinnerung dessen, dass wir nichts in die Welt gebracht haben, und nichts mit herausbringen werden.

1 Tim. 6, 7.

[Nachdem also oberwähntes erstes Kodicill, wegen göttl. vermehrten Segens, nicht zu reichlich war, allen weitläufigen Verwandten und nothdürfti-

gen Armen ein Genüge zu leisten, geräth es zu einem zweyten reichlichen
Vermächtnisses am 25. März, worin die Summe vergrössert auch sonst ein
und anderes verbessert worden ist.]
Der Sommer des 1761st Jahres gieng ziemlich gelinde, ohne Artzt oder
Artzney vorbey; da denn unter fleissigem meditiren, bey gutem Wetter
noch mancher Spaziergang auf dem Walle, zu Fusse, bey früher Morgenzeit
abgelegt wurde welches bey solchem Alter u. soviel ausgestandener Unge-
mach als was . . . . . . . . . . . . Nebst der Denkwürdigkeit, die
während der Zeit völlig ausgearbeitet, ins Reine gebracht, durch die gelehrte
Zeitung angemeldet und hiesigen Verlegern bekannt gemacht worden, erhielt auch ein anderes Werk, mit dem Titel eloquentia verticordia sonora
für Einrichtung, [mit dem] des Vorsatzes dasselbe den folgenden Winter
über mit Gottes Hülfe zum Standrecht bringen. Jenes [ist als sein] mein 89
stes . . . . . . bestimmtes Buch von mehr als 3 Alphabeten [führte zur
vollständigen Aufschrift diese Worte: Unbemerkte Denkwürdigkeiten
moralisch und musikalisch angezeiget von M. Am 28. Sept. beging [er] ich
[wie gewöhnlich] die 81ste Feyer [seines] meines Geburtstages] in Andacht und Vergnügen mit frölichem Herzen, legte die letzte Hand an das
Meloseysequinta welches bey seiner dereinstigen Einsenkung aufgeführet
werden soll, (Omnen crede diem tibi diluxisse supremum Grata superveniet
quae no sperabitur hora. Nicht nur alte, sonern auch junge mogen sich das gesagt sein lassen) und entzog sich je länger je mehr, soviel möglich und erlaubt,
von hier dem weltlichen Geschäfte: da indessen am europäischen Staatshim-
mel die Äspecte wunderlich durcheinander gingen wie die Saiten auf dem
Psalter ohne mit dem Unterschiede im geringsten zusammen zu lauten. Im
Grossfürstl. Holstein da ward ein Statthalter [gesetzt] bestimmt, der zu
Kirch residirte. Die beyden Schaubühnen des Krieges kehrten noch keine
Anstalt zu Fallung der . . . . . vor; das ankommende Friedenslicht ver-
kroch sich eine lange Zeit unter der Wolke; [aber in] England hingegen
schwamm alles in lauter Freude, bey Vermälung und Krönung, die ihres-
gleichen an Pracht und Hoheit schwerlich haben können.

1762     Erfolgt den 6. Jan. das Absterben der Czarin Elisabeth im 52sten
Jahre ihres Alters, und den 7. daruf bestieg der Herzog von Holstein, als [Gr.] bisheriger Grossfürst den erledigten Kaiserthron doch mit
[. . . . . . . .] schlechtem Glück unter dem Namen Petri III alt 34. Es ging
ihm aber im Julio übel. Frankreich aber wusste seine ziemlich delabrirte
Sache so zu karten, dass sich selbiges samt den ganzen lauenburgischen Hause
unvermuthlich mit Spanien vereinigte und dieses letztere den Krieg wider
England [deckl] declarirte. Diese weit aussehende Verbrüderung würde
ohne Zweifel in Europa nach grösserer Zerrüttung und Unruhe aussah
[?] wobei nicht etwas wir nur (Gottesbusserort . . . . . . . . . . . . .
. . . . . . . .) [unüberwindliche Flotte der alten . . . . . . . . . , und im
. . . . in der grossen Absicht machen sollte.] Unser [emeritus] wünschte
sich hiebey je länger je mahr Glück, dass er seine letzten Tage ohne grosse

Arbeit nunmehr in guter Ruhe mit ziemlicher Gesundheit zuzubringen Gelegenheit hatte. (quisquis dixit vixi quotidie ad lucrum fugit.) Er gab einen Zuschauer ab, las seine Bibel zum 24st mal, und polirte seine obwähnte eloquentiam verticordiam nebst den Denkwurdigkeiten [. . . . . . . . . . .] in Erwagung: Schedis adhuc inter positis delere dicebit. [Den 4.Febr. aber lieferte er der Michaelis Kirche abermal eine zweite Zugabe von 1000 fl. zur Beförderung der Orgel-Arbeit, dass sie also nunmehr wachsen statt 40.000 . . . . . . . . , 44000 . . . . . . . . . . . . erhalten und mit vielem öffentlichen Dank empfangen hat. Bey diesem Zustande ist eingetroffen, dass der Segen des Herrn auch ohne Mühe reich machen könne. Unbekümmert vor dem Morgen, doch kein Häusgen ohne Sorgen. [Sein] mein Denkspruch war:

| | |
|---|---|
| Sic cum transierint mei | nullo cum strepitudine |
| Plebeius moriar senex | illi mors gravis incubat |
| Quis nimis notus omnibus | ignotus meritu sibi |

Die öffentlichen Concerte welche verwichenen Winter angefangen, wurden auch diesen Winter uber fortgesetzt. Die erste Sängerin schrieb sich Madame de Cranchen, und erhält unsern Beyfall. Auch liessen sich noch im Junio die Gebrüder Colla daselbst auf ihren Instrumenten caelaesciencium und celesciene für Geld 3 mal hören. Item, ein Anselmi von Essen auf der Violen und den Violoncel. Der König von Dänemark aber kam nach Schleswig unter dem Vorwand seine Truppen zu mustern, in der That aber die Hamburger um etliche Summen 1000 000 Goldes, durch exortion in ihren Gärten, zu bringen. Der neue Baron Schimmelmann hatte ihnen dieses Bad zugerichtet. Der Pöbel wollte sein Haus stürmen. Evasit antem.

Ao. 1762 im Julio erfolgte die grosse unvermuthete revolution in Petersburg, dass Petrus III weil er die lutherische Religion einfuhren wollte, viele debauches darin ex d'amour bezogen gar zu gut Preussisch geworden, nach Petershof gefänglich hingebracht, [wo] seine Gemahlin aber Catharina II. auf den Thron gesetzt worden, welches d. 9.Juli geschah. Bald darauf erfolgt die Nachricht, dass in der Nacht zwischen dem 6ten und 7ten Julii a. St. Petrus III nach einer *heftigen Krankheit* gestorben sey.

In einem Schreiben aus Amsterdam vom 29. Julii N. St. wurde gemeldet dass daselbst abend um 7 Uhr vier Expressen mit der Nachricht angekommen seyn, dass die Präliminar Artikeln zu einem Frieden zwischen England Frankreich und Spanien zur Richtigkeit gebracht wären. Es befand sich aber zusichtlos und war eine Erfindung der Actionisten.

D. 19. Oct. erlebte M. in seinem 82sten Jar das Glück die sonderbare Freude, dass an solchem Tag die feyerliche Einrichtung der Michaeliskirche vor sich ging und sowohl der ganze Rath als das Ministerium, die Obwalter, die Sechziger und Hundertachtziger sich in corpore Prozessionsweise in selbige verfügten, wobey Trompeten und Pauken vom Thurm erschallten ein vortreffliches Oratorium vor und nach der Predigt aufgeführt, sodann nach Auftrags auf beyden Glockenspielen zu St. Peter und Nikolai vom 3.

bis 4 Uhr, und die ganze Feyerlichkeit mit Pauken und Trompeten von allen Thürmen der 5 Hauptkirchen zwischen 4 und 5 Uhr geendigt wurden. Glaubwürdigem Bericht nach, sind hierbey über 5000 Personen in der Kirche und auch 5470 fl. . . . . . . in die angesetzten Becken gewesen, ohne des gedenk was noch bey Handvoll Dukaten und Silbergeld in die Klingelbeutel gekommen. Den folgenden Sonntag 20. nach Trinit. geschah eine abermalige Kollecte in allen . . . . . . . . . . Kirchen, welche uberhaupt . . .

. . . . . . . . . . . eingebracht haben soll, um damit dasjenige was noch an dem Orgel-Spiel und an dem Bauwesen [. . . .] orgänzet [seyn] werden muss, besondermassen zu bestreiten.

Der Friede zwischen Oesterreich und Preussen ist (. . . . . .

. . . . . . . . . . . .) d. 15. Febr. (1763) zu Hubertburg endl. geschlossen.

# BIBLIOGRAPHY

Note—The purpose of this list is to give in full the titles of works most frequently referred to in the preceding pages. It aims in no way to be a complete bibliography of the subject or an exhaustive list of books, periodicals, etc., consulted in the preparation of this book.

ADLER, GUIDO. Handbuch der Musikgeschichte unter Mitwirkung von Fachgenossen. Berlin-Wilmeradorf, 1930. 2 vols.

BELL, W. G. The great plague in London in 1665. London, 1924.

BENTHNER, A. G. Jetzt-lebendes Hamburg worin von den Namen Characteren und Wohnungen aller hieselbst sich aufhaltenden Standes-Parsonen und accreditirten Ministern so dann E. Hoch Edelen und Hochweisen Raths, ferner des Hoch-Ehrwürdigen Dom-Capitula und Ministerii . . . Hamburg, 1725.

BEREND, FRITZ. Nicolaus Adam Strungk. Dissertation. Munich, 1913.

BODMER, JOHANN JAKOB. Anklagung des verderbten Geschmackes, oder critische Anmerkungen uber den Hamburgischen Patrioten, und die Hallischen Tadlerinnen. Frankfurt und Leipzig, 1728.

BRANDL, A. L. Barthold Heinrich Brockes . . . Ein Beitrag zur Geschichte der deutschen Literatur im achtzehnten Jahrhundert. Innsbruck, 1878.

BROCKES, B. H. Irrdisches Vergnügen in Gott, bestehend in physicalisch- und moralischen Gedichten . . . Hamburg, 1727–48. 9 Theile.

BRUFORD, WALTER HORACE. Germany in the eighteenth century. The social background of the literary revival. Cambridge [Eng.], 1935.

BURKE, J. and BURKE, J. B. A genealogical and heraldic history of the extinct and dormant baronetcies of England, Ireland and Scotland. 2d ed. London, 1844.

BUTTSTEDT, J. H. Ut, Re, Mi, Fa, Sol, La, Tota Musica et Harmonia Aeterna, Oder Neu-eröffnetes, altes, wahres, eintziges und ewiges Fundamentum Musices, entgegen gesetzt Dem neu-eröffneten Orcheste, und in zweene Partes eingetheilet. In welchen, und zwar im ersten Theile, des Herrn Authoris des Orchestre irrige Meynungen, in specie de Tonis seu Modis Musicis, wiederleget, Im andern Theile aber das rechte Fundamentum Musices gezeiget, Solmisatio Gvidonica nicht allein defendiret, sondern auch solcher Nutzen bey Einführung eines Comitis gewiesen, dann auch behauptet wird dass man dereinst im Himmel, mit eben den Sonis, welche hier in der Welt gebräuchlich, musiciren werde. Erfurt, [1717].

CHANCE, J. F. George I and the Northern War, a study of British-Hanoverian policy in the north of Europe in the years 1709 to 1721. London, 1909.

CHANCE, J. F. List of diplomatic representatives and agents, England and North Germany 1689–1727. In: Notes on the diplomatic relations of England and Germany, edited by C. H. Firth. Oxford, 1907.

CHRYSANDER, FRIEDRICH. G. F. Händel. Leipzig, 1919. 3 vols.

COBBETT, WILLIAM. Cobbett's Parliamentary History of England. From the Norman Conquest, in 1066, to the year, 1803. From which last-mentioned epoch it is continued downwards in the work entitled "Cobbett's Parliamentary Debates" . . . London, 1806–20. 36 vols.

COCKAYNE, G. E. Complete peerage of England, Scotland, Ireland, Great Britain, and the United Kingdom, extant, extinct, or dormant. London, 1887–98. 8 vols.

COFFMAN, BERTHA. The influence of English literature on Friedrich von Hagedorn. Dissertation. Chicago, 1914–15.

DEUTSCHES Anonymen Lexikon 1501–1850. Aus den Quellen bearbeitet von Dr. Michael Bohatta und Dr. Hanns Bohatta. Weimar, 1902–28. 7 vols.

DICTIONARY of anonymous and pseudonymous English literature (S. Halkett and J. Laing.) London, New and Enlarged Edition, 1926–34. 7 vols.

DICTIONARY of National Biography. Edited by Leslie Stephen. London, 1885–1901. 66 vols.

EITNER, ROBERT. Biographisch-Bibliographisches Quellen-Lexikon der Musiker und Musikgelehrten der Christlichen Zeitrechnung bis zur Mitte des neunzehnten Jahrhunderts. Leipzig, 1900–1904. 10 vols.

FAULWASSER, JULIUS. Die St. Michaelis Kirche in Hamburg. Hamburg, 1930.

FINDER, ERNST. Hamburgisches Bürgertum in der Vergangenheit. Hamburg, 1930.

FÜRSTENAU, MORITZ. Zur Geschichte der Musik und des Theaters am Hofe der Kurfürsten von Sachsen. Dresden, 1862.

GELEHRTE Neuigkeiten auf das Jahr 1749 (etc.) Hamburg, 1749–60 (?)

GERBER, E. L. Historisch-Biographisches Lexicon der Tonkünstler, welches Nachrichten von dem Leben und Werken musikalischer Schrifsteller, berühmter Componisten, Sänger etc. . . . enthält; Leipzig, 1790–92. 2 vols.

GERBER, E. L. Neues Historisch-Biographisches Lexikon der Tonkünstler, welches Nachrichten . . . etc. Leipzig, 1812–14. 4 vols.

GOLDSCHMIDT, HUGO. Die Musikästhetik des achtzehnten Jahrhunderts und ihre Beziehungen zu seinem Kunstschaffen. Zürich und Leipzig, 1915.

GRIESHEIM, LUDWIG VON. Die Stadt Hamburg in ihrem politischen, ökonomischen und sittlichen Zustand. Hamburg, 1760.

HAMBURGER Nachrichten aus dem Reiche der Gelehrsamkeit. Hamburg, 1759–65.

HAMBURGISCHE Berichte von den neuesten gelehrten Sachen. Hamburg, 1732–58.

HATFIELD, THEODORE. Moll Flanders in Germany. *The Journal of English and German Philology*, vol. XXXII, 1933.

HAZARD, PAUL. La Crise de la conscience européene (1680–1715). Paris, 1935. 3 vols.

HITZIGRATH, HEINRICH. Die Kompagnie der Merchants Adventurers und die englische Kirchengemeinde in Hamburg 1611–1835. Hamburg, 1904.

HORN, D. B. British diplomatic representatives 1689–1789 edited for the Royal Historical Society. London, 1932.

HÖRNER, HANS. G. P. Telemanns Passionsmusiken—Ein Beitrag zur Geschichte der Passionsmusik in Hamburg. Borna-Leipzig, 1933.

HOWELL, T. B. A complete collection of state trials and proceedings for high treason and other crimes and misdemeanors from the earliest period to the year 1783, with notes and other illustrations: compiled by T. B. Howell . . . London, 1816–1826. 33 vols.

JACOBY, KARL. Die erstes moralischen Wochenschriften Hamburgs am Anfange der achtzehnten Jahrhunderts. Hamburg, 1888.

JÖCHER, C. G. Allgemeines Gelehrten-Lexicon, darinne die Gelehrten aller Stände . . . vom Anfange der Welt bis auf ietzige Zeit . . . in alphabetischer Ordnung beschreiben werden. Leipzig, 1750–1751. 4 vols.

(JÖCHER, C. G.) Fortsetzung und Ergänzungen zu Christian Gottlieb Jöchers allgemeinen Gelehrten-Lexicon, von Johann Christoph Adelung. Leipzig, 1784–1897. 7 vols.

KELTER, EDMUND. Hamburg und sein Johanneum im Wandel der Jahrhunderte. Hamburg, 1929.

KLAGES, RICHARD. Johann Wolfgang Franck. Untersuchungen zu seiner Lebensgeschichte und zu seinen geistlichen Kompositionen. Dissertation. Hamburg, 1937.

KLEEFELD, WILHELM. Das Orchester der Hamburger Oper 1678–1738. In: Sammelbände der internationalen Musikgesellschaft. Erster Jahrgang 1899–1900.

KRETSCHMAR, HERMANN. Geschichte der Oper. Leipzig, 1919.

KROME, FERDINAND. Die Anfänge des Musicalischen Journalismus in Deutschland. Leipzig, 1896.

KRÜGER, LISELOTTE. Die Hamburgische Musikorganisation im XVII. Jahrhundert. Zurich, 1933.

LEWIS, CHARLES BARON DE PÖLLNITZ. Being the observations he made in his late travels thro' Poland, Germany, Italy, France, Spain, Flanders, Holland, England, etc., discovering not only the present state of the chief cities and towns; but the characters of the principal persons at the several courts. 2d ed., London, 1739–1740. 4 vols.

LINDNER, E. O. Die erste Stehende Deutsche Oper. Berlin, 1855. 2 vols.

LODGE, RICHARD. Great Britain and Prussia in the eighteenth century, being the Ford lectures delivered in the University of Oxford, Lent term, 1922. Oxford, 1923.

(MAINWARING, JOHN). Memoirs of the life of the late George Frederick Handel. London, 1760.

(MARPURG, F. W.). Kritische Briefe uber die Tonkunst, mit kleinen Clavier-stücken und Singoden begleitet von einer Musikalischen Gesellschaft in Berlin, 1759–1763.

MEINARDUS, LUDWIG. Johann Mattheson und seine Verdienste um die deutsche Tonkunst, No. 8, der Walderseeschen Vorträge. Leipzig, 1879.

MEINARDUS, LUDWIG. Rückblick auf die Anfänge der deutschen Oper in Hamburg. Hamburg, 1878.

MEYER, KATHI. Der chorische Gesang der Frauen mit besonderer Bezugnahme seiner Betätigung auf geistlichem Gebiet. 1. Teil bis zur Zeit um 1800. Dissertation Leipzig. Mittenwald, 1917.

MICHAEL, WOLFGANG. Englische Geschichte im achtzehnten Jahrhundert. Leipzig, 1896–1937. 4 vols.

MIESNER, HEINRICH. Philipp Emanuel Bach in Hamburg. Beiträge zu seiner Biographie und zur Musikgeschichte seiner Zeit. Dissertation. Berlin 1929.

NIEDERSÄCHSISCHE Nachrichten von Gelehrte Sachen. Hamburg, 1731–35.

NIEDERSÄCHSISCHE Neue Zeitungen von Gelehrte Sachen. Hamburg, 1727–31.

THE PRESENT STATE OF GERMANY; or, An account of the extent, rise, form, wealth, strength, weaknesses and interests of that Empire . . . By a Person of Quality. London, 1690. 2 vols.

THE PRESENT State of the republick of letters, giving a general view of the state of learning throughout Europe; and containing not only an early account, but accurate abstracts of the most valuable books published in Great Britain or foreign parts. Interspersed with dissertations on several curious and entertaining subjects; . . . London, 1728–1736. 18 vols.

PREUSSNER, EBERHARD. Die Bürgerliche Musikkultur—Ein Beytrag zur deutschen Musikgeschichte das 18 Jahrhunderts. Hamburg, 1935.

PRICE, L. M. The Reception of English Literature in Germany. Berkeley, Cal., 1932.

REINKE, H. Hamburg, ein Abriss der Stadtgeschichte von den Anfängen biss zur Gegenwart. Bremen, 1926.

RIEMANNS, HUGO. Musik Lexikon. Elfte Anflage bearbeitet von Alfred Einstein. Berlin, 1929. 2 vols.

RÖHLK. Geschichte des Hauptgottesdienstes in der evangelisch-lutherischen Kirche Hamburg's. Göttingen, 1899.

SCHÄFKE, RUDOLPH. Geschichte der Musik Aesthetik in Umrissen. Berlin-Schöneberg, 1934.

SCHIEDERMAIR, LUDWIG. Die Deutsche Oper. Leipzig, 1930.

SCHMIDT, HEINRICH. Johann Mattheson ein Förderer der deutschen Tonkunst im Lichte seiner Werke. Musikgeschichtliche Skizze. Leipzig, 1897.

SCHREIBER, IRMTRAUD. Dichtung und Musik der deutschen Opernarien. Dissertation. Berlin, 1934.

SCHÜNEMANN, GEORG. Geschichte der Deutschen Schulmusik, Handbücher der Musikerziehung. Leipzig, 1928.

SCHULZE, WALTER. Die Quellen der Hamburger Oper (1678–1738). Eine

# Bibliography

bibliographisch-statistische Studie zur Geschichte der ersten stehenden deutschen Oper. In: Mitteilungen aus der Bibliothek der Hansestadt Hamburg. Neue Folge. Ed. by Gustav Wahl, vol. IV. Hamburg-Oldenburg, 1938.

SCHRÖDER, HANS. Lexikon der Hamburgischen Schriftsteller bis zur Gegenwart. Hamburg, 1851–1883. 8 vols.

SCHWEITZER, ALBERT. J. S. Bach. London, reprinted 1935. 2 vols.

SPITTA, PHILIP. Johann Sebastian Bach; his work and influence on the music of Germany, 1685–1750. London, 1899. 3 vols.

SQUIRE, WILLIAM W. BARCLAY. J. W. Franck in England. *The Musical Antiquary.* 1912, pp. 181–190.

STIERLING, HUBERT. Leben und Bildnis Friedrich von Hagedorn. *Mitteilungen aus dem Museum für Hamburgische Geschichte.* Hamburg, 1911, no. 2. 4 Beiheft. 2 Teil zu, Jahrbuch der Hamburgischen Wissenschaftlichen Anstalten. XXVIII. 1910.

VOIGHT, F. A. Reinhard Keiser. Vierteljahrschrift für Musikwissenschaft, 1890.

WAHL, GUSTAV. Hamburgs Literatur und Theater im 17. und 18. Jahrhundert, unter Berücksichtigung englischer und französischer Kultureinflüsse.

WALTHER, JOHANN GOTTFRIED. Musicalisches Lexicon; oder Musicalische Bibliothec . . . Leipzig, 1732.

WEDGWOOD, C. V. The Thirty Years War. New Haven, 1939.

WEHL, FEODOR. Hamburgs Literaturleben im achtzehnten Jahrhundert. Leipzig, 1856.

WEICHMANN, C. F. Poesie der Nieder-Sachsen, oder allerhand mehrenteils noch nie gedruckte Gedichte von den berühmtesten Nieder-Sachsen, sonderlich einigen Mit-Gliedern der vormals in Hamburg blühenden Teutsch-übenden Gesellschafft. Hamburg, 1725–1738. 6 vols.

WERNER, ARNO. Musik und Musiker in der Landesschule Pforta. In: Sammelbände der internationalen Musikgesellschaft. Achter Jahrgang, Leipzig 1906–1907.

WINTERFELD, CARL VON. Der evangelische Kirchengesang und sein Verhältnis zur Kunst des Tonsatzes. Leipzig, 1843–1847. 3 vols.

ZELLE, FRIEDRICH. J. Theile und N. A. Strungk. Zweiter Beitrag zur Geschichte der ältesten deutschen Oper. In: Wissenschaftliche Beilage zum Programm des Humboldts-Gymnasiums zu Berlin, Ostern 1891. Berlin, 1891.

# INDEX

# Index

*Nachrichten zum Aufnehmen der Wissenschaften und der Historie überhaupt*, 205; *Hamburger Nachrichten aus dem Reiche der Gelehrsamkeit*, 96, 98, 108, 206, 213 f., 220; *Hamburgische Berichte von den Neuesten Gelehrten Sachen*, 101 f., 105, 205; *Historische Critische Beyträge zur Aufnahme der Musik*, 96; *The London Journal and Free Britain*, 82; *Mercure de France*, 206; *Mist's Journal*, 82; *Der Musicalische Patriot, see* Mattheson's Works; *Niedersächsische Nachrichten von Gelehrten Sachen*, 11, 75, 81–82, 87–88, 192–193, 196, 198; *Der Patriot*, 10, 86, 189; *The Political State*, 162; *The Present State of the Republic of Letters*, 81 f., 85, 192; *The Spectator Papers*, 10; *Staats und Gelehrte Zeitung des Hamburgischen unpartheyischen Correspondenten*, 108; *The Tatler*, 10, 76–78, 157–158; *Die Vernünftler, see* Mattheson's Works

# Index

200; uses opera singers as soloists in church music, 50–51, 52 n. 152, 163 n. 60, 174 n. 96; "Vicarius in Petro" of the Dom, 50, 61; writes "Official News Letters," 36, 70

WORKS:

As editor: Niedt, F. E., *Handleitung zur Variationen* (third part), 164 n. 63; *Friederich Erhard Niedtens Musicalische Handleitung, zur Variationen Des General-Basses,* 175 n. 97; Raupach, Christopher, *Veritophili Deutliche Beweis-Grunde,* 164 n. 63

Books on music: *Aristoxeni iunior, Phthongologia Systematica,* 95, 101, 207–208; *Behauptung der Himmlischen Musik,* 101, 207, 208; *Das Beschützte Orchestre,* 66, 84, 89, 138–139, 164–165, 201; *A Complete Treatise of Thorough Bass,* 196; *Critica Musica,* 66, 85, 139–143, 176–178, 181 f.; *Criticae Musicae,* 182–183; *Das erläuterte Selah,* 101, 204–205; *De eruditione Musica,* 193–194; *Etliche hundert erkohner Schriftstellen,* 204–205; *Das Exemplarische Organisten-Probe,* 84, 90, 170–171, 192; *Das Forschende Orchestre,* 84–85, 144, 175; *Grundlage einer Ehrenpforte,* 86, 89–90, 159, 200–201; *Gültige Zeugnisse über die jüngste Mattthesonisch-Musikalisch Kern-schrifft,* 199–200; *Johann Mattthesons Grosse General-Bass-Schule,* 90, 192; *Johann Mattthesons Kleine General-Bass-Schule,* 86 f., 196, 197; *Johann Mattthesons neuangelegter Freuden-Akademie zweyter Band,* 211; *Joh. Mattthesons Wahrer Begriff des Harmonischen Lebens,* 210; *Kern Melodischer Wissenschafft,* 88–89, 198–199; *Matthesonii Plus Ultra,* 95, 212–213; *Matthesons bewährte Panacea,* 209–210; *Mithridat wider den Gift einer Welschen Satyre,* 95, 96, 208; *Der Musicalische Patriot,* 58–59, 67, 85–86, 188–189; *Das Neu-Eröffnete Orchestre,* ix, 45, 83, 89, 113–121, 123–145, 157, 186; *Der neue Göttingische Ephorus,* 58, 185–186; *Die neuangelegte Freuden-Akademie,* 101–102, 210–211; *Die Neueste Untersuchung der Singspiele,* 94, 204; *Reflexions sur l'eclaircissement d'un probleme de Musique,* 172–173; *Sieben Gespräche der Weisheit u. Musik,* 96, 210; *Der Vollkommene Capellmeister,* 86, 88, 89, 144, 198, 200, 208–209.

Miscellaneous books, pamphlets, articles, etc.: *Abhandlung von den Pantomimen,* 208–209. *Etwas Neues unter der Sonnen,* 201; *Dem Hoch-Wohlgebohrnen Herrn, Herr Cyrillo von Wich,* 160; *Idioticon Hamburgense* (compiled by Michael Richey), 211–212; *Inimici Mortis,* 100, 207; *Kurtzer Begriff der vornehmsten Heilsamen Tugenden der Pyrmont-Wasser,* 195; *Matthesons Glückwunschungs Rede an Graf Schönborn,* 151–152; *Matthesons Philologisches Tresespiel,* 97, 211; *Ode auf des S. T. Hrn. Capellmeister Heinichen,* 188; *Prologo per il Sacro Re Christianissimo Ludovico XV,* 198; *Remèdes Chretiens et Philosophique contre la Medisance,* 205; *Versuch einiger Oden über die Gebote Gottes,* 205. Articles in: *Beyträge zur Cristischen Historie der Deutschen Sprache,* 201–202; *Beyträge zur Historie und Aufnahme des Theaters,* 209; *Freie Urtheile u. Nachrichten,* 205; *Die Hamburger Nachrichten aus dem Reiche der Gelehrsamkeit,* 213 f.; *Die Hamburgischen Berichte von den neuesten Gelehrten Sachen,* 211; *Niedersächsische Nachrichten,* 81–82, 192–193.

Miscellaneous translations: *Aesopus bey Hofe* [opera text], 189–190; *Die Automoton,* 70–73, 150–151; *Die Ausbündig-schönen Eigenschafften Der Tobacks-Pflantzen,* 72, 154–155; *Bischof Burnets Geschichte,* 79, 181–182, 197; *Deportatis nuper Londini,* 149–150; *Der Ehrsüchtige Arsaces* [opera text], 178; *Erlesener Davidischen Trost* [oratorio text], 183; *Freundschafft im Tode,* 79, 194; *George Friedrich Händels Lebensbeschreibung,* 107, 214; *Die Geschichte von dem Leben und von der Regierung Mariae, Königinn der Schotten,* 79, 184–185; *Historische Anmerckungen über Burnets Geschichte,* 79, 199; *Moll Flanders,* 78–79, 180; *Nero, in einem Sing-Spiele* [opera text], 180; *Pamela oder die belohnte Tugend,* 79–81, 202–203; *Des Ritters Ramsay Reisender Cyrus,* 79, 189; *M. H. J. Sivers Gelehrter Cantor,* 191; *Die Vernünftler,* 10, 76–78, 157–158; *Zenobia* [opera text], 178.

Translations of political and economic works: *Anmerckungen über die Aufführung abseiten Gross-Brittanniens,* 190; *Anmerckungen über die auffgefangene Briefe,* 166; *Anmerckungen über den Tractat,* 190–191; *Anrede des Lord Gross-Meisters,* 73, 162;

## 240 *Johann Mattheson*

# Index